KU-278-974

LIVERPOOL JMU LIBRARY

3 1111 01462 2383

Cambridge Studies in Biological and Evolutionary Anthropology 67

Bioarchaeological and Forensic Perspectives on Violence: How Violent Death is Interpreted from Skeletal Remains

Every year, there are over 1.6 million violent deaths worldwide, making violence one of the leading public health issues of our time. With the twentieth century just behind us, it is hard to forget that 191 million people lost their lives directly or indirectly through conflict.

This collection of engaging case studies on violence and violent deaths reveals how violence is reconstructed from skeletal and contextual information. By sharing the complex methodologies for gleaning scientific data from human remains and the context in which they are found, with complementary perspectives for examining violence from both past and contemporary societies, bioarchaeology and forensic anthropology prove to be fundamentally inseparable.

This book provides a model for training forensic anthropologists and bioarchaeologists, not just in the fundamentals of excavation and skeletal analysis, but in all subfields of anthropology, to broaden their theoretical and practical approach to dealing with everyday violence.

DEBRA L. MARTIN is Lincy Professor of Anthropology at the University of Nevada, Las Vegas. For the past 30 years, her research interests have focused on the analysis of ancient human remains to better understand the origin and evolution of violence and disease in culturally diverse human groups. Her primary research interests currently include bridging social theory with bioarchaeological data, the impact of raiding, warfare, and captivity on morbidity and mortality, and the ways in which social control creates marginalized individuals. Her popular course "The Anthropology of Violence" is offered every year at the University of Nevada.

CHERYL P. ANDERSON is a Ph.D. student at the University of Nevada, Las Vegas. Her primary research interests include the evolution of organized violence, the use of violence as a means of communication, and the impacts of social inequality on human health. Recently, she has investigated violence in a late precolonial skeletal collection from Northern Mexico. Additionally, she has been involved in projects analyzing human skeletal remains from a historic period family cemetery from southern Nevada, a Bronze Age population from the United Arab Emirates, and a Middle Bronze Age village in Anatolia.

Cambridge Studies in Biological and Evolutionary Anthropology 67

Series editors

HUMAN ECOLOGY
C. G. Nicholas Mascie-Taylor, University of Cambridge
Michael A. Little, State University of New York, Binghamton
GENETICS
Kenneth M. Weiss, Pennsylvania State University
HUMAN EVOLUTION
Robert A. Foley, University of Cambridge
Nina G. Jablonski, California Academy of Science
PRIMATOLOGY
Karen B. Strier, University of Wisconsin, Madison

Bioarchaeological and Forensic Perspectives on Violence

How Violent Death is Interpreted from Skeletal Remains

Edited by

DEBRA L. MARTIN
University of Nevada, Las Vegas

CHERYL P. ANDERSON
University of Nevada, Las Vegas

CAMBRIDGE
UNIVERSITY PRESS

CAMBRIDGE
UNIVERSITY PRESS

University Printing House, Cambridge CB2 8BS, United Kingdom

Published in the United States of America by Cambridge University Press, New York

Cambridge University Press is part of the University of Cambridge.

It furthers the University's mission by disseminating knowledge in the pursuit of education, learning and research at the highest international levels of excellence.

www.cambridge.org
Information on this title: www.cambridge.org/9781107045446

© Cambridge University Press 2014

This publication is in copyright. Subject to statutory exception
and to the provisions of relevant collective licensing agreements,
no reproduction of any part may take place without the written
permission of Cambridge University Press.

First published 2014

Printed in the United Kingdom by Clays, St Ives plc

A catalogue record for this publication is available from the British Library

Library of Congress Cataloguing in Publication data
American Association of Physical Anthropologists. Annual meeting (81st : 2012 : Portland, Or.)
Bioarchaeological and forensic perspectives on violence how violent death is interpreted from skeletal remains / edited by Debra L. Martin, University of Nevada, Las Vegas, Cheryl P. Anderson, University of Nevada, Las Vegas.
  pages cm. – (Cambridge studies in biological and evolutionary anthropology ; 67)
Includes bibliographical references and index.
ISBN 978-1-107-04544-6 (Hardback)
1. Human remains (Archaeology)–Congresses. 2. Violence–History–Congresses. 3. Wounds and injuries–History–Congresses. 4. Social archaeology–Congresses. 5. Forensic anthropology–Congresses. I. Martin, Debra L. II. Anderson, Cheryl P. III. Title.
CC79.5.H85A64 2014
930.1–dc23   2013034214

ISBN 978-1-107-04544-6 Hardback

Additional resources for this publication at www.cambridge.org/9781107045446

Cambridge University Press has no responsibility for the persistence or accuracy of URLs for external or third-party internet websites referred to in this publication, and does not guarantee that any content on such websites is, or will remain, accurate or appropriate.

Contents

Contributors

Cheryl P. Anderson, Department of Anthropology, University of Nevada, 4505 S. Maryland Pkwy Mailstop 455003, Las Vegas, NV 89154-5003, USA

Heidi J. Bauer-Clapp, Machmer Hall, Department of Anthropology, University of Massachusetts Amherst, Amherst, MA 01003, USA

Kathryn M. Baustian, Department of Anthropology, University of Nevada, 4505 S. Maryland Pkwy Mailstop 455003, Las Vegas, NV 89154-5003, USA

Ute Brinker, State Authority for Culture and Preservation of Monuments Mecklenburg-Vorpommern, Domhof 4/5, 19055 Schwerin, Germany

John J. Crandall, Department of Anthropology, University of Nevada, 4505 S. Maryland Pkwy Mailstop 455003, Las Vegas, NV 89154-5003, USA

Elizabeth M. DeVisser, University of Indianapolis, 200 S. Regent St., Lansing, MI 48912, USA

William N. Duncan, Department of Sociology and Anthropology, East Tennessee State University, 223B Rogers-Stout Hall, PO Box 70644, Johnson City, TN 37614-1702, USA

Stefan Flohr, Department of Biology, University of Hildesheim, Marienburger Platz 22, 31141 Hildesheim, Germany; Thuringian State Office for the Preservation of Historical Monuments and Archaeology, Humboldtstraße 11, 99423, Weimar, Germany

Laura C. Fulginiti, Maricopa County Office of the Medical Examiner, 701 W. Jefferson, Phoenix, AZ 85007, USA

Alison Galloway, Campus Provost/Executive Vice Chancellor, Chancellors Office, 1156 High St., University of California, Santa Cruz, CA 95064, USA

Michelle D. Hamilton, Department of Anthropology, Forensic Anthropology Center, Texas State University, 601 University Dr., San Marcos, TX 78666, USA

Ryan P. Harrod, Department of Anthropology, University of Alaska Anchorage, Anchorage, AK 99508, USA

Uwe Kierdorf, Department of Biology, University of Hildesheim, Marienburger Platz 22, 31141 Hildesheim, Germany

Laura M. King, Colorado College, 14 E Cache La Poudre St., Colorado Springs, CO 80903, USA

Anna Kjellström, Stockholm University, Department of Archaeology and Classical Studies, Sweden

Danielle Kurin, Department of Anthropology, HSSB 1002, University of California Santa Barbara, CA 93106, USA

Krista E. Latham, Departments of Biology and Anthropology, University of Indianapolis, 1400 East Hanna Ave., Indianapolis, IN 46227, USA

Marisol Intriago Leiva, Encargada de la Unidad Especial de Identificación Forense, Servicio Médico Legal, Avenida La Paz 1012, Independencia, Santiago, Chile

Debra L. Martin, University of Nevada, Las Vegas, Department of Anthropology, 4505 S. Maryland Pkwy Mailstop 455003, Las Vegas, NV 89154–5003, USA

Melissa Scott Murphy, Anthropology Department, 3431, University of Wyoming, 1000 E. University Avenue, Laramie, WY 82070, USA

Jörg Orschiedt, University of Berlin, Department of History and Cultural Studies, Institute of Prehistoric Archaeology, Altensteinstr. 15, 14195 Berlin, Germany

Ventura R. Pérez, 201 Machmer Hall, Department of Anthropology, University of Massachusetts Amherst, Amherst, MA 01003, USA

Annemarie Schramm, State Authority for Culture and Preservation of Monuments Mecklenburg-Vorpommern, Domhof 4/5, 19055 Schwerin, Germany

Andrew C. Seidel, Center for Bioarchaeological Research, School of Human Evolution and Social Change, Arizona State University, Tempe, AZ 85287, USA

Elena Spanagel, Department of Biology, University of Hildesheim, Marienburger Platz 22, 31141 Hildesheim, Germany

Brian Spatola, National Museum of Health and Medicine, 2500 Linden Lane, Silver Spring, MD 20910, USA

Vincent H. Stefan, Herbert H. Lehman, College – CUNY, Chair, Department of Anthropology, 250 Bedford Park Blvd. West, Bronx, NY 10468–1527, USA

Christopher M. Stojanowski, Center for Bioarchaeological Research, School of Human Evolution and Social Change, Arizona State University, Tempe, AZ 85287, USA

Rebecca Storey, Department of Comparative Cultural Studies, University of Houston, Houston, TX 77204–5020, USA

Christina Torres-Rouff, Anthropology – SSHA, University of California Merced, 5200 N. Lake Road, Merced, CA 95343, USA

Rick Weathermon, Anthropology Department, 3431, University of Wyoming, 1000 E. University Avenue, Laramie, WY 82070, USA

Part I

Introduction

1 Introduction: interpreting violence in the ancient and modern world when skeletonized bodies are all you have

DEBRA L. MARTIN AND
CHERYL P. ANDERSON

1.1 Introduction

If this collection of studies on interpreting violence has a single *raison d'être* it is that bioarchaeology and forensic anthropology make good bedfellows in thinking about the reasons and context for interpersonal violence. Bioarchaeology has emerged as an important and integrated approach to understanding human skeletal biology in the past. It combines analysis of skeletonized human remains with archaeological reconstruction of the grave and habitation site, and other aspects of the environment in which individuals lived. Forensic anthropology is the application of methods from bioarchaeology, but usually in a more recent historic or contemporary setting. The data from the skeleton are usually used in a legal setting while working with police, coroners, or human rights organizations. Both bioarchaeology and forensic anthropology share complex methodologies for gleaning every piece of scientific data from the human remains and the context in which they are found. Yet these two subdisciplines within biological anthropology often are separated in edited volumes, within departments, and across national conferences.

This is among the first organized symposia that we are aware of that presents a thematic set of case studies coming from both subdisciplines. At the 81st Annual Meeting of the American Association of Physical Anthropologists in Portland OR (April 11–14, 2012) the initial poster session focused on case studies that revealed sometimes surprising or counterintuitive interpretations of violence because a more nuanced approach was taken to understand both the bones and the context. The focus is on the theories and methods that are used to interpret violent interactions by identifying both the

Bioarchaeological and Forensic Perspectives on Violence: How Violent Death is Interpreted from Skeletal Remains, ed. D. L. Martin and C. P. Anderson. Published by Cambridge University Press.
© Cambridge University Press 2014.

perpetrators of violence and those who suffered as a result of their actions. The chapters in this volume all reveal how violence is reconstructed from skeletal and contextual information. However, they provide a range of approaches to foster multiple perspectives with regard to documenting and interpreting the meaning of violence. Individual chapters demonstrate how this can be operationalized on many different levels. In particular, the focus of these case studies is to identify the different participants in violent encounters (victims, witnesses, aggressors) in order to provide more detailed and nuanced interpretations of human behavior.

1.2   The complementarity of bioarchaeology and forensic anthropology

Bioarchaeology focuses on reconstructing ancient and historic cultures from burials and other archaeological evidence in an academic setting. Forensic anthropology deals primarily with more recent (and, most times, violent) deaths in local, national, and international arenas, and it is carried out within a framework that includes law enforcement, medical examiners, human rights organizations, lawyers, and surviving family members. Although both do work that involves excavation and analysis of skeletonized human remains, the career trajectory of bioarchaeologists and forensic anthropologists can be very different.

Bioarchaeology and forensic anthropology have largely developed in the USA as distinctively different career tracks, but there have been many scholars who practice both professionally and this has been the case for a long time (Buikstra and Beck 2006; Komar and Buikstra 2008). Physical (or biological) anthropology historically started out with individuals trained in anatomy and/ or medicine. Both Hooton and Hrdlička (dubbed the "father of physical anthropology") worked on forensic cases (Thompson 1982). Ubelaker (1999: 728) writes that Hrdlička worked directly with the FBI on solving cases for them in the 1930s. Thus there is a long and illustrious history of melding biological anthropology and forensic work.

Bioarchaeology and forensic anthropology present complementary perspectives for examining violence in both past and contemporary societies. An important goal of any investigation of conflict and trauma is to place the skeletal data into the larger social, political, or historical context. One way to get a deeper understanding of the motivations and consequences of violence for different categories of participants (e.g. victims, aggressors, captives, warriors) is to examine the different roles that individual agents and groups play and how they interact in a specific location.

An example of this approach is teasing out the victims from the attackers in cases of indigenous or colonial warfare or sectarian conflicts. Careful analysis of the human remains, detailed observations on the burial context, and ethnographic or witness reports all can aid in providing a more accurate and nuanced reconstruction of past events. Chapters in this volume highlight case studies of antemortem and perimortem trauma in contemporary, historic, and ancient contexts. These integrated bioarchaeological–forensic approaches are useful in constructing the contexts in which violence takes place. Ultimately, both subdisciplines aim to reconstruct and explain complex human behavior and so can benefit from directly sharing case studies, methods of analysis, and theoretical approaches to interpretation.

There is currently no umbrella term that would subsume both the work of forensic anthropologists, forensic archaeologists, and bioarchaeologists, although "forensic bioarchaeology" might be something to consider in the future. Increasingly, the work of the forensic anthropologist is highly varied, from work in academic settings and local homicide cases, to working at mass disasters and places where large numbers of people have perished from sectarian warfare and genocide (Crossland 2009). Bioarchaeologists are increasingly volunteering to aid in a wide variety of contexts that involve skeletonized remains, from historic cemeteries to mass disasters (Blau and Skinner 2005). This blurring of the roles of bioarchaeology and forensic anthropology is breaking down the largely artificial divisions between those who study the ancient dead and those who assist with the more recently dead.

Another reason why this is the moment to blend theory, method, and data from bioarchaeology with forensic anthropology is that bioarchaeology itself is emerging in a relatively new configuration (see Martin *et al.* 2013). Modern bioarchaeology is integrated into broader anthropological agendas of engagement and ethical action. Many bioarchaeologists incorporate theories about human behavior into their work and this has broadened and deepened the interpretations derived from human remains (Martin *et al.* 2013). Forensic anthropologists have provided a profound sense of what is at stake for the living when the dead cannot be located or identified (Sanford 2004). In addition, many forensic anthropologists also examine the direct impact of violent acts on the communities from which the victims were taken, and on eye-witnesses to the violence.

One of the issues facing the relatively young discipline of forensic anthropology is the need to create a balance between specialized knowledge embedded in the forensic sciences and training in the other subfields of anthropology. Through interdisciplinary inquiry and engagement across the subfields, anthropology provides a way to view the diversity of opinions about violence, warfare, and human rights issues that often result in death, trauma, and social upheaval.

1.3   A blended forensic–bioarchaeological approach

A variety of forms of violence, covert and vicious types of warfare, and a broad range of activities regarding surveillance or the elimination of human rights have created work for anthropologists that could not have been imagined 100 years ago. Future forensic anthropologists and bioarchaeologists will need to continue training not just in the fundamentals of excavation and skeletal analysis. They also will need training in all four subfields of anthropology to broaden their theoretical and practical approach to dealing with everyday violence. In this way, bioarchaeology (which is already deeply embedded in anthropological inquiry) and forensic anthropology can engage in an interdisciplinary inquiry of the theoretical and empirical issues within the study of violence, warfare, surveillance, and human rights. The approach and perspective that anthropology brings to the study of violence is a critical, self-reflective, and non-reductionist perspective that allows for a holistic examination of the dynamics that have led to the wide array of human atrocities committed throughout the world. It is this strength that is needed to keep forensic archaeology from falling into a trap of creating highly specialized technicians who are disconnected from the rest of anthropology.

Forensic anthropology and bioarchaeology may be considered two sides of the same coin (i.e. human osteology); however, this does not always have to be the case. The two applications of human skeletal analysis may have very different objectives and yet they are fundamentally inseparable in terms of methodology, theories about violence, and, sometimes, ultimate goals. The biggest difference between the two subdisciplines is that forensic analysis tends to focus on the individual while bioarchaeological analysis is more concerned with populations (although individuals can be a focus as well). Furthermore, forensic analysis may not have as much concern for skeletal evidence of events over the life course of the individual, something that has been more recently incorporated into broader bioarchaeological interpretation of individuals and their role within the population.

Bioarchaeology has the depth and cross-cultural breadth to help shape and understand the profound and complicated ways that humans think about and use violence and bodies. Bioarchaeologists use human remains as a lens through which to examine cultural processes. The ways that dead bodies are discussed, hidden, and displayed are used as a point of departure for examining the forms of violence that contributed to the deaths under study. Many of the most horrific genocidal events in the past 100 years demonstrate the relationship between violence and the expressive function that such acts and images have as vehicles of universal human communication. Covert operations are designed with the goal of unraveling culturally constructed webs of trust. Thus, the bodies have both real and symbolic properties.

1.4   Encompassing and cross-cutting themes

To continue building bridges and meshing methods and theory, the chapters in this book provide case studies that highlight the larger intellectual context within which this kind of scholarship falls. There are three broad sections, each with an emphasis on a particular approach and a particular contribution to new uses of methods and theories. While there is overlap among the sections, each provides a particularly nuanced set of case studies that show that there is no one way to interpret the meaning of violence – rather, there are many different pathways to getting at a more complete picture based on initial examination of human remains. The first section provides a variety of new approaches and methodologies for analysis of human remains. The next section provides a wide range of cases that fall into the broad category of ritual and performative violence. The last section takes up issues of identity and its dynamic interplay with a range of cultural factors. We end the volume with a thought-provoking chapter on what it means to do the kind of work that scholars in this book do in dealing with death and violence.

1.4.1   *Innovative methodologies in forensic anthropology and bioarchaeology*

Stefan Flohr, Ute Brinker, Elena Spanagel, Annemarie Schramm, Jörg Orschiedt, and Uwe Kierdorf (Chapter 2) investigate the demography of a commingled skeletal collection, located near the Tollense River in Germany, suspected to represent the victims of a battle. To accomplish this, Flohr and colleagues examine the cross-sectional properties of adult femora from this site to test whether the battlefield hypothesis is appropriate. Their results show the demography of the assemblage is largely consistent with what would be expected from a battlefield, mostly young and middle adult males, but that some females were also among the victims at this site. They discuss the important roles that women may have played during battles in the past, providing empirical evidence for the presence of females on the battlefield in this study. The approach taken by these authors contributes to understanding gender roles in violent events and how they may be identified bioarchaeologically.

Anna Kjellström and Michelle D. Hamilton (Chapter 3) reconstruct the events on the Royal Swedish Navy warship *Kronan* that led to sharp force trauma on some individuals using a forensic anthropological approach. They apply a detailed methodology to examine the sharp force defects present in this commingled collection. The authors demonstrate that the defects are not consistent with wounds resulting from explosions or combat, but rather reflect postmortem taphonomy. They show that the most likely scenario is that these remains, which would have been well preserved at the bottom of the ocean, were affected by the recovery of the cannons from the ship several years after it sank. This research demonstrates the utility of careful analysis of taphonomy, patterning, and context for providing nuanced interpretations of trauma and violence.

Vincent H. Stefan (Chapter 4) discusses the complexities associated with determining manner of death in cases of gunshot trauma. In this chapter he establishes criteria for the identification of victims of homicide vs. suicide, including examination of the context of the remains (buried, unburied, restrained, not restrained). He also suggests criteria based on location of wounds and number of gunshot wounds that will contribute to future investigations of gunshot trauma. He cautions, however, that, while these different criteria may be more consistent with homicide or suicide, in the end it is all of the observations about the trauma made by an investigator that will lead to determining the cause of death. This chapter provides an important, detailed method for considering key aspects of context and patterns of trauma for differentiating victims in both forensic and bioarchaeological investigations of gunshot trauma.

Andrew C. Seidel and Laura C. Fulginiti (Chapter 5) investigate victims and perpetrators of dismemberment cases in forensic contexts. This chapter provides important insight into trends in the nature of relationships between victims and perpetrators. They demonstrate that often in dismemberment cases the victims and perpetrators know each other prior to the violent act and also explore the degree of those relationships for Maricopa County (intimate relationships or not intimate). Significantly, this work also offers a unique analysis of sex differences among perpetrators of dismemberments. For example, they provide evidence that female perpetrators of dismemberments are far more likely to have intimate relationships with their victims. In considering the connections between victims and aggressors, this research illuminates the social patterning of this unique type of violence.

Cheryl P. Anderson (Chapter 6) examines commingled remains from a cave burial site in Northern Mexico to investigate whether the deceased represent victims or venerated ancestors. This research utilizes ethnographic and ethnohistoric information to investigate Rarámuri burial practices and beliefs about the dead. It also reconstructs some aspects of the political and social environment from Spanish accounts of groups living in the region. Based on the available evidence, the author concludes that, while most individuals likely were not victims of violence, at least one, and possibly a total of three, shows evidence of trauma that is more consistent with violence then burial ritual or ancestor veneration. This chapter demonstrates how consideration of these sources of information may be useful for identifying victims of violence in complex mortuary assemblages.

1.4.2   *Ritual and performative violence*

Ryan P. Harrod and Debra L. Martin (Chapter 7) examined the human remains from populations living in the ancient Southwest and found that some exhibit the "signature" of captivity and slavery on their bodies. Multiple healed head wounds, healed fractured bones, nutritional anemias, and infections all point to a life of violent beatings and inadequate living conditions. The violent acts involved with taking captives are usually very ritualized and performative, with males being murdered, and females and children being taken captive. The trauma on their bodies suggests multiple beatings across the course of the lifetime. From these case studies of captives who died young and with many traumatic and pathological injuries, a more detailed understanding of how captives were treated, as well as their symbolic and ritualized use as a show of power and domination, is gained.

Rebecca Storey (Chapter 8) explores the relationships between victims and aggressors in Maya warfare and sacrifice. This research discusses evidence for the importance of warfare among elite males in Maya society and the signifi-cance of trophies of war, specifically skull masks that were decorated and then worn by the aggressors. The author provides bioarchaeological evidence for the existence of these trophies and confirms that they likely represent elite victims of ritual violence. These trophies would have bestowed greater prestige to the perpetrators during life and the significance of these violent acts continued to link them to their victims after death. This contribution provides unique insight into considering the complex relationships between victims and perpetrators of ritual violence and how they may extend beyond the actual violent event.

Christina Torres-Rouff and Laura M. King (Chapter 9) consider patterns of cranial trauma, in particular nasal fractures, as evidence for face-to-face con-flict at oases in the San Pedro de Atacama during the Middle Period. They demonstrate a higher incidence of nasal fractures among males, although some females were also affected, and argue that this form of violence may have had social significance. The antemortem nature of these wounds provides evidence that, while this face-to-face violence was an important part of society, it was often non-lethal. This case may not have victims and perpetrators in the usual sense; rather the authors suggest that these fractures may result from some sort of culturally approved violence for resolving problems between adult individuals. This contributes to furthering our understanding of how violence may potentially be used for addressing social problems within a culture and how this type of violence may exhibit different patterns.

William N. Duncan and Christopher M. Stojanowski (Chapter 10) provide an analysis of a sixteenth-century calvaria from Georgia thought to belong to a martyred Spanish priest, Pedro de Corpa. Through the process of trying to determine whether or not this calvaria does in fact belong to Pedro de Corpa, the authors explore why some bodies are of greater interest to forensic anthropologists and bioarchaeologists than other bodies. They demonstrate that in this case there are two important factors leading to the high degree of interest. The first is that defacement of the body of the deceased has increased the degree to which it is held sacred. The second reason is that anthropological investigation of this calvaria has amplified the mystery surrounding it as well as the meaning associated with it. This chapter carefully considers how different groups within a community may be impacted differently by bioarchaeological and forensic research and represents an example of positive interaction between the anthropologists and the larger public.

1.4.3   *Violence and identity*

Heidi J. Bauer-Clapp and Ventura R. Pérez (Chapter 11) examine signs of structural and direct violence on the remains of Yaqui individuals killed in a massacre. The results of their analysis, demonstrating both trauma and signs of physiological stress, illuminate the extensive violence against the Yaqui perpetrated by the Mexican government during the nineteenth and early twentieth centuries. Through the repatriation of these remains to the Yaqui, the authors also aided in the transformation of the bodies of the victims into part of the Yaqui heritage, continuing to tell the story of violence and sacrifice to future generations. This research exemplifies how bioarchaeological and forensic research may further the understanding of violence while positively engaging the communities who are affected.

Kathryn M. Baustian (Chapter 12) explores signs of violence at the Ancestral Pueblo site Grasshopper Pueblo, finding evidence for antemortem trauma as well as scalping, and questions prior views of a peaceful community. The author considers a number of possibilities to explain the clear signs of violence on some of the remains, including warfare and raiding and different types of intra-community violence. She concludes that external violence likely played a role, especially among those with evidence for scalping, but cautions that identification of specific perpetrators is problematic based on the available evidence. The careful analysis presented in this chapter demonstrates the utility of considering the patterning of skeletal trauma when interpreting relationships between victims and perpetrators.

Elizabeth M. DeVisser, Krista E. Latham, and Marisol Intriago Leiva (Chapter 13) consider the impact of violence perpetrated by the Pinochet regime on Chilean national identity through the examination of the victims from the Patio 29 mass grave. The authors discuss the efforts put forward by the forensic anthropologists working on these human rights cases to use all available lines of evidence to identify victims correctly and provide closure for their families. They highlight the challenges associated with victim identification in the Patio 29 cases, but also the profound importance of these identifications for the families and the community impacted by the violence. This example demonstrates how forensic anthropologists, through identification of the remains of victims, can assist with the restoration of national identity.

Danielle Kurin (Chapter 14) discusses violence before and after the collapse of the Wari Empire in Peru through the examination of cranial trauma and how it affected different social groups, seen through different types of cranial modification. The results presented by the author show a relationship between social identity and trauma among the Chanka for both adults and subadults, suggesting that some groups may have been more at risk for violence and recidivism. This demonstrates that practices of violence changed following the Wari collapse, including the identification of a specific subgroup(s) among the Chanka to be targeted as the victims of violence. This chapter significantly contributes to growing literature that seeks to understand the social patterning of violence in different cultural contexts.

Melissa Scott Murphy, Brian Spatola, and Rick Weathermon (Chapter 15) examine colonial period violence and consider the ways trauma patterning might be used for inferring the potential identities of perpetrators. In this study, they compare injuries present on colonial period indigenous Andean human remains from Peru to different types of trauma in order to understand the types of weapons that may have been used on the victims. The authors point out that even the identification of weapon type may not lead to a clear picture of the identities of the perpetrators. In this case, while the victims from this site could have been killed by Spanish individuals they may also have been the victims of other native peoples, some of whom were aligned with the Spanish. Through their careful analysis, the authors demonstrate the utility of careful trauma comparison but show the necessity for researchers of violence to be cautious in their interpretations and consider the potential alternatives. They also demonstrate that individuals may have shifting roles as victims and aggressors, which must be considered in contexts of violence.

John J. Crandall, Ryan P. Harrod, Cheryl P. Anderson, and Kathryn M. Baustian (Chapter 16) present a historic double murder and suggest ways in which the events on the Kiel ranch may be interpreted. Originally thought to represent a murder–suicide, the authors confirm a previous anthropological analysis that these are the victims of a double murder. The results presented suggest an interpretation of the attack as possibly consistent with an ambush attack, with one victim being struck by both long-distance and close-range gunshot wounds and the other with a likely close-range shot. The violence at this ranch is then considered in the broader context of historic period violence on the American frontier. Through a comparative approach, the authors contribute to understanding aspects of ambush and massacre situations, their social significance, and their potential skeletal correlates.

1.5   Conclusions

Strong themes of ritual, performance, and identity run throughout these chapters and these tie violence to interpretive frameworks because of the multiple lines of evidence used. Various interpretations about the victims as well as the perpetrators were brought into focus with the use of innovative methodologies combined with theories about the ways that violence is shaped by cultural ideology, symbolism, and politics. From forensic cases to population–level studies of past peoples, violence is never a simple phenomenon to interpret. While the skeletons can reveal that some form of violence occurred, multiple lines of evidence are necessary to reconstruct the rich and detailed context within which the violent acts took place. Anthropology as a holistic approach to human behavior provides the "glue" that binds both forensic as well as archaeological approaches to understanding violence and explaining the role of culture and ideology in the use of violence. Alison Galloway (Chapter 17) provides the concluding thoughts for this volume on violence. In her chapter, she provides thoughtful commentary on what it means to work with the remains of the dead, and how this type of work is experienced by anthropologists.

References

Blau, S. & Skinner, M. (2005). The use of forensic archaeology in the investigation of human rights abuse: unearthing the past in East Timor. *The International Journal of Human Rights*, **9**, 449–63.

Buikstra, J. E. & Beck, L. A. (eds.) (2006). *Bioarchaeology: The Contextual Analysis of Human Remains*. Burlington: Academic Press.

Crossland, Z. (2009). Of clues and signs: the dead body and its evidential traces. *American Anthropologist*, **111**, 69–80.

Komar, D. A. & Buikstra, J. E. (2008). *Forensic Anthropology: Contemporary Theory and Practice*. Oxford: Oxford University Press.

Martin, D. L., Harrod, R. P. & Pérez, V. R. (2013). *Bioarchaeology: An Integrated Approach to Working with Human Remains*. New York: Springer.

Sanford, V. (2004). *Buried Secrets: Truth and Human Rights in Guatemala*. New York: Palgrave Macmillan.

Thompson, D. D. (1982). Forensic anthropology. In: Spencer, F. (ed.) *A History of American Physical Anthropology, 1930–1980*. New York: Academic Press, 357–65.

Ubelaker, D. H. (1999). Aleš Hrdlicka's role in the history of forensic anthropology. *Journal of Forensic Sciences*, **44**, 724–30.

Part II

Overview and innovative methodologies

2 Killed in action? A biometrical analysis of femora of supposed battle victims from the Middle Bronze Age site of Weltzin 20, Germany

STEFAN FLOHR, UTE BRINKER, ELENA
SPANAGEL, ANNEMARIE SCHRAMM,
JÖRG ORSCHIEDT, AND UWE KIERDORF

2.1 Introduction

Battles are outbreaks of massive intergroup violence that take place at a specific location, the battlefield, and within a rather short period of time. Battles are mostly fought by young adult to middle adult males, and therefore the age and sex composition of battle victims typically differs from that of the population from which they originated (Kjellström 2005; Lambert 2002). In contrast, a bone assemblage representing victims of a massacre mostly includes individuals of both sexes and all age classes in proportion to their presence in the population (Lambert 2002; Peter-Röcher 2006; Wahl and König 1987). Exceptions from this can occur when adult men were away from the settlement when it was attacked or where young females were captured and taken away by the raiders (Lambert 2002). In recent years, an increasing number of studies have focused on battlefield archaeology and the study of human skeletal remains from such archaeological contexts (Kjellström 2005; Fiorato *et al.* 2007). Identification of battlefields from historic periods is often possible based on historical records. Battlefields from prehistoric times are more difficult to identify, especially in the absence of distinctive features such as mass graves or earthworks. Hence, such prehistoric battlefields have to be identified based on other, indirect features. One of these features could be the demographic composition of the individuals represented in the bone assemblage associated with a presumed battle.

Bioarchaeological and Forensic Perspectives on Violence: How Violent Death is Interpreted from Skeletal Remains, ed. D. L. Martin and C. P. Anderson. Published by Cambridge University Press.
© Cambridge University Press 2014.

Reconstruction of demographic profiles on the basis of commingled bone assemblages is much more difficult than in the case of articulated skeletons. Pelves and skulls provide the most valid features for sex assessment and are therefore routinely used to this end when complete skeletons are available. In the case of disarticulated skeletons, the femora and tibiae are often the most frequent and best-preserved skeletal elements within the bone assemblage because of their high cortical content (Bennike 1985; Mays 1998). Therefore several studies have used the femur for sex assessment (Asala 2001, 2002; Black III 1978; Dittrick and Suchey 1986; Mall *et al.* 2000; Milner and Boldsen 2012). Femora of males are typically larger and more robust than those of females. However, the distinction between large and small or robust and gracile bones is meaningful only within single populations, given the amount of variation in skeletal dimensions between geographic regions and times. Reference data used for comparisons are therefore best obtained from populations that are close in time, region of origin, and ancestry to the studied population.

The purpose of the present study was to analyze metrical data obtained on femora of presumed battle victims from the Bronze Age of northern Germany in order to provide additional data relevant to the reconstruction of the demographic profile of the individuals represented in the assemblage.

2.2   Site background

Since the late 1970s, human skeletal remains and archaeological artifacts, including arrowheads made from flint stone and bronze as well as simple wooden clubs, have been recovered from several locations along a stretch of about 2 km in the valley of the Tollense, a small river in the federal state of Mecklenburg-Vorpommern in Northeastern Germany (Jantzen *et al.* 2011). The finds originate from excavations close to the River Tollense, underwater surveys, and from stray finds along the riverbanks. Since 2009, systematic investigations in the river valley have been conducted by an interdisciplinary research team. Radiocarbon dates from different skeletal elements and one of the wooden clubs revealed ages of *c.* 1200 cal BCE for the majority of these finds, corresponding to Period III of the Nordic Bronze Age (Jantzen *et al.* 2011). The consistent radiocarbon dates and the striking similarities in the find situations led to the assumption that the different locations along the river that yielded archaeological remains constitute a single "site-complex." However, thus far the extent of this presumed site-complex is unknown.

At present, *c.* 4700 human bones and *c.* 1800 animal bones have been recovered at 14 sites along the river. The majority of bones show an excellent state of preservation. Most of the human remains have been found commingled, with joining elements and larger articulated units being rare. As the excavations are still ongoing, the minimum number of individuals (MNI) is preliminary. Thus far, the femur is the most frequently found skeletal element and, based on its occurrence, an MNI of 108 has been established.

Currently, excavation activities concentrate on the sites Weltzin 20 and Weltzin 32, which have yielded the highest number of skeletal elements among the 14 sites. At Weltzin 20, a total of 3236 human bones from all regions of the skeleton and 1165 animal bones have thus far (summer 2012) been recovered from an area of slightly more than 161 m^2. At this site the femur is the most frequently represented skeletal element ($n = 90$), giving an MNI of 60. Calculations based on this MNI show that, on average, only 28% of the skeletal elements of the represented individuals have been recovered. Several bones show evidence of trauma. Three out of 34 skulls from Weltzin 20 exhibit signs of perimortem trauma, with two of them featuring depression fractures on the frontal bone caused by blunt force. The lesions are round to oval in shape and may have been caused by weapons like the wooden clubs that were found at the site. Another skull shows a lesion in the lower part of the right parietal bone that likely represents an arrow wound. The border of the lesion shows minor signs of healing, indicating that the trauma was survived for some days or weeks. In one humerus, a flint arrow head is embedded in the proximal portion of the bone between the head and the greater tubercle. Two of the 90 femora show perimortem comminuted peritrochanteric fractures. Additionally, some healed lesions were found in the assemblage. Signs of healed trauma have also been found on skeletal remains from other sites of the site-complex. Taking into account the commingled nature of the assemblage and the incompleteness of the skeletons, the frequency of trauma is rather high.

One of the most challenging questions regarding the site is how to interpret the unusual findings. Taphonomic considerations led to the assumption that the bodies were probably complete when they entered (were thrown into) the river and afterwards they became disarticulated. The skeletal elements were then transported in the river depending on their specific water transportation properties, thus becoming scattered over a stretch of the river (Brinker *et al.* 2013). Frequently occurring high water events in the formerly much shallower river bed led to local accumulations of bones on river banks, at "natural traps" such as roots or larger plants, or on adjacent drawdown zones. The fact that the skeletal remains lack gnawing damage by rodents or other animals indicates that, after deposition, the bones were always covered by sediment or water. The lack of bite marks from scavengers on the bones also indicates that the bodies had not lain on the presumed battlefield for a long period of time before being thrown into the water.

The commingled nature of the assemblage presents a problem for establishing the demographic composition of these remains, as age-at-death estimation and sex assessment are difficult on isolated bones. This is even more problematic, if, as in the present case, reference data from comparable assemblages (of similar archaeological age and region of origin) are largely missing. In the human skeletal material from the Tollense river valley, sex assessment was performed mainly on skulls and pelvic bones. In addition, postcranial bones with a particularly robust or gracile appearance were assumed to represent most likely males and females, respectively. Age-at-death estimation was based on macroscopic standard references for cranial sutures, dental attrition, age-related changes on the auricular surface of the ilium, and the pubic face (Buikstra and Ubelaker, 1994). In a few cases, the non-fusion of the epiphyses of long bones also provided information for age-at-death estimation. According to these analyses, the Weltzin 20 assemblage is composed mainly of young adult and middle adult males (Brinker *et al.* 2013). Preliminary data for the other sites along the Tollense River indicate a similar demographic profile. Thus, the skeletal assemblage found in the Tollense river valley clearly does not represent a population with a "normal" demographic composition, where a largely balanced sex ratio and a higher percentage of non-adult and also senile individuals can be expected. It can, for instance, be ruled out that these remains represent bodies from a cemetery that were washed into the river during a high flood. Rather, the high percentage of young adult and middle adult males represented in the assemblage, in combination with the observed cases of perimortem trauma, suggests that the remains are those of battle victims (Bishop and Knüsel 2005; Jantzen *et al.* 2011). The battle hypothesis is supported by the finding of flint and bronze arrow heads along the river (Jantzen *et al.* 2008). However, thus far neither larger weapons like swords have been found, nor have a battlefield, earthworks, or graves been identified. Also, a Bronze Age settlement or camp has thus far not been discovered. Therefore, the interpretation of the site has remained controversial. In this situation, the skeletal material from the site remains the basic source of information for testing the hypothesis that the assemblage represents battle victims, and the demographic composition of the assemblage is of crucial importance for the interpretation of the finding situation. Since so far mainly hip bones and skulls have been studied to obtain information on the demographic composition of the assemblage, we performed additional studies on the femora, since these are currently the most frequently represented skeletal elements at Weltzin 20. It is suggested that gross morphological features as well as cross-sectional properties of the femora can provide additional information on the composition of the assemblage, which is of relevance for testing the "battle victim hypothesis."

2.3   Materials and methods

In the present study, only femora from the site Weltzin 20 were investigated. As of summer of 2012, a total of 90 femora have been recovered. However, metric data have only been obtained for 74 of these. Among these 74 femora, 22 pairs could be matched on the basis of gross morphological comparisons, reducing the number of individuals represented to 52. Femora from juveniles ($n = 16$), as shown by the presence of unfused epiphyses, were excluded from the study. Therefore, the femora of 36 adult individuals formed the basis for the present study. When both femora were available, only the left one was considered for the study.

For these femora, bicondylar length (BL), head diameter (FHD), sagittal (SMD) and transverse midshaft diameter (TMD), and midshaft circumference (MC) were measured with calipers and an osteometric board. Since in certain bones some of these external measurements could not be taken, the number of observations can vary between the different variables.

Femora of 37 individuals from Weltzin 20 were scanned by computed tomography (CT) to analyze mid-diaphyseal (50% biomechanical length) cross-sectional properties. The bones were analyzed basically following the sequence of excavation and were not selected according to specific morphological or other criteria. The 37 femora scanned so far include some bones from juveniles, incomplete bones, and cases in which the femora of single individuals could be matched. Again, bones from juveniles were excluded from the study and in the case of bone pairs, only the left femur was included in the analyses, thereby reducing the sample to 27 specimens. All of these 27 femora were also part of the sample ($n = 36$) for which external measurements were obtained. Analyses were performed using ImageJ 1.45s with the plugin MomentMacroJ v1.3 (www.hopkinsmedicine.org/fae/mmacro.htm). The following areas (in mm^2) of the cross-sections were determined: (1) total area (TA); the TA includes the complete area within the subperiosteal bone surface and represents the gross dimension (size) of the bone; (2) cortical area (CA); CA was calculated as TA minus the medullary area (MA) and is a measure that can serve as a proxy for the rigidity of the bone to axial forces, both compression and tension (Ruff, 2008). For the present study, MA and relative cortical area (%CA; i.e. the relative area of the TA formed by CA) are considered to represent an approximation of the age at death, assuming that, after reaching peak bone mass at a young adult to middle adult age, MA increases and, thus, %CA decreases slightly, leading to osteopenia and osteoporosis in old adult age. Areas were adjusted by body mass (BM; kg). The latter was calculated based on the FHD (mm). Although the FHD does not yield optimal results for BM calculation, it is still widely used in bioarchaeological and paleoanthropological studies (e.g. Grine *et al.* 1995; McHenry 1992; Sládek *et al.* 2006). To enable comparisons between the Weltzin 20 individuals and published data, we used the procedure of Sládek *et al.* (2006), who studied femora of Late Eneolithic and Early Bronze Age individuals. To calculate BM, these authors used the mean of the results obtained from the following two formulae:

$$BM = 2.239 \times FHD - 39.9 \ (McHenry \ 1992)$$

and

$$BM = 2.268 \times FHD - 36.5 \ (Grine \ et \ al. \ 1995).$$

Moments of area (in mm^4) are considered to reflect bending rigidity properties (Ruff 2008). Here, the maximum (I_{max}) and minimum (I_{min}) second moments of area as well as the second moments of area related to, respectively, the anterior–posterior axis (I_y) and the mediolateral axis (I_x) were calculated. Torsion rigidity is best reflected by the polar second moment of area (J), which is calculated as twice the average bending rigidity. Moments of area were standardized by the product of BM and bone length (Ruff 2000).

The external measurements for the Weltzin 20 individuals were compared with published data for adult individuals from Franzhausen I, an early Bronze Age site in Austria (Berner 1988). The cemetery from which the assemblage was recovered was excavated completely, yielding a total of 716 burials (Neugebauer *et al.* 1997). The site is culturally associated with the Unterwölbling culture that is characterized by highly gender-specific burial practices (Neugebauer 1994). This fact was used to validate the results of the morphological sex assessment of the buried individuals (M. Berner, pers. comm. 2012). Metric data for the femora from Franzhausen I analyzed by Berner (1988) were kindly provided by this author and used in the present study. In her study, Berner (1988) distinguished several degrees of reliability with respect to sex assessment and osteometric measurement. For the present study, only individuals whose sex could be reliably assessed according to this classification and only measurements that could be taken with the highest degree of reliability were included in the comparison.

The results of the cross-sectional analysis were compared with data for adults from Eneolithic samples of the Bell Beaker and the Corded Ware cultures and with Bronze Age samples from the Únětice, the Unterwölbling, and the Wieselburger cultures, using data from Sládek *et al.* (2006). The sample of the Unterwölbling culture studied by Sládek *et al.* (2006) includes individuals from the site Franzhausen I.

Since not all data from Weltzin 20 and Franzhausen I were normally distributed (Shapiro–Wilk test), differences between groups were compared with the non-parametric Mann–Whitney U test. Because multiple significance tests were performed on the data, P values were Bonferroni-adjusted. For that, we multiplied the nominal P values from the U test by the number of tests performed. Resulting adjusted P values exceeding 1.0 were reduced to 1.0 (Bland and Altman 1995). Reported in this study are the adjusted P values, with values <0.05 being considered to indicate significance.

For the cross-sectional analyses, the data available for the reference samples were means and standard errors (SE) of the means (Sládek *et al.* 2006). For comparisons, we therefore used the 95% confidence interval (95% CI) for the population mean calculated from these data (sample mean − 1.96 × SE to sample mean + 1.96 × SE). Groups with non-overlapping 95% CIs were considered significantly different. We are aware of the deficiencies of examining overlap between CIs for judging the significance of the difference between two point estimates (Schenker and Gentleman 2001); however, the data needed for a more appropriate test were unavailable. All statistical analyses were performed using SPSS statistics v20.

2.4   Results

2.4.1   *Comparison of external measurements between Weltzin 20 and Franzhausen I*

Mean values for BL, FHD, and MC of the Weltzin 20 assemblage are closer to those of the males from Franzhausen I than to those of the females from that site, while the mean values for the midshaft diameters (SMD and TMD) are intermediate between the corresponding values of the Franzhausen males and females (Table 2.1). For example, BL of the Weltzin 20 femora (mean ± SE = 448.7 ± 3.1 mm; median = 449.0 mm) is only slightly lower than that of the femora from the Franzhausen I males (453.1 ± 4.7 mm; 451.5 mm) and clearly larger than that of the Franzhausen I females (415.5 ± 4.3 mm; 416.5 mm). The difference in BL between the Weltzin 20 femora and the female femora from Franzhausen I is significant (U test; P <0.001), while there is no significant difference between the Weltzin 20 femora and the male femora from Franzhausen I (U test; $P = 1.00$). Regarding FHD, the values for Weltzin 20 (46.6 ± 0.4 mm; 46.3 mm) are slightly, but significantly (U test; $P = 0.045$) lower than those for the Franzhausen I males (48.5 ± 0.4 mm; 48.0 mm), and significantly higher (U test; P <0.001) than those for the Franzhausen I females (42.5 ± 0.3 mm; 42.0 mm).

An indicator for the uniformity of the sex composition of an assemblage could be the amount of intrasample variation. It is assumed that in a purely male or

Table 2.1. *Values of the external measurements (mm) of the Weltzin 20 femora compared with the values from Franzhausen I (Berner* 1988*).*

Measurement	Site	*n*	Min–max	Median	Mean	SE	CV(%)
Bicondylar	Weltzin 20	29	418–480	449.0	448.7	3.13	3.75
length	Franzhausen I males	18	409–482	451.5	453.1	4.65	4.35
	Franzhausen I females	20	383–446	416.5	415.5	4.29	4.62
Head diameter	Weltzin 20	36	43–53	46.3	46.6	0.39	4.99
	Franzhausen I males	28	45–53	48.0	48.5	0.44	4.78
	Franzhausen I females	42	39–48	42.0	42.5	0.31	4.76
Sagittal midshaft	Weltzin 20	36	23–34	27.4	27.8	0.46	9.91
diameter	Franzhausen I males	87	25–35	30.0	29.6	0.25	8.01
	Franzhausen I females	91	21–31	25.0	25.1	0.19	7.27
Transversal	Weltzin 20	36	21–34	27.0	26.7	0.38	8.60
midshaft	Franzhausen I males	88	25–33	28.0	28.1	0.18	6.05
diameter	Franzhausen I females	93	23–29	26.0	25.7	0.15	5.68
Midshaft	Weltzin 20	35	70–95	86.0	85.5	1.06	7.30
circum-	Franzhausen I males	87	76–98	88.0	87.4	0.57	6.07
ference	Franzhausen I females	92	66–88	77.0	76.8	0.45	5.68

SE = standard error; CV(%) = coefficient of variation.

female sample variation is smaller than in a mixed sample. In the Weltzin 20 assemblage, the coefficient of variation (CV) is slightly lower for the BL, similar for the FHD, but markedly higher for the midshaft measurements than in the purely male and female reference assemblages from Franzhausen I (Table 2.1).

The distributions of the TMD values for male and female femora from Franzhausen I overlap partly, while some values are located outside (lower values in females and higher ones in males) this overlap zone (Figure 2.1). Assuming that values below the overlap zone of the Franzhausen I male and female femora are indicative of females, six of the Weltzin 20 femora might be classified as probably female by their TMD alone. Two of these six femora exhibit the lowest values of all specimens included in the study. It therefore seems warranted to classify at least these two individuals as females.

For FHD, nine individuals from Weltzin 20 exhibit values below the minimum of the males from Franzhausen I. However, none of the values for

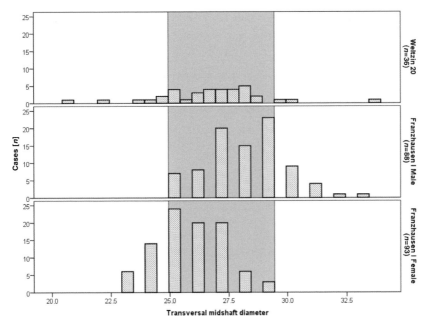

Figure 2.1. Comparison of transversal midshaft diameters (TMD) of the femora from Weltzin 20 and of male and female femora from Franzhausen I (data from Berner 1988). In the Weltzin 20 assemblage, values for six femora are below the overlapping zone between males and females from Franzhausen I. These femora probably represent females.

Weltzin 20 is below the lowest value for the females from Franzhausen I. Therefore the possibility remains that some of these nine femora stem from males.

When FHD and MC are combined in a bivariate scatterplot, males and females from Franzhausen I are clearly separated with only a small overlapping zone (Figure 2.2). The values of the Weltzin 20 femora overlap mostly with those of the Franzhausen I males and only to a lesser extent with those of the Franzhausen I females.

2.4.2 *Cross-sectional analyses*

Like external dimensions, cross-sectional properties are also considered to differ between sexes, with males exhibiting larger dimensions than females. It is further assumed that younger individuals tend to possess a higher %CA than older individuals.

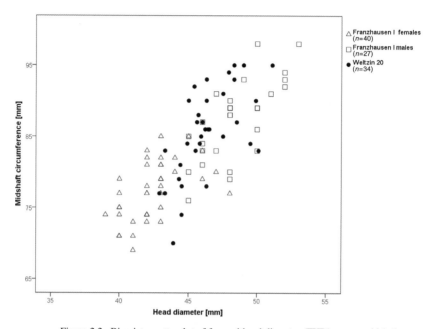

Figure 2.2. Bivariate scatterplot of femoral head diameter (FHD) versus midshaft circumference (MC) for the Weltzin 20 femora (filled circles) and males (squares) and females (triangles) from Franzhausen I. Most of the values for the Weltzin 20 femora cluster with those for the Franzhausen I males.

Except for MA, which shows the lowest average of all samples compared, all average values for the Weltzin 20 femora exceed those of the mixed male–female reference assemblages (Table 2.2). For CA, the 95% CI for the Weltzin 20 femora does not overlap with those of the femora from the other assemblages. Average TA for the Weltzin 20 femora (834.3 mm^2) is close to that for the Bell Beaker sample (828.9 mm^2). Mean values for the second moments of area (I_x, I_y, and J) are highest in the Weltzin 20 femora; however, the 95% CIs overlap with those from some other assemblages. These results could indicate either that the proportion of males is much higher in the Weltzin 20 assemblage compared with the other assemblages, or that the Weltzin 20 individuals were more robust and of a taller stature than those of the other assemblages.

The interpretation that the individuals from Weltzin 20 represent taller and more robust individuals appears less feasible when the Weltzin 20 means are compared with those for males only from the other assemblages. For several parameters (adjusted TA, I_x, I_y, J), the means for Weltzin 20 femora lie close to TA or within the range of those for the other assemblages (Table 2.3). Average CA for the Weltzin 20 femora is, however, markedly higher than those of the others, although there is overlap in 95% CI with some of them.

Table 2.2. *Body mass, femoral cross-sectional areas, and second moments of area for the Weltzin 20 assemblage compared with data for male–female mixed samples from different Eneolithic and Bronze Age contexts (Sládek et al. 2006). Data are given as means (n) and standard errors (SE).*

Parameter	Weltzin 20	Bell Beaker (T)	Corded Ware	Únětice	Unterwölbling	Wieselburger
Body mass [kg]	66.3 (27) ± 0.84	64.7 (23) ± 1.51	64.2 (31) ± 1.47	63.6 (23) ± 1.68	62.1 (37) ± 1.25	61.3 (31) ± 1.31
TA adj. [mm^2]	834.3 (27) ± 16.49	828.9 (19) ± 15.26	814.1 (25) ± 13.25	793.8 (22) ± 16.54	803.4 (26) ± 12.58	746.1 (30) ± 12.52
CA adj. [mm^2]	670.5 (27) ± 12.94*	597.2 (19) ± 13.04	610.8 (25) ± 10.45	593.4 (22) ± 10.20	588.4 (26) ± 9.60	570.7 (30) ± 11.12
MA adj. [mm^2]	163.9 (27) ± 9.04	231.7 (19) ± 13.57	203.3 (25) ± 10.55	200.4 (22) ± 13.22	215.0 (26) ± 9.44	175.3 (30) ± 5.99
I_x (= I_{a-p}) adj. [mm^4]	816.0 (27) ± 39.41	797.4 (19) ± 35.60	779.2 (25) ± 29.70	735.2 (22) ± 36.71	739.0 (26) ± 22.97	677.1 (30) ± 33.52
I_y (= I_{m-l}) adj. [mm^4]	809.3 (27) ± 41.00	791.3 (19) ± 25.98	771.7 (25) ± 27.79	762.9 (22) ± 34.86	726.3 (26) ± 26.27	647.2 (30) ± 28.34
J adj. [mm^4]	1625.2 (27) ± 76.16	1588.8 (19) ± 55.47	1550.9 (25) ± 48.20	1498.2 (22) ± 60.21	1465.2 (26) ± 44.67	1324.3 (30) ± 58.43

Asterisk (*) indicates that the 95% CI for the Weltzin 20 femora does not overlap with that of any other assemblage.

Table 2.3. Body mass, femoral cross-sectional areas, and second moments of area for the Weltzin 20 assemblage compared with data for male-only samples from different Eneolithic and Bronze Age contexts (Sládek et al. 2006). Data are given as means (n) and standard errors (SE).

Parameter	Weltzin 20	Bell Beaker (T)	Corded Ware	Únětice	Unterwölbling	Wieselburger
Body mass [kg]	66.3 (27) ± 0.84	68.6 (13) ± 1.34	69.4 (15) ± 1.36	70.0 (9) ± 1.99	71.8 (11) ± 1.17	69.4 (12) ± 0.92
TA adj. [mm^2]	834.3 (27) ± 16.49	840.5 (11) ± 21.59	839.7 (12) ± 18.16	802.2 (9) ± 24.73	802.7 (9) ± 22.76	798.7 (12) ± 18.10
CA adj. [mm^2]	670.5 (27) ± 12.94	596.9 (11) ± 20.18	629.4 (12) ± 12.42	594.9 (9) ± 15.47	594.7 (9) ± 15.19	621.8 (12) ± 14.91
MA adj. [mm^2]	163.9 (27) ± 9.04	243.6 (11) ± 18.24	210.3 (12) ± 12.80	207.4 (9) ± 23.38	208.0 (9) ± 19.15	176.9 (12) ± 8.83
I_x (= I_{a-p}) adj. [mm^4]	816.0 (27) ± 39.41	858.8 (11) ± 51.66	899.1 (12) ± 26.65	767.9 (9) ± 53.84	816.9 (9) ± 23.59	861.3 (12) ± 36.95
I_y (= I_{m-l}) adj. [mm^4]	809.3 (27) ± 41.00	823.6 (11) ± 39.92	811.7 (12) ± 41.93	824.2 (9) ± 60.13	796.6 (9) ± 41.60	783.2 (12) ± 42.79
J adj. [mm^4]	1625.2 (27) ± 76.16	1682.4 (11) ± 83.20	1710.8 (12) ± 48.60	1592.1 (9) ± 84.30	1613.5 (9) ± 53.81	1644.5 (12) ± 68.50

Mean BM and mean MA, in contrast, are lowest for the Weltzin 20 individuals, although again there is overlap in 95% CIs with some of the other assemblages (for MA only with the Wieselburger culture).

Relative CA (%CA; calculated on the basis of the group means for TA and CA) is much higher (mean of 80.37) in the Weltzin 20 assemblage than in both the male (means from 71.02 to 77.85) and the mixed (means from 72.05 to 76.49) samples. This suggests a higher proportion of young individuals in the Weltzin 20 assemblage compared with the other assemblages.

2.5   Discussion

In humans, the femur is one of the most extensively studied bones in regard to its potential for sex determination (e.g. Asala 2001, 2002; Black III 1978; Dittrick and Suchey 1986; Mall *et al.* 2000; Milner and Boldsen 2012). The high number of studies performed reflects a common issue in sex determination based on skeletal remains – that is, the question of which reference data should be used for comparison with a particular sample. Many studies have been performed on modern femora to obtain valid data in forensic contexts for comparison with individuals from different geographic and ethnic origins. It is, however, problematic to use these reference data for comparisons with prehistoric femora, especially in the case of commingled assemblages (Hoppa 2002). At first glance, information on sexual dimorphism in historic or prehistoric femora may seem more suitable for comparison with data from other historic or prehistoric cases. Such studies were, for example, performed by Black III (1978), who provided a method to sex archaeological skeletal remains by measuring femoral shaft circumference. The data were generated on individuals from the prehistoric Libben site (Ohio, USA). Dittrick and Suchey (1986) studied sexually dimorphic traits in prehistoric femora from California. However, the latter authors caution against sexing individuals of different origin using the same discriminant functions. Considering this caveat, we chose to compare the values of the Weltzin 20 femora with those obtained for assemblages that were relatively close in time (Bronze Age, Eneolithic) and origin (Central Europe), assuming that, the closer the assemblages are with respect to these parameters, the more similar they probably are with respect to the analyzed morphological traits (Weiss 1972).

The results obtained for the Weltzin 20 femora are consistent with earlier interpretations based on gross morphological analyses of skeletal remains in suggesting that the assemblage consists predominantly of the remains of male individuals. The high TA, CA, and %CA values are in line with the view that the femora largely represent young and middle adult males, who are assumed to have been killed in battle. However, both the results of the gross morphological sex assessment on skulls and pelvic bones (Brinker *et al.* 2013) and the results of the present metrical analyses on the femora suggest that some female individuals are also represented in the assemblage.

Although fighting and warfare are typically regarded as male behavior, there is evidence from many time periods and cultures that females were also present at or close to battlefields and sometimes even took part in the actual fighting. For instance, it is accepted that women participated in various functions of warfare in ancient Greek and Roman societies (Wintjes 2012). Authors like Plutarch (*Life of Gaius Marius*), Caesar (*Gallic War*), and Tacitus (*Germania*) described that, in Germanic tribes, females accompanied males to battle and their presence was an important motivation for the warriors to protect their families and tribes. Especially when it came to defending the camp and wagons, women became actively engaged in fighting, as is reported by Plutarch for the battle of the Romans against the Ambrones (Plutarch 1988). The phenomenon of "female warriors" is also documented from the European Middle Ages (McLaughlin 1990), and in Napoleon's Grande Armée females acted in a number of important logistic roles, including assisting surgeons and helping the wounded back from the firing line (Elting 1997). Warfare was never just fighting, but was always associated with logistical challenges, and women were commonly involved in solving these challenges. The presence of a number of female bones at the Bronze Age Weltzin 20 site in the Tollense river valley does, therefore, not come as a surprise and does not contradict the battlefield hypothesis.

The age-at-death composition of the assemblage from Weltzin 20 basically supports the battlefield hypothesis. Thus, bones of children and very old persons, who are unlikely to be active participants in a battle, are (largely) missing. Instead, the assemblage consists of the remains of juveniles and young adult and middle adult individuals, i.e. those age groups that can be expected to represent the majority of active participants in a battle. As in the case of female remains, it would, however, not be surprising also to find the remains of a few children and old adults if the warriors were accompanied by their families. Thus far, only a single infant bone has been recovered at the Weltzin 20 site; however, its affiliation to the Bronze Age context is unclear and radiocarbon dating failed because of poor collagen preservation. In contrast, the 178 bones from juvenile individuals (MNI = 9) recovered so far are clearly associated to the Bronze Age context. Juvenile femora were not considered in the present study owing to non-fusion of the epiphyses. Based on studies of adult femora, MA might be seen as an indicator for age at death. It is assumed that, after peaking at middle adult age, bone mass decreases, leading to higher MA and lower %CA values. Average MA in the Weltzin 20 femora is the lowest and %CA the highest of all assemblages, indicating an on-average younger age at death for the Weltzin 20 individuals. Clearly, these measurements provide only very rough estimates for the age at death; however, the results are in line with the findings based on other, established methods of age-at-death estimation.

2.6   Conclusions

The present study showed that the adult femora of the Weltzin 20 assemblage originate mostly from young adult to middle-aged males. This is in line with the hypothesis, put forward based on the analyses of skulls and pelves, that the skeletal remains from the site represent battle victims (Brinker *et al.* 2013). However, results of external bone measurements suggest that some adult females are represented in the assemblage and were thus present at or close to the presumed battlefield.

The study demonstrated that demographic data relevant for the interpretation of archaeological sites can be obtained by analyzing femora in addition to the more commonly studied skulls and pelves. Femora are often among the most frequent and best-preserved human skeletal elements at archaeological sites (Bennike 1985). They constitute a valuable source of information for osteoarchaeological studies, especially if suitable reference data are available.

Acknowledgments

Margit Berner is gratefully acknowledged for providing raw data from her doctoral thesis on the bones from Franzhausen I. We thank Jürgen Piek for CT scanning of the bones at the University of Rostock. The investigation in the Tollense river valley was supported by the Ministry of Education, Science and Culture of Mecklenburg-Western Pomerania and since 2010 by the Deutsche Forschungsgemeinschaft (German Research Foundation).

References

Asala, S. A. (2001). Sex determination from the head of the femur of South African whites and blacks. *Forensic Science International*, **117**, 15–22.

(2002). The efficiency of the demarking point of the femoral head as a sex determining parameter. *Forensic Science International*, **127**, 114–18.

Bennike, P. (1985). *Palaeopathology of Danish Skeletons. A Comparative Study of Demography, Disease and Injury.* Copenhagen: Akademisk Forlag.

Berner, M. (1988). Das Gräberfeld Von Franzhausen I: Metrische und demographische Analyse. Vienna: Unpublished doctoral thesis.

Bishop, N. A. & Knüsel, C. (2005). A palaeodemographic investigation of warfare in prehistory. In: Parker Pearson, M. & Thorpe, I. J. (eds.) *Warfare, Violence and*

Slavery in Prehistory: Proceedings of a Prehistoric Society Conference at Sheffield University. Oxford: Archaeopress, 201–16.

Black III, T. K. (1978). A new method for assessing the sex of fragmentary skeletal remains: femoral shaft circumference. *American Journal of Physical Anthropology*, **48**, 227–31.

Bland, J. M. & Altman, D. G. (1995). Multiple significance tests: the Bonferroni method. *British Medical Journal*, **310**, 170.

Brinker, U., Flohr, S., Piek, J. & Orschiedt, J. (2013). Violent death and injury in bronze age human remains from riverine contexts in the Tollense Valley, Germany: victims of a battle? In: Knüsel, C. & Smith, M. (eds.) *The Bioarchaeology of Human Conflict: Traumatized Bodies from Early Prehistory to the Present.* London: Routledge.

Buikstra, J. E. & Ubelaker, D. H. (eds.) (1994). *Standards for Data Collection from Human Skeletal Remains. Proceedings of a Seminar at the Field Museum of Natural History.* Fayetteville: Arkansas Archeological Survey, Research Series, No. 44.

Dittrick, J. & Suchey, J. M. (1986). Sex determination of prehistoric central California skeletal remains using discriminant analysis of the femur and humerus. *American Journal of Physical Anthropology*, **70**, 3–9.

Elting, J. R. (1997). *Swords Around a Throne: Napoleon's Grande Armée.* New York: Da Capo Press.

Fiorato, V., Boylston, A. & Knüsel, C. (eds.) (2007). *Blood Red Roses: The Archaeology of a Mass Grave from the Battle of Towton AD 1461.* Oxford: Oxbow Books.

Grine, F. E., Jungers, W. L., Tobias, P. V. & Pearson, O. M. (1995). Fossil Homo femur from Berg Aukas, Northern Namibia. *American Journal of Physical Anthropology*, **97**, 151–85.

Hoppa, R. D. (2002). Paleodemography: looking back and thinking ahead. In: Hoppa, R. D. & Vaupel, J. W. (eds.) *Paleodemography: Age Distribution from Skeletal Samples.* Cambridge: Cambridge University Press, 9–28.

Jantzen, C., Jantzen, D. & Terberger, T. (2008). Der Fundplatz Weltzin, Lkr. Demmin – ein Zeugnis bronzezeitlicher Konflikte? In: Piek, J. & Terberger, T. (eds.) *Traumatologische und pathologische Veränderungen an prähistorischen und historischen Skelettresten – Diagnose, Ursachen und Kontext: Interdisziplinärer Workshop in Rostock-Warnemünde, 17.-18. November 2006.* Rahden, Westf: Leidorf, 89–98.

Jantzen, D., Brinker, U., Orschiedt, J., Heinemeier, J., Piek, J., Hauenstein, K., Krüger, J., Lidke, G., Lübke, H., Lampe, R., Lorenz, S., Schult, M. & Terberger, T. (2011). A Bronze Age battlefield? Weapons and trauma in the Tollense Valley, North-Eastern Germany. *Antiquity*, **85**, 417–33.

Kjellström, A. (2005). A sixteenth-century warrior grave from Uppsala, Sweden: the Battle of Good Friday. *International Journal of Osteoarchaeology*, **15**, 23–50.

Lambert, P. M. (2002). The archaeology of war: a North American perspective. *Journal of Archaeological Research*, **10**, 207–41.

Mall, G., Graw, M., Gehring, K. & Hubig, M. (2000). Determination of sex from femora. *Forensic Science International*, **113**, 315–21.

Mays, S. (1998). *The Archaeology of Human Bones*. London, New York: Routledge.

McHenry, H. M. (1992). Body size and proportions in early hominids. *American Journal of Physical Anthropology*, **87**, 407–31.

McLaughlin, M. (1990). The woman warrior: gender, warfare and society in medieval Europe. *Women's Studies*, **17**, 193–200.

Milner, G. R. & Boldsen, J. L. (2012). Humeral and femoral head diameters in recent white American skeletons. *Journal of Forensic Sciences*, **57**, 35–40.

Neugebauer, C., Neugebauer, J. & Gattringer, A. (1997). *Franzhausen: Das frühbronzezeitliche Gräberfeld 1*. Horn: Berger.

Neugebauer, J. (1994). Die frühe und beginnende mittlere Bronzezeit in Ostösterreich südlich der Donau. *Zalai Múzeum*, **5**, 85–111.

Peter-Röcher, H. (2006). Spuren der Gewalt – Identifikation und soziale Relevanz in diachroner Perspektive. *Beiträge zur Ur- und Frühgeschichte Mecklenburg-Vorpommerns*, **41**, 163–74.

Plutarch (1988). *Demetrius and Antony, Pyrrhus and Caius Marius*, 1st edn, Harvard: Harvard University Press.

Ruff, C. B. (2000). Body size, body shape, and long bone strength in modern humans. *Journal of Human Evolution*, **38**, 269–90.

(2008). Biomechanical analyses of archaeological human skeletons. In: Katzenberg, M. A. & Saunders, S. R. (eds.) *Biological Anthropology of the Human Skeleton*, 2nd edn. Hoboken: Wiley-Liss, 183–206.

Schenker, N. & Gentleman, J. F. (2001). On judging the significance of differences by examining the overlap between confidence intervals. *The American Statistician*, **55**, 182–6.

Sládek, V., Berner, M. & Sailer, R. (2006). Mobility in central European late Eneolithic and Early Bronze Age: femoral cross-sectional geometry. *American Journal of Physical Anthropology*, **130**, 320–32.

Wahl, J. & König, H. (1987). Anthropologisch-traumatologische Untersuchung der menschlichen Skelettreste aus dem bandkeramischen Massengrab bei Talheim, Kreis Heilbronn. *Fundberichte Baden-Württemberg*, **12**, 65–193.

Weiss, K. M. (1972). On the systematic bias in skeletal sexing. *American Journal of Physical Anthropology*, **37**, 239–49.

Wintjes, J. (2012). "Keep the Women out of the Camp!": women and military institutions in the Classical World. In: Hacker, B. C. & Vining, M. (eds.) *A Companion to Women's Military History*. Leiden, Boston: Brill, 17–60.

3 The taphonomy of maritime warfare: a forensic reinterpretation of sharp force trauma from the 1676 wreck of the Royal Swedish Warship Kronan

ANNA KJELLSTRÖM AND

MICHELLE D. HAMILTON

3.1 Introduction

By the end of the Age of Discovery, European expansionist policies to establish commercial and political supremacy were in full effect, accomplished largely via maritime expertise with large-scale exploration and colonization initiatives. In addition to nation-building activities abroad, disputes over internal European lands and possessions also relied heavily on maritime forces, and these engagements often resulted in mass casualties when ships were lost at sea during combat hostilities. This chapter explores osteological signatures of seventeenth-century naval warfare via examination of human skeletal remains recovered from one such catastrophic maritime disaster.

In 1676 the battleship *Kronan*, the flagship vessel of the Royal Swedish Navy, sank in the midst of combat maneuvers during the Scanian War. Of the 850 men originally on board, only 42 survived the sinking event. Accounting for the 200 or so bodies that washed ashore in the 2-week period immediately after the disaster, the remains of approximately 600 men rested with the ship (Einarsson 1990).

The wreck of the *Kronan* remained on the ocean floor for over 300 years before it was rediscovered by Anders Franzén in 1980. Since the rediscovery, annual nautical archaeological excavations have been carried out at the site (Einarsson 2013; Einarsson and Mörzer Bruyns 2003). Within the first few years of excavations, approximately 370 kilograms (815 pounds) of commingled human bones, primarily found on the lower gun deck, were recovered.

Bioarchaeological and Forensic Perspectives on Violence: How Violent Death is Interpreted from Skeletal Remains, ed. D. L. Martin and C. P. Anderson. Published by Cambridge University Press. © Cambridge University Press 2014.

While some articulated bone elements were recovered together (i.e. humerus, radius, ulna), most of the skeletal elements were commingled. An initial analysis was conducted in 1997 by the late Professor Ebba M. During of the Osteoarchaeological Research Laboratory at Stockholm University. After completing the preliminary osteological analysis, During estimated the minimum number of individuals recovered during the excavations to be around 260. This number is likely an underestimation, since During did not have access to an additional 150 kilograms (330 pounds) of bones recovered after she passed away.

Many of the bones show striking (and completely unexpected) evidence of sharp force traumatic defects. This research evaluates that trauma in the context of what is known about the sinking of the ship, analysis of the sharp force injury patterns and appearance, consideration of the burial environment, and examination of possible taphonomic processes, in order to provide a new interpretation for the ambiguous sharp force skeletal trauma present on the bones from the men of the *Kronan*.

3.2   The Battle of Öland and loss of the battleship *Kronan*

In Scandinavia, the Swedish empire saw threats to her land holdings as a result of a number of martial conflicts in the region harkening back to the Northern Seven Years' War (1563–1570). The Scanian War of 1675–1679 was fought between Sweden and the allied forces of Brandenberg and a Danish–Dutch and Austrian alliance, and resulted from the 1675 Danish invasion of Scania, a Danish border region originally ceded to Sweden in 1658 (Lindkvist and Sjöberg 2010).

Construction of the Swedish man-of-war *Kronan* ("Crown") was begun in 1665 by English shipwright Francis Sheldon under the direction of the Swedish monarch King Charles XI (Delgado 1997; Einarsson 1990). At the time of her construction, the *Kronan* was among the largest naval war vessels in the world, with a crew consisting of 850 men and heavy armament that included over 120 cannons, each varying in weight up to 4.5 metric tons (5 tons) (Einarsson 2001; 2006). As the new flagship of the Royal Swedish Naval fleet, the outbreak of regional hostilities necessitated her entry into the Scanian War, where she made her last stand at the Battle of Öland.

On June 1, 1676 the *Kronan* met the pursuing Danish–Dutch enemy fleet near the island of Öland in the Baltic Sea. Historic eye-witness statements report that, as the *Kronan* attempted to confront the enemy fleet, the ship turned too quickly and began to keel over. As she foundered in the water, munitions and powder magazines aboard the ship then exploded, destroying

Figure 3.1. "The Battle of Öland," 1686 oil painting by Danish artist Claus Møinichen. The *Kronan* is in the foreground, foundering in the water as her on-board munitions explode.

the entire bow structure and causing the *Kronan* to disappear very quickly below the waves (Figure 3.1). In addition to the large numbers of sailors, soldiers, and crew on board, the Admiral of the Realm Commander Lorentz Creutz and numerous upper echelon naval officers also perished, decimating a large portion of the command structure of the entire Swedish naval force at the time. As noted previously, of the 850 crew members on board, only 42 survived. After the *Kronan* sank a number of bodies washed ashore, but the remains of approximately 600 men remained entombed 26 meters (85.3 feet) deep at the bottom of the sea for the next three centuries (Einarsson 1990).

3.3   Recovery of the *Kronan*'s cannons

Despite the depth of the wreck, soon after the sinking the Swedish monarchy approved an expedition to recover the valuable cannons from the *Kronan*, an operation that lasted from 1682 to 1686 (Einarsson 1990). Twenty years previously, a number of cannons from another sunken Swedish warship named the *Vasa* were successfully recovered with the use of a simple diving bell that stood almost 1.5 meters (5 feet) tall (Bevan 1999), and similar techniques were employed with the *Kronan* to salvage her armament.

At the time of the wreck of the *Kronan*, diving bells had been deployed for the better part of a century for the purposes of recovering equipment and treasure from sunken vessels. Diving bells are deep-sea diving chambers that provide divers a limited air supply, allowing them to work at depth on the ocean floor. They were typically built of wood in the shape of an inverted cup with an opening at the base. Divers would first position themselves inside the bell, and the weighted bell would then be lowered from a ship into the ocean, open base first. The internal pressure of the air inside the bell kept the ocean water from rushing inside, allowing the divers an air supply source while they engaged in salvage and recovery work. Prior to 1690, diving bells were primitive and not equipped with renewable air sources, which meant that divers were working in dark and dangerous conditions and with limited time constraints (i.e. 30 minutes at a time) and the bell had to be regularly raised to renew and replenish the air supply (Bevan 1999).

The use of diving bells and recovery equipment such as hooks to attach to the cannons so that they could be hauled out of the water made it possible to save almost half of the cannons aboard the *Kronan* during the 4-year salvage operation, with the largest recovered cannon weighing almost 4 metric tons (4.5 tons).

3.4 Taphonomic environment

Despite resting on the floor of the Baltic Sea for over 300 years, the condition of the osteological material is surprisingly very good, but three centuries of diagenetic processes are nevertheless apparent. Most notable are the consequences of direct contact with the ship's metal structures, staining many bones a dark brown to orange color, and in one case leaving corroded metal precipitate merged to the bone surface (Figure 3.2). A number of distal and proximal portions of long bones also show postmortem scuffing and abrasion damage (Figure 3.3).

In the region of the Baltic Sea where the *Kronan* was discovered, the condition and preservation of organic material is known to range from very good to excellent. A number of factors characterize the depositional environment, including weak subsurface ocean currents, the deep depth of the wreck at 26 m (85.3 feet), brackish water of low salinity, temperatures seldom exceeding 5° Celsius (41° Fahrenheit), and the complete absence of aquatic scavengers and bone modifiers that all contribute to favorable conditions for the preservation of bone, wood, and other organic material, even after three centuries. In fact, in addition to the skeletal remains, the wreck of the *Kronan* has yielded a large quantity of excellently preserved organic materials such as textiles, articles of fine clothing, butchered cow and pig bones, garlic cloves, leaves of tobacco, wooden ship figureheads, and other items characterizing shipboard life in the seventeenth century.

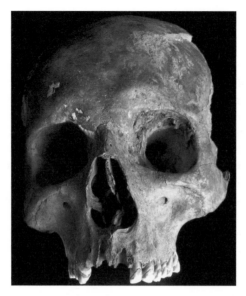

Figure 3.2. Cranium infused with rusted metal. Also note traces of multiple horizontal straight-line defects on left zygomatic bone.

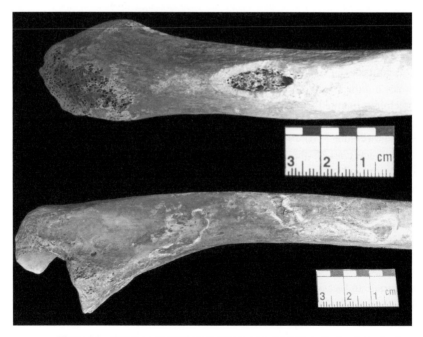

Figure 3.3. Abrasion and scuffing alterations on a distal fibula (top) and proximal ulna (bottom).

3.5   Demography, health, and trauma aboard the *Kronan*

While the crew of the *Kronan* was composed of men from all social strata, titles of officers and working men fluctuated during the seventeenth century. Nevertheless, generally the Admiral was in command, followed by a Captain, a Lieutenant-Commander, several skippers and foremen, and then seamen of lower rankings. Other professional classes on board included administrative personnel, physicians, pharmacists, soldiers, the ship's priest, carpenters, sail makers, trumpeters, and a timpanist (Skenbäck 1985). Most of the occupational groups were subdivided according to rank (i.e. apprentices, journeymen, and masters). Based on archived letters from some of the widows and mothers of the fallen men, the age of the crew ranged from young boys serving in apprentice positions to professional mariners who had served in the Royal Navy for more than 40 years (Olsson 1985).

The biological profile assessed by During as part of the preliminary osteological analysis confirmed the historical documentation, and showed that the skeletal assemblage was composed of males ranging from the age of 9 to individuals in their 60s. A variety of pathological conditions consistent with both the historical period and the occupation class are represented in the skeletal material. A range of antemortem trauma and disease is observed on both cranial and postcranial bone elements, including signs of cribra orbitalia, enamel hypoplasia, caries, chronic infections in the form of periapical changes and periostitis, and degenerative disorders such as osteoarthritis and osteochondritis dissecans.

Beside these antemortem conditions and pathologies, intriguing evidence of violent trauma was also found. Throughout her analysis, During identified perimortem defects characteristic of sharp force trauma on at least 27 of the 260 individuals (10.4%) (see Figure 3.4 for examples charted on long bones). This was not an expected finding, since the presence of sharp force defects is not in accordance with percussive or blast injuries that might be expected as a result of the ship-board explosions that blew the bow off, leading to the quick sinking of the ship. Additionally, according to contemporary ethnohistoric sources, at no time did any enemy forces board the fast-sinking ship to engage in close quarter, hand-to-hand combat (Grandin 1985).

In her analysis, During suggested that these sharp force injuries were incurred while the ship was sinking, and are the result of the actions of trapped and panicked men wielding their knives and swords on each other in a desperate attempt to slash their way out of the confines of the sinking ship:

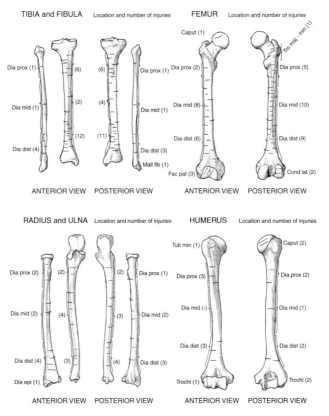

Figure 3.4. Locations and numbers of sharp force defect distributions on the long bones originally charted by Professor Ebba M. During. Dia prox, proximal diameter; dia mid, midshaft diameter; dia dist, distal diameter; mall fib, malleolus of the fibula; fac pat, patellar facet on the distal femur; tro maj–min, greater and lesser trochanter; cond lat, lateral condyle; dist epi, distal epiphysis; tub min, lesser tubercle; trochl, trochlea.

Probably what we are looking at, and what these injuries are indicating, is a situation on board the sinking ship characterized by chaos and panic. Members of the crew are desperately trying to get out of the rapidly sinking ship, using all the means at their disposal, both physical as well as psychological (During 1997: 594).

This explanation, while initially plausible, requires further examination based on what we know of the circumstances of the sinking, as well as the conflicting appearance, patterning, and distribution of the trauma. A convincing clarification of the cause and timing of the defects has never been formulated, and other potential scenarios have not been addressed.

A collaboration between the authors from the Osteoarchaeological Research Laboratory at Stockholm University and the Forensic Anthropology Center at Texas State University-San Marcos began in 2010, with the goal of reassessing the sharp force defects in detail and providing more information on the patterning and timing of wound occurrence. This chapter explores alternative interpretations for the injuries present on the skeletal remains using a forensic anthropological perspective, in an attempt to both build upon and enhance previous bioarchaeological assessments.

3.6   Sharp force trauma

Sharp force trauma (often abbreviated, "SFT") is a collective term for injuries inflicted by bladed or pointed tools possessing edges, bevels, or points (Komar and Buikstra 2008; SWGANTH 2011). Typical weapon classes capable of producing sharp force trauma include knives, swords, axes, machetes, hatchets, and saws. Bladed weapons capable of inflicting sharp force trauma were present aboard the *Kronan* in the form of personal knives carried by the common sailors, and rapier swords belonging to many of the soldier and officer classes on board.

The trauma analysis protocol utilized in this project incorporates descriptions and recommendations utilized in forensic anthropological praxis, survey, and research contexts (e.g. Kimmerle and Baraybar 2008; Komar and Buikstra 2008; Merbs 1989; Ong 1999; Quatrehomme 2007; Sauer and Simson 1984; Stewart 1979; SWGANTH 2011; Symes *et al.* 2001, 2010; Tegtmeyer 2012) in an effort to elucidate information about the patterning and timing of the specific sharp force injuries observed on the men of the *Kronan*.

Signatures of sharp force trauma on bone include defects such as straight-line incisions, stab wounds, chop and hack marks, punctures, saw marks, gouges, and kerfs (Kimmerle and Baraybar 2008; Symes *et al.* 2010). There are also ancillary and associated injuries, including chop and crush marks, that may mimic blunt force injuries or may present as a combination of sharp force and blunt force injuries known as "sharp blunt" or "corto-contundente" trauma that results from dual contact from a weapon's sharp and non-sharp components in a single wounding episode (i.e. an axe blade can leave an incised cut mark at the initial contact point, but additionally the non-bladed portions of the axe head may also leave defects on the bone that are blunt force in nature and appearance) (Komar and Buikstra 2008; SWGANTH 2011).

A standard analysis protocol was developed for this project to document the defects present on the bones:

1. The bones were examined macroscopically and microscopically, and all sharp force defects were identified and described according to element, location, side, length, width, and depth.
2. The anatomical positioning and number of the defects present on each bone were documented together with shape, length, depth, and direction (where possible). All kerf walls and floors were microscopically examined under a light microscope (magnification ranging from 8× to 35×), measured, and photographed (a "kerf" is the actual incised cut or channel; Symes *et al.* 2010). Existence and morphology of striae, if present, were noted and described.
3. Since the bones were commingled, no attempts could be made to identify wound patterns specific to any single individual, although overall patterns of defect locations were documented (Figure 3.5).

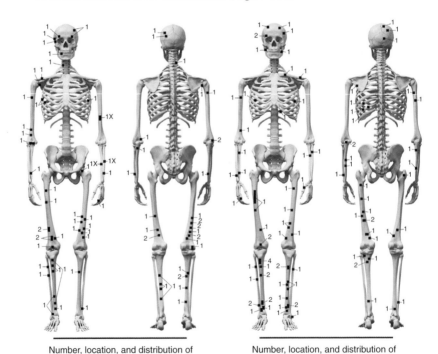

Number, location, and distribution of sharp force chop wound defects (note: an "X" denotes defects located on the same individual).

Number, location, and distribution of sharp force incised (straight line) defects.

Figure 3.5. Overall number, location, and distribution of sharp force defects (chop marks and incisions) found throughout the commingled assemblage (after Lodén 2008).

4. Butchered cow and pig bones (*Bos taurus, Sus scrofa*) from barrels containing the crew's subsistence provisions were also recovered from the wreck, and they exhibit clear sharp force butchering marks. The cow and pig bones were used as a reference sample of known sharp force defects inflicted during the early postmortem interval to compare against the trauma observed on the human remains.

3.7   Timing of defects – antemortem, perimortem, and postmortem considerations

Establishing the timing of injuries in skeletal material – especially during the perimortem and early postmortem interval – can be a difficult endeavor. Diagnostic criteria to identify the temporal timeframe in which defects are sustained are dependent on features such as the presence of healing, or the "fresh" or "dry" response state of the bones derived from the organic collagen content and associated elasticity levels (Aufderheide and Rodríguez-Martin 1998).

While determining whether skeletal trauma is associated with the perimortem or postmortem interval has important legal consequences in modern forensic investigations, in bioarchaeological and historic skeletons, understanding the timing of these defects can also aid in understanding the cause and/or manner of death, as well as the circumstances surrounding the depositional environment. In the case of the *Kronan*, we are confronted with historic eye-witness accounts that do not initially match with the osteological evidence at hand, and thus the question of timing is significant.

3.7.1   Antemortem trauma

The recognition of antemortem injuries, suffered while the individual was living, is relatively straightforward because of the presence of active bone response and healing around the site of injury or disease process (Ortner 2003). According to standardized forensic anthropology guidelines (SWGANTH 2011: 2), characteristics that indicate antemortem trauma include:

• Evidence of healing or healed defects
• Development of a pseudarthrosis
• Trauma-induced degenerative joint disease
• Infectious response
• Dental fractures with worn edges
• Surgical implants or other medical devices.

3.7.2   *Perimortem trauma*

Perimortem injuries are those sustained by the individual in the period surrounding the death event itself (Bennike 2008). In the absence of soft tissue, it can be difficult to assess injuries sustained in the perimortem interval on skeletonized individuals. This is because bones may retain the same signatures of trauma and damage sustained in the perimortem interval as defects inflicted in the early postmortem interval, owing to the inherent plastic properties of fresh bone retained for some period even after an individual's death (White *et al.* 2012). This inability to estimate accurately the timing of wound occurrence from the perimortem to early postmortem interval may confound interpretations and lead to incorrect assumptions about the mechanism and causes of trauma, because bone may still show perimortem bone response even if the defects were incurred in the postmortem period. According to standardized forensic anthropology guidelines (SWGANTH 2011: 3), characteristics that indicate perimortem trauma include:

• A lack of osteological activity such as healing or infectious response
• The presence of fresh bone fracture characteristics (e.g. plastic response)
• The absence of dry bone fracture characteristics (e.g. angular fractures)
• An overall fracture pattern characteristic of a terminal event (e.g. rapid deceleration).

3.7.3   *Postmortem defects*

Postmortem defects are taphonomic alterations that occur after the individual has died, and are unassociated with the death event itself. Postmortem defects in dry bone from archaeological, historic, or forensic depositional contexts can be comparatively easy to identify because, once bone loses its organic content, it reacts differently than fresh bone would to similar pressures or forces, producing identifiable defects (i.e. angular fractures), and coloration changes (i.e. lighter edges of more recently fractured bone). According to standardized forensic anthropology guidelines (SWGANTH 2011: 3), characteristics that indicate postmortem damage include:

• Differentially stained or recently exposed surfaces
• A lack of healing
• Characteristics of the break lacking evidence of a plastic component
• Pattern of damage.

The challenge in interpreting the category and timing of defects on the skeletal material from the *Kronan* not only involves distinguishing perimortem from postmortem defects, but is made all the more difficult by the fact that the bones were never in a dry postmortem state until they were recovered some three centuries later. They remained waterlogged in conditions conducive to organic preservation for over 300 years, likely retaining organic content and biomechanical properties of fresh bone for quite some time.

3.8   Results of analysis of sharp force trauma

Using standard forensic anthropological protocols and macroscopic and microscopic analysis, a sample of 18 out of the total 27 human bone elements recovered from the *Kronan* displaying traumatic sharp force defects was analyzed.

Given the known circumstances surrounding the sinking of the *Kronan*, the first question we asked is whether these defects were more consistent with blast force trauma (expected) or sharp force trauma (unexpected). The analysis confirmed that the morphology of these injuries was wholly consistent with sharp force trauma (Figure 3.6) and that no conclusive evidence of blast force, percussive, or explosive injuries or fractures was noted within the remainder of the collection, with the possible exception of a scapula clearly displaying a square impalement defect (Figure 3.7).

Next, the sharp force defects were examined to determine if the perimortem versus postmortem timing of these injuries could be assessed. Potential

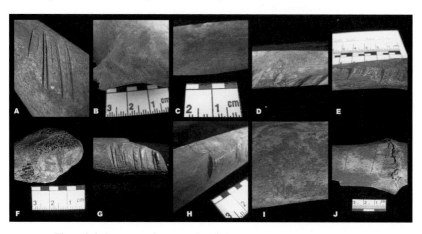

Figure 3.6. Representative examples of sharp force trauma (incisions and chop marks) found throughout the *Kronan*'s skeletal assemblage. A = Right distal femur. B = Right frontal. C = Right ulnar shaft. D = Left tibial shaft. E = Right proximal ulna. F = Right distal fibula. G = Right humeral shaft. H = Left fibular shaft. I = Right distal tibia. J = Cow rib.

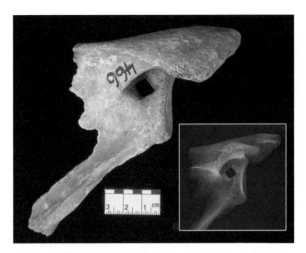

Figure 3.7. Photo of right scapula (left) and inset radiograph (right) displaying a square impalement defect.

indicators of fresh bone response to certain types of sharp force trauma can include such features as breakaway notches or spurs, chipping, chattering, or bone shaving with attendant polish (Kerley 1973; Ong 1999; Symes *et al.* 2010). However, where these defects were noted (i.e. the chattering shown in Figure 3.6E, or the polish shown in Figure 3.6G), it is unknown if they resulted from an injury sustained in the perimortem interval or if they were incurred in the postmortem interval and merely mimic a perimortem defect because of the waterlogged (and hence potentially plastic) nature of the bone. Because of the inherent complexity of the submerged depositional context, we were unable to determine definitively whether the sharp force defects were inflicted in the perimortem or postmortem period. Despite this, we do have known comparative samples against which to compare these defects. The butchered cow and pig bones recovered from the wreck of the *Kronan* provide exemplars for what waterlogged postmortem sharp force defects look like on bone. These animal bones were protected in barrels and a majority show clear signs of being slaughtered units of meat. Among the commingled animal bones are elements demonstrating trauma similar to that found on the human bones. For example, a butchered cow rib displays straight-line incisions that bear a striking resemblance to the morphology of the sharp force trauma seen on many of the human bones (compare Figure 3.6A and 3.6J), so postmortem infliction of these defects should not be ruled out.

The final question we explored was whether the morphology, distribution, and patterning of sharp force defects reflected what would be expected in hand-to-hand combat by men wielding knives and swords. Our examination showed that the sharp force defects are not distributed on the expected bone elements if combatants were engaged in face-to-face (or even face-to-back) combat (Ong 1999), i.e. we might expect bones of the head, chest, arms, and back to sustain the most damage, but, in fact, the patterning and location of trauma appears to be distributed across many elements (see Figures 3.4 and 3.5), and appears to be focused on the arms and especially the legs, with many incisions located in atypical areas such as internal joint surfaces that would have been difficult to access in living, fleshed individuals (see Figure 3.6F).

3.9   Alternative interpretation of the ambiguous sharp force trauma

This current project was undertaken to better define the trauma type, location, and patterning present on a number of skeletal elements recovered from the wreck of the *Kronan*. In terms of differentiating between perimortem and postmortem trauma, no definitive assessment can be offered owing to the complexities of estimating timing of these defects in waterlogged bone subject to three centuries of diagenetic modifications. However, the results of this current osteological analysis show the following:

- If the defects reflect close-quarter combat, they are not distributed on expected bone elements
- If the defects reflect close-quarter combat, many are located in anomalous regions (i.e. cut marks located in between joint surfaces in the legs and feet)
- Butchered cow and pig bones with postmortem sharp force trauma show very similar wound signatures to the human osteological material.

The forensic analysis confirmed that the defects were not caused by explosive blast events, and that multiple bones do in fact have clear evidence of the type of damage classified as sharp force trauma, i.e. injuries caused by sharp-edged objects. Given the known facts of the sinking of the *Kronan* and the analysis of the traumatic defects and patterning of the wound characteristics, it does not appear that these defects resulted from the violent actions of panicked men trying to escape the ship, as was previously proposed (During 1997). Patterns, locations, and morphology of the cuts do not rule out postmortem timing, so what might instead account for the variety and number of sharp force traumatic injuries observed on many of the skeletal elements from the *Kronan* if they did not, in fact, result from close-quarter conflicts?

We suggest an alternative hypothesis for the sharp force trauma signatures. We propose the defects are taphonomic in nature, and likely reflect postmortem damage sustained during the cannon recovery efforts undertaken only 6 years after the loss of the *Kronan*.

Organic and inorganic material was excellently preserved, and the ship's rigging, sails, masts, metallic components, and other structures were still intact even hundreds of years after she sank. Additionally, it is not unreasonable to propose that only 6 years after the wreck, at that depth and under those conditions, adipocere may have been present on many of the bodies, leading to the presence of wholly fleshed or partially fleshed individuals. (In fact, one of the authors worked on a forensic case involving a body that had been submerged in a deep, cold, freshwater quarry for over 20 years, and when it was recovered and brought to the surface, many of the elements still retained adipose tissue.) Adipose tissue, also referred to as grave soap or grave wax, results from a chemical conversion of the body's lipids into a substance that is greasy, coagulated, dense, and most often formed in aquatic contexts and lasting upwards of a century in the right environment (Sorg *et al.* 2012). This means that only 6 years after the sinking, when the diving bells were deployed to raise the valuable armament, a large and complex debris field was still present where fleshed bodies, ropes, sails, rigging, masts, and other items were likely entangled with some of the cannons. This would have presented a challenge to the divers in the diving bell who were working in dangerous conditions and in near darkness with hooks, knives, hatchets, and other recovery gear. The bodies or body parts likely would have been manipulated (i.e. cut, chopped, removed) to clear the cannons for transport to the surface. This scenario may fully explain the ambiguous patterning and location of the cut marks; they are postmortem artifacts caused by divers using bladed instruments on entangled bodies during the 4-year expedition to salvage the *Kronan*'s valuable cannons.

References

Aufderheide, A. C. & Rodríguez-Martin, C. (1998). *The Cambridge Encyclopedia of Human Paleopathology*. Cambridge: Cambridge University Press.

Bennike, P. (2008). Trauma. In: Pinhasi, R. & Mays, S. (eds.) *Advances in Human Palaeopathology*, Chichester: John Wiley & Sons, 309–28.

Bevan, J. (1999). Diving bells through the centuries. *South Pacific Underwater Medicine Society Journal*, **29**, 42–50.

Delgado, J. P. (1997). *Encyclopedia of Underwater and Maritime Archaeology*. New Haven: Yale University Press.

During, E. (1997). Specific skeletal injuries observed on the human skeletal remains from the Swedish seventeenth century man-of-war, *Kronan*. *International Journal of Osteoarchaeology*, **7**, 591–4.

Einarsson, L. (1990). Kronan – underwater archaeological investigations of a 17th-century man-of-war. The nature, aims and development of a maritime cultural project. *The International Journal of Nautical Archaeology and Underwater Exploration*, **19**, 219–97.

(2001). *Kronan*. Kalmar: Kalmar läns Museum.

(2006). *Kronanprojektet, Rapport Om 2006 Års Marinarkeologiska Undersökningar Av Regalskeppet Kronan*. Kalmar: Kalmar läns Museum.

(2013). *Kronanprojektet, Rapport Om 2012 Års Marinarkeologiska Undersökningar Av Regalskeppet Kronan*. Kalmar: Kalmar läns Museum.

Einarsson, L. & Mörzer Bruyns, W. F. J. (2003). A cross-staff from the wreck of the Kronan (1676). *The International Journal of Nautical Archaeology*, **32**, 53–60.

Grandin, G. (1985). Kronan Går Under. In: Axel, J. B. (ed.) *Regalskeppet Kronan*. Höganäs: Bra Böcker, 138–9.

Kerley, E. R. (1973). Forensic anthropology. In: Wecht, C. H. (ed.) *Legal Medicine Annual*. New York: Appleton-Century-Crofts, 161–98.

Kimmerle, E. H. & Baraybar, J. P. (eds.) (2008). *Skeletal Trauma: Identification of Injuries Resulting from Human Remains Abuse and Armed Conflict*. Boca Raton: CRC Press.

Komar, D. A. & Buikstra, J. E. (2008). *Forensic Anthropology: Contemporary Theory and Practice*. Oxford: Oxford University Press.

Lindkvist, T. & Sjöberg, M. (2010). *Det Svenska Samhället 800–1720. Klerkernas Och Adelns Tid*. Lund: Studentlitteratur.

Lodén, M. 2008. Svärdshugg eller explosion? En osteogisk analys ay skelettelment med perimortala huggmärken från regalskeppet Kronan. Master Thesis, Stockholm University.

Merbs, C. F. (1989). Trauma. In: Iscan, M. Y. & Kennedy, K. A. R. (eds.) *Reconstruction of Life from the Skeleton*. New York: Alan R. Liss, 161–99.

Olsson, E. L. (1985). Kronans Änkor. In: Axel, J. B. (ed.) *Regalskeppet Kronan*. Höganäs: Bra Böcker, 166–7.

Ong, B. B. (1999). The pattern of homicidal slash/chop injuries: a 10 year retrospective study in University Hospital Kuala Lumpur. *Journal of Clinical Forensic Medicine*, **6**, 24–9.

Ortner, D. J. (2003). *Identification of Pathological Conditions in Human Skeletal Remains*, 2nd edn. London: Academic Press.

Quatrehomme, G. (2007). A strange case of dismemberment. In: Brickley, M. B. & Ferllini, R. (eds.) *Forensic Anthropology: Case Studies from Europe*. Springfield: Charles C. Thomas, 99–119.

Sauer, N. J. & Simson, L. R. (1984). Clarifying the role of forensic anthropologists in death investigations. *Journal of Forensic Sciences*, **29**, 1–6.

Skenbäck, U. (1985). Timmermän, Befäl Och Andra. In: Axel, J. B. (ed.) *Regalskeppet Kronan*. Höganäs: Bra Böcker, 82–3.

Sorg, M. H., Haglund, W. D. & Wren, J. A. (2012). Current research in forensic taphonomy. In: Dirkmaat, D. C. (ed.) *A Companion to Forensic Anthropology*. Chichester: Wiley-Blackwell Publishing, 477–527.

Stewart, T. D. (1979). *Essentials of Forensic Anthropology: Especially as Developed in the United States*. Springfield: Charles C. Thomas.

SWGANTH. (2011). *Trauma Analysis* [Online]. Available: http://swganth.startlogic. com/Trauma%20Rev/.pdf. [Accessed September 28, 2013.]

Symes, S. A., Williams, J. A., Murray, E. A., Hoffman, J. M., Holland, T. D., Saul, J. M., Saul, F. P. & Pope, E. J. (2001). Taphonomic context of sharp-force trauma in suspected cases of human mutilation and dismemberment. In: Haglund, W. D. & Sorg, M. (eds.) *Advances in Forensic Taphonomy: Method, Theory, and Archaeological Perspectives*. Boca Raton: CRC Press, 403–34.

Symes, S. A., Chapman, E. N., Rainwater, C. W., Cabo, L. L. & Myster, S. M. T. (2010). *Knife and Saw Toolmark Analysis in Bone: A Manual Designed for the Examination of Criminal Mutilation and Dismemberment* [Online]. National Institute of Justice Technical Report. Available: http://www.ncjrs.gov/pdffiles1/ nij/grants/232227.pdf.

Tegtmeyer, C. E. (2012). A comparative analysis of serrated and non-serrated sharp force trauma to bone. Texas State University-San Marcos: MA thesis.

White, T. D., Black, M. T. & Folkens, P. A. (2012). *Human Osteology*, 3rd edn. San Diego: Academic Press.

4   *The determination of homicide vs. suicide in gunshot wounds*

VINCENT H. STEFAN

4.1   Background

When examining a set of human skeletal remains in a bioarchaeological or forensic context, the assessment of perimortem trauma and the collection of evidence that can be utilized to determine the cause and/or manner of death are just a couple of the critical objectives facing a biological/forensic anthropologist. When evidence of perimortem gunshot wound (GSW) trauma is evident in a set of human remains the question needs to be asked as to how the decedent obtained that trauma, i.e. accident, suicide, or homicide. In most situations involving homicidal GSW trauma, it is difficult to determine whether the decedent was truly a victim (non-participant in a conflict) or a perpetrator of violence shot in the course of a conflict (justifiable homicide). The presence of ligatures, blindfolds, etc. may aid in those distinctions; otherwise, each individual dying from a GSW is a "victim" to a varying degree. A similar point of potential confusion and difficulty is found in recognizing suicidal vs. homicidal GSWs in certain situations. In many cases, the context of the remains and the scene will aid in the determination of suicide vs. homicide. "Context accounts for the intention of those perpetrating crimes and the fatal environment (i.e. where the incident took place). Were the victims fighting, detained, bound, crowded into a small concrete room, or lying in a field at the time of their deaths?" (Kimmerle and Baraybar 2008).

This chapter will attempt to address these issues and lines of potential evidence that can be utilized to assess the manner of death involving GSWs.

Bioarchaeological and Forensic Perspectives on Violence: How Violent Death is Interpreted from Skeletal Remains, ed. D. L. Martin and C. P. Anderson. Published by Cambridge University Press. © Cambridge University Press 2014.

51

LIVERPOOL JOHN MOORES UNIVERSITY
LEARNING SERVICES

4.2   Context of remains

As should be evident to all, GSW victims tend not to be able to bury themselves following their death, so some subsequent activity facilitated their burial. Careful examination of the burial needs to be conducted to determine if the grave is "homicide-related" or owing to natural taphonomic activity (Roksandic 2002; Schmitt 2002). Graves, either single burials or mass graves, are often utilized to conceal human remains in an attempt by the perpetrator(s) to hide the evidence of a crime (Schmitt 2002). The presence of blindfolds and restraints on the victims within the burials would further indicate the burial was a result of "homicide-related" activity. "Evidence of executions, such as blindfolds, ligatures, wounds to the back of the head, or those inflicted when the individual was in a kneeling or lying position and witness testimony or other investigative/documentary forms of evidence are all indicative of murder" (Kimmerle and Baraybar 2008).

Surface deposition of GSW victims poses a more difficult task of assessing manner of death. The specific context of the victim at the time of death, as well as the postmortem context of the victim's remains, could provide invaluable information as to the manner of death.

Figure 4.1a illustrates an example of a "clandestine" burial, with the victim lying in a supine position, approximately 4–6 inches below ground level. Although the decedent had sustained an entrance GSW to the right frontal bone (Figure 4.1b), with an exit GSW near the osteometric landmark "lambda," resulting in a trajectory consistent with a suicidal, self-inflicted GSW, the lack of a weapon within the grave and the fact the decedent was buried all indicate this individual had died as a result of homicidal activity.

The next figures present two cases of GSW victims with surface deposition of their remains. Figure 4.2a is of a homicidal GSW victim, while Figure 4.2b is of a suicidal GSW victim. The decedent in Figure 4.2a possessed a tangential entrance GSW to the posterior left parietal bone, with an incomplete exit in the superior frontal squama. The trajectory of the GSW is more consistent with a homicidal GSW than with a suicidal GSW. A distinct entrance GSW could not be determined with the decedent in Figure 4.2b; however, a clear exit GSW is present in the occipital bone, indicating an anterior–posterior trajectory, consistent with a suicidal GSW. Also found at the scene was a rifle, suspected to be the weapon which inflicted the GSW. Although the presence of the weapon with the decedent does not preclude homicide as a possible manner of death, in an undisturbed crime scene, the weapon is more likely to be found in close proximity to suicide victims (Spitz 1993).

Figure 4.1. **a** Clandestine burial of GSW homicide victim.

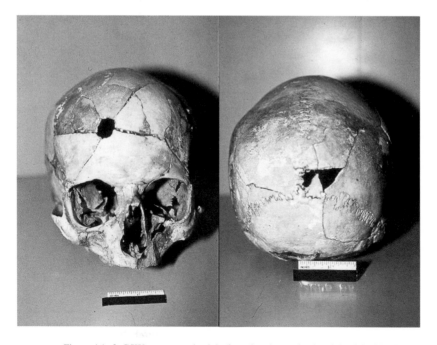

Figure 4.1. **b** GSW – entrance in right frontal, exit near landmark lambda. Homicide.

Figure 4.2. **a** Surface deposition of GSW homicide victim.

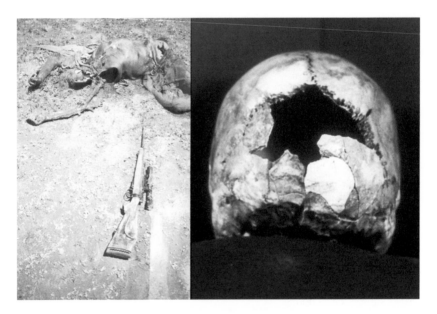

Figure 4.2. **b** Surface deposition of GSW suicide victim. Probable anterior splanchnocranial entrance, exit through the occipital bone.

4.3   Defensive wounds

In some incidents involving assaults with a firearm, the victims make attempts to protect themselves by positioning themselves to minimize the target area presented by their body or by placing their arms in front of their faces in an attempt to protect their face and head. Distinctive wounds to the bones of the forearm, the ulna and radius, and the hand may be observed, indicating that such self-defense posturing was attempted by the victim. For example, a victim apprehending that the bullet/projectile is approaching to hit them in the head may instinctively attempt to protect their head either by turning it away or by raising the arms, with the bullet passing-off just by grazing the scalp or striking/hitting the arm (Vij *et al.* 2012).

When examining and evaluating a potential self-defensive GSW, special attention must be made to determine the trajectory of the projectile, taking into account possible changes in body orientation. A GSW to the radius may have the appearance of a posterior–anterior trajectory when considering the body in a standard anatomical position, but may in fact have been an anterior–posterior trajectory if the arm was raised in front of the face and head for protection. There can never be 100% certainty about the position/orientation of the victim and the perpetrator of GSWs, but the careful evaluation and consideration of all possible positions/orientations in conjunction with the GSWs can result in the inclusion and exclusion of certain scenarios, which in turn can assist in the assessment of manner of death.

4.4   Multiple wounds

In cases involving suicidal GSWs it is rare, though not impossible, to observe multiple GSW traumas (Kury *et al.* 2000; Spitz 1993). In a study of 288 firearm deaths, Druid (1997) found that 57% of homicide victims possessed multiple GSWs, while only 3% of suicides possessed multiple GSWs. Hejna *et al.* (2012) discuss three cases of multiple, suicidal GSWs to the head. Kury *et al.* (2000) discuss two cases of multiple, suicidal GSWs to the head and discuss the scientific literature that document other such cases. In their assessment, the vast majority of multiple suicidal GSWs to the head involve the utilization of handguns (revolvers and pistols), while "high-velocity guns and large-caliber bullets with high stopping power obviously tend to cause immediate incapacitation" (Kury *et al.* 2000), limiting the victim's ability to inflict subsequent wounds.

The presence of multiple GSW traumas in a single victim, or GSW trauma defects in close anatomical proximity may indicate the assault was inflicted by an independent assailant. Meddings and O'Conner (1999) state the location, number, and severity of GSWs could demonstrate homicidal intent. Molina and DiMaio (2008), in a study of rifle GSWs, found that in cases with multiple rifle wounds it was 21.6 times more likely to be a result of homicide than suicide. Additionally, Molina and DiMaio found that multiple wound locations were the most common "location" for homicidal rifle wounds, followed by the head and chest (Molina and DiMaio 2008).

4.5   Trajectory and range of fire

As mentioned previously, "Evidence of executions, such as blindfolds, ligatures, wounds to the back of the head, or those inflicted when the individual was in a kneeling or lying position and witness testimony or other investigative/documentary forms of evidence are all indicative of murder" (Kimmerle and Baraybar 2008). Bullet trajectory cannot definitively prove manner of death – it can, however, provide evidence "consistent with" a particular manner of death. Site of entrance is one component of trajectory of fire. Desinan and Mazzolo (2005) note that "shooting in inaccessible sites cannot be suicide" and that "it is not true that suicides always shoot themselves in the head on the same side as their dominant hand." Karger and DuChesne (1997) document a case where the handedness of the decedent and the trajectory of the projectile excluded the possibility that the GSW was self-inflicted accidentally or by suicide.

However, range of fire can rule out suicide as a manner of death. With suicides, the range of fire must be within arm's length, depending on the type of weapon and excluding some mechanical device to assist in firing the weapon (Desinan and Mazzolo 2005). An example of mechanically assisted, suicidal shotgun GSW to the back is presented by Durak *et al.* (2006). In this example, the decedent utilized a string to pull the trigger of a shotgun, resulting in a GSW to the back at a range of approximately 140.0 cm.

The presence or absence of soot, powder burns, and stippling (powder tattooing) on the skin, as well as clothing or skin rupture from trapped gases, will indicate whether an entrance GSW was contact, near contact or greater range, and thus provide evidence consistent with or not consistent with suicide, homicide, or other (Tokdemir *et al.* 2007). Intermediate GSWs typically produce powder tattooing and/or stippling of the skin. The size and density of such powder-induced injuries around an entry wound are used to estimate the separation distance between the muzzle of the responsible firearm and the entry site through test firings at selected muzzle-to-target distances, with ammunition comparable to the injury-producing round and the evidence firearm (Haag 2005). Therefore, in addition to the distance between the firearm muzzle and surface of the body, the pattern of powder burns and stippling are influenced by the type of firearm, as well as the type of ammunition and propellant within that round, producing distinctive patterns (Haag 2005).

In a retrospective study of 288 GSW fatalities, Druid (1997) determined that suicidal GSWs were predominantly contact wounds, while only 33 of 112 (approximately one-third) of the homicidal GSWs were contact, near-contact, or intermediate-range wounds. Suicide entrance wound sites tended to occur at the mouth, right temple, or left chest, while homicide entrance wound sites tended to be more variable. Although 38% of the homicidal GSWs had entrance wounds to the right temple and the left side of the chest (sites common to suicidal GSWs), the trajectory of these wounds differed significantly from suicidal wounds (Druid 1997). A back-to-front trajectory is more common in homicide, even with a GSW to the right temple, and an intraoral GSW with a downward trajectory is not likely to occur in a suicide, but is more common in homicide. A study by Karger *et al.* (2002) supports the findings discussed by Druid, yet they caution that certain trajectories cannot be utilized to exclude suicide.

In an exhaustive study of rifle GSWs, Molina and DiMaio (2008) found that the location of suicidal rifle GSWs tended to be intraoral, while homicidal head wounds tended to be temporoparietal or occipital. Yet, a wound to the head is 3.5 times more likely to be a result of suicide than homicide. With regard to wounds to specific locations on the head, wounds to the back of the head are 28 times more likely to be a homicide, as are wounds to the face (33 times more likely). Additionally, the presence of multiple rifle wounds was 21.6 times more likely to be a result of homicide than suicide. With regard to range-of-fire, distant rifle wounds are 1000 times more likely to be homicide; intermediate rifle wounds are 2.5 times more likely to be homicide; and contact rifle wounds are 170 times more likely to be suicide.

Similar results were obtained when these researchers examined cases involving shotgun GSWs (Molina *et al.* 2007). As with rifle GSWs, Molina *et al.* (2007) found that the location of suicidal shotgun GSWs tended to be in the head and was predominantly intraoral or submental, while homicidal shotgun wounds tended to occur in the chest and head, with the specific location of head wounds in the face. Multiple wounds and multiple locations of wounds were seen more frequently in cases involving homicide than in cases of suicide. Contact wounds were observed more frequently in suicides than homicides, while distant wounds were observed more frequently in homicide cases (Molina *et al.* 2007).

Figures 4.3a and 4.3b illustrate several examples of multiple GSW traumas, as well as GSW trajectory. The decedent in Figure 4.3a received three GSWs,

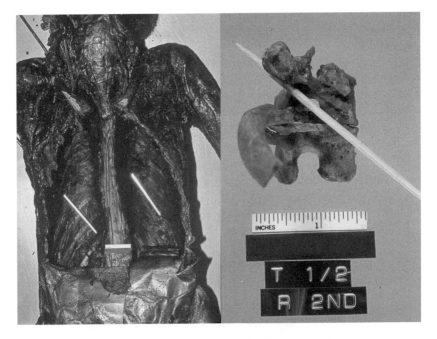

Figure 4.3. **a** Multiple GSWs to thoracic cavity. Posterior–anterior trajectory.

one in each of the right, left, and mid upper torso. Evaluation of the wounds indicated the trajectory of fire was posterior–anterior, and slightly superior–inferior, a trajectory that is most clearly recognized when examining the damage present to the first and second thoracic vertebrae. Figure 4.3b presents two cases, one involving wounds to the occipital and posterior parietal bones and the second involving wounds to adjacent right ribs. The entrance wounds to the cranium clearly indicate a trajectory of posterior–anterior, and slight left–right. The presence of multiple GSWs, the close anatomical proximity of the wounds, and the trajectory of these wounds are all consistent with homicide.

4.6   Discussion

"The distinction between homicide, suicide and accident can sometimes be extremely difficult" (Desinan and Mazzolo 2005). As illustrated by the cases presented, in many situations the determination of manner of death can be deduced through the assessment of context, presence of defensive wounds, and presence of multiple GSWs, as well as the trajectory of the GSWs. Despite the importance of determining manner of death in a forensic context, an exhaustive

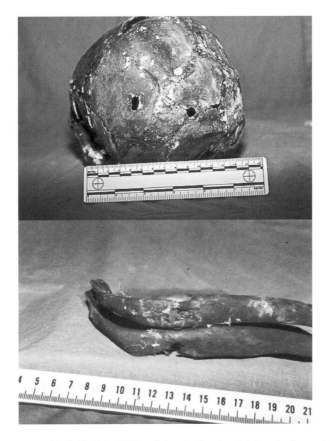

Figure 4.3. **b** Multiple GSWs to left parietal and occipital, and adjacent right ribs.

search of the scientific literature has revealed that few articles have been published dealing with assessing and determining manner of death in GSWs. Most of the articles found are either case studies dealing with unusual GSW deaths (Durak *et al.* 2006; Kury *et al.* 2000; Sekula-Perlman *et al.* 1998; Zietlow and Hawley 1993) or surveys of GSW cases examining wound location, number of wounds, and/or range of shot (Karger and DuChesne 1997; Karger *et al.* 2002; Molina and DiMaio 2008; Molina *et al.* 2007).

Some features and lines of evidence utilized to evaluate manner of death in GSWs, and all mechanisms of death for that matter, are so "self-evident" that almost no scientific literature is dedicated to their discussion and review, making any mention of them seem "anecdotal," as is the case with this chapter. Some of these features are the presence of ligatures and blindfolds, evidence of possible defensive wounds, and the disposition of the remains (i.e. buried, unburied, etc.). When encountered by forensic practitioners and investigators, immediate and often "obvious" conclusions are reached with regard to manner of death.

A review of the available literature, however, does present informative data that can be utilized in the assessment of manner of death involving GSWs. Some general conclusions are as follows.

1. Intentional, clandestine burial of decedents with GSWs tends to be "homicide-related."
2. The presence of blindfolds and restraints on the decedents indicates "homicide-related" activity.
3. Multiple GSWs are more commonly observed in cases involving homicide.
4. Multiple wound location is more consistent with homicide.
5. Suicidal GSWs are predominantly contact or near-contact wounds.
6. Gunshot entrance wounds located in inaccessible sites are more consistent with homicide.
7. Back-to-front and downward bullet trajectories are more consistent with homicide.

As can be inferred from the usage of such terms as "consistent with," "more commonly observed," and "would tend to be," these general conclusions are not absolute by any stretch of the imagination. Each case needs to be examined carefully to determine if the observed evidence supports or contradicts these generalized conclusions.

4.7   Summary and conclusions

There is no single feature or wound characteristic that can be exclusively attributed to a single manner of death. The best any forensic practitioner can do is to evaluate the GSW traumas present in a decedent and make an evaluation as to which manner of death the evidence is more consistent with. The features of the victim and GSW trauma that are routinely evaluated to assess manner of death include context of remains, presence of ligatures/ blindfolds, presence of defensive wounds, presence of powder burns and stippling (powder tattooing), presence of multiple wounds, wound location/ trajectory, and range of fire. Some of these features tend to be "more consistent" with suicide, while others tend to be "more consistent" with homicide. In the end, it is the total, summed weight of the objective/subjective observations of these features that will lead a forensic investigator to make the determination as to whether a GSW victim died as a result of suicidal or homicidal activity.

To many readers, this chapter will seem "simplistic" and "anecdotal," and in all honesty it is. The paucity of scientific literature dealing with this topic is a reflection of how most of these features become "common knowledge" and "obvious" as forensic practitioners gain more experience and exposure to more cases. The correct assessment of manner of death depends on the accurate observation, evaluation, and interpretation of all evidence related to the case. The knowledge base that is required by forensic practitioners, that which is necessary to make these accurate investigations, is often acquired through first-hand experience. For each case involving GSWs, there is physical evidence that can be scientifically, "objectively" examined and empirical data that can be collected. It is the "subjective" interpretation of this evidence and empirical data to determine manner of death that has garnered little scientific evaluation and, as a result, there are few publications in the scientific literature.

References

Desinan, L. & Mazzolo, G. M. (2005). Gunshot fatalities: suicide, homicide or accident? A series of 48 cases. *Forensic Science International*, **147S**, S37–40.

Druid, H. (1997). Site of entrance wound and direction of bullet path in firearm fatalities as indicators of homicide versus suicide. *Forensic Science International*, **88**, 147–62.

Durak, D., Fedakar, R. & Türkmen, N. (2006). A distance-range, suicidal shotgun wound of the back. *Journal of Forensic Sciences*, **51**, 131–3.

Haag, L. C. (2005). Physical forms of contemporary small-arms propellants and their forensic value. *The American Journal of Forensic Medicine and Pathology*, **26**, 5–10.

Hejna, P., Šafr, M. & Zátopková, L. (2012). The ability to act – multiple suicidal gunshot wounds. *Journal of Forensic and Legal Medicine*, **19**, 1–6.

Karger, B. & DuChesne, A. (1997). Who fired the gun? A causistic contribution to the differentiation between self-inflicted and non-self-inflicted gunshot wounds. *International Journal of Legal Medicine*, **110**, 33–5.

Karger, B., Billeb, E., Koops, E. & Brinkmann, B. (2002). Autopsy features relevant for discrimination between suicidal and homicidal gunshot injuries. *International Journal of Legal Medicine*, **116**, 273–8.

Kimmerle, E. H. & Baraybar, J. P. (eds.) (2008). *Skeletal Trauma: Identification of Injuries Resulting from Human Rights Abuses and Armed Conflict*. Boca Raton: CRC Press.

Kury, G., Weiner, J. & Duval, J. V. (2000). Multiple self-inflicted gunshot wounds to the head: report of a case and review of the literature. *The American Journal of Forensic Medicine and Pathology*, **21**, 32–5.

Meddings, D. R. & O'Conner, S. M. (1999). Circumstances around weapon injury in Cambodia after departure of a peacekeeping force: prospective cohort study. *British Medical Journal*, **319**, 412–15.

Molina, D. K. & DiMaio, V. J. (2008). Rifle wounds: a review of range and location as pertaining to manner of death. *The American Journal of Forensic Medicine and Pathology*, **29**, 201–5.

Molina, D. K., Wood, L. E. & DiMaio, V. J. (2007). Shotgun wounds: a review of range and location as pertaining to manner of death. *The American Journal of Forensic Medicine and Pathology*, **28**, 99–102.

Roksandic, M. (2002). Position of skeletal remains as a key to understanding mortuary behavior. In: Haglund, W. D. & Sorg, M. H. (eds.) *Advances in Forensic Taphonomy. Method, Theory, and Archaeological Perspectives*. Boca Raton: CRC Press, 99–117.

Schmitt, S. (2002). Mass graves and the collection of forensic evidence: genocide, war crimes, and crimes against humanity. In: Haglund, W. D. & Sorg, M. H. (eds.) *Advances in Forensic Taphonomy. Method, Theory, and Archaeological Perspectives*. Boca Raton: CRC Press, 277–92.

Sekula-Perlman, A., Tobin, J. G., Pretzler, E., Ingle, J. & Callery, R. T. (1998). Three unusual cases of multiple suicidal gunshot wounds to the head. *The American Journal of Forensic Medicine and Pathology*, **19**, 23–9.

Spitz, W. U. (1993). *Spitz and Fisher's Medicolegal Investigation of Death: Guidelines for the Application of Pathology to Crime Investigation*. Springfield, IL: Charles C. Thomas.

Tokdemir, M., Kafadar, H., Turkoglu, A. & Bork, T. (2007). Forensic value of gunpowder tattooing in identification of multiple entrance wounds from one bullet. *Legal Medicine (Tokyo, Japan)*, **9**, 147–50.

Vij, K., Garg, A., Sandhu, S. S., Langeh, S. & Bakshi, I. (2012). Medicolegal implications of defence wounds. *Journal of Punjab Academy of Forensic Medicine & Toxicology*, **12**, 54–6.

Zietlow, C. & Hawley, D. A. (1993). Unexpectedly homicide: three intraoral gunshot wounds. *The American Journal of Forensic Medicine and Pathology*, **14**, 230–3.

5   The first cut is the deepest: looking for patterns in cases of human dismemberment

ANDREW C. SEIDEL AND LAURA C. FULGINITI

5.1   Introduction

More so than most murders, homicides involving postmortem dismemberment tend to capture the imagination of the public and spur on speculation as to the identity and motives of the perpetrator. Owing in part to the influence of popular culture, there is the unwarranted tendency to associate dismemberments with serial killers (Konopka *et al.* 2007). Yet, despite the morbid interest that such cases draw, there is little that can be definitively said about either the victims of dismemberment or the authors of such crimes. The lack of knowledge concerning this type of crime can be attributed primarily to their rarity (Dogan *et al.* 2010; Konopka *et al.* 2007; Rajs *et al.* 1998) as well as to the difficulties involved with solving homicide cases involving fragmented remains.

We begin this chapter with an overview of the literature concerning dismemberment cases, detailing classification schemes that have been introduced and inferences that are typically drawn from case characteristics. We then present a series of recommended protocols when dealing with dismembered human remains. Following this, brief descriptions of eight dismemberment cases from Maricopa County, Arizona, are provided. The results of previous surveys of dismemberment cases from other countries are discussed, especially in regard to characteristics that are common in such cases. These outcomes, as well as a brief discussion on the differences between male and female homicide offenders, are used to suggest that homicides involving dismemberments might have different characteristics depending on the sex of both their victim and their perpetrator. We conclude by presenting and discussing the results of a preliminary analysis of 102 dismemberment cases taken primarily from published accounts.

Bioarchaeological and Forensic Perspectives on Violence: How Violent Death is Interpreted from Skeletal Remains, ed. D. L. Martin and C. P. Anderson. Published by Cambridge University Press. © Cambridge University Press 2014.

5.2   Classification of dismemberments

Dismemberment of the human body, here defined as the intentional removal of a body segment or segments (adapted from Kahana *et al.* 2010), is often viewed by both the public and the media as more heinous than homicide alone and is frequently accompanied by speculations about serial killers (Konopka *et al.* 2007). Despite popular imagination, it seems that most cases involving dismemberment of the corpse, although certainly not all, are driven by less exotic motives – namely the desire to facilitate the disposal of the body and/or to attempt to conceal the identity of the deceased (Delabarde and Ludes 2010; Di Nunno *et al.* 2006; Hyma and Rao 1991; Kahana *et al.* 2010; Reichs 1998). Within the literature, cases involving dismemberment are often categorized by the perceived (or sometimes known) motive underlying the act itself as well as by the pattern of actual defects inflicted upon the corpse.

Dismemberment is considered to be a subset of mutilation, defined by Rajs *et al.* as "the act of depriving an individual of a limb, member, or other important part of the body; or deprival of an organ; or severe disfigurement" (1998: 563). As such, dismemberments are frequently classified in the literature by their perceived underlying motivation as: (1) defensive; (2) aggressive; (3) offensive; or (4) necromanic (Di Nunno *et al.* 2006; Häkkänen-Nyholm *et al.* 2009b; Konopka *et al.* 2006; 2007; Rajs *et al.* 1998). Defensive mutilation refers to acts carried out to facilitate the transportation or disposal of the remains, to make it difficult to identify the deceased, or to conceal evidence of the crime. Aggressive mutilations are carried out as a result of a state of outrage that persists after the death of the victim and frequently the act of dismemberment itself contributes to the cause of death (e.g. death by decapitation). Offensive mutilations are brought about by the need to kill and then carry out sexual urges or by the need to inflict pain, injury, or death while carrying out sexual urges (Rajs *et al.* 1998). As such, this type of mutilation typically accompanies lust or necrosadistic murders and frequently involves the severing or disfigurement of the face and genitalia of the victim. Necromanic mutilation may or may not involve homicide and is primarily concerned with trophy-taking or the acquisition of a "keepsake," sometimes involving the exhumation of a corpse. With the increasing efficacy of DNA analyses, a fifth category of postmortem mutilation has appeared – those committed solely in order to remove evidence that could lead to the identification of the perpetrator (Di Nunno *et al.* 2006; Karger *et al.* 2000).

Dismemberments have also been classified as either localized or generalized based on the patterning of cuts evident on the body (Delabarde and Ludes 2010; Kahana *et al.* 2010; Reichs 1998). Localized dismemberment typically involves the removal of the head, the hands (or fingers), or both. This is usually done in an effort to mask the identity of the victim, although this motivation is less likely when all of the removed body parts are deposited in the same place (Konopka *et al.* 2006; Reichs 1998). Generalized dismemberment usually involves the removal of the limbs and/or the head and is typically inferred to have been done to facilitate transportation or concealment of the corpse (Figure 5.1). Generalized dismemberments can be further subdivided into: (1) body bisections, in which the corpse is separated by a horizontal cut through the torso (Kahana *et al.* 2010); (2) limb bisections, in which the limbs are cut through the diaphyses or metaphyses of the long bones; and (3) disarticulations, in which limb removal is accomplished by severing the joints themselves; this is characterized by cut marks in the intracapsular area, surrounding muscle insertions, and near articular surfaces (Kahana *et al.* 2010; Reichs 1998). Of these three patterns of generalized dismemberment, disarticulations are frequently described as reflecting some degree of knowledge concerning anatomy or butchering (Kahana *et al.* 2010; Reddy 1973; Reichs 1998). This assertion has been challenged by Konopka *et al.* (2007) who, in their analysis of 23 dismemberment cases from Poland, found only one instance out of four disarticulations in which the perpetrator's profession (a cook) even loosely related to anatomical knowledge. However, the profession of a perpetrator does not necessarily reflect their interests, education, or training.

5.3   Recommended protocols

Regardless of the pattern of cuts or whether or not it was the intended effect, dismemberment introduces complications into the investigation of the accompanying crime. As discussed earlier, the act of dismembering may serve to obscure the identity of the victim. Furthermore, the damage to the body incurred during the dismemberment may conceal the actual cause of death, thereby leaving open the possibility of the death being ruled accidental, suicidal, or natural, and consequently the effective erasure of a crime (Di Nunno *et al.* 2006; Rajs *et al.* 1998). As a result of these and other difficulties, dismemberment cases are typically more challenging to close. In Japan, for instance, the clearance rate for dismemberment cases is 78%, as opposed to a reported 90% clearance rate for all homicides in that country (Watanabe and Tamura 2001), and an even lower clearance rate is reported for Poland (Konopka *et al.* 2007). For the cases presented below from Maricopa County, seven out of eight were solved.

Such difficulties have led many researchers to advocate extensive documentation of cases involving dismemberment. The scene of recovery itself should

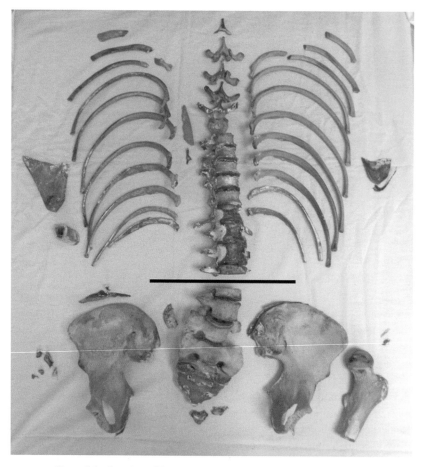

Figure 5.1. Case 1 provides an example of a generalized dismemberment. Solid line indicates the location where the torso was bisected.

be carefully documented. A complete inventory and description of all recovered remains should be undertaken, along with extensive photographic documentation of the remains prior to undertaking any maceration or analysis. Any present soft tissue should be examined for the presence of scars, tattoos, signs of drug use, trauma, and other potentially informative features. All associated clothing and personal effects should be carefully documented, paying special attention to manufacturer labels, laundry tags, and unique clothing attributes. Where possible, fingerprints, palm prints, and footprints should be taken, as well as radiographs to look for foreign matter which may help to elucidate cause of death or potentially reveal prior surgical

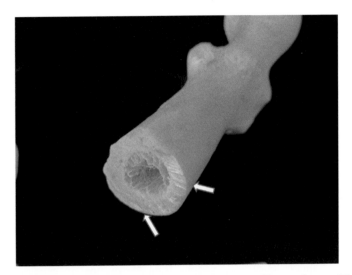

Figure 5.2. Kerf wall from femur of Case 6. White arrows illustrate the two different orientations of striae. Note the breakaway spur.

interventions. DNA samples and dental radiographs should also be taken when possible. Lastly, casts of the cut specimens or the specimens themselves should be retained for possible future analyses (Di Nunno *et al.* 2006; Hyma and Rao 1991; Reichs 1998). Furthermore, if specimens are retained, then reapproximation of remains can be attempted should additional body segments be discovered at a future date (Buikstra and Gordon 1980).

After maceration, additional important information regarding tool type used, cutting sequence, and the directionality of blade progress can and should be gleaned from examination of the skeletal tissue. Reichs (1998) advocates the retention of sections of bone extending at least 3 inches from the cut surface to preserve any potential false start defects. False starts are particularly good indicators of saw tooth shape and size (Symes *et al.* 1998). Further, both halves of a cut should be investigated whenever possible as differences in the characteristics of the kerf walls can provide information about the type of cutting implement used. Directionality of the cut can be traced from the aspect of the bone exhibiting false starts to the aspect of the cut exhibiting breakaway spurs (Figure 5.2). This information, in combination with the observation and recording of any super-positioning of defects on the bone, can help shed light on the sequence of dismemberment as well as body positioning during the act of dismemberment (Reichs 1998). Determining the sequence of injuries is especially important to rule out dismemberment itself as the cause of death (Delabarde and Ludes 2010).

This suite of variables can be used to provide behavioral information concerning the perpetrator, to link victims together, to winnow down a list of potential suspects, and to corroborate eye-witness accounts (Reichs 1998).

5.4   Description of cases from Maricopa County, Arizona

The following brief descriptions of the osseous traumata evident in a series of dismemberment cases derive from Maricopa County, Arizona between 1984 and 2012.

5.4.1   Case 1

Exhumation of an unidentified female yielded two portions of a well-preserved torso. Scene photographs from the original investigation depict two wrapped packages, each containing a section of the body, placed in a dumpster. The first portion consisted of the thorax from the level of the second thoracic vertebra to the level of the third lumbar vertebra. Neither arm was present. The second portion consisted of all elements from the inferior portion of the third lumbar vertebra to the proximal femora. The lower legs, arms, neck, and head of this individual were never recovered. The pattern of epiphyseal union indicates that the victim was between the ages of 16 and 18 at the time of her death.

  Following maceration, examination of the remains revealed that the femora were bisected at a level approximately 12.0 cm inferior to the tip of the greater trochanter. The cut surface exhibited uneven striae, indicating a minimum of two attempts to sever the femoral diaphysis. Several smaller sharp force defects accompanied the bisecting cut. To remove the arms, transverse cuts were made through both scapulae, leaving intact only the inferior angles. There are additional sharp force defects oriented roughly parallel to the bisecting cut located on the vertebral borders of both scapulae. The removal of the head was accomplished in a puzzling manner. A transverse cut bisects the spinous process of the second thoracic vertebra. One continuous sharp force defect, oriented nearly coronally, bisects the right pedicles of the third, fourth, and fifth thoracic vertebrae, while a second continuous sharp force defect, oriented at an oblique angle to the first, bisects the left laminae of the third and fourth thoracic vertebrae, and the left pedicle of the fifth. The vertebral bodies of the second through fifth thoracic vertebrae were not recovered. Both cuts terminate in a transverse cut that bisects the body of the sixth thoracic vertebrae (Figure 5.3). A series of sharp force defects evident on left and right ribs 1–6

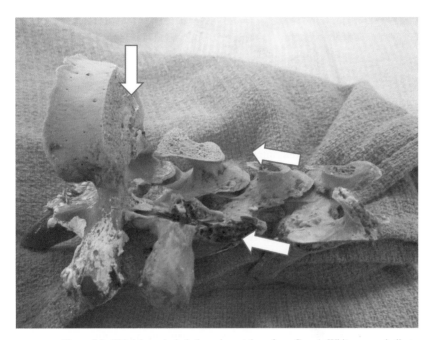

Figure 5.3. Third through sixth thoracic vertebrae from Case 1. White arrows indicate the three different sharp force defects used to remove the victim's head and neck.

appear to be associated with these cuts as well as the removal of the arms. In addition to this unorthodox removal of the head and neck, the sternum of the victim was bisected sagittally.

5.4.2   Case 2

These remains consisted of an adult male torso that was placed in a sealed Rubbermaid tub and deposited in a remote commercial dumpster. The victim was decapitated by a transverse cut through the third cervical vertebra and sectioned again at the level of the third lumbar vertebra. In addition, the left humerus was cut at a level approximately 9.0 cm inferior to the humeral head, and the right humerus was bisected approximately 11.0 cm inferior to the head. The head, lower portion of the upper limbs, abdomen, pelvis, and lower limbs were never recovered.

Macroscopic and microscopic investigation of the cut surfaces of the vertebrae and the humeri revealed that all cuts were made in a single event and exhibited fine, fairly uniform striations. Experimental cut marks made by a Milwaukee Heavy Duty "Sawzall" Brand saw using a 12-inch blade on donated human femora were found to match the defects evident on the cut surfaces of the vertebrae and humeri from this case.

5.4.3   Case 3

These remains consisted of a nearly complete adult female recovered from a residential trash container. Minimal thermal injury was evident on the right foot, leg, and a portion of the abdomen. The body was severed in four locations: at the level of the third and fourth cervical vertebrae, at the level of the third and fourth lumbar vertebrae, and at the level of the knees. Radiographic examination revealed an unhealed "parry" fracture on the right distal ulna.

Following maceration, examination of the cranium revealed evidence of blunt force osseous traumata. A small number of superficial incised defects accompanied the cut between the third and fourth cervical vertebrae. The third lumbar vertebra was bisected, exhibiting two transverse, irregular striations, and associated damage to the second lumbar vertebra. The inferior portion of the left femoral condyles had been sheared off and this was associated with sharp force defects on the left tibial plateau and fibular head. The right tibia and fibula were bisected approximately 5.0 cm inferior to the tibial plateau. Morphological attributes of these defects suggest that cutting initiated from the posterior aspect of the legs and proceeded anteriorly.

5.4.4   Case 4

Portions of remains from a dismembered adult male discovered in a Rubbermaid tub disposed of in the desert were submitted for maceration and examination of the dismemberment sites. After maceration, an oblique cut was revealed on the right tibial plateau, initiating approximately 3.2 cm inferior to the plateau on the medial side and terminating at the level of the articular condyle on the lateral side. This defect did not involve the right fibula. A second cut bisected the left tibial diaphysis approximately 7.0 cm inferior to the medial condyle and 8.0 cm inferior to the lateral condyle. This cut involved the right fibular diaphysis, as well. Both of these cuts exhibited undulating striations of various depths through the trabecular bone along with microscopic, roughly parallel striations evident in the cortical bone. The first lumbar vertebra was missing the superior surface along its anterior half and associated damage was evident on the twelfth thoracic vertebra. Sharp force trauma was also evident on the left tenth through twelfth ribs and the right twelfth rib. Experimental cut marks made by a jigsaw on a donated human femur were found to match the defects evident on the cut surfaces of the vertebrae and tibiae from this case. Additionally, there was microscopic evidence that the torso had been frozen prior to dismemberment.

5.4.5   Case 5

The remains of a decomposed, dismembered, and charred adult male were discovered in a residential trash container that had been left in the parking lot of a church. The skull, atlas, right femur minus the head, and the left and right humeri were submitted for maceration and examination. After maceration, the skull was reconstructed to facilitate examination and description of osseous traumata. Upon reconstruction, the skull was found to exhibit fracture patterns indicative of at least eight, and probably ten, separate impacts. The proximal end of the right femur exhibited comminuted fracturing, separating the femoral neck from the head. The diaphysis was found to be held together by surgical interventions and an elaborate healed callus. A complete fracture was located inferior to this callus. Transverse incised marks were found to be located near both sites of fracturing. The left humerus exhibited a complete comminuted fracture located approximately 9.0 cm inferior to the humeral head. A series of transversely oriented incised defects were found on the proximal portion of the humerus near this level. The combination of fractures and incisions suggest that the limbs were removed from this individual using a combination of both blunt and sharp force.

5.4.6   Case 6

Portions of a decomposed adult male were discovered inside a suitcase that had been placed within a commercial dumpster. Remains initially submitted for analysis consisted of a partial human torso, including the inferior half of the fourth cervical vertebra, the right and left proximal humeri, and the right and left proximal femora. A separate portion included the distal portion of the right femur as well as the proximal two-thirds of the right tibia and fibula.

Upon maceration, the fourth cervical vertebra was found to be bisected transversely. The cut surface exhibited parallel striations that measured approximately 0.1 cm in width and were oriented roughly mediolaterally. The right humerus was bisected approximately 10.0 cm inferior to the humeral head. The cut surface exhibited a breakaway spur on the anterior aspect of the bone as well as two false starts on the lateral edge of the bone located superior to the cut surface. Striae evident on the cut surface measured approximately

0.1 cm in width and were generally oriented mediolaterally. The left humerus was also bisected at a level approximately 10.0 cm inferior to the humeral head and exhibited a breakaway spur on the medial aspect of the bone. Three false starts were evident on the lateral aspect of the bone located superiorly to the bisection. The cut surface exhibited roughly parallel striae, oriented antero-posteriorly in direction, and measuring approximately 0.1 cm in width. The left femur was bisected approximately 19.1 cm inferior to the femoral head and exhibited a breakaway spur on the medial aspect of the bone. The cut surface exhibited roughly parallel striations that measured approximately 0.1 cm in width and were oriented both anteroposteriorly and mediolaterally. The right femur was bisected approximately 20.3 cm inferior to the femoral head and exhibited a breakaway spur on the posteromedial aspect of the bone. The cut surface exhibited roughly parallel striae that were oriented more-or-less antero-posteriorly. The inferior portion of the femur exhibited false starts on both the lateral and the anterior aspects. The right tibia was bisected approximately 29.1 cm inferior to the proximal end and the cut exhibited a step-off at the lateral edge. The cut surface exhibited roughly parallel striae that measured approximately 0.1 cm in width and were oriented both mediolaterally and anteroposteriorly. There were two false starts on the medial aspect of the bone. The right fibula was bisected approximately 27.3 cm below the proximal end and exhibited a breakaway spur on the lateral aspect. There was a false start on the medial side of the bone. The inferior portion of the fourth cervical vertebra could be reassociated with its superior portion, which was submitted along with the remainder of the cervical vertebrae and the skull under a separate case number. Nine months later, the right ankle and foot; the left hand, radius, ulna, and distal two-thirds of the humerus; the left knee, including the distal femoral shaft and the proximal tibia and fibula; and the left foot of the same individual were recovered from a separate location (Figure 5.4).

5.4.7   Case 7

The skeletonized remains of an adult male were discovered concealed under some brush in a desert area. The ribcage, right radius and ulna, sternum, right clavicle, third through seventh cervical vertebrae, and a disc of cranial vault bone were submitted for maceration following an autopsy for the purpose of evaluating any osseous traumata as well as assisting in the identification of a partially skeletonized set of decapitated remains. Approximately 2 weeks later, the cranium from this individual was found in a separate location and confirmed to belong to the same individual by means of fitting the disc of cranial vault bone into an ovoid defect on the cranium.

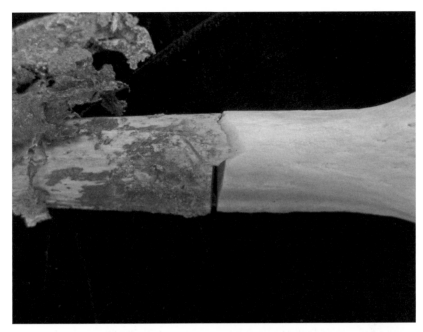

Figure 5.4. Retention of remains can facilitate reapproximation of skeletal elements recovered at different times. The two limb segments depicted here, from Case 6, were recovered approximately 9 months apart. Note the breakaway spur and the false starts.

After maceration, several long, linear, V-shaped sharp force defects were identified on the cranium, some of which were associated with areas of missing bone. Several more sharp force defects were located on the third cervical vertebra, which had fractured into three pieces, as well as the fourth and fifth cervical vertebrae. These defects are consistent with decapitation. The left eighth rib and right seventh rib exhibited defects along their shafts. The right radius and ulna both exhibited complete fractures of the distal shaft associated with a sharp force defect. The radius exhibited two additional sharp force defects, and the ulna exhibited an additional four. These defects were all consistent with self-defense wounds. Over 1 year later, additional portions of the cranium, as well as the mandible and the atlas, were recovered.

5.4.8   Case 8

The body of an adult female was discovered in the hallway of her home with a hacksaw embedded in her right lower leg. The right proximal tibia and fibula of an adult female were submitted for maceration and the evaluation of osseous traumata. The medial aspect of the right tibial shaft exhibited multiple incised defects, V-shaped in profile. Multiple incised defects were also present on the anteromedial and lateral aspects of the tibia, although these were shallower in depth than those on the medial aspect. A single incised defect, square-shaped in cross-section, was present further down the tibial shaft. The morphology of this latter defect was consistent with that produced by a saw blade known to have been used on the decedent. Although incomplete, this defect was meant to dismember the victim; however, the suspect "got tired."

5.5   Characteristics of dismemberment cases

Despite their overall rarity (Dogan *et al.* 2010; Konopka *et al.* 2007; Rajs *et al.* 1998), several studies have been carried out utilizing samples of homicides with postmortem mutilation, typically involving dismemberment. Results of these studies suggest that several characteristics of this kind of crime are fairly common. To begin with, most dismemberment cases are classified as defensive in nature, and most perpetrators are male. In Maricopa County, while the majority of cases appear to be defensive in nature, the majority of the perpetrators were female.

Research suggests that the bulk of dismemberments are committed by perpetrators who knew their victims, and often were related to them either by blood or marriage (Häkkänen-Nyholm *et al.* 2009b; Konopka *et al.* 2007; Rajs *et al.* 1998; Watanabe and Tamura 2001). For example, in only 8.7% of Polish cases were the victim and the offender unknown to each other (Konopka *et al.* 2007) and the corresponding proportion for a sample of Japanese cases is 13.3% (Watanabe and Tamura 2001). In Maricopa County, the victims and suspects knew each other in all seven instances in which both parties were identified. In only three of these cases, however, were they intimate relations.

Most dismemberments took place at the scene of the preceding homicide, often the private residence of the victim, the perpetrator, or both, and most cases involved tools that were readily available, such as kitchen knives, axes, woodworking saws, or hacksaws (Konopka *et al.* 2007). This holds true in Maricopa County as well.

Dismemberment cases are more common in large urban areas (Rajs *et al.* 1998), but this observation may be caused by other factors such as increased population density or increased presence of law enforcement agencies and hence an increased chance of detection. Most offenders who dismember their victims have a history of psychiatric treatment (Häkkänen-Nyholm *et al.*

2009b; Rajs *et al.* 1998). However, the majority of dismemberments are not planned in advance and they are only rarely serial in nature (Konopka *et al.* 2007).

Although some studies have attempted to identify characteristics associated with specific categories of dismemberment (i.e. defensive, aggressive, offensive, and necromanic) (e.g. Häkkänen-Nyholm *et al.* 2009b; Rajs *et al.* 1998), few studies seem to address the possibility of differences based on sex, either of the victim or of the offender. One notable exception is the work of Watanabe and Tamura (2001), who analyzed a series of 134 homicides with subsequent dismemberment that took place in Japan between 1947 and 1998. Based on the application of a non-linear canonical correlation analysis to a series of victim factors (e.g. sex, age), offence factors (e.g. cause of death, number of body parts removed), and offender factors (e.g. age, sex, relationship to victim), Watanabe and Tamura divided their cases into three categories: (1) those cases in which the victim is less than 20 years of age; (2) those cases in which the victim is 20 years old or more and female; and (3) those cases in which the victim is 20 years old or more and male. Differences observed in these categories suggest that an investigation of the sex of both the victim and the suspect in dismemberment cases may be a fruitful line of inquiry.

5.6   Differences between the sexes pertaining to homicide

The majority of homicides are committed by males. Although the value varies from place to place and year to year, most studies report that females only commit between 7% and 15% of homicides annually (Goetting 1988; Häkkänen-Nyholm *et al.* 2009a; Jurik and Winn 1990; Karlsson 1998; Kellerman and Mercy 1992; Ormstad *et al.* 1986; Putkonen *et al.* 2001; Rogde *et al.* 2000). The victims of female homicide offenders are typically male, and more likely to be family members or intimates, especially (ex)spouses or (ex) lovers, with between 60% and 78% of the victims reported as falling into these categories (Goetting 1988; Häkkänen-Nyholm *et al.* 2009a; Jurik and Winn 1990; Mann 1990; Ormstad *et al.* 1986; Putkonen *et al.* 2001; Weizmann-Henelius *et al.* 2003). Conversely, women are far less likely to kill strangers than are males (Mann 1990; Weizmann-Henelius *et al.* 2003). A study of female homicide offenders in Finland found that the victims had no relationship with the offender in only two out of 125 cases (Putkonen *et al.* 2001). Women are almost twice as likely as males to participate in victim-precipitated killings (i.e. the victim initiated the conflict by acting violently towards their eventual slayer) (Goetting 1988; Jurik and Winn 1990). Perhaps related to this component of self-defense, women have also been found to be more likely than males to remain at the scene and to notify somebody after the crime has been committed (Goetting 1988; Häkkänen-Nyholm *et al.* 2009a). Likely related to all of the above observations, women have also been found to kill in private settings more often than males – either in their own home, that of the victim, or the residence that they share with the victim (Goetting 1988; Häkkänen-Nyholm *et al.* 2009a; Jurik and Winn 1990; Mann 1990).

Within the larger population of female homicide offenders, there seems to be some meaningful variation. According to one study, based in Finland, women who attacked (but did not necessarily kill) strangers or acquaintances were more likely to have a history of violence, to have a higher rate of violent recidivism, and to have a higher rate of alcohol abuse. Women who attacked individuals who were emotionally close to them tended to be older (mean age 37 as opposed to mean ages of 30.1 and 28.7 for women who attacked acquaintances and strangers, respectively), were more usually married, more often mothers, more often employed, and typically were better educated (Weizmann-Henelius *et al.* 2003). Another study found that personality disorders and psychoses among female homicide offenders show some degree of segregation based on their victim profile. Women who attacked adults tended to be diagnosed with personality disorders, while those individuals who victimized children tended to be diagnosed with psychotic disorders (Putkonen *et al.* 2001).

Further differences become apparent between male and female homicide offenders when the murder weapon is considered. Häkkänen-Nyholm *et al.* (2009a) found that firearms, punching, and kicking are more likely to be employed by male offenders, while suffocation was found more often among female offenders. They suggest that this pattern is likely associated with the higher number of children that are killed by women in their Finnish sample. In another sample from Finland, Putkonen *et al.* (2001) found that stabbing was the most common means of homicide, accounting for 65% of cases, followed by strangulation and blunt force (12% and 11%, respectively). Studies based in the USA found that female homicide offenders most often used a handgun to commit the crime, but that they also resorted to stabbing their victim more often than male homicide offenders (Goetting 1988; Jurik and Winn 1990; Kellerman and Mercy 1992). Regarding female homicide victims, a study carried out in the USA between 1976 and 1987 reported that almost 30% of female victims were bludgeoned, strangled, or suffocated. The comparable proportion for male homicide victims is 12% (Kellerman and Mercy 1992).

Given these reported differences in the victim profiles and manner of killing between male and female homicide offenders, is it not possible that similar sex-based differences exist in the population of individuals who dismember their victims?

5.7 Sex-based differences in dismemberment cases

To investigate whether or not male and female perpetrators who dismembered their victims differ in any discernible way, as well as whether or not characteristics of the crime vary with the sex of the victim, a database was compiled using both published dismemberment cases as well as the selection of cases presented above. Sources for this database are listed in Table 5.1. A total of 102 dismemberment cases was located and information, where available, was recorded concerning the date of occurrence, the age and sex of the victim, the age and sex of the suspect, the relation of the victim to the suspect, the manner of death, the implement used for dismemberment, the body segments that were recovered, the minimum number of segments that the body was sectioned into, and the disposal method of the remains. Not all categories of information were available for each case. Results are presented in Table 5.2.

When sex of the victim of dismemberment is considered, males and females account for nearly equal proportions of the total sample (52% and 48%, respectively). Male victims are slightly older, but not significantly so ($t = 0.82$; P value $= 0.21$). For victims of both sexes, the age of the suspects was comparable. A slightly lower percentage of male dismemberments were committed by females than female dismemberments. Further, the mean

Table 5.1. *Sources used in database and number of cases from each source.*

Sources used in database	Number of cases per source
Andrews 2003	2
Delabarde & Ludes 2010	2
Di Nunno *et al.* 2006	2
Dogan *et al.* 2010	1
Hyma & Rao 1991	4
Kahana pers. comm., May 16, 2013	20
Karger *et al.* 2000	1
Konopka *et al.* 2006	1
Konopka *et al.* 2007	23
Rajs *et al.* 1998	20
Randall 2009	1
Reddy 1973	1
Reichs 1998	7
Sugiyama *et al.* 1995	3
Symes *et al.* 2001	2
Toms *et al.* 2008	2
Tümer *et al.* 2012	2
Unpublished cases	8

Table 5.2. *Select descriptive statistics for males and females both as victims of dismemberment and as perpetrators.*

Victims (n = 102)	Mean Age	Median Age	Range	% Killed by female	Mean age of suspect
Male victims (n = 53)	38.3 (n = 46)	38	12–73	22.6 (7/31)	37.8 (n = 23)
Female victims (n = 49)	34.9 (n = 48)	31	3–85	27.3 (9/33)	38.5 (n = 36)

	Mean minimum number of segments		Mean age male suspect		Mean age female suspect
Male victims (n = 53)	5.2 (n = 40)		38.3 (n = 17)		37.3 (n = 4)
Female victims (n = 49)	5.9 (n = 40)		39.7 (n = 19)		37.0 (n = 5)

Perpetrators (n = 60)	Mean Age	Median Age	Range	% Victims female	Mean age of victims
Male suspects (n = 46)	39.0 (n = 36)	33.5	18–71	50.0 (23/46)	37.9 (n = 46)
Female suspects (n = 14)	37.1 (n = 9)	33	22–50	57.1 (8/14)	37.9 (n = 14)

	Mean minimum number of segments		Mean age male victims		Mean age female victims
Male suspects (n = 46)	6.7 (n = 39)		37.7 (n = 23)		38.2 (n = 23)
Female suspects (n = 14)	4.6 (n = 9)		47.5 (n = 6)		30.8 (n = 8)

minimum number of body segments produced by the dismemberment was not significantly different between male and female victim populations (t = 0.99; P value = 0.327). While some differences exist in the number of deaths attributed to each of sharp force, blunt force, strangulation, and gunshot wounds between the sexes, these differences are also not significant ($\chi^2 = 4.13$; $v = 3$; $P = 0.25$).

When sex of the suspect is examined, males account for 76.7% of the perpetrators of dismemberments while females account for the remaining 23.3%. The mean age of the victims of male perpetrators is the same as that of female perpetrators. An interesting pattern emerges when the victims are segregated by sex in that the mean age of the female victims of female suspects is nearly 17 years younger than the mean age of their male victims (mean age for female victims is 30.8 and mean age for male victims is 47.5). No such separation occurs amongst the victims of male suspects. Unfortunately, sample size is too small for statistical validation of this result. The mean number of body segments produced throughout the course of the dismemberment is slightly higher among male suspects, but not significantly so ($t = 1.36$; P value $= 0.18$). The number of deaths attributed to sharp force, blunt force, strangulation, and gunshot wounds seem to differ, with female suspects rarely employing strangulation or firearms, but again, the sample is too small for statistical comparison. Roughly in line with characteristics of female homicide offenders, 12 out of 14 female suspects in this sample (85.7%) dismembered an intimate relation. In comparison, intimate relations were the victims of dismemberment for 23 out of 42 male suspects (54.8%).

5.8   Discussion and conclusions

Very few differences emerge between the populations of male and female victims of dismemberments or between the populations of male and female offenders. In comparison to the general population of homicides, both males and females share relatively equal representation as victims of dismemberment (as opposed to a predominance of males as victims in the general homicide population). Likewise, while females tend to account for approximately 15% of the homicides committed, they account for a larger proportion of dismemberments committed (23.3% of the current sample). Proportionally more females were killed by strangulation and proportionally more males were killed by gunshot wounds. Likewise, although sample size was small, female suspects appeared to prefer either blunt or sharp force as a means of dispatching their victims, while males also employed strangulation and, rarely in this sample, firearms. Despite an already documented predilection for female suspects to kill intimate relations, the female suspects who carried out dismemberments killed intimate relations almost exclusively.

The results of this analysis are extremely limited. The data employed were compiled from published sources, and with little consistency of the kinds of information presented between publications. This served to drastically reduce the sample size for any given comparison of variables. Further, many published case studies are published because of their spectacular nature. Inclusion of such cases in the current study may skew the dataset in unpredictable ways. Additional problems exist in compiling a dataset of cases from several different places and time periods. Removing such cases from their cultural and temporal context may destroy the evidence for any regional patterns that exist in this kind of violence. Nevertheless, the relative rarity of dismemberment cases necessitates such compilation in the hopes of creating statistically viable comparative samples.

Despite the limitations of the current dataset, some intriguing differences were suggested between both male and female dismemberment victims and perpetrators. The possibility of differences in weapon choice between male and female perpetrators of dismemberment is especially interesting since, if such a difference is shown to be real and not simply an artifact of sample size, it may have some small amount of utility for identifying suspects in novel dismemberment cases. Further analyses should be performed with larger, more controlled samples of dismemberment cases to pursue this line of inquiry as well as to further characterize the differences (or lack thereof) between males and females both as victims and perpetrators of postmortem dismemberment.

Acknowledgments

The authors would like to thank Dr. Tzipi Kahana for her assistance in providing us with details concerning a series of dismemberment cases that she analyzed. We would also like to acknowledge the Maricopa County Office of the Medical Examiner.

References

Andrews, J. M. (2003). Central nervous system consequences of an unusual body disposal strategy: case report and brief experimental investigation. *Journal of Forensic Sciences*, **48**, 1–5.

Buikstra, J. E. & Gordon, C. C. (1980). Individuation in forensic science study: decapitation. *Journal of Forensic Sciences*, **25**, 246–59.

Delabarde, T. & Ludes, B. (2010). Missing in Amazonian jungle: a case report of skeletal evidence for dismemberment. *Journal of Forensic Sciences*, **55**, 1105–10.

Di Nunno, N., Costantinides, F., Vacca, M. & Di Nunno, C. (2006). Dismemberment: a review of the literature and description of 3 cases. *The American Journal of Forensic Medicine and Pathology*, **27**, 307–12.

Dogan, K. H., Demirci, S., Deniz, I. & Erkol, Z. (2010). Decapitation and dismemberment of the corpse: a matricide case. *Journal of Forensic Sciences*, **55**, 542–5.

Goetting, A. (1988). Patterns of homicide among women. *Journal of Interpersonal Violence*, **3**, 3–19.

Häkkänen-Nyholm, H., Putkonen, H., Lindberg, N., Holi, M., Rovamo, T. & Weizmann-Henelius, G. (2009a). Gender differences in Finnish homicide offence characteristics. *Forensic Science International*, **186**, 75–80.

Häkkänen-Nyholm, H., Weizmann-Henelius, G., Salenius, S., Lindberg, N. & Repo-Tiihonen, E. (2009b). Homicides with mutilation of the victim's body. *Journal of Forensic Sciences*, **54**, 933–7.

Hyma, B. A. & Rao, V. J. (1991). Evaluation and identification of dismembered human remains. *The American Journal of Forensic Medicine and Pathology*, **12**, 291–9.

Jurik, N. C. & Winn, R. (1990). Gender and homicide: a comparison of men and women who kill. *Violence and Victims*, **5**, 227–42.

Kahana, T., Aleman, I., Botella, M. C., Novoselsky, Y., Volkov, N. & Hiss, J. (2010). Postmortem dismemberment in two Mediterranean countries. *Journal of Forensic Identification*, **60**, 557–72.

Karger, B., Rand, S. P. & Brinkmann, B. (2000). Criminal anticipation of DNA investigations resulting in mutilation of a corpse. *International Journal of Legal Medicine*, **113**, 247–8.

Karlsson, T. (1998). Sharp force homicides in the Stockholm Area, 1983–1992. *Forensic Science International*, **94**, 129–39.

Kellerman, A. L. & Mercy, J. A. (1992). Men, women, and murder: gender-specific differences in rates of fatal violence and victimization. *The Journal of Trauma*, **33**, 1–5.

Konopka, T., Bolechała, F. & Strona, M. (2006). An unusual case of corpse dismemberment. *The American Journal of Forensic Medicine and Pathology*, **27**, 163–5.

Konopka, T., Strona, M., Bolechała, F. & Kunz, J. (2007). Corpse dismemberment in the material collected by the Department of Forensic Medicine, Cracow, Poland. *Legal Medicine*, **9**, 1–13.

Mann, C. R. (1990). Black female homicide in the United States. *Journal of Interpersonal Violence*, **5**, 176–201.

Ormstad, K., Karlsson, T., Enkler, L., Law, B. & Rajs, J. (1986). Patterns in sharp force fatalities – a comprehensive forensic medical study. *Journal of Forensic Sciences*, **31**, 529–42.

Putkonen, H., Collander, J., Honkasalo, M.-L. & Lönnqvist, J. (2001). Personality disorders and psychoses form two distinct subgroups of homicide among female offenders. *Journal of Forensic Psychiatry*, **12**, 300–12.

Rajs, J., Lundström, M., Broberg, M., Lidberg, L. & Lindquist, O. (1998). Criminal mutilation of the human body in Sweden – a thirty-year medico-legal and forensic psychiatric study. *Journal of Forensic Sciences*, **43**, 563–80.

Randall, B. (2009). Blood and tissue spatter associated with chainsaw dismemberment. *Journal of Forensic Sciences*, **54**, 1310–14.

Reddy, K. S. N. (1973). Identification of dismembered parts: the medicolegal aspects of the Nagaraju case. *Forensic Science*, **2**, 351–74.

Reichs, K. J. (1998). Postmortem dismemberment: recovery, analysis, and interpretation. In: Reichs, K. J. (ed.) *Forensic Osteology: Advances in the Identification of Human Remains*, 2nd edn. Springfield: Charles C. Thomas, 353–88.

Rogde, S., Hougen, H. P. & Poulsen, K. (2000). Homicide by sharp force in two Scandinavian capitals. *Forensic Science International*, **109**, 135–45.

Sugiyama, S., Tatsumi, S., Noda, H., Yamaguchi, M., Furutani, A., Izumi, M., Wakatsuki, R., Yoshimura, M. *et al.* (1995). Investigation of dismembered corpses found during the past 10 years in Osaka. *Hanzaigaku Zasshi*, **61**, 192–200.

Symes, S. A., Berryman, H. E. & Smith, O. C. (1998). Saw marks in bone: introduction and examination of residual kerf contour. In: Reichs, K. J. (ed.) *Forensic Osteology: Advances in the Identification of Human Remains*, 2nd edn. Springfield: Charles C. Thomas, 389–409.

Toms, C., Rogers, C. B. & Sathyavagiswaran, L. (2008). Investigation of homicides interred in concrete – the Los Angeles experience. *Journal of Forensic Sciences*, **53**, 203–7.

Tümer, A. R., Akçan, R., Karacaoğlu, E., Balseven-Odabaşi, A., Keten, A., Kanburoğlu, C., Unal, M. & Dinç, A. H. (2012). Postmortem burning of the corpses following homicide. *Journal of Forensic and Legal Medicine*, **19**, 223–8.

Watanabe, K. & Tamura, M. (2001). Mutilation-murder cases in Japan. In: Farrington, D. P., Hollin, C. R. & McMurran, M. (eds.) *Sex and Violence: The Psychology of Crime and Risk Assessment*. New York: Psychology Press, 229–41.

Weizmann-Henelius, G., Viemerö, V. & Eronen, M. (2003). The violent female perpetrator and her victim. *Forensic Science International*, **133**, 197–203.

6 Victims of violence? A methodological case study from precolonial Northern Mexico

CHERYL P. ANDERSON

6.1 Introduction

Bioarchaeology is significant for the study of violence as it provides direct evidence of violent acts in the past through the identification of lethal and non-lethal wounds. These data, combined with other evidence, may lead to the identification of patterns of violence. Recent research in bioarchaeology has demonstrated how human skeletal data may allow for the identification of victims as well as considerations about the perpetrators of violence (Martin and Harrod 2012). La Cueva de Dos Cuchillos (The Cave of the Two Knives) presents one example of how current methodology for investigating violence may be applied to reinterpret older skeletal collections, potentially leading to the identification of victims and perpetrators in the past.

La Cueva de Dos Cuchillos was originally excavated and reported on by Richard and Sheilagh Brooks in the 1950s, and the human skeletal remains they recovered are currently curated in the Department of Anthropology at the University of Nevada, Las Vegas. In 2010, a preliminary examination of the remains revealed trauma potentially consistent with violence and thus a reanalysis of the collection was undertaken to investigate implications for conflict in the region (Anderson et al. 2012). This proved challenging as the age of the remains was then unknown, some of the remains originally excavated were no longer with the rest of the collection, and some of the records were no longer available. Moreover, little archaeological work has been done in this portion of Mexico, and, of the studies that have been performed, few have focused on bioarchaeological evidence. To interpret the data collected from the human remains from La Cueva de Dos Cuchillos, the use of multiple

Bioarchaeological and Forensic Perspectives on Violence: How Violent Death is Interpreted from Skeletal Remains, ed. D. L. Martin and C. P. Anderson. Published by Cambridge University Press.
© Cambridge University Press 2014.

83

lines of evidence was necessary. In this case, ethnographic data on the Rarámuri (Tarahumara Indians) and their mortuary practices, ethnohistoric data written by Spanish colonial sources that describe groups living in the region, and archaeological data from other sites in the Sierra Madre Occidental were used. These lines of evidence, combined with the bioarchaeological data, were used to explore whether the remains represent victims of violence or if the trauma present on some of the individuals and the state of the remains may be explained by burial rituals and/or ancestor veneration. Ultimately, the analysis proved to be successful in providing a reasonable explanation for the signs of trauma found on some individuals.

6.2   Case study: La Cueva de Dos Cuchillos

La Cueva de Dos Cuchillos (The Cave of the Two Knives) is a cave burial site located in the Sierra Madre Occidental near the town of San Francisco de Borja in Chihuahua, Mexico (see Anderson *et al.* 2012; Brooks and Brooks 1990). Human remains and artifacts from this site were collected by Richard and Sheilagh Brooks during 1956 and 1957 while they were surveying and excavating archaeological sites in Chihuahua and Durango (Brooks and Brooks 1990). The site has been described by Brooks and Brooks (1990) as a small cave with a midden inside that contained human remains and artifacts. The La Cueva de Dos Cuchillos site is located in a region that is now populated by people of the modern Rarámuri culture (Bennett and Zingg 1976; Brooks and Brooks 1990; Kennedy 1996; Merrill 1988; Pennington 1963). The topography of this region of the Sierra Madre Occidental is described as foothills, with channels running down them, resulting from the erosion of rivers and arroyos. Inside the channels there are a number of rock shelters and caves (Brooks and Brooks 1990).

During excavation of the cave, human skeletal remains were discovered commingled and scattered in the cultural deposits of the midden. Some of the skeletal remains were also burned, although evidence for fire within the cave was not discovered by the excavators (Brooks and Brooks 1990). Artifacts in the cave included corn cobs, ceramics, basket fragments, spindle whorls, beads, burned wooden sticks, the foreshaft of an arrow, gourd ladles, red ocher, a scraper, manos, smoothing stones, a chopper, stone flakes, stone bowl pieces, and shell pendants. Additionally, two metal knives, thought to date to the seventeenth or eighteenth century, were found with blue trade beads from the colonial period. There was no specific association between the human remains and either the historic or precolonial artifacts. Because of the types of artifacts present in the cave, it was originally thought that remains represented a closely related group of people that dated between the late precolonial period and the eighteenth century (Brooks and Brooks 1990; Brooks and Brooks n.d.). A recent radiocarbon date of cal AD 1280–1400 now shows that at least some individuals date to the late precolonial period, although it is possible that other burials are from later time periods. The radiocarbon date was obtained from the mandible of burial 1–118; this is an old adult (50+ years) male to be discussed in more detail below (Anderson *et al.* 2012).

A reanalysis of the human remains from La Cueva de Dos Cuchillos was performed using standard osteological procedures (Bass 2005; Brooks and Suchey 1990; Buikstra and Mielke 1985; Buikstra and Ubelaker 1994; Hillson 1996; Johnston 1962; Phenice 1969; Scheuer and Black 2000; Smith 1991) to document and explain signs of trauma and potential violence. The minimum number of individuals was estimated based on the most represented skeletal element (Stodder and Osterholtz 2010; White 1992; White *et al.* 2012). At least 17 individuals were interred in the cave, including ten adults and seven subadults. During the analysis, one old adult male, burial 1–118 (mentioned above) was found to exhibit perimortem chop marks on the left os coxa, left femur, and right tibia (Anderson *et al.* 2012). The chop mark located on the proximal right tibia is shown in Figure 6.1. Additionally, two isolated second

Figure 6.1. Proximal right tibia with chop mark (adapted from Anderson *et al.* 2012).

cervical vertebrae were found to have perimortem teardrop fractures (Anderson *et al.* 2012), which are often associated with hyperextension of the neck and head trauma (Galloway 1999; Shapiro *et al.* 1973). This type of fracture is infrequent in modern times (Korres *et al.* 1994) and no other bioarchaeological examples are known (Anderson *et al.* 2012). No other definitive signs of trauma were found on the other human remains from the site, although the occipitals of two subadults had possible perimortem breakage. In addition to trauma, the bones of three individuals, one adult and two subadults, showed signs of burning. The burning on the adult was quite extensive and covered the ribs and vertebral column (Anderson *et al.* 2012). One of the burned subadults was an individual with potential perimortem breakage on the base of the skull. Owing to the complex mortuary context and the presence of perimortem trauma on at least three individuals, a comprehensive review of the ethnographic, ethnohistoric, and archaeological records was performed to make sense of this unusual assemblage.

6.3   Ethnographic data

Ethnographic data can be a powerful tool for investigating mortuary practices and potential evidence for violence in the past. This type of data has been utilized in other archaeological studies of violence in the Southwest, e.g. by Darling (1998), who employs these ethnographic and ethnohistoric reports to explore the reasons behind Ancestral Pueblo violence in the Greater Southwest. This type of data has also been used to investigate burial practices in the past, such as by Ellis (1968), who used ethnographic reports to aid in interpreting precolonial mortuary patterns from the American Southwest. Of course it should not be expected that practices exhibited by cultural groups will remain consistent over time. In some cases, however, ethnographic information can be an important line of evidence and, when combined with other types of data, can add to bioarchaeological interpretations of the past.

To interpret the mortuary context of the remains in this case and determine if the burial data were consistent with standard mortuary practices or indicative of violence, a review of the ethnographic information on the Rarámuri was critical. At La Cueva de Dos Cuchillos, the presence of multiple, disarticulated and commingled human remains, and the presence of burning on some individuals could have been further evidence for a violent death for some of these people in addition to the perimortem trauma found on three burials. In their original report, Brooks and Brooks (1990) suggest that a number of circumstances could account for the state of the human remains, including mortuary ritual, interment of only token pieces of the dead, and colonial period violence, or disease. In this case, the ethnographic data made it possible to rule out some of these scenarios through an understanding of the principal components of Rarámuri burial rituals and their social meaning.

According to the ethnographic reports, the Rarámuri have been described as a semi-nomadic, semi-agricultural people living in Western Chihuahua, Mexico. At the time of Spanish contact the Rarámuri were surrounded by several cultural groups, including the Tubar, Témori, Tepehuán, Concho, Jova, Pima Bajo, Guazapar, and Varohío. All of these peoples speak closely related Uto-Aztecan languages (Bennett and Zingg 1976; Pennington 1963). Traditionally, Rarámuri subsistence included mainly corn, beans, and squash, accompanied by fish and wild plants (Pennington 1963). Residential practices have been described by Lumholtz (1902) and suggest that Rarámuri were generally mobile and would inhabit different locations throughout the year. Residence type was described as variable, with some groups living in houses, some in caves, and some groups alternating between caves and houses at different times during the year (Lumholtz 1902).

Ethnographic reports also describe distinct Rarámuri burial practices and ideas about the dead. Death, according to modern Rarámuri beliefs, occurs when an individual's soul separates from the rest of the body. This results in a deceased individual that is still perceived to be alive by the community, although in an altered state. The dead can be encountered by the living while they are asleep or sometimes also while they are awake (Merrill 1988). The potential for interaction between the living and the dead is a cause for concern, however, among the Rarámuri as the living can become ill if they come into contact with the soul of a deceased person (Lumholtz 1902; Merrill 1988) or if they consume any food or drink contaminated by the deceased (Merrill 1988). The souls of the dead do not reside solely in the world of the living and some suggest that the souls can move between heaven and earth or that, after all of the necessary burial rituals are completed, the dead will go to heaven permanently (Merrill 1988).

Because of the potential for the dead to harm the living, people commonly fear the dead and do what is required to convince them to leave the living alone (Lumholtz 1902; Merrill 1988). To accomplish this, the Rarámuri must satisfy the needs of the deceased. One of the first required actions of the living is to give the deceased a proper burial (Merrill 1988). Specific burial practices can include wrapping the deceased in a blanket and placement of their hands tied together on their chest with a cross or down at their sides (Bennett and Zingg 1976; Kennedy 1996; Lumholtz 1902; Merrill 1988). After wrapping a deceased individual, a fire is built next to the body (Bennett and Zingg 1976; Kennedy 1996; Merrill 1988). On the ground a cross and rosary are placed and near the cross there are items such as food, clothes, and knives.

These are the possessions the deceased used during their lifetime (Bennett and Zingg 1976; Kennedy 1996). Food items interred with the dead will often include corn and beans. The body of the dead individual is then placed in a house by itself and everyone else in the household sleeps elsewhere (Bennett and Zingg 1976; Kennedy 1996; Merrill 1988). People often do not wish to touch the body and are afraid of being in close proximity (Kennedy 1996; Merrill 1988). The dead are generally left in the house for one night and then buried the next day (Bennett and Zingg 1976; Kennedy 1996; Merrill 1988).

The actual burial ceremony practiced by the Rarámuri can be variable, with the biggest contrast between Christian and non-Christian groups. During a non-Christian burial family members and neighbors generally assemble at the house, uncover the head of the deceased, and make crosses of incense smoke over the body (Bennett and Zingg 1976; Kennedy 1996). The family speaks to the deceased and encourages them not to return and frighten the family or damage the crops or animals (Bennett and Zingg 1976; Kennedy 1996; Lumholtz 1902). The family promises the deceased that they will provide food and perform the required number of death fiestas (Kennedy 1996). The body is then brought to a cave that contains the remains of other people who have already been buried. The body and burial items are set down near the burial cave with a fire kindled at the feet of the deceased. The body is then pushed inside the cave along with the food and any other grave items. Once the body and grave items are inside the cave is closed with stones and mud. After the burial is finished, any individuals who carried the body are cured in a special ceremony (Bennett and Zingg 1976; Kennedy 1996).

6.4   Ethnohistoric data

Ethnohistoric reports can also be useful for understanding intragroup and intergroup interactions in the past. While it is understood that historic reports will not necessarily present an entirely accurate picture of the past, they may still provide invaluable information and are often the only type of record available (Spielmann et al. 2009). Ethnohistoric evidence has been used extensively by other researchers working with late precolonial or colonial period assemblages in the New World (e.g. Duncan 2005; Gaither et al. 2008; Klaus and Tam 2009; Nelson et al. 1992; Pérez et al. 2008; Spielmann et al. 2009; Stojanowski 2009). Some of these have focused on violence, veneration, or both. For example, Spielmann et al. (2009) examines ethnohistoric documents about the Pueblo Revolt of 1680 and Duncan (2005) uses ethnographic and ethnohistoric accounts to investigate Postclassic Maya assemblages, including examples of ancestor veneration and violation of the deceased. These examples exemplify the utility of combining ethnohistoric data with skeletal and archaeological evidence.

In the case of La Cueva de Dos Cuchillos, ethnohistoric data were used to understand the relationships between the Rarámuri and other groups residing in the region. These reports were often written by Spanish Jesuits who were living among the Rarámuri or in nearby settlements. According to the ethnohistoric literature, intergroup violence was common in the early seventeenth century AD. This violence included acts such as scalping and the taking of trophy heads (Beals 1933, 1973; Moser 1973; Nelson *et al.* 1992). Spanish reports discuss how the heads of captured enemies were removed with hatchets. The heads were then perforated and displayed, and this has been compared to the Aztec practice of placing heads on skull racks (Kelley 1978; Moser 1973). Groups identified as practicing head-taking included the Rarámuri, Yaqui, Tepahue, Acaxee, Cora, Xixime, and Tepehuan, among others (Kelley 1978; Moser 1973). Cannibalism may have been part of the ceremonies surrounding the treatment of dead enemies, although this may have also been a part of ritual human sacrifice among some cultures (Beals 1973). One example concerns the Acaxee, whose practice of decapitating enemies, followed by ritual cannibalism, was tied to their ideology, with the remains being offered to a deity (Beals 1973). Another account of the Acaxee, Xixime, and Tepehuan in Durango, Mexico, written by Father Andrés Pérez de Ribas in 1645, discusses frequent warfare in the past between groups that sometimes spoke the same language. In some instances entire communities would be involved in the conflict (de Ribas 1971 [1645]). De Ribas (1971 [1645]) also specifically mentions the Tepehuan as being hostile to the Rarámuri, as well as to other groups. The ethnohistoric reports of the groups living in Northern Mexico also describe some of the weapons that would have been used in violent conflict in the past. These weapons included obsidian or flint-edged wooden swords, hatchets, bows and arrows, and spears (Beals 1973; de Ribas 1971 [1645]).

Another type of violence that has been discussed in the ethnohistoric (and ethnographic) reports as perhaps relevant to the Rarámuri is sacrifice. Human sacrifice is known to have occurred in various parts of the Americas during the precolonial period. Many bioarchaeological reports have provided skeletal evidence for human sacrifice (e.g. Berryman 2007; De Anda Alanis 2007; Eeckhout and Owens 2008; Gaither *et al.* 2008; Mendoza 2007). In Northern Mexico, among some cultures, ritual human sacrifice is reported in the ethnohistoric literature. For example, child sacrifice is thought to have occurred in this region to cure an adult from illness (Beals 1973). It has been suggested by some (Bennett and Zingg 1976; Pastron and Clewlow Jr. 1974) that the Rarámuri may have practiced human sacrifice at some point in the past. Pastron and Clewlow Jr. (1974), however, interpret their findings in a historic cave, where all the adult skulls were missing, as more likely the result of witchcraft. In contrast, Beals (1973) suggests that the Rarámuri may have practiced animal sacrifice but maintains that there is no indication of human sacrifice, although it did likely occur among at least one cultural group in Northern Mexico. There has thus far been no study that has demonstrated that the Rarámuri practiced human sacrifice.

6.5   Archaeological data

In addition to ethnographic and ethnohistoric data, archaeological evidence is, of course, critical for providing a comparative context. For this reason, archaeological reports from sites near La Cueva de Dos Cuchillos were used to identify other examples of potential violence from the same time period in the region. A number of cave burial sites from this region have been described (see Ascher and Clune 1960; Green 1985; Lister 1958; Lumholtz 1902; Pastron and Clewlow Jr. 1974; Pinter 1985; Walker 2006; Zingg 1940), and they provide the comparative data necessary for understanding the assemblage at La Cueva de Dos Cuchillos.

6.5.1   *Mortuary practices*

In addition to ethnographic reports of Rarámuri mortuary practices, archaeological reports of burial sites were reviewed and demonstrated a regional pattern. Overall, the archaeological record is fairly consistent with the ethnographic reports of Rarámuri burial practices. The use of burial caves, often containing multiple individuals, is very similar to the practices reported in the ethnographic literature. Also, the types of grave goods reported mirror those described in later times, and include food and personal items. Additionally, at some sites there are signs of wrapping of bodies and occasionally signs of fire are detected.

One example of this comes from Waterfall Cave, where the remains of 10 individuals were recovered. This site is thought to be precolonial (1000–1600 AD) based on associated artifacts found in the cave, including a lack of colonial period items. Both individual and multiple interments were present inside the burial cave. The burials were found in flexed positions and the heads of the individuals were facing toward the cave entrance. The bodies of the deceased appear to have been wrapped in blankets and then mats and stones were placed on top of the wrappings. Adult males, adult females, and subadults were present in the cave and a fire pit was also discovered in the cave near the burials. Materials within the cave consisted of pottery, textiles, plant remains, lithics, and faunal remains (Ascher and Clune 1960).

Another example comes from an unnamed burial cave reported by Pastron and Clewlow Jr. (1974), although this cave was thought to be only 70–125 years old. The human remains in this cave indicated that multiple individuals were interred and were placed in flexed positions. There was also evidence suggesting that the heads of these individuals were facing toward the east, which is a common burial practice. Both adults and subadults were represented in the cave but, interestingly enough, no adult crania were present. All of the cranial fragments that belonged to infants were bleached white, indicating that they had been exposed to sunlight (Pastron and Clewlow Jr. 1974). While these remains are from no earlier than the late nineteenth century AD, and are therefore not contemporaneous with La Cueva de Dos Cuchillos, similar mortuary practices suggest some potential continuities with earlier behaviors or customs.

More recently, Walker (2006) investigated 13 burial caves in the Sierra Madre Occidental. The dates of these caves ranged from AD 1099 to AD 1769 but the one cave that dated to approximately 1769 (AD 1720–1819) was the only historic cave (Walker 2006). The burial practices observed by Walker (Walker 2006) are consistent with the burial practices described in ethnographic and ethnohistoric reports of the Rarámuri. For example, all of the caves except one contained multiple individuals that were generally placed in flexed positions. Evidence that some of the bodies were wrapped in mats was found in some instances as well. Additionally, one of the caves contained evidence for a fire. Grave goods in the caves included ceramics, corn, and lithics (Walker 2006).

6.5.2 Evidence for violence

To date, very little skeletal evidence for violence has been identified in archaeological assemblages in this portion of the Sierra Madre Occidental. It is possible that violence was relatively rare in this region or that signs of violence have been obscured by taphonomy. Alternatively, the lack of evidence may be due to the paucity of archaeological investigations in this area. Of the available archaeological publications, human remains reported have been subjected to very few in-depth skeletal analyses. One exception, however, is recent work by Walker (2006), who included modern bioarchaeological analysis of the human remains from 13 burial caves. Walker (2006) provides full bioarchaeological reports of the skeletal remains, including any evidence for trauma. Of the 13 burial caves examined, two contained the remains of individuals exhibiting perimortem trauma. One of these, Hedionda cave

(AD 1262–1511), contained the remains of two individuals with perimortem blunt force trauma to the head. This included a young adult woman with both antemortem and perimortem trauma to the basicranium. A young adult male found in the cave also had both antemortem and perimortem trauma, including perimortem blunt force trauma to both the right and left sides of the head (Walker 2006). The second cave, Cueva Juárez (AD 1208–1302), contained the remains of an adolescent (probable) female with perimortem blunt force trauma to the basicranium that resulted in decapitation. Walker (2006) suggests that this decapitated female may have suffered an accident or been the victim of violence. The blows to the right and left side of the head on the male individual are interpreted as being the result of a fall where the head strikes the ground on both right and left sides. No interpretation is offered by Walker (2006) as to the potential cause of trauma on the third individual.

6.6   Discussion

When investigating signs of trauma on an individual, there are often multiple possible interpretations of the cause of such trauma (Walker 2001). Walker (2001) points out that bodily injury observed by the bioarchaeologist could result from dramatically different causes. For example, skeletal trauma may be caused by violence or it could result from funerary preparations of a venerated ancestor. Because of the diversity of possible interpretations, it is important to examine all lines of evidence to decide which interpretation is the most probable. As more contextual evidence is compiled, the number of reasonable hypotheses that could be used to explain the trauma should decrease (Walker 2001). In investigating the evidence of traumatic injury found on at least three individuals at the site of La Cueva de Dos Cuchillos, skeletal, ethnographic, ethnohistoric, and archaeological data were used to explore two potential scenarios. The first scenario is that the perimortem trauma and state of the remains may be explained by standard Rarámuri burial practices and/or ancestor veneration. The alternative scenario is that perimortem injury and burning would not be expected to occur during burial ritual and these individuals more likely represent victims of violence.

6.6.1   *Ancestor veneration and burial ritual*

Veneration of the dead has been documented among multiple modern and precolonial cultures. According to Duncan (2005), veneration can include honoring certain deceased members of a community and/or helping the soul of the dead journey to its final destination. Certain individuals can be selected for this treatment, including leaders and those of religious significance. Veneration can be complex to differentiate in the archaeological record and may incorporate acts of violence (Duncan 2005). Several disarticulated processed skeletal assemblages in the precolonial Americas have been interpreted as the result of ancestor veneration (e.g. Duncan 2005; Pérez 2012a). In cultures that practice processing of the deceased, body parts may become important symbols and a source of comfort for the living (Pérez 2012a). An example of this type of ancestor veneration is seen at La Quemada, which includes the disarticulation and display of the bodies of ancestors in special burial contexts (Nelson *et al.* 1992; Pérez 2012b; Pérez *et al.* 2008). Alta Vista, Chalchihuites similarly contained disarticulated remains, primarily males, with cut marks and perforated skulls (Kelley 1978; Nelson *et al.* 1992). Ancestor veneration was considered a possibility during the analysis of the trauma and state of the assemblage at La Cueva de Dos Cuchillos. Standard mortuary ritual, separate from veneration of specific individuals, was also considered as an explanation.

Upon examination of the ethnographic and archaeological data on Rarámuri burial practices, it seems unlikely that the perimortem trauma found on the three individuals at La Cueva de Dos Cuchillos resulted from either standard mortuary ritual or ancestor veneration. First, there are no other known cases of chop marks reported, such as those found on burial 1–118, or neck fractures on other contemporaneous Rarámuri burials. If this were a standard practice, even for only select individuals, it would be expected to be more common. The trauma on burial 1–118 is actually quite different from some of the reported cases of veneration as the body of 1–118 does not appear to have been dismembered and there is no evidence for removal of body parts. Also, this individual was placed with the rest of the deceased community members, not in a special location. Second, there are no reports in the ethnographic or ethnohistoric literature that suggest that the Rarámuri ever processed the remains of the deceased in any way that would lead to this type of trauma. In contrast, the Rarámuri are fearful of the deceased and consider them to be a threat to the living. The Rarámuri avoid contact with the body of the deceased and do not wish to even be close to the body (Kennedy 1996; Merrill 1988). For example, the deceased person is encouraged to leave the living alone and any person who touches the deceased must be cured afterwards. Also, the home of the deceased will be immediately abandoned by the family if they die in the home (Bennett and Zingg 1976). This does not just occur in more recent times, however, as Joseph Neuman in 1681 described that when a death occurs in a dwelling, that habitation will be destroyed and never lived in again. Additionally, in 1683 Juan María Ratkay also discussed similar behaviors, writing that, after a death, the family of the deceased would move immediately to another home and may even burn the old home (Pennington 1963). It appears that, for the Rarámuri to encourage the deceased to leave them alone, they quickly provide all the necessary things to help the deceased successfully make the journey to the afterlife (Bennett and Zingg 1976). This process seems to include a minimal amount of physical contact between the living and the dead, and the placement of the bodies of the deceased away from the community.

In contrast to the perimortem trauma, the commingled, disturbed state of the remains is very consistent with reported Rarámuri burial practices and other Rarámuri archaeological sites. This is likely an unintentional consequence of the interment of multiple individuals over time and, according to the ethnographic accounts, the Rarámuri may forget the location of previous burial spots and will dig a grave on top of an older burial. Also significant for understanding burial assemblages, the Rarámuri reportedly do not take or use bones of their own deceased nor do they practice secondary burial (Merrill 1988). In addition, there is not much variability in terms of burial treatments and all members of a community appear to be treated similarly. This, combined with the fear of the dead, suggests that the state of the assemblage may best be explained by standard mortuary ritual.

6.6.2   Violence

Violence has been documented throughout human history and is perhaps one of the most universal characteristics of human interpersonal relationships (Martin and Harrod 2012; Walker 2001). Despite the long history of violence and its prevalence in modern societies, however, it is not well understood (Martin and Harrod 2012; Schröder and Schmidt 2001). While there are different ways of defining violence, some ways of conceptualizing it include the "assertion of power" (Schröder and Schmidt 2001: 2) or, as stated by David Riches (1986: 8), "an act of physical hurt deemed legitimate by the performer and illegitimate by (some) witness." Similarly to contemporary societies, in the past violence was likely important for demonstrations of power and for solving disputes (Martin 1997). Violence is not just a reaction to outside factors, however, but has complex cultural significance (Pérez 2012a). One of the goals of this project was to determine whether La Cueva de Dos Cuchillos provided direct evidence that violence affected at least some Rarámuri communities during the late precolonial period.

Considerable bioarchaeological evidence for violence during the precolonial period has been documented in the Americas (e.g. Kuckelman *et al.* 2002; Martin *et al.* 2008; Osterholtz 2012; Pérez 2006; Turner and Turner 1999;

White 1992), but very little of this work has focused on the Sierra Madre Occidental. Other than La Cueva de Dos Cuchillos, Hedionda cave and Cueva Juárez present the only other known examples of potential violence at precolonial Rarámuri sites. The evidence from these sites is significant, however, in that the remains from these two caves are approximately contemporaneous with the remains exhibiting trauma from La Cueva de Dos Cuchillos. It has also been argued that the injuries on all three of these individuals could be consistent with violence, possibly similar to ethnohistoric descriptions of intergroup conflict in the region (Anderson *et al.* 2012).

In understanding the patterning of injuries on the remains from La Cueva de Dos Cuchillos, comparisons with the mortuary practices of the Rarámuri were critical. These practices generally include the use of burial caves, presence of multiple individuals, grave goods such as food and other small items, evidence for fire, and wrapping of the bodies. Because of this information, when interpreting the human remains from this site, any signs consistent with these burial practices would be considered normal and not indicative of violence. For example, the burning that was observed on three individuals, two of whom did not exhibit noticeable perimortem trauma, and one of whom had potential perimortem breakage on the base of the skull, was ruled out as a sign of violence. This is because the Rarámuri practice of lighting fires next to the deceased could lead to accidental burning, although the extensive burning found on one adult individual might still be unexpected. The presence of multiple individuals was also ruled out as evidence for violence as this mortuary pattern is standard for the Rarámuri cultural group and most of these individuals did not exhibit any trauma. After determining that 14 of the 17 individuals in this cave did not demonstrate any signs of violence, the pattern of injuries on the remaining three individuals were examined.

Out of the possibilities considered during the analysis, the perimortem trauma patterns observed on three individuals from La Cueva de Dos Cuchillos were most consistent with violence. The injuries on burial 1–118, for example, consisted of multiple chop marks made by a sharp implement. This included blows to both the front and back of the individual (Anderson *et al.* 2012). These sharp force wounds could have been caused by one of the weapons described in the ethnohistoric record and are unlikely to be accidental. The neck fractures on the other two individuals could also indicate violence, although this is less definite. The type of fracture observed on these two individuals, the teardrop fracture, is very uncommon (Korres *et al.* 1994) but when it occurs it is the result of severe head trauma (Galloway 1999; Shapiro *et al.* 1973). While accidental falls could potentially cause this kind of head trauma, it seems suspicious that two individuals from the same community would suffer the same type of fall and receive the same type of neck fracture. The type of trauma that leads to teardrop fractures could be similar to the cause of the head trauma observed at Hedionda cave and Cueva Juárez (Anderson *et al.* 2012). Unfortunately, it was not possible to associate these vertebrae with any of the other remains, preventing examination of the entire individual in these two cases.

6.7   Conclusion

Bioarchaeology often involves examining and interpreting human remains from a variety of complicated contexts. In the case of La Cueva de Dos Cuchillos, this skeletal assemblage presented a unique and challenging puzzle as to whether or not certain individuals were the victims of violence. To form a reasonable interpretation of the remains, ethnographic, ethnohistoric, and archaeological data were combined with skeletal evidence to reconstruct the cultural context. This approach was ultimately successful, leading to an interpretation that at least one, and possibly three, individuals from La Cueva de Dos Cuchillos were victims of violence. While conclusions about specific practices of violence among the Rarámuri and other local groups cannot be made based on such a small sample size, La Cueva de Dos Cuchillos, combined with the two other reported sites examined by Walker (2006), provide empirical evidence that violence may have impacted individuals in this region. This could include intergroup violence between the Rarámuri and another local group if a regional pattern of this type of violence was present, as suggested in the ethnohistoric accounts. It is also possible, however, that there may have been violence between the Rarámuri and non-local groups traveling through the Sierra Madre or possibly intragroup conflict among the Rarámuri (Anderson *et al.* 2012). After their deaths, these victims appear to have been provided the standard Rarámuri mortuary rituals by their community, interment in a cave with grave items and other local individuals. The remaining 14 individuals in the cave, however, do not appear to have been victims as they do not have any noticeable traumatic injuries and their treatment was consistent with Rarámuri burial practices.

   The case study from La Cueva de Dos Cuchillos presents another example of the utility of using these types of data together to aid in the identification and understanding of violence in the precolonial past. In this case, the method allowed for the identification of previously unknown victims but could not provide any definite conclusions as to the identities of the perpetrators. Walker (2001) discusses how bioarchaeology, through the accumulation of multiple lines of evidence, can provide a clearer and more nuanced understanding of violence in the past. Using this approach to bioarchaeology, the analysis of the remains from La Cueva de Dos Cuchillos presents an additional example of how the use of multiple types of evidence provides rich contextual data that allow for better understanding of the skeletal data and their behavioral implications.

Acknowledgments

This research would not have been possible if not for the careful documentation, excavation, and curation of these remains by the late Drs. Richard and Sheilagh Brooks. The author would also like to thank Dr. Debra Martin for her guidance and support. Funding for this project was provided by the University of Nevada, Las Vegas Graduate and Professional Student Association grant and a Department of Anthropology Edwards and Olswang scholarship.

References

Anderson, C. P., Martin, D. L. & Thompson, J. L. (2012). Indigenous violence in northern Mexico on the eve of contact. *International Journal of Paleopathology*, **2**, 93–101.

Ascher, R. & Clune, F. J. (1960). Waterfall Cave, Southern Chihuahua, Mexico. *American Antiquity*, **26**, 270–4.

Bass, W. M. (2005). *Human Osteology: A Laboratory and Field Manual*, 5th edn. Columbia: Missouri Archaeological Society.

Beals, R. L. (1933). *The Acaxee: A Mountain Tribe of Durango and Sinaloa*. Berkeley: University of California Press.

(1973). *The Comparative Ethnology of Northern Mexico before 1750*. New York: Cooper Square Publishers Inc.

Bennett, W. C. & Zingg, R. M. (1976). *The Tarahumara: An Indian Tribe of Northern Mexico*. Glorietta: The Rio Grande Press, Inc.

Berryman, C. (2007). Captive sacrifice and trophy taking among the ancient Maya. In: Chacon, R. J. & Dye, D. H. (eds.) *The Taking and Displaying of Human Body Parts as Trophies by Amerindians*. New York: Springer US, 377–99.

Brooks, S. & Suchey, J. (1990). Skeletal age determination based on the os pubis: a comparison of the Acsádi-Nemeskéri and Suchey-Brooks methods. *Human Evolution*, **5**, 227–38.

Brooks, S. T. & Brooks, R. H. (1990). *Skeletal Remains from La Cueva De Dos Cuchillos, San Francisco De Borja, Chihuahua, Mexico. Para Conocer Al Hombre: Homenaje a Santiago Genovés a 33 Años Como Investigador En La Unam*. Universidad National Autónoma de México, 261–71.

Brooks, S. T. & Brooks, R. H. (n.d.) Unpublished Site Report.

Buikstra, J. E. & Mielke, J. H. (1985). Demography, diet, and health. In: Gilbert, R. I. & Mielke, J. H. (eds.) *The Analysis of Prehistoric Diets*. Orlando: Academic Press, 359–422.

Buikstra, J. E. & Ubelaker, D. H. (eds.) (1994). *Standards for Data Collection from Human Skeletal Remains. Proceedings of a Seminar at the Field Museum of Natural History*. Fayetteville: Arkansas Archeological Survey, Research Series, No. 44.

Darling, A. J. (1998). Mass inhumation and the execution of witches in the American Southwest. *American Anthropologist, New Series*, **100**, 732–52.

De Anda Alanis, G. (2007). Sacrifice and ritual body mutilation in postclassical Maya society: taphonomy of the human remains from Chichén Itzá's Cenote Sagrado. In: Tiesler, V. & Cucina, A. (eds.) *New Perspectives on Human Sacrifice and Ritual Body Treatments in Ancient Maya Society*. New York: Springer Press, 190–208.

De Ribas, A. P. (1971) [1645]. Excerpts from the account of the triumphs of our holy faith among the most fierce and savage people of the New World... Vol. 3. In: Hedrick, B. C. Kelley, J. C. & Riley, C. L. (eds.) *The North Mexican Frontier*. Carbondale: Southern Illinois University Press, 154–68.

Duncan, W. N. (2005). Understanding veneration and violation in the archaeological record. In: Rakita, G. F. M., Buikstra, J. E., Beck, L. A. & Williams, S. R. (eds.) *Interacting with the Dead: Perspectives on Mortuary Archaeology for the New Millennium*. Gainesville: University Press of Florida, 207–27.

Eeckhout, P. & Owens, L. S. (2008). Human sacrifice at Pachacamac. *Latin American Antiquity*, **19**, 375–98.

Ellis, F. H. (1968). An interpretation of prehistoric death customs in terms of modern southwestern parallels. In: Schroede, A. H. (ed.) *Collected Papers in Honor of Lyndon Lane Hargrave*. Santa Fe: Museum of New Mexico Press, 57–75.

Gaither, C., Kent, J., Sánchez, V. V. & Tham, T. R. (2008). Mortuary practices and human sacrifice in the middle Chao valley of Peru: their interpretation in the context of Andean mortuary patterning. *Latin American Antiquity*, **19**, 107–21.

Galloway, A. (ed.) (1999). *Broken Bones: Anthropological Analysis of Blunt Force Trauma*. Springfield: Charles C. Thomas.

Green, J. S. (1985). Ethnographic analysis of a 12th century female mummy from Chihuahua, Mexico. In: Tyson, R. A. & Elerick, D. V. (eds.) *Two Mummies from Chihuahua, Mexico: A Multidisciplinary Study*. San Diego: San Diego Museum Papers No. 19, San Diego Museum of Man, 121.

Hillson, S. W. (1996). *Dental Anthropology*. Cambridge: Cambridge University Press.

Johnston, F. E. (1962). Growth of long bones of infants and young children at Indian Knoll. *American Journal of Physical Anthropology*, **20**, 249–53.

Kelley, E. A. (1978). The temple of the skulls at Alta Vista, Chalchihuites. In: Riley, C. L. & Hedrick, B. C. (eds.) *Across the Chichimec Sea*. Carbondale: Papers in Honor of J. Charles Kelley: Southern Illinois University Press, 102–26.

Kennedy, J. G. (1996). *Tarahumara of the Sierra Madre*. Pacific Grove: Asilomar Press.

Klaus, H. D. & Tam, M. E. (2009). Surviving contact: biological transformation, burial, and ethnogenesis in the colonial Lambayeque Valley, North Coast of Peru. In: Knudson, K. J. & Stojanowski, C. M. (eds.) *Bioarchaeology and Identity in the Americas*. Gainesville: University of Florida Press, 126–52.

Korres, D. S., Zoubos, A. B., Kavadias, K., Babis, G. C. & Balalis, K. (1994). The "tear drop" (or avulsed) fracture of the anterior inferior angle of the axis. *European Spine Journal*, **3**, 151–4.

Kuckelman, K. A., Lightfoot, R. R. & Martin, D. L. (2002). The bioarchaeology and taphonomy of violence at Castle Rock and Sand Canyon Pueblos, Southwestern Colorado. *American Antiquity*, **67**, 486–513.

Lister, R. H. (1958). *Archaeological Excavations in the Northern Sierra Madre Occidental, Chihuahua and Sonora, Mexico, with Reports by Paul C. Mangelsdorf and Kate Peck Kent*. Boulder: University of Colorado Press.

Lumholtz, C. (1902). *Unknown Mexico: a Record of Five Years' Exploration among the Tribes of the Western Sierra Madre; in the Tierra Caliente of Tepic and Jalisco; and among the Tarascos of Michoacan*, Vol. 1. New York: C. Scribner's Sons.

Martin, D. L. (1997). Violence against women in the La Plata River Valley (A.D. 1000–1300). In: Martin, D. L. & Frayer, D. W. (eds.) *Troubled Times: Violence and Warfare in the Past*. Amsterdam: Gordon and Breach, 45–75.

Martin, D. L. & Harrod, R. P. (2012). Body parts and parts of bodies: traces of violence in past cultures, editorial. *International Journal of Paleopathology*, **2**, 49–52.

Martin, D. L., Akins, N. J., Crenshaw, B. J. & Stone, P. K. (2008). Inscribed in the body, written on the bones: the consequences of social violence at La Plata. In: Nichols, D. L. & Crown, P. L. (eds.) *Social Violence in the Prehispanic American Southwest*. Tucson: University of Arizona Press, 98–122.

Mendoza, R. G. (2007). The divine gourd tree: Tzompantli skull racks, decapitation rituals, and human trophies in Ancient Mesoamerica. In: Chacon, R. J. & Dye, D. H. (eds.) *The Taking and Displaying of Human Body Parts as Trophies by Amerindians*. New York: Springer, 400–43.

Merrill, W. R. (1988). *Rarámuri Souls: Knowledge and Social Process in Northern Mexico*. Washington D.C.: Smithsonian Institution Press.

Moser, C. M. (1973). *Human Decapitation in Ancient Mesoamerica*. Washington, D. C.: Dumbarton Oaks.

Nelson, B. A., Darling, J. A. & Kice, D. A. (1992). Mortuary practices and the social order at La Quemada, Zacatecas, Mexico. *Latin American Antiquity*, **3**, 298–315.

Osterholtz, A. J. (2012). The social role of hobbling and torture: violence in the prehistoric Southwest. *International Journal of Paleopathology*, **2**, 148–55.

Pastron, A. G. & Clewlow Jr. C. W. (1974). The ethno-archaeology of an unusual Tarahumara burial cave. *Man*, **9**, 308–11.

Pennington, C. W. (1963). *The Tarahumar of Mexico: Their Environment and Material Culture*. Salt Lake City: University of Utah Press.

Pérez, V. R. (2006). The politicization of the dead: an analysis of cutmark morphology and culturally modified human remains from La Plata and Peñasco Blanco (A.D. 900–1300). University of Massachusetts Amherst: Unpublished PhD dissertation.

(2012a). The politicization of the dead: violence as performance, politics as usual. In: Martin, D. L., Harrod, R. P. & Pérez, V. R. (eds.) *The Bioarchaeology of Violence*. Gainesville: University of Florida Press, 13–28.

(2012b). The taphonomy of violence: recognizing variation in disarticulated skeletal assemblages. *International Journal of Paleopathology*, **2**, 156–65.

Pérez, V. R., Nelson, B. A. & Martin, D. L. (2008). Veneration or violence? A study of variations in patterns of human bone modification at La Quemada. In: Nichols, D. L. & Crown, P. L. (eds.) *Social Violence in the Prehispanic American Southwest*. Tucson: University of Arizona Press, 123–42.

Phenice, T. W. (1969). A newly developed visual method of sexing the os pubis. *American Journal of Physical Anthropology*, **30**, 297–301.

Pinter, S. A. (1985). Descriptions of two mummies from Chihuahua, Mexico. In: Tyson, R. A. & Elerick, D. V. (eds.) *Two Mummies from Chihuahua, Mexico: A Multidisciplinary Study*. San Diego: San Diego Museum Papers No. 19, San Diego Museum of Man, 13.

Riches, D. (1986). The phenomenon of violence. In: Riches, D. (ed.) *The Anthropology of Violence*. New York: Blackwell, 1–27.

Scheuer, L. & Black, S. M. (2000). *Developmental Juvenile Osteology*. San Diego: Elsevier Academic Press.

Schröder, I. W. & Schmidt, B. E. (2001). Introduction: violent imaginaries and violent practices. In: Schmidt, B. E. & Schröder, I. W. (eds.) *Anthropology of Violence and Conflict*. London, New York: Routledge, 1–24.

Shapiro, R., Youngberg, A. S. & Rothman, S. L. (1973). The differential diagnosis of traumatic lesions of the occipito-atlanto-axial segment. *Radiologic Clinics of North America*, **11**, 505–26.

Smith, B. H. (1991). Standards of human tooth formation and dental age assessment. In: Kelley, M. A. & Larsen, C. S. (eds.) *Advances in Dental Anthropology*. New York: Wiley-Liss, 143–68.

Spielmann, K. A., Clark, T., Hawkey, D., Rainey, K. & Fish, S. K. (2009). "...Being weary, they had rebelled": Pueblo subsistence and labor under Spanish Colonialism. *Journal of Anthropological Archaeology*, **28**, 102–25.

Stodder, A. L. W. & Osterholtz, A. J. (2010). Analysis of the Phr: methods and data collection. In: Perry, E. M., Stodder, A. L. W. & Bollong, C. A. (eds.) *Animas La Plata Project Volume Xv – Bioarchaeology*. Phoenix: SWCA, 243–78.

Stojanowski, C. M. (2009). Bridging histories: the bioarchaeology of identity in postcontact Florida. In: Knudson, K. J. & Stojanowski, C. M. (eds.) *Bioarchaeology and Identity in the Americas*. Gainesville: University of Florida Press, 59–81.

Turner, C. G., II & Turner, J. A. (1999). *Man Corn: Cannibalism and Violence in the Prehistoric American Southwest*. Salt Lake City: The University of Utah Press.

Walker, C. M. (2006). The bioarchaeology of newly discovered burial caves in the Sierra Tarahumara. University of Oregon: Unpublished PhD dissertation.

Walker, P. L. (2001). A bioarchaeological perspective on the history of violence. *Annual Review of Anthropology*, **30**, 573–96.

White, T. D. (1992). *Prehistoric Cannibalism at Mancos 5mtumr-2346*. Princeton: Princeton University Press.

White, T. D., Black, M. T. & Folkens, P. A. (2012). *Human Osteology*, 3rd edn. San Diego: Academic Press.

Zingg, R. M. (1940). *Report on Archaeology of Southern Chihuahua*. Denver: Contributions of the University of Denver, Center of Latin American Studies, No 1.

Part III

Ritual and performative violence

7 Signatures of captivity and subordination on skeletonized human remains: a bioarchaeological case study from the ancient Southwest

RYAN P. HARROD AND DEBRA L. MARTIN

7.1 Introduction

In early May of 2013, three young women were rescued from a horrific scene of modern-day captivity and enslavement in Cleveland, Ohio. Taken hostage and held captive for approximately 10 years, the released women revealed details about their abduction and subsequent physical beatings, rapes, restraint with chains and ropes, verbal assaults, pregnancies, forced miscarriages, periods of starvation, confinement to small spaces, and denial of access to medical care through daily violent acts of subordination and exploitation by a single male (accessed on May 10, 2013, on page A21 of the *New York Times* edition with the headline: *Officials, Citing Miscarriages, Weigh Death Penalty in Ohio Case.* www.nytimes.com/2013/05/10/us/cleveland-kidnapping. html?_r=0). As forensic anthropologists and bioarchaeologists, we wondered what story their bones might tell that could provide an empirical reality to these kinds of violence visited upon the women. While this kind of information may be forthcoming in the future from radiography or CT scans, it is clear from their testimonies that the bones may reveal the effects of periodic starvation, misaligned broken and healed bones, healed cranial depression fractures, unusual patterns of muscular markings (from either habitual use or no use), and a histological signature of poorly mineralized bones. These physical assaults may be the tip of the iceberg in terms of other kinds of psychological and emotional damage from being stripped of their identities and their humanity.

In a sweeping and grand overview of slavery in world prehistory, Patterson (1982) provides ample evidence that culturally sanctioned captivity, particularly

Bioarchaeological and Forensic Perspectives on Violence: How Violent Death is Interpreted from Skeletal Remains, ed. D. L. Martin and C. P. Anderson. Published by Cambridge University Press.
© Cambridge University Press 2014.

of women and children, has been found to occur in almost every ancient and historic society since the Neolithic and the domestication of plants and animals. He writes persuasively about the ways that captured humans come to be owned as personal property, and the underlying power structures that keep these kinds of systems in place. He notes that, while males were sometimes taken as captives for ritual purposes, it was females who were the most prized, not only for sexual purposes, but also as farm hands and laborers (Patterson 1982: 179). Females were also more easily assimilated into the captor societies, and, if their children were also abducted, they would resist captivity even less.

Thus, while captivity is well documented for early city-states, much less has been written about non-state societies. Cameron (2011) notes the ubiquity of captives and the central role that they have played in both cultural and economic terms. She documents for many cultures on a global scale the ways in which female captives were subordinated and often labored at craft production and other activities that demanded skill and hard work. Females as currency and bodies as wealth is a common theme in much of the writing about the ways that captivity and slavery operate within economic systems of owned property, purchasing power, and debt (Peebles 2010).

For pre-state indigenous groups in North America, Cameron (2008; Cameron in press) provides an extensive review of warfare, raiding, abduction, and captivity of primarily females and children across the Americas. Using ethnohistoric, archival, and archaeological sources, she provides compelling data that suggest the indigenous systems of warfare and captive-taking that had been in places for centuries before contact with the Spanish were quickly usurped and exploited by the early colonists. Tung and Knudson (2011) have likewise documented the role of warfare and captive-taking in precolonial groups in South America.

What all of these reviews of captive-taking in non-state and state-level ancient societies have in common is the underlying and institutionalized practices of violence that keep the cycle of raiding and captive-taking in place over hundreds of years. Captives are by definition used without their consent as part of these larger systems of social control. How can captives and the violence used to subordinate them be read on the skeletonized remains?

Interpreting captive violence in bioarchaeological or forensic settings is always challenging because it must be reconstructed with evidence pieced together from the human remains as well as all other available lines of evidence. While reconstructing what was done to the body by examination of the skeletonized remains has limits, getting at the ultimate meaning and motivation is even more difficult. Nevertheless, as the chapters in this volume demonstrate, there is much that can be learned by forensic anthropologists and bioarchaeologists about the meaning and even the motivations with careful and integrative analyses. Peebles (2010: 233) implores that ". . . [A]nthropology may be uniquely situated to insist continually on the relationship between . . . debt and bodily punishment." Violence is at the core of capturing, subduing, subordinating, and enforcing desired behaviors for those unfortunate enough to become captives.

7.2   Captives in the ancient Southwest (AD 850–1150)

Using ethnohistoric and archival sources, Barr (2005), Brooks (2002), and Gutiérrez (1991) have documented widespread forms of slavery at contact at the Pueblo borderlands in the historic Southwest, with captive women and children at the center of a complex web of trade, prestige, and cultural exchange. They suggested, but did not have data to support, that systems of raiding and capture of Pueblo women were in place long before the colonial period.

With the extensive study of a series of ancestral Pueblo burials of women exhibiting signs of violence and pathology from La Plata, evidence was provided that Barr, Brooks, and Gutiérrez were correct. Captives were identified at the La Plata archaeological sites near Farmington, New Mexico dating to around AD 1100. This study is a follow-up to and expansion of previous studies published by the authors on this group of females from La Plata (Martin 1997, 2008a, 2008b; Martin and Akins 2001; Martin *et al.* 2001, 2008, 2010).

The current research expands upon the original data from the La Plata archaeological sites to demonstrate the presence of captives as a more wide-ranging phenomenon in the ancient Southwest, especially during a period of cultural transformation (AD 850–1150) dubbed the Chaco Phenomenon. Harrod (2013) has examined many more skeletal collections from this period and has found other cases of captivity.

The Chaco Phenomenon is a large regional complex characterized by trade and shared architecture, and a system of functional and symbolic roads that developed during the Pueblo II and early Pueblo III periods (*c.* AD 850–1150) (Irwin-Williams 1972; Sebastian 1992; Washburn 2011). This study further expands on the original La Plata dataset by considering the presence of males and subadults who possess biological indicators of captivity and subordination as well, suggesting that it was not just females who were taken captive in the Southwest context.

Demonstrating that there was a system of captivity and exploitation in the past requires the identification of individuals within a larger segment of society that show indicators on the skeletonized remains of violence and abuse. In the past, bioarchaeological studies often were most focused on population-level studies so that paleoepidemiological patterns could be established. This population-level approach was an important corrective to the historical development of the discipline. Prior to the late 1970s, studies of ancient human remains were very descriptive and focused upon severe expressions of disease. These were important as case studies, but they did not speak to the general level of health and adaptation at the population level.

Thus, in the 1980s, bioarchaeologists began to ask questions about health and wellbeing at the community (or population) level. Questions were formulated about selective adaptations, the effects of diet, and shifts in nutrition and health that impacted morbidity and mortality (Cohen and Armelagos 1984; Gilbert and Mielke 1985; Huss-Ashmore *et al.* 1982; Larsen 1987). Since this time, the majority of the studies in bioarchaeology have become very population-centric, often losing track of unique individuals who can offer additional information.

A recent edited volume by Stodder and Palkovich (2012) addresses this issue by challenging researchers to identify and extensively examine unique individuals to uncover clues about their lives. Focusing on individuals, however, does not mean that population-level analyses are ignored. Practice theory suggests that the structure and nature of populations is a consequence of the complex interactions that exist between all individuals within a society. Thus, the only way to put an individual into context is to understand the population of which they were a part, because, taken together, each level of analysis provides a more complete picture of the social, economic, and political structure of past societies.

It is possible that, in reporting population frequencies of male and female trauma, individuals within the larger population that might have been unique in their expression or patterning of trauma could be masked. For example, Morgan (2010: 36) reported on frequencies of trauma for individuals from Pecos Pueblo and surrounding sites over a 1000-year period (*c.* AD 600–1600) using population frequencies. These included the percentage of all individuals who had cranial trauma, postcranial trauma, healed trauma, and perimortem trauma by age, sex, and period. The only thing that can be said of data presented in population summaries such as this one is that more males than females showed trauma, and that trauma increased over time. The population-level presentation has obscured the patterning of trauma across individual bodies and the ability to provide a more nuanced understanding of the empirical data. About 10% of the females showed healed trauma, but it is not clear if this is in the form of cranial depression fractures, ribs, or long bones.

Presenting trauma data, the closest thing available to understanding interpersonal violence, in this way prevents any kind of interpretation on the suspected causes of these trauma data.

Harrod and Martin (in press) explore the concept of captivity in the past by examining individual patterns of trauma and linking these to larger population trends. They illustrate that the term captivity is a broad term and that individuals identified as captives can, and often do, vary in terms of their perceived social status and the ways in which they are exploited within each society. Despite the variation in lived experience, and whether or not the individuals epitomize the traditional concept of captives or not, this research shows that there is a distinct pattern associated with the subordination of individuals and that this can be identified on skeletonized remains. Thus, even though the term captive is used, it is important to remember that the experience of each captive may differ from individual to individual and site to site. This kind of variation and complexity demands analyses that move from individual to population and from population to population within and between regions.

The ancient Southwest presents a good place to examine the variable use of captives, the ways in which they were subdued and subordinated, and how widespread the practice was spatially and temporally. As mentioned previously, the ethnohistoric research by Barr (2005) and Brooks (2002) is especially important because they both provide detailed accounts of a highly structured system of captivity in the Southwest shortly after contact. Barr (2005: 21) writes that "... the very heterogeneity of Indian bondage suggests comparisons with the range of slave practices in Africa, Asia, the Mediterranean, and other parts of the world where at different times and places persons, primarily women, were held and used as not only economic but also social and political capital – comparisons that resonate with growing scholarly discussion of slavery in a global perspective." Reconstruction of population demographics of sites throughout the Southwest by Kohler and Turner (2006) that reveal a disproportionate amount of women and children at some sites provides additional support for the existence of pre-existing systems of captivity.

7.2.1   *Identifying captives from skeletonized human remains*

The La Plata females provided a rich source of data that included multiple lines of evidence that some of them were captives. As outlined more explicitly in the following section, data from the human remains provided one kind of patterning, but other patterns emerged when the archaeological context was examined.

The use of the term archaeological in this instance refers to the context in which the individuals are situated, including the mortuary context (i.e. burial location, body position, and presence or absence of grave goods), as well as the overall spatial context of the site itself (i.e. its location on the landscape, its place in time, and its complexity or simplicity compared to surrounding sites). By looking at the entire archaeological context, it is possible to start to ascertain the ways in which individuals that appear to be captives differed from other individuals at that site and across the region. The interpretation of these multiple lines of evidence (skeletons, mortuary context, site) from the archaeological context was enhanced by ethnohistoric and archival research on captivity in the past (Brooks 2002; Patterson 1982; Ruby and Brown 1993). The importance of these ethnohistoric accounts is that they provide some first-person accounts of what captivity involved or written records of how captivity was initiated and maintained. Using multiple lines of evidence in reconstructing any activity having to do with trauma and violence is crucial. While archaeology provides the context, the importance of bioarchaeological data is that the body records the accumulated life history. The value of analyzing human skeletal remains is that the quality of an individual's life in terms of exposure to violence, overall health, and level of activity is recorded on the bones. Prior bioarchaeological work has revealed that, oftentimes, individuals who have lower social status are at greater risk of traumatic injury, health disparities, and degeneration of the musculoskeletal system as a result of strenuous labor (Blakey 2001; Corruccini *et al.* 1982; Harrod *et al.* 2013; Rankin-Hill *et al.* 2000). When trauma and these other indicators of stress accumulate within a lifetime on the skeleton, they reveal much more information than when indicators of pathology and stress are viewed in isolation.

7.3   Identifying captives from skeletonized human remains

The approach to analyzing the burials recovered from each site was to identify the basic identity of each individual, which involves assessing changes in health, nutrition, activity, and trauma (Harrod 2013: 64). "These data were essential because they revealed differences between individuals at each site, which allowed for a more comprehensive understanding of how and why violence and social inequality, a ubiquitous yet poorly understood human behavior, existed in the Puebloan world" (Harrod 2013: 70). The importance of reconstructing the identity in this project is that it provides a profile of each individual that can be used to identify the coercive and violent activities that captives could be subject to that would result in changes to the skeleton associated with this activity (Table 7.1).

Table 7.1. *Skeletal correlates of subordination and captivity. Modified from Martin* et al. *(2010: 6–7, Martin 2008b: 163).*

	Hypothesized skeletal changes with captivity	
Activity	Skeletal, demographic, and archaeological correlates	
Capture and forced abduction	• Healed cranial depression fractures • Healed broken ribs and long bones	
Desire for prestige or trade	• High occurrence of reproductive-aged women • Increase in the amount of rare, exotic materials	
Subordination, beatings	• Cranial and postcranial fractures • Recidivism, co-occurrence of trauma and pathology	
Hard physical or domestic labor	• Entheseal changes, ossified ligaments, and asymmetries • Work-related osteoarthritis • Postcranial fractures (accident/occupation-related)	
Punishment	• Non-specific infections • Evidence of torture • Early death	
Not recognized member of community	• Skeletal changes (head shape and cradle boarding) • Irregular burial • Differential amounts of grave goods	
Food restriction, forced poverty	• Nutritional stress (cribra orbitalia and porotic hyperostosis) • Differences in stature	
Poor sanitation, living conditions	• Non-specific infections (staph. and strep.) • Tuberculosis, treponematosis	

7.4 Raiding and captivity: interpreting the patterning of violence from skeletal remains

The data for this project were obtained from the excavation of two communities in the La Plata River Valley, along with the analysis of previously excavated skeletal collections housed at the American Museum of Natural History (AMNH). The burials analyzed in this study included only those sets of human skeletal remains that were identified as individual burials, so commingled and poorly preserved remains were not included.

The individuals identified as captives in this project are associated with the sites of La Plata, Kin Bineola, and Aztec Ruins. The importance of each of these sites is that they are outliers or satellite communities associated with the Chaco Phenomenon, described earlier. The site referred to as La Plata in this project actually consists of two sites, Barker Arroyo and Jackson Lake, that were excavated between 1988 and 1991 (Martin *et al.* 2001). These sites are dated to AD 1000–1200 and are located in an area of the Four Corners that is described as being fertile and a veritable "bread basket" (Toll 1993). The site of Kin Bineola is the site closest to the center of the Chaco Phenomenon. This site is the second largest of the satellite communities, second only to Aztec Ruins (Lekson 2007: 38). Finally, the last site is Aztec Ruins, which consists of three independent communities. Only one of the communities is of interest in this study and that is the site of West Ruin or Aztec West because it is from where the burials were excavated (Morris 1924).

7.4.1   La Plata

The data on violence, trauma, and pathology from the La Plata site have been published in several venues and will only be briefly summarized here (for detailed accounts see Martin 2008a, 2008b; Martin *et al.* 2001, 2010). Of the 66 burials retrieved from the two La Plata sites, 43 were complete enough to do thorough analyses. One subadult had a healed postcranial fracture. Three males had healed fractures in a rib, a hand, and a toe bone. Nine females had multiple and serious healed trauma in the form of cranial depression fractures, and face, nose, and rib fractures. There was vertebral and pelvic trauma and displacement in several of the females. In addition, these females had the most severe cases of infection and nutritional anemia. They also exhibited more marked lesions related to extreme enthesis development on some of the upper and lower extremities. Each of these females were thrown and buried in abandoned pit structures without grave goods, which is in direct contrast with females without trauma and all other males. Isotopic data revealed that these females were not non-local, but Pueblo women from other areas within the region.

From these multiple indicators of stress markers and trauma, a profile of raiding for women and abduction was constructed (Martin *et al.* 2010). A modified version of this profile is shown in Table 7.1, presenting a more concise set of indicators for the bioarchaeological signature of captives. The skeletal and mortuary data on the subset of La Plata women who experienced interpersonal violence and other stressors match many, if not all, of the indicators presented in this table (see Martin *et al.* 2008a for a full description of these multiple indicators of stress).

One of the more striking patterns on the La Plata females was the presence of well-healed cranial depression fractures. Walker (1997) presented a detailed examination of historic patterns of violence in wife-beating and found there to be a distinctive pattern of hitting women on the head. Hitting individuals on the head is the most expedient way to subdue but not cause death. It often renders individuals unconscious for some period of time and, when they awaken, they are disoriented, in pain, and often unable to make decisions or communicate clearly. This condition renders the victim relatively easy to subordinate and control.

The La Plata females with trauma all had some form of single or multiple cranial depression fractures. In one study (Martin *et al.* 2008), a neuropathologist examined the head wounds and reasoned that these blunt force trauma blows to the head would have likely led to mild or moderate traumatic brain injury (TBI). There are a multitude of side effects associated with even mild TBI, such as cognitive, motor, and speech deficits, and fatigue, irritability, and migraine headaches. TBI can also lead to poor concentration and blurred vision, the inability to process information, and emotional instability. Given the nature of the healed cranial depression fractures on the La Plata females, it is highly likely that they survived the original blows to the head but suffered from any or all of the behavioral sequelae or abnormal bodily conditions of TBI. It was also discovered that individuals who had one trauma also had other pathologies and trauma in various stages of healing (Martin *et al.* 2001). For example, one female aged 30–35 survived a crushing blow to the top of her head that affected three separate regions of the cranium, and healed with an uneven and problematic knitting together of the bones. Given the location of the injury, she would have had problems with motor control and emotions, balance, and general coordination. She also had a trauma-induced partial dislocation of her pelvis, perhaps sustained in a fall. She had osteoarthritis at this site as well. This is likely indicative of injury recidivism, the pattern of having one problem from trauma or pathology leading to additional problems.

7.4.2 Kin Bineola

Kin Bineola is a large Pueblo site located approximately 11 miles south of the center of Chaco Canyon. This site is less understood than La Plata because the burials from the site were recovered by Hrdlička at the turn of the nineteenth century, which has led to ambiguity in the dates and mortuary context. All that is known about the mortuary context is that the burials were recovered from a location outside the Pueblo, about one-third of a mile away (Akins 1986: 165). Additionally, the dates for the burials are not well understood, with the exception of a single burial that was recently dated to AD 891–1147 (Coltrain *et al.* 2007: 306). The rest of the burials are assumed to be from the Pueblo II period based on the fact that archaeological reconstruction of the site itself, such as tree-ring dates, indicates that the site was built during the Pueblo II period (Bannister *et al.* 1970; Marshall *et al.* 1979).

At the site of Kin Bineola, like at La Plata, the rate of violence against women was very high. Seven of the eleven (63.6%) adult females had trauma, in contrast to only one of five (20.0%) males and two of the fourteen (14.3%) children having evidence of trauma. In a recent study (Harrod 2013), the rate of trauma among women at Kin Bineola was compared to that at other sites in the region during the Pueblo II, and it was found that the occurrence of trauma at Kin Bineola was significantly higher than at the other sites. The site of La Plata is the only other site with a comparable rate of trauma. Being that Kin Bineola is one of the largest sites in the region, outside of Chaco Canyon, it has been suggested that it may have been an important satellite community, so it is possible that the women with evidence of violence were captives in a system of labor exploitation.

7.4.3   Aztec Ruins

Aztec Ruins is a slightly later site that dates to between the early to mid Pueblo III period. It is the largest pueblo outside of Chaco Canyon (Brown *et al*. 2008: 235). Unlike La Plata and Kin Bineola, the rate of trauma among females at Aztec Ruins is not noticeably higher than trauma among males. Instead, it appears that there may be select individuals of both sexes that have indicators of possibly being captives.

First, there is a young adult female at Aztec Ruins buried in Room 182 who has both cranial and postcranial trauma that is indicative of having suffered repeated injury (i.e. injury recidivism). According to Morris (1924: 195) she was in a tightly flexed position. Both this individual and the one interred directly above her in Room 135 were noted by Morris (1924: 173, 195) to be individuals that were short in stature and upon burial wrapped in feather cloths, with no evidence of grave goods.

There is a second young adult at Aztec Ruins who has multiple indicators of potential captivity on the body. Although Morris (1924: 183) suggests that this individual is "apparently female," analysis by Harrod (2013) and Martin and Stone (2003) suggest that this is likely a developing male. Despite there being no evidence of a cranial depression fracture, he has two healed broken ribs, the right hip appears to have been dislocated, asymmetry of the upper arms where the left humerus is noticeably smaller, and there are degenerative changes of the lower spine. Analysis of the entheseal development seems to suggest that he has moderate buildup for a young adult, which could indicate a heavier workload during his lifetime.

Finally, there is an individual that was recovered from a kiva that may have been a captive at Aztec Ruins. This individual is only represented by cranial remains and, according to Morris (1924: 193), the head appears to have been thrown into the structure with other refuse or trash. Based on robust morph-ology, this individual appears to be a probable male; however, without the postcranial remains it is not certain if this individual is a male or a very robust female. The importance of this skull is that there are several healed cranial injuries as well as perimortem injuries that occurred around the time of death. This individual is also unique because "[t]his skull is the first example of oblique deformation exhumed in the Aztec Ruin" (Morris 1924: 193). Morris had suggested that these isolated cranial remains came from a burial interred in another part of the site, but it is possible that this represents a trophy skull.

The importance of each of these burials is that they not only have traumatic injuries but an accumulation of other pathological conditions that seems to suggest that they may have been at more risk than other members of the community.

7.5   The ongoing and multiple forms of violence related to captivity

Many of the individuals in these studies that are noted to be captives have multiple traumatic injuries or trauma associated with other pathological conditions. The importance of these overall findings is that these individuals all demonstrate a pattern of injury recidivism and comorbidity factors that suggest a life history fraught with hazardous activities, interpersonal violence, and hard labor.

Looking at individuals with multiple traumatic injuries provides a method for identifying injury recidivism as a pattern of re-injury and related pathologies. The presence of individuals with both cranial and postcranial trauma provides one more insight into the role that violence played among the ancestral Pueblo. Thus, all cranial injuries were evaluated with consideration of postcranial trauma and were scrutinized for patterns that may have represented a single injury event, such as falls from heights (Galloway 1999; Lovell 1997, 2008).

Injury recidivism is not limited to trauma alone, however; it is also important to look at individuals who have trauma in association with evidence of activity-related changes and pathological conditions. Similar to repeated trauma, the presence of trauma and other health-related changes may indicate that some people within a particular society were a subclass or subaltern group who worked harder and were at more risk of being targeted for violence.

In terms of activity-related changes, these studies all included analyses of both robusticity differences and entheseal development. For both robusticity and entheseal development, which are age-dependent phenomenon, individuals were compared by age-specific categories. The pathological conditions of interest in this project were primarily those that are indicative of nutritional anemia conditions such as cribra orbitalia, porotic hyperostosis, and infections such as periosteal reactions.

The importance of understanding the process of injury recidivism is that severe head trauma or TBI may have predisposed people to other types of injury. Using methods established by Judd (2002) and insights gained from a recent project with modern Turkana populations in Kenya (Harrod *et al.* 2012), this project was not only focused on identifying cranial trauma but attempted to understand the consequence of a severe head injury in the form of TBI. TBI is essentially severe, long-term damage to the brain that causes cognitive deficiencies. The type of cognitive impairment that develops depends on where the damage to the brain occurs.

For example, according to Stern (2004: 179), damage to the frontal or temporal lobes often results in personality or social dysfunctions. The Centers for Disease Control also report a number of problems that arise, and these include a decrease in attention and focus, reduced emotional control (e.g. aggression and impulsivity), memory problems, as well as a deterioration of verbal and physical abilities (Centers for Disease Control 2010). TBI is a worldwide problem as "head injuries account for the majority of all trauma-related deaths; and at least 6.2 million people in Europe and 5.3 million in the United States live with disability, impairment, or handicap from TBI" (Vagnerova *et al.* 2008: 206). Well-documented cognitive side effects from this type of injury include cognitive, motor, and speech problems, migraines and dizziness, poor concentration, emotional instability, increased aggressiveness and antisocial behavior, and amnesia (Centers for Disease Control 2010; Cohen *et al.* 1999; Leon-Carrion and Ramos 2003; The Brain Injury Association of Wyoming 2004). Aside from cognitive impacts, TBI can also have social effects that include the increased likelihood of re-injury (i.e. injury recidivism), imprisonment, or of becoming homeless (Centers for Disease Control 2010).

The increased risk of future injury is due to the fact that the original TBI, whether it was mild, moderate, or severe, causes lingering neurological and behavioral side effects (Bazarian and Atabaki 2001; Glaesser *et al.* 2004; Hwang *et al.* 2008; Stern 2004). This increased risk of repeated injury has been documented for ancient populations as well (Judd 2002; Martin *et al.* 2008). Although TBI may be one reason for recidivism it is not the only explanation, as the culture in which an individual was raised or social learning (Bandura 1973) is also a probable factor for why people exposed to violence tend to accrue more injuries throughout their lifetime. For example, among children it has been well documented that the exposure to violence has an effect on the level of violence in which one is involved as an adult (Wilson and Daly 1995). Additionally, it may be entirely possible that a person's personality

8.2   The Sibun Valley

Excavations of more modest-sized sites in the middle and lower reaches of the Sibun Valley, Belize, indicate that these settlements survived the period of decline and abandonment in the adjacent Petén area (part of the famous Classic Maya collapse) and thrived during the Terminal Classic period (800–950 CE). This late fluorescence appears to mirror the rise and historical trajectory of sites in northern Yucatán, such as Chichén Itzá, which were also to be abandoned by the eleventh century CE in the last wave of the Classic Maya collapse. Fueled by the growing hegemony of the north, the coastal Caribbean trade network assumed an increased importance (Masson and Mock 2004). Location on the Sibun River would allow sites to take advantage of this increasing trade.

At the mid-valley site of Pakal Na, there is evidence of this late fluorescence and coastal interaction, and the influence of the important site of Chichén Itzá. Within Structure 130 (the largest at the site), an elaborate mortuary deposit intruded into the eastern (front) central axis of this elongated platform (Harrison-Buck *et al.* 2007). Both the quality and nature of the grave offerings, including evidence of postmortem body processing and the extended period over which the mortuary ritual occurred, indicate that the central individual (Burial 1-A) was of high rank and probably a prominent and successful warrior. The style and content of grave goods again point to northern influence, likely stemming from Chichén Itzá.

The large burial pit at Pakal Na measures roughly 1.3 m wide, 3.0 m in length, and over 1.0 m in depth (Figure 8.1). The burial includes a total of six individuals: a primary interment (1-A), who was accompanied by the partial remains of four other individuals, who are represented by three discrete clusters of disarticulated remains (1-B, 1-C, 1-D, and 1-E), plus an individual represented by a carved human skull mask. Most appear to be male and older than 35 years of age (the sex of one individual is undetermined); the primary interment (1-A) was probably over 60 years of age at death and possibly close to 80 years.

Burial 1-A was laid in an extended, supine position, with his legs crossed. A robust individual, the old male showed pronounced muscle attachments on the shoulder girdle and a prominent linea aspera of the femur. Thus, an active lifestyle is indicated, which might be expected of a successful leader and warrior. The skull of Burial 1-A had been removed and replaced with an inverted bowl. The left arm and right forearm were also missing.

The disarticulated remains of Burial 1-B were located just east of 1-A. Burial 1-B included a skull with atlas vertebra and pieces of the left shoulder. Considerable wear on the teeth (one drilled for an inlay) and the closure of

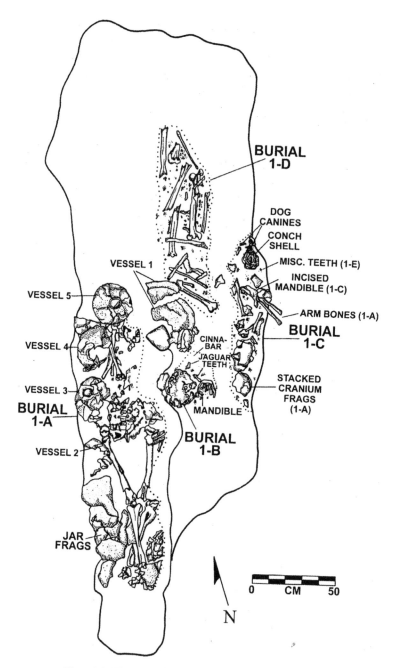

Figure 8.1. Plan Map of Burial 1, Pakal Na. Skull mask was in the Burial 1C skeletal cluster. (Reproduced with permission of the Xibun Archaeological Research Project.) Drawing by K. Acone and S. Morandi, reprinted with permission.

some sutures indicate that Burial 1-B was an older adult, probably the oldest of the secondary interments. The morphological features of the skull suggest a more gracile male, indicating that the skull probably did not belong to the 1-A interment. Drilled jaguar teeth and a deposit of cinnabar 5.0–10.0 cm thick found over an area 20.0 cm diameter were associated with this skull.

Burial 1-D, located just north of 1-B, may be part of the 1-B individual, but there is a clear separation between these two bone clusters (Figure 8.1). Thus, 1-D has been treated as a separate person. Burial 1-D consists primarily of arm and leg bones with few other skeletal elements and they appear to have been scattered, rather than bundled. The robusticity of these elements indicate that this is also a male, but they also do not show any cortical bone loss that might indicate an older individual like 1-B.

The Burial 1-C deposit, like 1-D, did not appear bundled, but rather was a collection of bones with associated grave goods that had been placed on an earthen shelf on the eastern side of the mortuary pit. At first, this was considered to be another individual, but the analysis indicated that the skeletal elements present were exactly those missing from Burial 1-A. Other human remains within the 1-C deposit included a left arm and partial shoulder girdle, most of a right forearm, and parts of the cervical vertebrae. Comparison of this left humerus with the right humerus of Burial 1-A was sufficient to indicate that these elements belonged to Burial 1-A, and to attribute all to that individual. There was no separate 1-C individual. There was no skull modification, but two upper anterior teeth had been drilled for inlays that were not present at the time of excavation. Because of the position of the forearms, some articulation might have been still present when these were removed and then deposited here, so the removal and redeposition occurred not too long after death. There was also a cluster of six teeth, mostly molars and premolars, from another individual (Burial 1-E). No cranial fragments could be linked to this individual, so it appears to be a deposit solely of teeth from a middle-aged to an older individual, based on tooth wear. Sex is undetermined.

Mortuary ritual surrounding the main interment (1-A) included the burning or smoking of the deceased, which likely included torching a wooden litter upon which the old male had been placed. Charcoal was scattered throughout the base of the pit, particularly under the lower legs of Burial 1-A where a dense deposit of charcoal 15.0 cm thick had accumulated on top of a bed of large sherds from a red-neck, striated olla (the sherds also were blackened and coated with charcoal residue). The bones of the focal individual bear evidence of smudging and scorching from smoke, although the bone is well preserved and is not calcined as it would have been if cremated. A charcoal sample (AA55938) collected from the burned wood beneath the legs of the primary interment yielded a 2-sigma calibrated radiocarbon range of 687–959 CE.

Another sample (AA55936) with a calibrated range of 776–979 CE was associated with the later construction that capped the burial pit. A Terminal Classic date for the Pakal Na burial is confirmed. Further evidence of posthumous manipulation of the primary interment is provided by traces of red and yellow ocher paint on the bones, some in places like the promontory of the sacrum that could only be accessed if bones were exposed and physically removed. Despite removal and painting of the bones, mortuary specialists preserved the articulated position of the skeleton (see Figure 8.1).

Notably, all individuals (including that represented by the skull mask) show significant dental calculus deposits. This not only indicates poor dental hygiene practices among these populations, but also signals a highly acidic diet that can result from ingestion of large amounts of protein (Hillson 1996). This dietary indicator, plus the robust health and advanced age of the primary interment, suggests that these interments were individuals of high status, at least as adults. Additionally, teeth from 1-A and 1-B had been modified through filing or inlays, perhaps originally of jade. The main interment and the other individuals had clear evidence of healed infections. Again, it is probably a tribute to the generally good lifestyle and prestige accorded to these individuals that they were able to survive systemic infection.

The complex mortuary ritual probably included the following events. First, Burial 1-A was placed, likely on a perishable litter, in an extended position on his back with feet crossed and hands placed on the pelvis. The body appears to have been left to skeletonize, a process that would have been expedited by burning and smoking the body. At some point, the skeletal elements were painted and the left arm, partial torso, and cranium were removed and eventually placed on the ledge in deposit 1-C. The robust cranium appears to have been partially bundled as a stack of vault pieces, although other skeletal elements were just scattered in this area. This seems to indicate that at some point the skull was deliberately broken, perhaps to weaken its power, before final interment. It is also possible that the skeletal elements and skull were displayed or served in rituals after removal from the body, and some unknown period of time has passed since the original interment.

At this point, or perhaps earlier, additional human remains (1-B, 1-D, and 1-E) were added to the base of the burial pit. There is no evidence of cut marks or perimortem violence on the bones of the main interment, nor are signs of violence present on any of the disarticulated remains of deposits 1-B, 1-C, and 1-D. There were not, however, very many joint areas preserved to be positive that no dismemberment took place, but seven leg and arm long bones with sufficient preservation definitely lack such marks. On the other hand, the skull mask is covered with cut marks and this individual was probably the victim of perimortem violence (see below).

All individuals appear to have been in a skeletonized state (i.e. defleshed) when they were interred and the burial pit backfilled. Apparently, the disarticulated individuals (1-B, 1-C, and 1-D) had been curated and likely functioned as special companions for the primary interment. These could represent sacrificial victims or other war trophies of the main individual but are just as likely to represent a group of venerated ancestors who may have served to ritually charge the burial ground. The curated remains of Burial 1-B, with offerings of jaguar teeth and cinnabar (items often found with high-ranking Maya burials), especially favor that interpretation.

A number of grave goods – including four perforated dog canines and the inner spiral of a Queen Conch marine shell – were placed with the bones deposited in 1-C. Most notable, however, is the carved human skull mask that was part of this bone cluster (Figure 8.2). The mask is similar, though far more elaborate, to skull masks found with Classic period elite burials at the site of Copán in Honduras (Storey 2005) and those at the Terminal Classic site of Xochicalco in the central Mexican highlands (Hirth 1989). In Classic Maya art and sculpture, trophy masks were worn as pectorals by elite warriors and likely were fashioned from captives taken in war. The only age indicator on the Pakal Na specimen is moderate tooth wear, which probably indicates a young to middle-aged adult at the time of death. The marks of skinning are very clear, indicating that the head of the decapitated captive was flayed and the skull carved shortly after death (see Figure 8.3). Along the jaw line, there are vertical cut marks where the mandible was defleshed. Additionally, the bone appears to have been "smoked"; areas of scorching are concentrated on the interior surface of the skull, with only limited scorching on the exterior surface. The skull mask could have been ceremonially burned as part of the mortuary ritual or perhaps the head was burned to reduce the presence of soft tissue. Once skeletonized, the back half of the skull was removed and the edges polished. Then, the top of the skull was carved with a mat motif and drilled holes placed at the interstices of the woven design (Figure 8.3). Triangular designs line the sides of the square-shaped mat motif. Mock (1997) notes the link between the mat design and rulership. The mat design is complemented by another iconographic element, the smoke affix of the Mayan *k'ahk'* glyph, carved on the glabella and centered between the eye sockets (Figure 8.2). This element also resembles the serpent tongues that form part of the warrior-on-serpent images seen in both the Lower and Upper Temple of the Jaguars (Ringle *et al.* 1998) at Terminal Classic Chichén Itzá. There is some evidence of incision on the infraorbital area as well, so all of the face was probably decorated, but only small fragments of this portion of the skull were preserved.

Two cartouches containing animal imagery – canines or felines paired with an unidentified avian species – were carved on each side of the mandible of the Pakal Na skull mask (Figure 8.4). Additionally, the partial remains of other

Figure 8.2. The surviving pieces of carved skull mask, Pakal Na.

Figure 8.3. Close-up of mat pattern on skull mask with defleshing marks visible.

Figure 8.4. The carved mandible of skull mask. Cartouche and cut marks visible.

cartouches that appear to contain the same imagery are visible on the sides of the cranial portion of the skull mask, along the edge of the mat motif. This avian and canine or feline imagery is likely analogous to the paired images of jaguars and eagles found in Terminal Classic iconography at Chichén Itzá, such as the images on the *Tzompantli* or Temple of the Skulls and the adjacent Platform of the Eagles, where both animals are seen devouring sacrificial human hearts (Harrison-Buck *et al.* 2007). Again, this illustrates the focus of the Terminal Classic Pakal Na site towards the northern Yucatán capital and most powerful site of the period.

The mandible of the Pakal Na skull mask was drilled in several places along the inferior margin (Figure 8.4). Feathers or other decorative elements could have been attached to the mask, or the mandible could have been attached to the skull and worn around the neck of the warrior, presumably by the individual who had claimed the life of the captive. According to Hirth (1989), trophy heads validated a warrior's capture of a sacrificial victim and accorded him elevated status through successful participation in warfare. With evidence of foreign connections and martial prowess, it is no surprise that the focal burial – an older male – received elaborate mortuary treatment upon his death. During the Late Classic period, skull masks as burial offerings and extended mortuary ritual involving elaborate body processing, such as the smoking and painting of bones, appear limited to high-ranking individuals and members of royal families (Storey 2005). Such royal treatment has been documented for the ruling elite at a number of large Classic Maya centers, including Copán (Storey 2005), Piedras Negras (Fitzsimmons 1998), and Caracol (Chase and Chase 1996). The Pakal Na mortuary facility, located at a modest-sized Maya site, provides information on changes in sociopolitical organization during the Terminal Classic period, when successful warriors even in peripheral settlements might be accorded a status equal to rulers in the earlier larger centers.

The northern-style ceramics and iconography associated with an important deceased warrior and ruler of Pakal Na may indicate a materialization of an allied northern relationship. The increased conflict and warfare in the Terminal Classic is expressed through the inclusion of a skull mask suggestive of captive-taking in the burial of the high-status male at the site of Pakal Na. The Sibun Valley was a strategic production area for cacao, a prestige drink, and much valued resource in the long-distance trade (McAnany *et al.* 2002), so the evidence of elite wealth and elaborate mortuary treatment here is really not surprising.

8.3   Late classic example from Copán, Honduras

Copán was one of the major centers of the Late Classic Maya and was abandoned during the Terminal Classic. Extensive excavations have been conducted at the site for the past 30+ years in both the central Acropolis, which was the domicile and ritual space of the ruling dynasty, and in residences of the neighborhood of Las Sepulturas, 1 km east of the Acropolis. Both the Acropolis and elite residences have evidence of skeletal trophies, which is not surprising as it was probably expected of all able-bodied elite males that they partake in the wars of their polities. One elite compound, 9N-8, was almost completely excavated, containing 10 patios and over 50 structures. This was clearly the residence of an important elite lineage that had clear links to court positions with the royal dynasty at the Acropolis (Webster 1989). The main patios here were A and B, the former with sculpture and a carved bench in the principal building. Interestingly, it was in a subsidiary patio, Patio D, that a skull mask was found; this was the only such trophy found at this residence. The individual was a young, gracile male, but clearly male by morphology, with the skull mask lying on his chest. This was the only grave offering with this individual, who was buried under the staircase in front of a large and centrally placed residence, a position of honor. He did have moderate cranial modification and mesial notches on the mandibular central incisors. Such dental and cranial modification is found with many, although not all, individuals in the 9N-8 residence and probably, in my estimation, indicates elite or noble status.

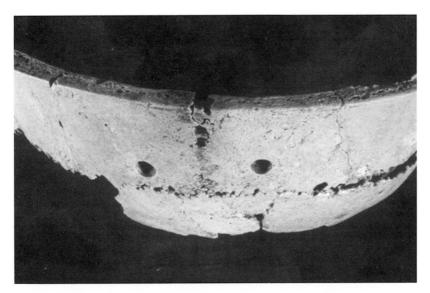

Figure 8.5. The skull vault of skull mask, with polished edge and drilled holes.

The skull mask had been cut just beyond the coronal suture, with the edge polished and holes drilled for suspension (Figure 8.5). The cut went inferior between the temporal fossa and the mastoid. The fossa is also drilled, so that the mandible, drilled at the tops of the rami, could be suspended from the mask. The mandible also had a series of holes at the inferior border (Figure 8.6), probably so that decorations such as feathers could be attached. There are also at least eight holes drilled in the vault, and probably two more lost through lack of preservation, which may be more than was needed to suspend it or tie it to the face as a mask. It is possible that some of these holes were also for feathers or other decoration. The face was present, but in too many pieces for reconstruction. The individual was male, probably slightly older than the "owner," but elite status was indicated by the drilled and inlaid (probably pyrite?) maxillary central incisors. While the main interment does not seem robust enough to be a successful warrior, the skull mask is, as expected, from an important captive. There is no reason to think that the aggressor and the victim are not linked here; it obviously was important enough to the main interment that it was buried with him.

Several broken skull masks, with the same drill holes and cuts as the one just described, were recovered from a four-room structure on the northeastern corner of the Great Plaza near the Acropolis. The excavators suggested that it was a communal or young men's house (Cheek and Spink 1986), which are known from ethnohistoric sources to be present among the Maya.

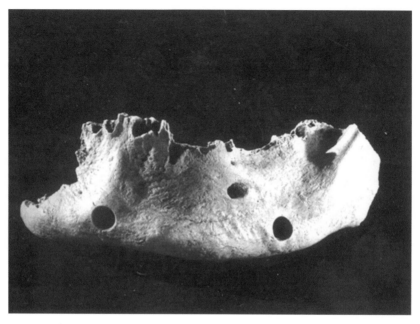

Figure 8.6. Partial mandible of skull mask with drill holes.

The presence of the skull masks is strong evidence that this communal house was probably occupied by young, unmarried elite men training for war and ritual duties. Unlike the skull mask in Patio D of the 9N-8 residence, these were incomplete and lacked face pieces. Because they were found among the refuse, it appears that these were probably deliberately broken and discarded and were not considered the personal property of any of the residents. It is also possible that these were considered a cohort trophy of a group of warriors, and it was important at some point to destroy these ritually, rather than link them to any particular individual. Such cohort skeletal trophies are known from the earlier Classic site of Teotihuacan, for example (Sugiyama 2005).

8.4   Conclusion

While some trophy heads are known, skull masks made from captives appear to be an important trophy, to judge from the iconography of the Late/Terminal Classic Maya. Maya elite men, especially, were expected to be warriors and to be successful had to capture and sacrifice elite warriors from the opposing polity (Webster 1998). Archaeologically, several of these skull masks have been found. These have been elaborately modified to be used as pectorals, hung from belts, or else to be worn as masks. Defleshing marks indicate that such modifications were undertaken fairly soon after death. They also appear to have holes drilled for decorations – usually feathers are depicted in the art. Those from Copán and Pakal Na have been studied by the author. When associated with a single interment, these definitely appear to be important properties of the individuals. The skull masks have clear evidence of coming from elite individuals. In this case, it is likely that both the aggressor and the victim are linked in the mortuary treatment.

In one case, the aggressor was a robust individual, while in the other, he was a rather gracile individual, indicating that elite males were expected to be warriors, even if they were not physically impressive. At Pakal Na, the warrior was probably also the ruler of the site during his lifetime, while at Copán, the individual was simply an honored member of the residential group. Copán also provides evidence of skull masks that do not appear to be linked to particular individuals. Except for the individual in Patio D of the 9N-8 residence, the skull masks seem to have been deliberately broken, especially to obliterate the face. At Pakal Na, this was probably done at final interment, to terminate whatever power it may have embodied when whole. There were only pieces of the face of the skull mask at 9N-8, especially the maxilla, so it is possible that the face was broken at the interment of the main individual, although it remained on his chest. Skeletal trophies were powerful reminders of war and its dangers, and probably gave the "owners" power and prestige in their society.

Maya iconography has many examples of the stress on elite warfare, the treatment of captives, and the use of skeletal elements from probable captives (see Cucina and Tiesler 2007). However, the bioarchaeological evidence of warriors and their trophy skull masks make this violence personal and materialized, as involving individuals whose archaeological context and skeletal features support the information that is in the art and accompanying texts – namely that both perpetrators and victims were elites, even in the case of the skull masks within a young men's house. This was violence within Maya society between individuals who shared very much the same culture and seemed to involve only adult males. The ritual nature of this violence, and that being able to exhibit the results of ritual violence was important, is revealed by both the art and the skeletons. Maya warfare was fought for status, for control and tribute, and to prove the favor of the gods between competing polities; the results had a dampening effect on losers and seemed to bring prosperity to winners, at least until the next conflict (Webster 1998). Maya ritual violence was both performance and political (Pérez 2012). In that, it aligns with other New World pre-Columbian cultures, such as the Wari Empire of Peru (Tung 2012) and Cahokia, near St. Louis today, of the Mississippian period of the central and southeastern United States (Koziol 2012), where sacrifice and skeletal trophies are also found bioarchaeologically in particular patterns for each culture. The association of skull masks with meanings of power, control, and supernatural favor is crucial to what it meant to be an elite Maya warrior. The victims undoubtedly understood the risks when they went to war, and that it was a risk that was inherent in an elite status in Classic Maya society. The roles and meanings attached to perpetrators and victims of warfare violence were well understood among the Classic period Maya and served to link the individuals in death.

Acknowledgments

The Xibun Archaeological Research Project received financial support from the National Science Foundation (BCS-0096603). It was conducted with the permission of the Institute of Archaeology, Belize. The Copán research is conducted with the permission of the Instituto Hondureño de Antropología e Historía, Tegucigalpa, Honduras, and has financial support from the World Bank, the Fulbright Foundation, and the University of Houston.

References

Chase, D. Z. & Chase, A. (1996). Maya multiples: individuals, entries, and tombs in structure A34 of Caracol, Belize. *Latin American Antiquity*, **7**, 61–79.
Cheek, C. D. & Spink, M. L. (1986). Excavaciones En El Groupo 3, Estructure 223 (Operacion Vii). In: Sanders, W. T. (ed.) *Excavaciones En El Area Urbana De Copán, Tomo 1*. Tegucigalpa: Instituto Hondureno de Antropologia e Historia, 27–154.
Cucina, A. & Tiesler, V. (eds.) (2007). *New Perspectives on Human Sacrifice and Ritual Body Treatments in Ancient Maya Society*. New York: Springer.
Fitzsimmons, J. L. (1998). Classic mortuary anniversaries at Piedrs Negras, Guatemala. *Ancient Mesoamerica*, **9**, 271–8.
Harrison-Buck, E., McAnany, P. A. & Storey, R. (2007). Empowered and disempowered during the late to terminal classic transition: Maya burial and terminal rituals in the Sibun Valley, Belize. In: Tiesler, V. & Cucina, A. (eds.) *New Perspectives on Human Sacrifice and Ritual Body Treatments in Ancient Maya Society*. New York: Springer, 74–101.
Hillson, S. (1996). *Dental Anthropology*. Cambridge: Cambridge University Press.
Hirth, K. G. (1989). Militarism and social organization at Xochicalco, Morelos. In: Diehl, R. A. & Berlo, J. C. (eds.) *Mesoamerica after the Decline of Teotihuacan*. Washington, D.C.: Dumbarton Oaks, 69–82.
Koziol, K. M. (2012). Performances of imposed status: captivity at Cahokia. In: Martin, D. L., Harrod, R. P. & Pérez, V. R. (eds.) *The Bioarchaeology of Violence*. Gainesville: University Press of Florida, 226–250.

Masson, M. & Mock, S. (2004). Ceramics and settlement patterns at terminal classic period lagoon sites in Northern Belize. In: Demarest, A. A., Rice, P. M. & Rice, D. S. (eds.) *The Terminal Classic in the Maya Lowlands*. Boulder: University Press of Colorado, 367–401.

McAnany, P., Thomas, B., Morandi, S., Peterson, P. A. & Harrison, E. (2002). Praise the ahaw and pass the kakaw: Xibun Maya and the political economy of Cacao. In: Masson, M. A. & Friedel, D. A. (eds.) *Ancient Maya Political Economies*. Walnut Creek: Altamira Press, 123–39.

Mock, S. B. (1997). Monkey business at northern river lagoon: a coastal-inland interaction sphere in Northern Belize. *Ancient Mesoamerica*, **8**, 165–83.

Pérez, V. R. (2012). The politicization of the dead: violence as performance, politics as usual. In: Martin, D. L., Harrod, R. P. & Pérez, V. R. (eds.) *The Bioarchaeology of Violence*. Gainesville: University of Florida Press, 13–28.

Ringle, W. M., Gallareta, T. N. & Bey, G. (1998). The return of Quetzalcoatl: evidence for the spread of a world religion during the epiclassic period. *Ancient Mesoamerica*, **9**, 183–232.

Storey, R. (2005). Lifestyles (before and after death) of the rich and famous at Copán. In:Webster, D. L., Freter, A. C. & Gonlin, N. (eds.) *Copán: The Rise and Fall of a Classic Maya Kingdom*. Santa Fe: SAR Press, 315–43.

Sugiyama, S. (2005). *Human Sacrifice, Militarism, and Rulership: Materialization of State Ideology at the Feathered Serpent Pyramid, Teotihuacan*. Cambridge: Cambridge University Press.

Tung, T. A. (2012). Violence against women: differential treatment of local and foreign females in the heartland of the Wari Empire, Peru. In: Martin, D. L., Harrod, R. P. & Pérez, V. R. (eds.) *The Bioarchaeology of Violence*. Gainesville: University of Florida Press, 180–98.

Webster, D. L. (ed.) (1989). *The House of the Bacabs, Copán, Honduras. Studies in Pre-Columbian Art and Archaeology, No. 29*, Washington, D.C.: Dumbarton Oaks.

(1998). Warfare and status rivalry: lowland Maya and Polynesian comparisons. In: Feinman, G. & Marcus, J. (eds.) *Archaic States*. Santa Fe: School of American Research Press, 311–51.

9   Face me like a man! (or, like a woman): antemortem nasal fractures in pre-Columbian San Pedro de Atacama

CHRISTINA TORRES-ROUFF AND
LAURA M. KING

9.1   Introduction

Exploring the nature of conflict when confronted only with archaeological data can be daunting. However, unlike the more circumstantial evidence from weaponry or defensive settlements, the human body can provide one of the only direct sources of the acts of violence experienced by an individual (Walker 2001). From a bioarchaeological perspective, the remains of the human body can be studied to document the scarring of acts of violence, which may leave bones broken and permanently altered. These provide us with an interesting lens through which to consider violence in antiquity that is more intimate than the scale of analyses employed by other disciplines. Similarly, while certain events of warfare or imperial conquest may have clear histories or understandable outcomes, small-scale conflicts or interpersonal disputes require close readings to explore context and meaning. Tying these things together, a bioarchaeological perspective can afford a more intimate and contextualized view into violent injury, allowing a means with which to analyze small-scale conflict.

This, then, leaves certain episodes of violence open to myriad interpretations. Here, we use this bioarchaeological approach to explore possible scenarios and conflicts resulting in face-to-face confrontations and, ultimately, bleeding and broken noses for numerous individuals in the Middle Period (AD 400–1000) Atacameño oases. These particular incidences of violence pose a number of interesting questions. The oases are home to long-term occupation and these villages are found near permanent sources of freshwater (Llagostera 2004). The Middle Period is considered a time of

Bioarchaeological and Forensic Perspectives on Violence: How Violent Death is Interpreted from Skeletal Remains, ed. D. L. Martin and C. P. Anderson. Published by Cambridge University Press.
© Cambridge University Press 2014.

peace, prosperity, increased population, and growing spheres of interregional interaction, suggesting that resource stress and competition for land were not overt reasons for conflict. Finally, previous studies have shown that the Middle Period, despite having rates of violence that vary over contemporary cemeteries, is a time of considerably less violent injury than the subsequent Late Intermediate Period (Torres-Rouff 2011; Torres-Rouff and Costa Junqueira 2006). As such, it provides an interesting context in which to explore particular manifestations of violence. Additionally, consideration of patterns of violent injury during times of affluence and peace provides an intriguing perspective into topics such as gendered practices, ritual violence, and increasing social inequality. Therefore, this type of study can provide us with a more nuanced perspective into the different social personae at play in the Middle Period. As such, the presence of a number of cranial fractures during the Middle Period in the Atacameño oases that overwhelmingly affect the nasal bones and maxillae suggest that face-to-face confrontation merits a closer exploration.

9.2   Background

San Pedro de Atacama (Figure 9.1) comprises a series of small oases at 2450 meters above sea level in northern Chile's Atacama Desert, and has a long history of occupation (Hubbe *et al.* 2011; Llagostera and Costa 1999). By the Middle Period (AD 400–1000; encompassing the local Quitor, AD 400–700, and Coyo, AD 700–1000, phases), the time period we focus on here, the oases included numerous permanent settlements inhabited by camelid pastoralists who practiced agriculture. At this time, grave wealth began to include many more goods than seen previously, as well as gold materials and highly decorated and finely crafted objects such as wooden snuff trays (Llagostera 2004). This time also witnessed a surge in interregional interaction, with the San Pedro Atacama oases serving as a node in an elaborate mesh of exchange and interaction (Llagostera 1996). The most prominent player in these exchanges was the Tiwanaku polity, located in the Bolivian altiplano, whose presence in the Atacama oases was made visible in portable elite goods, including gold keros and elaborately carved snuff trays (Berenguer and Dauelsberg 1989; Llagostera 2004). However, contacts during this time also extended toward the Chilean coast and over the Andes into areas of northwest Argentina (Bravo and Llagostera 1986; Conklin and Conklin 2007; Costa Junqueira *et al.* 2009; Rivera 2008; Torres and Conklin 1995). Despite the general view that local populations were prosperous and even affluent during the Middle Period and that they were enjoying the benefits of the aforementioned increase in

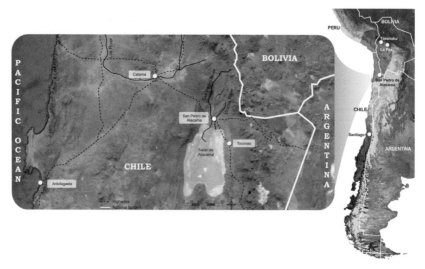

Figure 9.1. Map of Chile indicating the location of the San Pedro de Atacama oases.

long-distance interactions, we suggest that this period was not without conflict, and, moreover, that perhaps that conflict took on a standardized structure.

Human skeletal remains from the length of the occupation of the Atacama oases have been studied by a number of anthropologists. Bioarchaeological analyses of skeletal remains from several Middle Period cemeteries, most notably Solcor 3, suggest that Tiwanaku influence resulted in an increase in quality of life or standard of living as assessed through bioarchaeological indicators (Costa Junqueira *et al.* 2004; Neves and Costa Junqueira 1998). Interestingly, while there is no indication of investment in military activities during the period, a fact that supports a peaceable Middle Period, there is evidence of a slight increase in interpersonal violence from the Late Formative to the Middle Period and of the differential distribution of violent injury (Torres-Rouff 2011; Torres-Rouff and Costa Junqueira 2006). Similarly, the rates of postcranial trauma do not differ significantly before and after the Middle Period, suggesting that part of the population continued to engage in potentially high-risk activities (Costa *et al.* 1998). These data suggest that this time was not as peaceful as archaeologists have argued.

9.3   Research problem

While the common narrative for the Middle Period describes a time of unparalleled prosperity and peace, this account masks the variability inherent in societies where elites are concentrating power. It seems clear from earlier studies that the abundant prosperity and increasing levels of foreign interaction of the Middle Period had tangible benefits for Atacameños; however, the distribution of that benefit, and the concomitant costs for individual wellbeing, merit further exploration. Archaeological evidence suggests that these individuals lived through a time of peace and affluence; however, this does not imply that they were immune to violence. While it did not affect everyone, some portion of this population experienced pain and violent injury while others thrived. Moreover, we argue that some of the violence was regulated through social norms or organized dispute resolution, resulting in a shift toward one particular sort of injury pattern (e.g. Tung 2007; Walker 1997). Through analyses of traumatic injury likely related to face-to-face confrontation, we attempt here to explore the nature of interpersonal conflict in a time of a peace.

9.4 Materials and methods

The skeletal remains of 493 individuals from eight cemeteries are considered in this analysis of the distribution of trauma patterns in Middle Period San Pedro de Atacama. The extremely arid environment of the Atacama Desert results in the excellent preservation of skeletal material, allowing for the large sample size considered here. These skeletal remains are curated at the Instituto de Investigaciones Arqueológicas y Museo R.P. Gustavo Le Paige in San Pedro de Atacama. Father Gustavo Le Paige, an amateur archaeologist and pioneer in the study of Atacameño prehistory, excavated six of these cemeteries in the 1950s and 1960s. As a result of his collection practices there are no postcranial remains from these cemeteries, although he did meticulously document the tombs and their contents in his field notes and many of his later publications (e.g. Le Paige 1964). Archaeologists from the Universidad Católica del Norte's Instituto de Investigaciones Arqueológicas y Museo R.P. Le Paige excavated the final two cemeteries, Solcor 3 and Quitor 6 Tardío, in the 1980s (Bravo and Llagostera 1986; Llagostera *et al.* 1988; Llagostera and Costa Junqueira 1990). These remains are complete skeletons. In sum, this study involved analysis of the cranial remains of 493 individuals.

All the cemeteries date to between AD 400 and 1000, thereby covering the expanse of the Quitor and Coyo phases that are discussed here. One cemetery, Solor 3, occupies a transitional time between the Late Formative Period (AD 1–400) and the Middle Period (Torres-Rouff and Hubbe, 2013). Similarly, three of the cemeteries analyzed here, Quitor 6 Tardío, Yaye 3, and Yaye 4, occupy the end of the Middle Period and the beginning of the subsequent Late Intermediate Period (AD 1000–1450). Finally, it is worth noting that these mostly contemporary cemeteries represent various *ayllus* in the oases. The *ayllu* is the traditional form of Andean kin-based community structure that reflects lineage and political groupings (ascriptive descent groups; Abercrombie 1998; Cock 1981). Locally, these also reflect contemporary geographic and populational separations. The Larache and Solcor *ayllus* are traditionally associated with greater wealth (Goldstein and Rivera 2004; Llagostera 1996; Tamblay 2004). Nevertheless, even within particular *ayllus*, it is likely that certain groups in the population had more access to resources than other groups, and this may have resulted in increased conflict between certain individuals.

Human skeletal remains were analyzed using standard bioarchaeological methods (i.e. Buikstra and Ubelaker 1994a; Buzon *et al.* 2005). To form part of this analysis, a cranium needed to be over 75% complete and include the majority of the facial bones (and, of course, the nasal region). As a result of the large number of individuals who are represented only by crania, sex was mainly determined based on sexually dimorphic features of the skull, although the os coxae were examined when available ($n = 143/493$). Similarly, rough age categories (juvenile, 0–18; young adult, 18–30; middle adult, 30–45; old adult, 45+) were made based on cranial suture closure and using postcranial remains when available. Pelvic bones were used to determine sex in 121 individuals, while only crania were available for the remainder of the sample. While cranial suture closure is notoriously difficult to use to assess age, the majority of our questions and interpretations do not hinge on age-based differences. These broad categories were used to assess whether an individual's age resulted in biased results, given that trauma is among those biocultural patterns that may have a "cumulative impact" over the course of a life (Glencross and Sawchuk 2003). In our dataset, age (outside of childhood) did not seem to impact the distribution of trauma, as there were no significant differences between adult age categories ($\chi^2 = 2.156$, df = 2; $P = 0.340$).

For this study we recorded not just traumatic injury to the nasal region, but all instances of cranial trauma. Evidence of healed trauma was documented as depressions on the vault, facial fractures, and weapon wounds. Convincing perimortem trauma, injuries that were sustained at or around the time of death, was also documented. Trauma was recorded in a number of ways. Details used to document perimortem trauma included radiating fractures, color, and adhering bone fragments (Buikstra and Ubelaker 1994b; Lovell 1997; Roberts and Manchester 2007; Tung 2008). The affected bone of the skull, side, and state of healing were described, as were the shape and size of the injury and any evidence of weapon use. Data were also collected as to those individuals with multiple injuries or injuries to both the nasal region and elsewhere on the skull. All data were analyzed for patterns based on age and sex and compared among sites and over time.

9.5 Results and discussion

The analysis shows that 78 of 493 individuals (15.8%) had antemortem cranial fractures; the overwhelming majority of these fractures were to the nasal bones (63/78; 80.8%), suggesting face-to-face confrontations as a dominant form of violent interaction (Table 9.1; Figures 9.2–4). We documented very few cases of possible perimortem trauma (all involving the cranial vault) and they are not discussed here. Surprisingly, individuals with fractures involving the nasal region showed no evidence of fractures elsewhere on the cranium. There is a significant difference between the sexes in the presence of traumatic injury ($\chi^2 = 8.604$; df = 1; $P = 0.003$), with fractures more common among males (46/199 vs. 23/194). Similarly, there is a significant difference between the sexes when only injuries to the nasal region are considered ($\chi^2 = 6.854$; df = 1; $P = 0.009$), with males, again, displaying the great majority of these traumas (38/199 vs. 19/194). There are no significant differences when all sites are compared; however, pairwise comparisons yield some statistically significant differences between sites, suggesting that these could be affected by differences in social personae, be it through kin relations or sociopolitical roles. For example, closer examination of cemeteries from the Solcor *ayllu*, considered socially distinct based on studies of material culture (Nado *et al.* 2012; Torres-Rouff 2011), supports this, with 8.6% of individuals from the more elite cemetery of Solcor 3 injured in contrast to 18.6% from Solcor Plaza, a difference for males that is statistically significant ($\chi^2 = 7.022$; df = 1; $P = 0.008$). Below we detail the results of our bioarchaeological analyses and break down the types of distinctions and similarities that we see in the nature of these violent encounters.

Table 9.1. *Presence and distribution of traumatic injury in the sample.*

Site	Time	Absent	Trauma to the nasal region	Other cranial trauma	Total
Larache	MP	22	2	3	27
Quitor 6 T.	MP/LIP	44	5	1	50
Solcor Plaza	MP	54	13	3	70
Solcor 3	MP	81	9	3	93
Solor 3	LF/MP	45	4	1	50
Tchecar	MP	137	20	3	160
Yaye 3	MP/LIP	18	4	1	23
Yaye 4	MP/LIP	14	6	0	20
	TOTAL	415	63	15	493

MP, Middle Period; LIP, Late Intermediate Period; LF, Late Formative Period.

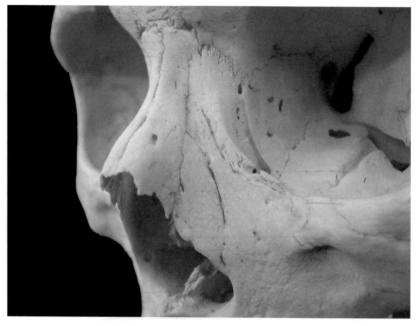

Figure 9.2. Healed fracture to the nasal region (Tchecar Túmulo Sur, t. 1107).

9.5.1   *Presence of nasal fractures*

Despite assertions that the Middle Period was peaceful and prosperous, our evidence suggests that the population still engaged in violent activity, perhaps even with some frequency. In total, 63 of 442 adults showed evidence of nasal fractures (14.3%; increasing to 19.1% [38/199] when only adult males are taken into account). These data argue for a social role for this type of violent injury, especially considering the low rates of traumatic injury to the rest of the skull (15 of 78 fractures did not involve the nasal bones; however, of these, 10 involved other bones of the face, continuing to support the idea that the population engaged in frontal attacks). The confrontational nature of the violent encounters that produced these fractures is dramatic. In sum, it appears that frontal assaults played something of an important role in Middle Period Atacameño society.

9.5.2   *Age*

It is worth noting that one of the clearest results of this study is that interpersonal violence that causes serious injury in the form of skeletal trauma appears

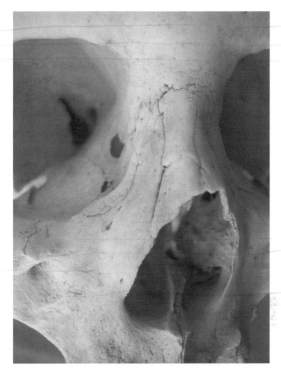

Figure 9.3. Healed fracture to the nasal region (Tchecar Túmulo Sur, t. 854).

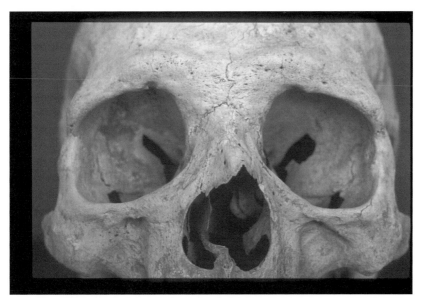

Figure 9.4. Healed fracture to the nasal region (Quitor 6 Tardío, t. 32).

to be the domain of adults. None of the 51 children nor adolescents from the eight cemeteries included in this study (no infants or neonates were analyzed) showed evidence of nasal fractures, or, for that matter, any type of trauma to the cranium. Although it is possible that the rapid remodeling of children's bones affects these data, it would be unexpected if every incidence of trauma was erased from children (Glencross and Stuart-Macadam 2000). Given the frequency with which violent injury is seen in the adult portion of the sample, this suggests that age was a decisive factor in whether one could participate in these more regularized violent activities.

9.5.3   Sex

At some level, sex also appears to be a determining factor in the pattern of nasal fractures ($\chi^2 = 6.854$; df $= 1$; $P = 0.009$), and violent injury more generally ($\chi^2 = 8.604$; df $= 1$; $P = 0.003$). Twice as many males (38/199; 19.1%) as females (19/194; 9.8%) showed evidence of nasal fractures. These patterns hold for the presence of non-nasal trauma as well, although this difference is not significant (females: 4/194, 23 total injuries; males: 8/199, 46 total injuries; $\chi^2 = 1.939$; df $= 1$; $P = 0.165$). Despite this majority, it is clear that individuals of both sexes participated in these violent encounters. In this sample, we are not looking at a pattern that suggests, for example, organized warfare involving only young men. While our data do not rule out the possibility of some form of ritualized confrontation, the structured patterns seen here suggest that this was an activity that could have involved the entire adult population. Other scholars (e.g. Arriaza *et al.* 1994; Lessa and Mendonça de Souza 2006) have posited some form of ritual activity involving bloodletting among males. In their analysis of violent injury at Coyo Oriente, another cemetery in the Atacameño oases that was in use during the Middle Period, Lessa and Mendonça de Souza (2006: 136) interpret the patterns they document (25/226 or 11.1% of the population injured; 18/25 are nasal injuries) as the product of "ceremonial fights dedicated to the gods."

This type of activity has been documented in the historic period for the Andes in the form of the *tinku*. The *tinku* is a ritual battle in which individuals engage in direct confrontation with fists or weapons and where the goal is injury and not death (e.g. Orlove 1994). For example, Bandelier (1910) describes regular hostilities on the Island of the Sun in Bolivia's Lake Titicaca. During these annual events men engaged in confrontations by throwing sling stones at men from other social groups. While women were not directly engaged in these specific fights, they provided men with the stones, which they kept in their skirts. This could suggest the possibility of injuries across both sexes. While we cannot extrapolate the specifics of the *tinku* to the Chilean case considered here, this kind of regularized and socially sanctioned violence may stand as an example of the kind of standardized non-lethal violence engaged in by a community that could result in the patterns of nasal and facial fractures we see reflected in our sample. Given that all the injuries in our sample show evidence of healing, this suggests that lethal violence was not the focus of these face-to-face conflicts.

9.5.4   *Temporal differences over the Middle Period*

We have a temporal spread in the sample considered here that not only includes the heart of the Middle Period, but also smaller samples from the preceding Late Formative Period ($n = 50$; Solor 3) as well as the subsequent Late Intermediate Period ($n = 93$; Quitor 6 Tardío, Yaye 3, and Yaye 4). Together these give us the opportunity to assess whether there might be temporal distinctions in these patterns of nasal trauma and whether they could be particular to the events of the Middle Period. Nevertheless, there are no significant differences between the time periods ($\chi^2 = 1.703$; df $= 2$; $P = 0.427$) in the presence of traumatic injury, or in trauma to the nasal region ($\chi^2 = 1.974$; df $= 2$; $P = 0.373$). Additionally, there appears to be no significant differences between the sexes over time. All of this information suggests that the patterns of nasal and facial fractures, and consequently of violent face-to-face encounters, documented in this collection span the whole of the Middle Period and may reflect a long-established tradition for conflict resolution.

9.5.5   *Sites and status*

When the different cemeteries are compared there is no significant difference in the presence of nasal trauma among them. This also holds for other events of traumatic injury to the cranium. When the sites are compared in a pairwise chi-square analysis, only Yaye 4 is distinct from the other sites. It has the highest presence of nasal fractures (30.0%; 6/20), although the small sample size may be contributing to the occurrence of a significant difference here. However, it should be noted that the other cemetery from the same *ayllu*, Yaye 3, also has very high rates of nasal trauma (17.4%; 4/23), suggesting consistency among these two very poor cemeteries from the end of the Middle Period and the early Late Intermediate Period. It raises the issue that rates of violent injury may have increased at the end of the Middle Period; however, our third late cemetery, Quitor 6 Tardío, only has six fractures (five of which are in the nasal region) out of the 50 individuals interred there, a pattern that is consistent with the core Middle Period sites. The Quitor cemeteries, in contrast to the Yaye ones, have typically been associated with more material wealth (e.g. Le Paige 1964).

Despite the general lack of significant differences, there is a substantive range in the presence of nasal fractures, from the aforementioned 30% at Yaye 4 to the very low rates at Solcor 3 (9/93; 9.7%) and Larache (2/27; 7.4%). The more opulent mortuary assemblages from Solcor 3 and Larache suggest that these were the burial places for an elite segment of the population during the Middle Period. As mentioned above, this period saw a substantial increase in interregional interaction, and the oases were incorporated into the Tiwanaku sphere of influence. This association with the powerful and influential foreign state seems to have conveyed elite status to a number of individuals within the oases (Llagostera 1996). The two cemeteries with the strongest evidence for Tiwanaku influence, Larache and Solcor 3, also include the highest number of other high status goods, including gold and foreign objects from locations outside of Tiwanaku as well as the greatest number of goods in the mortuary assemblage (Torres-Rouff 2011). Finally, while apparent elite standing in this time of growing social inequality did not protect the individuals buried in these two cemeteries from the injuries sustained during violent encounters, it did seem to lessen the impact on or involvement of certain individuals.

9.6   Conclusions

This exploration of traumatic injury in the Middle Period aimed to shed some light on the practices that resulted in nasal fractures becoming nearly commonplace. However, the consistency with which this activity was engaged in during the length of the Middle Period suggests that more than acts of interpersonal violence we may be documenting some form of socially sanctioned activity that involved face-to-face confrontation. Without more detailed study we are unable to identify what these individuals shared that resulted in injury. While it seems unlikely that there were "attackers" and "victims" in the traditional sense, what this may be is evidence of a local means of conflict resolution involving direct confrontation between adult individuals. Moreover, it is possible that there was a regularized quality to these contests that produced standardized injury patterns. Unsurprisingly, it is evident that the peace and prosperity that characterized the Middle Period was not tied to a complete lack of hostilities between different social groups and this leaves open the possibility for a deeper exploration of violence in this time of growing prosperity and increasing social hierarchization.

Acknowledgments

We would like to express our gratitude to Dr. Mark Hubbe and the Instituto de Investigaciones Arqueológicas y Museo R.P. Gustavo Le Paige. NSF BCS-0721229, Colorado College Jones Fund and Venture Grants, and the Fulbright Foundation supported this research. Our thanks also go to Blair Daverman for her assistance during data collection and to Debra Martin and Cheryl Anderson for the invitation to participate in the original AAPA symposium.

References

Abercrombie, T. A. (1998). *Pathways of Memory and Power: Ethnography and History among an Andean People*. Madison: University of Wisconsin.

Arriaza, B. T., Oakland, A., Cassman, V. & Costa Junqueira, M. A. (1994). Ritualistic battles in a Tiwanaku colony [abstract]. *Abstracts of the 59th Annual Meeting of the Society for American Archaeology*, Anaheim, CA.

Bandelier, A. F. A. (1910). *The Islands of Titicaca and Koati*. New York: The Hispanic Society of America.

Berenguer, J. & Dauelsberg, P. (1989). El norte grande en la órbita de Tiwanaku (400 a 1200 D.C.). In: Hidalgo, J., Schiappacasse, V., Niemeyer, H., Aldunate, C. & Solimano, I. (eds.) *Culturas De Chile: Prehistoria Desde Sus Orígenes Hasta Los Albores De La Conquista*. Santiago de Chile: Andrés Bello, 129–80.

Bravo, L. & Llagostera, A. (1986). Solcor 3: un aporte al conocimiento de la cultura San Pedro, Período 500 Al 900 D.C. *Chungara*, **16–17**, 323–32.

Buikstra, J. E. & Ubelaker, D. H. (eds.) (1994). *Standards for Data Collection from Human Skeletal Remains. Proceedings of a Seminar at the Field Museum of Natural History*. Fayetteville: Arkansas Archeological Survey, Research Series, No. 44.

Buzon, M. R., Eng, J. T., Lambert, P. M. & Walker, P. L. (2005). Bioarchaeological methods. In: Maschner, H. A. & Chippendale, C. A. (eds.) *Handbook of Archaeological Methods*. Lanham, MD: Altamira Press, 871–918.

Cock, G. (1981). El ayllu en la sociedad Andina: alcances y perspectivas. *Etnohistoria y Antropología Andina*, **17**, 231–53.

Conklin, W. J. & Conklin, B. M. (2007). An Aguada textile in an Atacamenian context. *Andean Past*, **8**, 407–48.

Costa, M. A., Neves, W., Barros, A. M. & Bartolomucci, R. (1998). Trauma y estrés en poblaciones prehistóricas de San Pedro de Atacama, Norte de Chile. *Chungara*, **30**, 65–74.

Costa Junqueira, M. A., Neves, W. A. & Hubbe, M. (2004). Influencia de Tiwanaku en la calidad de vida biológica de la población prehistórica de San Pedro de Atacama. *Estudios Atacameños*, **27**, 103–16.

Costa Junqueira, M. A., Matheson, C., Iachetta, L., Llagostera, A. & Appenzeller, O. (2009). Ancient leishmaniasis in a highland desert of northern Chile. *PLoS One*, **4**, e6983.

Glencross, B. & Sawchuk, L. (2003). The person-years construct: aging and the prevalence of health related phenomena from skeletal samples. *International Journal of Osteoarchaeology*, **13**, 369–74.

Glencross, B. & Stuart-Macadam, P. (2000). Childhood trauma in the archaeological record. *International Journal of Osteoarchaeology*, **10**, 198–209.

Goldstein, P. & Rivera, M. (2004). Arts of greater Tiwanaku: an expansive culture in historical context. In: Young-Sánchez, M. (ed.) *Tiwanaku: Ancestors of the Inka.* Lincoln: University of Nebraska Press, 150–85.

Hubbe, M., Oviedo, M. & Torres-Rouff, C. (2011). Estado de conservación y contextualización cronológica de la colección osteológica "Gustavo Le Paige." *Estudios Atacameños*, **41**, 29–44.

Le Paige, G. (1964). Los cementerios de la época agroalfarera en San Pedro de Atacama. *Anales de la Universidad del Norte*, **3**, 43–93.

Lessa, A. & Mendonça de Souza, S. (2006). Broken noses for the gods: ritual battles in the Atacama desert during the Tiwanaku period. *Memorias del Instituto Oswaldo Cruz*, **101**(suppl 2), 133–8.

Llagostera, A. (1996). San Pedro de Atacama: nodo de complementariedad reticular. In: Revesz, B. (ed.) *La Integración Surandina Cinco Siglos Después.* Cusco: Centro de Estudios Regionales Andinos Bartolomé de las Casas, 17–42.

(2004). *Los Antiguos Habitantes Del Salar De Atacama: Prehistoria Atacameña.* Santiago: Pehuén Editores.

Llagostera, A. & Costa, M. A. (1999). Patrones de asentamiento en la época agroalfarera de San Pedro de Atacama (norte de Chile). *Estudios Atacameños*, **17**, 175–206.

Llagostera, A. & Costa Junqueira, M. A. (1990). Inventario Solcor 3, San Pedro De Atacama. Manuscript on File. Archives of the Museo Arqueologico R.P. Gustavo Le Paige, San Pedro de Atacama, Chile.

Llagostera, A., Torres, C. M. & Costa Junqueira, M. A. (1988). El complejo psicotrópico en Solcor 3 (San Pedro De Atacama). *Estudios Atacameños*, **9**, 61–98.

Lovell, N. C. (1997). Trauma analysis in paleopathology. *Yearbook of Physical Anthropology*, **40**, 139–70.

Nado, K. L., Marsteller, S. M., King, L. M., Daverman, B. M., Torres Rouff, C. & Knudson, K. J. (2012). Examining local social identities through patterns of biological and cultural variation in the Solcor Ayllu, San Pedro de Atacama, Chile. *Chungara*, **44**, 239–55.

Neves, W. A. & Costa Junqueira, M. A. (1998). Adult stature and standard of siving in the prehistoric Atacama Desert. *Current Anthropology*, **39**, 278–81.

Orlove, B. (1994). Sticks and stones: ritual battles and play in the southern Peruvian Andes. In: Poole, D. (ed.) *Unruly Order: Violence, Power, and Cultural Identity in the High Provinces of Southern Peru.* Boulder: Westview Press, 133–64.

Rivera, M. (2008). The archaeology of Northern Chile. In: Silverman, H. & Isbell, W. (eds.) *Handbook of South American Archaeology.* New York: Springer, 963–97.

Roberts, C. A. & Manchester, K. (2007). *The Archaeology of Disease.* Ithaca: Cornell University Press.

Tamblay, J. (2004). El cementerio larache, los metales y la estratificación social durante el horizonte Tiwanaku en San Pedro de Atacama. In: Rivera, M. & Kolata, A. (eds.) *Tiwanaku: Aproximaciones a Sus Contextos Históricos Y Sociales.* Santiago, Chile: Colección Estudios Regionales, 31–66.

Torres, C. M. & Conklin, W. J. (1995). Exploring the San Pedro de Atacama/Tiwanaku relationship. In: Dransart, P. (ed.) *Andean Art: Visual Expression and Its Relation to Andean Beliefs and Values.* Hampshire: Avebury, 78–108.

Torres-Rouff, C. (2011). Hiding inequality beneath prosperity: patterns of cranial injury in middle period San Pedro de Atacama, northern Chile. *American Journal of Physical Anthropology,* **146,** 28–37.

Torres-Rouff, C. & Costa Junqueira, M. A. (2006). Interpersonal violence in prehistoric San Pedro de Atacama, Chile: behavioral implications of environmental stress. *American Journal of Physical Anthropology,* **130,** 60–70.

Torres-Rouff, C. & Hubbe, M. (2013). The sequence of human occupation in the Atacama Oases, Chile: a radiocarbon chronology based on human skeletal remains. *Latin American Antiquity,* **24,** 330–44.

Torres-Rouff, C., Knudson, K. J. & Stovel, E. M. Ms. Considering power and the display of exotica: Northern Chile's Larache Cemetery and Tiwanaku. *Journal of Anthropological Archaeology.*

Tung, T. A. (2007). Trauma and violence in the Wari Empire of the Peruvian Andes: warfare, raids, and ritual fights. *American Journal of Physical Anthropology,* **133,** 941–56.

(2008). Violence after imperial collapse: a study of cranial trauma among late intermediate period burials from the former Huari Capital, Ayacucho, Peru. *Ñawpa Pacha,* **29,** 101–18.

Walker, P. L. (1997). Wife beating, boxing, and broken noses: skeletal evidence for the cultural patterning of violence. In: Martin, D. L. & Frayer, D. W. (eds.) *Troubled Times: Violence and Warfare in the Past.* Amsterdam: Gordon and Breach, 145–80.

(2001). A bioarchaeological perspective on the history of violence. *Annual Review of Anthropology,* **30,** 573–96.

10 Why some bodies matter: defacement and narrative in historical forensics cases

WILLIAM N. DUNCAN AND CHRISTOPHER

M. STOJANOWSKI

10.1 Introduction

Since the 1980s, ethnographers have increasingly explored the ways that dead bodies and body parts may have significant and dynamic afterlives by virtue of their psychological, social, political, and economic potential. The study of topics ranging from organ trafficking (Scheper-Hughes 2002) and transplantation (Sharp 1995), to the legacy of immortal stem cell lines (Bharadwaj 2012), to repatriation of border crossers' bodies in the American Southwest (Magaña 2011), has demonstrated that dead bodies are highly dynamic loci through which a host of competing interests, and social and politically oriented narratives may intersect and emerge. In the past decade, this and related ethnographic research on the body has sufficiently permeated the broader anthropological sciences such that a "body focus" has emerged as a principal research theme throughout the social and biological subfields of anthropology (Borić and Robb 2008; Csordas 1990; 1999; Joyce 2005; Lorentz 2008; Rebay-Salisbury *et al.* 2010; Scheper-Hughes and Lock 1987; Sharp 2000; Shilling 1993). This orientation has largely stemmed from feminist and gender-focused research (Haraway 1991; Strathern 1988).

Bioarchaeologists have long been aware of the fact that differential funerary treatments of human bodies reflect a range of psychological, sociopolitical, and cosmological concerns (Brown 1971; Hertz 1960 [1907]; Shanks and Tilley 1982), and that the narratives surrounding dead bodies can unfold long after an individual dies. As such, bioarchaeologists are uniquely situated to engage efforts to understand how and why some dead bodies are incorporated into historical narratives and thus become potent social, political, or economic

Bioarchaeological and Forensic Perspectives on Violence: How Violent Death is Interpreted from Skeletal Remains, ed. D. L. Martin and C. P. Anderson. Published by Cambridge University Press. © Cambridge University Press 2014.

symbols while others are not. Sarah Tarlow's (2008) micronarrative of Oliver Cromwell's head and Annia Cherryson's (2010) discussion of the commodification of bodies for dissection and medical training through time are two examples of such research.

In the wake of the Native American Graves Protection and Repatriation Act (NAGPRA; Fine-Dare 2002; 2005; 2009; Kakaliouras 2008; 2012), bioarchaeologists and forensic anthropologists have also become acutely aware of the fact that anthropologists play active roles in shaping the historical narratives surrounding certain bodies (collectively and individually). The debates about NAGPRA unfortunately pitted scientists against Native Americans in a discussion about who ultimately decided the fate of human remains and what constituted reasonable or legitimate cultural affinity between the living and the dead (Brooks and Rumsey 2007; Watkins 2004). However, anthropologists play active roles in driving discourse in criminal and war contexts as well. In many criminal contexts, the discourse surrounding dead bodies occurs between the survivors, the state, and the anthropologist. Anthropologists frequently think of themselves as speaking for the deceased, which is undoubtedly true; however, in many circumstances the discourse surrounding dead bodies is anything but straightforward. Rocío Magaña (2011) has shown, for example, that border crossers' bodies in the American Southwest are symbols of the Mexican state's lack of ability to provide for its citizens. However, he also argues that border crossers' bodies are a medium by which the state establishes control over its citizenry through an unnecessarily complex bureaucracy. The location, identification, and repatriation of the bodies of the deceased are among the principal interests of the surviving loved ones in Mexico as a part of mourning and an attempt to achieve closure. However, the bureaucratic hurdles that are set up (on both sides of the border) present a significant delay, of up to a year, even after bodies are located and potential family members are identified. The Mexican government requires that all DNA testing occur at Baylor University and then data and samples must be processed in the Foreign Ministry Center in Mexico City, for example (Magaña 2011). Thus, Magaña (2011: 170) has argued that "through strategic management ... the dead bodies that could be indexical of the state's failures at its borders are turned into political resources that help strengthen its claims to authority over people and territory."

Outside of discussions about NAGPRA, forensic anthropologists and bioarchaeologists have spent relatively little time reflecting upon our roles in the narratives that surround the bodies we study. To this end, we ask what makes some bodies more likely to receive attention from forensic anthropologists and bioarchaeologists than others? Why do some interest groups pursue anthropological consultation on certain bodies and, furthermore, why do anthropologists agree to collaborate? What causes some bodies to receive merely an inventory and description in a report and others to be identified as worthy of greater investment of time, money, technical expertise, and, ultimately, publication? To put it even more bluntly, why do some bodies collect dust in museums while others become part of larger historical narratives, sociopolitical symbols, or enduring case studies that help define emerging research foci within the academy? One area in which these questions are particularly salient is historical forensic research or biohistory (Komar and Buikstra 2008). We consider historical forensics to overlap with, but be distinct in spirit from, both contemporary forensic anthropology and bioarchaeology. These are not discrete disciplines. We argue that it is worth considering historical forensics as a separate, or at least a specific, area of inquiry because doing so can shed light on anthropologists' roles in the processes that determine whether some bodies become part of a larger historical narrative and thus accrue or receive particular social or political meaning. The narrative and discourse surrounding bodies in some historical forensic cases is obvious because the individuals are well known or are immediately connected to a well-known historical context. Examples of such cases include the study of Dr. Carl Austin Weiss, who killed Huey Long (Ubelaker 1996) and the identification of the Romanovs (Coble *et al.* 2009). Less famous cases include the study of remains associated with a mutiny on a Dutch ship in the 1600s (Franklin 2012) and the study and display of Esther, a mummy from Colorado, in Mesa Verde National Park (Fine-Dare and Durkee 2011).

We suggest that reflecting on anthropologists' roles in less famous historical forensic cases can inform on the dynamics that characterize and (to some degree) drive forensics and bioarchaeology in general. Here we explore the role of anthropologists in defining and extending the social lives of past bodies in a historical forensic case study of a partial human "skull," or calvaria. The calvaria was found at the site of Fort King George (Darien, Georgia) and was thought to be that of a sixteenth-century Spanish priest martyred in defense of the Sacrament of Marriage. We outline the history of the Spanish priest, the skull, and our involvement in its analysis. We argue that the concept of defacement, originally described by Michael Taussig (1999), is a useful way to theorize biopolitics in this case. Taussig argues that violence often functions to sacralize objects by unleashing their latent sacred potential through their destruction. This is not only true for bodies and objects, but can also occur when closely held beliefs and myths are unmasked. We argue that defacement was a driving force in the historical narrative surrounding the Fort King George "skull" and triggered interest in its study from the standpoint of the Catholic Church, the local historical and archaeological community, and ourselves. Acknowledging and exploring how forensic anthropologists can trigger defacement highlights our role in the unfolding narratives that surround dead bodies.

10.2   The Fort King George "skull," the Georgia Martyrs, and the Juanillo Revolt of 1597

As the title of this section indicates, we are dealing with multiple histories – of historical figures, of an historical landscape, of an archaeological exploration of that landscape, and of an object, a person, a partial human skull – that combined in an intersection of local knowledge, archaeological discovery, and forensic anthropological intrigue. Before understanding the manner in which these histories have come to intersect, however, we must first tease them apart.

10.2.1   Spanish Florida and the Juanillo Revolt of 1597

Outside of the southeastern USA, the history of seventeenth-century Spanish occupation of La Florida (generally most of the southeastern USA but in practice northern Florida and coastal Georgia) is little known (Figure 10.1). This fact was made apparent to us during lectures when members of the public relate that they had no idea the Spanish built missions in Florida and Georgia at such an early date. Indeed, there is little of the religious architecture visible above ground today, and, despite the mission system lasting for over 100 years (from 1573 to 1706), this is a history filled with challenges and missteps. After Pedro Menéndez de Avilés secured La Florida for Spain he established the city of St. Augustine in 1565 (Barcia 1951 [1723]). The city has remained occupied ever since. Franciscan missionaries arrived in 1573 as part of the *conquista de almas* and began building mission outposts in the area of St. Augustine and along the Florida and Georgia coast. Described by one noted scholar as a "makeshift period" (Geiger 1937: 69), what progress the missionaries had made at bringing Christianity to the New World was dramatically ended in 1597 when a widespread uprising erupted in the province of Guale – a coastal chiefdom (or series of chiefdoms) located between the Altamaha and Ogeechee rivers (Jones 1978; Saunders 2009; Worth 2004b). During the course of several weeks of unrest (occurring in September and October of that year), five Franciscans were killed (Pedro de Corpa at Tolomato, Blas de Rodríguez and Miguel de Auñón on the island of Guale, Antonio de Bádajoz at Tupiqui, and Francisco de Veráscola at Asao) and a sixth (Francisco de Avila) was captured and tormented, although he eventually escaped and provided testimony (Barcia 1951 [1723]; Geiger 1937; Gómez-González 2007; Habig 1944; Harkins 1990, n.d.; Johnson 1923; Lanning 1935; López 1931; Omaechevarría 1955; de Oré 1936; Pou y Martí 1927; Wyse, 1982;

Figure 10.1. Map of the southeastern US states showing the location of Fort King George (asterisk) located along the southern coast of Georgia.

1985). Most missions were razed. The principal instigator of the rebellion was a young Guale named Juanillo (but see Francis and Kole 2011), heir to the local paramount chiefdom, who was publicly reprimanded and stripped of his claim to title for practicing polygyny. This occurred at the village of Tolomato and the rebuke came at the hands of the resident friar Pedro de Corpa.

Although tensions had likely been broiling below the surface for some time, it was this one event that historians of the time (Barcia 1951 [1723]; Gómez-González 2007; Torquemada 1944) and through the mid twentieth century (de Oré 1936; Geiger 1937; Habig 1944; Lanning 1935) say ignited the short but intense period of violence. The suddenness and ferocity of the violence was shocking to the colonial administrators, who launched a full investigation leading to the capture, interrogation, torture (by water boarding) and, in at least one case, execution of the few witnesses (almost all teenagers) they could capture. During the Spanish military's investigation into the events, the bodies of three of the friars were identified. The remains of Pedro de Corpa and Francisco de Veráscola were never recovered, with de Corpa reportedly beheaded and his body hidden so that it would never be discovered. Although recent scholarship has called into question many of the details and motivations of the Juanillo Revolt (Francis and Kole 2011), the story just outlined is well known to most local historians and students of Florida and Georgia archaeology, a fact that itself reflects the power of defacement for defining regional histories. The story also forms the basis for the claim of martyrdom and is part of the active postulation for canonization (Harkins 1990; n.d.; Wyse 1982, 1985).

10.2.2   The Darien Bluff and the Fort King George "skull"

The calvaria in question was found in the 1950s during excavation of British and Spanish period archaeological deposits along the Darien Bluff, a promontory of land bordering the Altamaha River near present-day Darien, Georgia (Figure 10.1). As a dry bluff overlooking a major river it is no surprise that the history of human occupation of the area spans several millennia, as reconstructed through numerous archaeological investigations of the site (Baker 1970; Caldwell 1943, 1952, 1953, 1954, 1970, n.d.-a, n.d.-b, n.d.-c; Johnson 1983; Joseph *et al.* 2004; Kelso 1968; Steinen 1985; Watkins 1970). The bluff witnessed the construction of two Spanish period missions for the local Guale population during the late sixteenth and early-to-mid seventeenth centuries (Caldwell 1953; 1954; Lewis 1953), was abandoned in 1661 at the initiation of slave raids along the coast (Worth 1995), and was re-settled by Yamasee Indians in 1715 (Barnwell 1926), followed by the building of an English fort at the site (Fort King George), in existence from 1721 until 1727 (Cook 1990; Ivers 1996; Lewis 1967).

During these 6 short years dozens of aged and infirmed English soldiers died and were buried in the nearby cemetery, which visitors to the Fort King George museum today can still see (Figure 10.2; see also Hulse n.d. for a discussion of these remains). The fort also temporarily housed Swiss deserters from French Louisiana as well as African slaves (Barnwell 1926). The area was re-settled by Scottish Highlanders in 1736, who established the modern town of Darien (Lewis 2002). By 1820 sawmilling operations were established on the bluff, the site served a defensive purpose during the Civil War (the mills and the town were destroyed by Sherman); by 1878 a second sawmilling operation began at the site. Interspersed among these major foundation events were various Creeks, New Englanders, Carolinians, Irish and English expats, and free and escaped slaves.

Initial excavations at the Fort King George site uncovered evidence of the prehistoric occupation of the area (Caldwell 1943). Subsequent work identified elements of the Spanish period mission (likely the later one built) as well as the English cemetery associated with the fort (the fort, to our knowledge,

Figure 10.2. Commemorative grave stones at the Fort King George site marking the location of the British period cemetery.

has not actually been found; Caldwell 1952; 1953; 1954; n.d.-a; n.d.-b). Details about the Spanish missions are most relevant here. Although at the time of excavation the mission was thought to be Nuestra Señora de Guadalupe, associated with the important Guale village of Tolomato where Pedro de Corpa served and was killed (Jones 1978), subsequent historiographic work (Francis and Kole 2011; Worth 2004a) suggests that the sixteenth-century mission was actually Santo Domingo de Talaje, associated with the Guale village of Asao where Francisco de Veráscola lived and was killed. Regardless of which attribution is correct, a Spanish priest was killed at the site and it is this documented history that intersected with the discovery of the Fort King George "skull" and led us to this point in the calvaria's history.

The calvaria in question has limited provenance and is not mentioned in any of the excavator's reports about the site (Caldwell 1952; 1953; 1954; n.d.-a; n.d.-b). Given the clarity and specificity of these reports in other details, we find this curious and wonder if Caldwell herself thought the skull belonged to Pedro de Corpa (we suspect not, since she apparently assigned the mission to Talaje or Espogache, not Nuestra Señora de Guadalupe – Caldwell 1970; n.d.-c). The formal museum accession record indicates it was donated by Caldwell between 1952 and 1954, that it was found "on the bank of the river in what had been the Guale Indians' trash pile," and that, because of this location and the Mediterranean type (a reference to old racial typology) of the skull, it "is believed to be that of the Franciscan priest, Father Corpa [who] was beheaded by the Indians…[h]is head placed on a stake in the trash pile and [the] rest of his body was feed (sic) to the dogs. (Fort King George accession record for FKG.52–54.1.121/FK2001.1.1.)." The calvaria was on display in the Fort King George museum but the only references to the attribution are by David Hurst Thomas (1993) in an unpublished report on the archaeology of the region and by Alexander Wyse (1985), which provides the only known image of the calvaria on display at the museum. However, given the occupational history of the site, the calvaria could have been that of any number of individuals that lived along the Georgia coast during the post-contact period.

10.2.3　Anthropological involvement

Because Pedro de Corpa and the other Georgia Martyrs are the subject of an ongoing canonization case, the Franciscan Order needed expert opinion on the calvaria's potential identification as one of the friars. Our involvement began with the receipt of a letter addressed to one of the authors (CMS) dated September 23, 2003. Having completed a dissertation on the bioarchaeology of the Florida missions, CMS was familiar with the story of the Georgia Martyrs and naturally found the project of interest, useful in its applied focus, and a relatively simple matter to resolve. That CMS was 1 month into his first tenure track job may have helped matters along as well. However, the initial examination of the calvaria asked more questions than it answered; falsification was not possible. As the literature review for the various components expanded, CMS enlisted the aid of the senior author (WND, his then research assistant) to evaluate specific leads and survey specific literatures. We returned to Georgia in tandem to examine the calvaria jointly. Then, with more questions remaining, the specimen was loaned to CMS at Arizona State University for a third consideration. As of this writing, a fourth visit is likely as we have yet to exhaust all possibilities.

　　The actual results of the analysis are not the most germane elements to be presented here and have been published elsewhere (Stojanowski and Duncan 2008; 2009). Briefly, the calvaria displays a morphological profile consistent with a male (Figure 10.3a, b). The age of the individual, as could be determined best using only cranial vault sutures (and considering the pathological condition of some of them – see below), is consistent with an adult of the approximate age of the Georgia Martyrs (about 30–40 years). The calvaria is not pristine – breakage is apparent in that the facial skeleton is missing, as

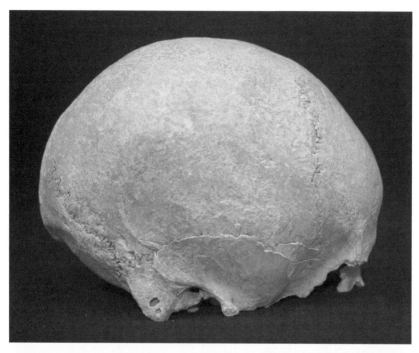

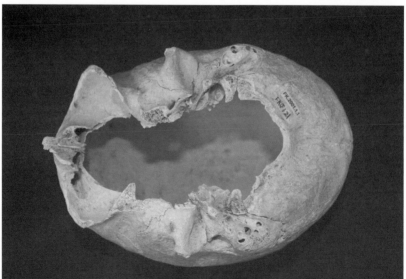

Figure 10.3. The Fort King George calvaria, thought to be that of Pedro de Corpa. (a) Right lateral view; (b) inferior view. Note the damage to the cranial base.

is a portion of the cranial base (Figure 10.3b). In fact, a complete skull would have been inconsistent with the reported brutality with which the friars were dispatched.

Rather than simply using FORDISC to assess ancestral affiliation, we instead followed the advice of Brues (1992) and used populations known to have resided in the area during the post-contact period to generate appropriate comparative samples for discriminant function analysis of cranial vault variation. In total, over 5000 individuals were data-mined from published sources (primarily *Biometrika* and the Archives of the National Museum of Natural History), representing three centuries and multiple ancestral groups (Stojanowski and Duncan 2009; 2010). An Iberian/Basque affiliation was not only possible given the range of craniometric variation – it appeared to be the most likely option (Stojanowski and Duncan 2009; 2010). Extraction of DNA was, of course, attempted but was ultimately unsuccessful. Radiocarbon assay was also unable to falsify the attribution. Oxygen, nitrogen, carbon, and strontium isotopic analyses are ongoing.

Considerable effort was also expended exploring a relatively rare pathological condition – partial frontal and squamosal unilateral craniosynostosis (Duncan and Stojanowski 2008). Ironically, such a condition would be sufficient for positive identification in a modern forensic context but did little for positive identification in this case (not for lack of trying to link noted changes in facial asymmetry to historical descriptions of the friars). We spent considerable time documenting the calvaria's various taphonomic signatures – cortical exfoliation, sun bleaching, microfractures, post-excavation damage, and the pattern of breakage (Stojanowski and Duncan 2008). We considered whether the lack of a face is consistent with a LeFort III fracture or whether it is the result of the natural taphonomic process of skull fragmentation. We mined the various historical sources for information on what weapons may have been used, which led us down the wormhole of non-specific, non-English terms for weaponry in the Americas. We asked whether the damage to the cranial base was consistent with impalement, whether impalement could also cause the face to detach from the vault, and whether any experimental work had been done documenting the effect of impalement on the cranial base. We considered the lack of evidence of scalping in light of ethnohistoric reports of what the natives of Georgia actually used for such practices, specifically whether or not reeds would have left evidence on the frontal bone. Soil samples were extracted from the inner ear to assess whether the soil type was local and whether it could be matched to specific archaeological reports of the stratigraphic profile of the Georgia Bluff where the calvaria was found. The bodies of head lice were also found within the ear and considered for potential DNA extraction if blood was preserved in their stomachs. We worked very hard to falsify the attribution to one of the Georgia Martyrs and equally as hard to establish some means, a hint even, of positive identification. As falsification becomes less and less likely, our attention has turned to trying to identify, with as much evidence as possible, who this is likely to be, if not one of the Georgia Martyrs.

10.3   Discussion

Throughout this chapter we have documented the lengths we went to to falsify the association between the Fort King George "skull" and Pedro de Corpa. Ultimately we were unsuccessful, but, at the same time, neither were we able to find any reason why anyone ever thought the calvaria was specifically his. This outcome raises questions about how narratives emerge about dead bodies, why some bodies realize or are imbued with greater meaning than others, and the role that anthropologists play in the construction of those narratives and their meaning. We will consider why the body was important from the perspective of the church, the museum, the anthropologists, and also Native Americans, but first we suggest that a useful tool for understanding this unfolding in the case of Pedro de Corpa is the concept of defacement. Defacement was originally described by Michael Taussig (1999) to account for the fact that destruction of a thing can sacralize it. Although the potential for violence to make something sacred is well-trod ground in ritual discussions (Hubert and Mauss 1964), for Taussig the defacement need not be in a ritualized context. The history of the World Trade Center in New York presents a straightforward example. On September 10, 2001, the twin towers were a center for commerce. They were symbolically important on that date, of course, both within the United States and abroad, which is why they (along with the Pentagon and other structures of obvious national importance) were ultimately targeted for violence. However, their destruction the following day unleashed their latent sacrality and created an enduring symbol of the USA as being under attack from outsiders. The violence unleashed the towers' sacred potential.

10.3.1   Unmasking secrets: revelation and explanation

Taussig (1999) explores another facet of defacement that is relevant to anthropology, and particularly to historical forensics and bioarchaeology: the unmasking of a public secret in initiation rites on the Isla Grande of Tierra del Fuego during the early 1900s. He describes both the Selk'nam and

Yamana cultures, but we focus only on the former here. During initiation to men's groups, men dressed like spirits by painting their naked bodies and wearing masks. The initiates encountered the spirits in the Big Hut, during which the spirit approached the young men, fondled their genitals, and wrestled with them. After this, the initiates were forced to unmask the spirit and the men began laughing as the secret (the trick) was revealed: the men are the spirits and only the men may know it. Part of being a man in Selk'nam society was knowing and keeping this secret, and the rite in the Big Hut consisted of unmasking that secret. Ultimately, the women knew the secret as well as the men, and the men knew that the women knew. However, the identities of the spirits were openly acknowledged only in the ceremony; destroying the secret served to make it (more) sacred (Taussig 1999). As Taussig (1999: 162; italics removed) notes, "all along revelation was part of the secret's secret."

Unmasking the secret made it sacred but there is another facet to the Selk'nam example concerning the framing of the unmasking, one that high-lights the anthropologist's relationship to defacement in this case. Martin Gusinde was a German Austrian priest–anthropologist who lived with the Selk'nam in the early 1900s and Taussig (1999) analyzes his relationship to the ritual and the unmasking in the Big Hut. Gusinde was clearly interested in understanding the entire ritual process and paid the Selk'nam to re-create it for him (Taussig 1999: 128). More than that, though, Gusinde wanted to docu-ment the ritual so badly that he was willing to risk offending the Selk'nam and thus jeopardize his work there. Although he was permitted to take photographs of the men, he was expressly forbidden from doing so until they were completely dressed as the spirits, lest the photographs provide proof to the women that the spirits were only men in disguise. Gusinde proceeded to take pictures of the half-dressed men and immediately found a hand around his throat demanding an explanation for the violation, which he managed to provide only with a "dramatic act of submission" (Gusinde, cited in Taussig 1999: 120). Given the state of photographic technology in the early 1900s, Gusinde must have known taking a picture clandestinely was impossible. Yet he so wanted to unmask the secret in his own way that he ignited a magnesium flash to photograph his subjects in precisely the state (half-costumed) that he had promised not to photograph.

Taussig (1999) explored how Gusinde's potential unmasking through photography differed from the Selk'nam unmasking in the Big Hut. He argues that, for Gusinde, attraction was not just to the secret itself, but to the need to unmask it on his own terms, which in this case was to explain it away. Gusinde wanted to account for the ritual (unsuccessfully in the end) in terms of its function, history, or origin to explain why such an elaborate rite and secret existed. He tried to reduce the ritual to a product of a specific cause or process. This is problematic, in part, because reductionism failed to account for the mystery, intensity, elaborate preparation, and potential sanctions that came with violating the unspoken rules. It did not explain why the men were obsessed with the women not finding out or why the rite lasted more than a year (Taussig 1999).

Gusinde's focus on understanding the rite was not only incomplete – it changed his relationship to the secret. The Selk'nam unmasking in the Big Hut maintained the potency of the mystery surrounding the secret even as it was revealed. The mystery for Gusinde, on the other hand, was what function the rite and secret served to begin with. When Gusinde engaged the secret, he tried to demystify it in a way that would have just reduced it to a hoax resulting from some larger historical or functional process. His unmasking did not increase the mystery and sacrality of the original secret; it detracted from it. Moreover, Gusinde's approach, in Taussig's view, would have added to the mystery and sacrality of the search for function or origin, reinforcing the value of scientific inquiry and enlightenment reductionism. This is why the epigraph for Taussig's (1999) book is a quote from Walter Benjamin: "Truth is not a matter of exposure which destroys the secret, but a revelation which does justice to it." Gusinde engaged the secret from a functionalist (scientific) point of view. Rather than use the sacrality that emerges from its destruction to add mystery to the ritual, he appropriated and redirected the sacrality to his own goals, and relegated the experience of the ritual to details that did not fit his explanation, which in itself was an act of violence.

10.3.2 Defacement: parallelism and divergence

With this in mind, we can consider the case of Pedro de Corpa from the perspective of the relevant interlocutors (the church, the museum, the anthropologists, and the Native Americans). Highlighting parallels and divergences between the Pedro de Corpa and the Selk'nam cases sheds light on the case's relevance to larger issues in bioarchaeology. The Franciscan Order's initial interest in the calvaria was to gain insight into the historical narrative of the Georgia Martyrs as a contribution to their possible canonization. Martyrdom is historically a common route to canonization. The willingness to suffer and die for the faith is, of course, a powerful symbol (and tool) for the Catholic Church. The violence suffered by the priests unleashed the potential sacrality that could be used as a symbol by the Church. However, confirming that the priests suffered both bodily harm and desecration after death was important for the Church's case for canonization. In other words, the church solicited and required anthropological involvement to confirm that such violence had occurred and, ultimately, the establishment of truth or falsification in this case was handed over to outsiders (the anthropologists). This highlights two principal differences between the Pedro de Corpa and Selk'nam cases. In the former, anthropological involvement was sought as an arbiter in an actual case; in the latter the anthropologist sought out and paid for a re-creation of an indigenous ritual. Thus the role and contribution of the anthropologist to the respective cases is inherently different (see below).

The museum's perspective mimicked that of Gusinde, the anthropologist in Tierra del Fuego, to a greater degree. The narrative surrounding the Georgia Martyrs was sufficiently magnetic that the museum displayed the calvaria for years advertised as Pedro de Corpa even though we were unable to find reason to connect the skull to Pedro de Corpa, biologically or historically. You can understand why; museums' goals include attracting, informing, and entertaining (edu-taining?) the public. This display and its surrounding narrative would have engaged the public in a specific narrative about local history, and in turn educated them on some of the dynamics that characterized the colonial period.

The anthropological interest, which is to say our own, was driven by factors ranging from professional obsessiveness to the need to publish, but defacement drove our interest for the same reason as the museum. The narrative was magnetic, and it presented an opportunity to serve the public, and to have some greater relevance outside of the narrow audience of academia. Frankly, as bioarchaeologists working in the NAGPRA era, we were thrilled to have someone want anthropological input. This is where our involvement in the case differed from that of Gusinde in Tierra del Fuego. In this case, anthropological input was solicited and had the potential to offer clarity about the skull, but it never detracted from the mystery surrounding it. In fact, anthropological involvement added to its mystery, and it would have done so whether or not we had determined with certainty that the skull was one of the Georgia Martyrs. In this sense anthropological engagement occurred on the terms of the people who asked us to study it. Our involvement occurred, so to speak, in the Big Hut, and accordingly did justice to the mystery rather than explaining it away, in Walter Benjamin's terms (see above). This is not to say that we did not consider purely anthropological issues in this case. We published a case study on a pathology exhibited by the skull as well as a craniometric analysis, but, initially and ultimately, our involvement was on the terms of the Church and the museum. Our involvement and unmasking of the fact that there was no

LIVERPOOL JOHN MOORES UNIVERSITY
LEARNING SERVICES

reason to have thought the calvaria was specifically Pedro de Corpa in no way undermined their (or the public's) enchantment with it.

The final interlocutors in the discourse surrounding the Fort King George "skull" are the Native Americans. Even asking the question of whether or not the priests were martyrs frames the role of Native Americans as the perpetuators of violence. It is worth re-stating the fact that the uprising in which the priests were killed stemmed from their prohibition of indigenous marriage practices. Thus, ultimately even though Native Americans were not actively engaged in this discourse, they were and are part of the larger political context of the case by virtue of their (passive) portrayal. In this regard the church, the museum, and the anthropologists were engaged in re-creating a narrative of contact and conquest.

If you juxtapose this case to the circumstances surrounding NAGPRA, you see a different relationship between the anthropologists and Native Americans. The initial steps that eventually led to NAGPRA began with a road project in Iowa when a cemetery that contained both Native American and European remains was uncovered. The European remains were taken for reburial and the Native American remains were taken to a museum. The Native Americans saw the movement of their ancestors to the museum and subsequent study as an act of violence. In this way, the differential treatment served as a form of violence and unleashed their symbolic and political potential. In retrospect, this seems like an obvious violation, but the differential treatment and questions of reverence ignore the other facet of defacement – that of demystification and appropriation of sacred potential. In terms of defacement, viewing remains as a medium to inform on past lifeways turned the remains into datapoints and appropriated their potential sacrality to serve (and valorize) scientific goals. Scientists hope to explain nature in terms of function, origin, and process, and the value of those goals is self-explanatory. We are part of this science and in no way question its value. However, as anthropologists, we should be aware of the fact that, like Gusinde in Tierra del Fuego, our mysteries about the lifeways of the past (origins, diet, disease, demography, cultural affinity, migration, ritual, etc.) are not necessarily the mysteries of other groups, and that we are just one of many groups that may intersect through a particular body.

This brings us back to the initial question for this chapter – why do some bodies receive more detailed forensic analysis than others? Engaging the concept of defacement permits us to identify two reasons. The first is the direct result of violence. The destruction of a body, as much as with other media, can unleash a latent sacred potential. In the case of the Fort King George "skull," it was acknowledged and used for religious, economic, educational, and professional purposes by the Catholic Church, the museum, and ourselves. The second reason, though, is that in this case the information that anthropological investigation brought to bear served to enhance the mystery of the initial narrative, rather than explaining it away, and in doing so imbued the calvaria with greater social and religious meaning and value than it had prior to our involvement. The nature of inquiry that characterized anthropological involvement was entirely consistent within the framework of the relevant soliciting groups that intersected through the Fort King George "skull" and, as a result, this particular body received more detailed investigation than it might have otherwise.

Acknowledgments

We have enjoyed working on this project tremendously, not least because it has given us an opportunity to contribute to a fascinating historical question. It has also brought us in contact with a number of people who have been happy to help since we began in 2005. We would like to thank Father Conrad Harkins for contacting us and inviting us to begin the project, and for his continued support through the past couple of years. We are also grateful to the staff of Panola Mountain State Park for accommodating our visits to their facilities. We are particularly indebted to Linda Bitley and Debbie Wallsmith, who helped arrange for the temporary loan of the Fort King George specimen to our lab for more detailed analysis. Josephine Caldwell has and continues to provide important historical information about her parent's work along the Darien Bluff. Clark Spencer Larsen also facilitated data collection for some of the comparative samples used in this analysis. We would like to thank Dr. Debra Martin and Cheryl Anderson for soliciting our participation in this volume, and Dr. Kathy Fine-Dare for her constructive review. Funding for this project was provided by a St. John Fisher Faculty Development Grant.

References

Baker, S. G. (1970). Fort King George archaeology, spring 1970. Unpublished manuscript. Onfile at the Fort King George Museum. Darien, GA.

Barcia, A. (1951) [1723]. *Ensayo Cronologico Para La Historia General De La Florida (in English)*. Gainesville: University of Florida Press.

Barnwell, J. W. (1926). Journal of Col. John Barnwell (Tuscarora) in the construction of the Fort on the Altamaha in 1721. *The South Carolina Historical and Genealogical Magazine*, **27**, 189–203.

Bharadwaj, A. (2012). Enculturating cells: the anthropology, substance, and science of stem cells. *Annual Review of Anthropology*, **41**, 303–17.

Borić, D. & Robb, J. (2008). *Past Bodies. Body-Centred Research in Archaeology.* Oxford: Oxbow Books.

Brooks, M. & Rumsey, C. (2007). *The Body in the Museum. Human Remains: Guide for Museums and Academic Institutions.* New York: Altamira Press, 261–89.

Brown, J. A. (1971). The dimensions of status in the burials at Spiro. *Approaches to the Social Dimensions of Mortuary Practices.* Society for American Archaeology Memoir, **25**, 92–112.

Brues, A. M. (1992). Forensic diagnosis of race – general race vs. specific populations. *Social Science and Medicine*, **34**, 125–8.

Caldwell, J. (1943). Cultural relations of four Indian sites on the Georgia coast. University of Chicago: Unpublished MA thesis.

Caldwell, S. K. (1952). Field notes 1952 season. Unpublished records. On file at the Fort King George Museum. Darien, GA.

  (1953). Excavations at a Spanish Mission site in Georgia. *Southeastern Archaeological Conference Newsletter*, 31–2.

  (1954). A Spanish mission site near Darien. *Early Georgia*, **1**, 13–17.

  (1970). Editor's note. *Artifacts from the Sites of Three Nineteenth Century Houses and Ditches at Darien Bluff.* Athens, GA: University of Georgia Laboratory of Archaeology Series Report Number 9.

  (n.d.-a). Fort King George archaeological catalog, Caldwell 1952–1954. Unpublished records. On file at the Fort King George Museum. Darien, GA.

  (n.d.-b). Preliminary report on Fort King George. Unpublished manuscript. On file at the Fort King George Museum. Darien, GA.

  (n.d.-c). Tentative conclusions regarding Spanish mission and village on Darien Bluff. Unpublished manuscript. On file at the Fort King George Museum. Darien, GA.

Cherryson, A. (2010). In the pursuit of knowledge: dissection, post-mortem surgery and the retention of body parts in 18th- and 19th-century Britain. In: Rebay-Salisbury, K., Stig Sørensen, M. L. & Hughes, J. (eds.) Body Parts and Bodies Whole. Oxford: Oxbow Books, 135–48.

Coble, M. D., Loreille, O. M., Wadhams, M. J., Edson, S. M., Maynard, K., Meyer, C. E., Niederstätter, H., Berger, C., Berger, B., Falsetti, A. B., Gill, P., Parson, W. & Finelli, L. N. (2009). Mystery solved: the identification of the two missing Romanov children using DNA analysis. *PLoS One*, **4**, e4838.

Cook, J. (1990). *Fort King George. Step One to Statehood.* Darien, GA: Darien News.

Csordas, T. (1990). Embodiment as a paradigm for anthropology. *Ethos*, **18**, 5–47.

  (1999). The body's career in anthropology. In: Moore, H. (ed.) *Anthropological Theory Today.* Cambridge: Polity, 172–205.

de Oré, L. G. (1936). *The Martyrs of Florida (1513–1616).* New York: Joseph F. Wagner, Inc.

Duncan, W. N. & Stojanowski, C. M. (2008). A case of squamosal craniosynostosis from the 16th century southeastern United States. *International Journal of Osteoarchaeology*, **18**, 407–20.

Fine-Dare, K. S. (2002). *Grave Injustices: The American Indian Repatriation Movement and NAGPRA*. Lincoln: University of Nebraska Press.

—— (2005). Anthropological suspicion, public interest and NAGPRA. *Journal of Social Archaeology*, **5**, 171–92.

—— (2009). Bodies unburied, mummies displayed: mourning, museums, and identity politics in the Americas. In: Fine-Dare, K. S. & Rubenstein, S. L. (eds.) *Border Crossings: Transnational Americanist Anthropology*. Lincoln: University of Nebraska Press, 67–118.

Fine-Dare, K. S. & Durkee, B. N. (2011). Interpreting an absence: Esther's legacy at Mesa Verde National Park. *Journal of the West*, **50**, 43–50.

Francis, J. M. & Kole, K. M. (2011). *Murder and Martyrdom in Spanish Florida. Don Juan and the Guale Uprising of 1597*. New York: American Museum of Natural History, Anthropological Papers, Number 95.

Franklin, D. (2012). Human skeletal remains from a multiple burial associated with the mutiny of the Voc Retourschip Batavia, 1629. *International Journal of Osteoarchaeology*, **22**, 740–8.

Geiger, M. (1937). The Franciscan conquest of Florida (1573–1618). Catholic University of America: Unpublished PhD dissertation.

Gómez-González, J. (2007). *La Florida: Fray Alonso Gregorio de Escobedo, (Manuscrito del Siglo XVI, Conservado en la Biblioteca Nacional de España)*. http://archivo.bitacoramedica.com/wp-content/uploads/2007/04/LaFlorida.pdf. [Accessed September 25, 2013.]

Habig, M. A. (1944). The Franciscan provinces of Spanish North America. *The Americas*, **1**, 88–96.

Haraway, D. (1991). *Simians, Cyborgs and Women: The Reinvention of Nature*. New York: Routledge.

Harkins, C. (1990). On Franciscans, archaeology, and old missions. In: Thomas, D. H. (ed.) *Columbian Consequences Volume 2. Archaeological and Historical Perspectives on the Spanish Borderlands East*. Washington, D.C.: Smithsonian Institution Press, 459–74.

—— (n.d.) *The Five Franciscan Martyrs of Georgia, Postulator of the Cause*. 1235 University Boulevard, Franciscan University of Steubenville. Manuscript on file with authors.

Hertz, R. (1960) [1907]. *Death and the Right Hand*. Glencoe, IL: The Free Press.

Hubert, H. & Mauss, M. (1964). *Sacrifice: Its Nature and Function*. London: Cohen & West.

Hulse, F. S. (n.d.) Certain Caucasian skeletal remains from the site at Ft. King George. Unpublished manuscript. On file at the Fort King George Museum. Darien, GA.

Ivers, L. E. (1996). British occupation of the Altamaha. *Drums Along the Altamaha, A Historic Symposium Held at Fort King George State Historic Site*. November 10, 1996.

Johnson, J. G. (1923). The Yamasee revolt of 1597 and the destruction of the Georgia missions. *Georgia Historical Quarterly*, **7**, 44–53.

Johnson, R. E. (1983). An archaeological reconnaissance survey of the proposed Saw-grass Cove apartment complex, Darien Lower Bluff, Mcintosh County, Georgia. Unpublished report. On file at the Fort King George Museum. Darien, GA.

Jones, G. D. (1978). The ethnohistory of the Guale coast through 1684. In: Thomas, D. H., Jones, G. D., Durham, R. S. & Larsen, C. S. (eds.) *The Anthropology of St. Catherines Island. 1. Natural and Cultural History. Anthropological Papers 55, pt 2*. New York: American Museum of Natural History, 178–210.

Joseph, J. W., Hamby, T. M. & Long, C. S. (2004). *Historical Archaeology in Georgia*. Athens, GA: University of Georgia Laboratory of Archaeology Series Report Number 39.

Joyce, R. A. (2005). Archaeology of the body. *Annual Review of Anthropology*, **34**, 139–58.

Kakaliouras, A. M. (2008). Leaving few bones unturned: recent work on repatriation by osteologists. *American Anthropologist*, **110**, 44–52.

(2012). An anthropology of repatriation: contemporary physical anthropological and Native American ontologies of practice. *Current Anthropology*, **53**, S210–21.

Kelso, W. M. (1968). *Excavations at the Fort King George Historical Site, Darien, Georgia. The 1967 Survey*. Atlanta, GA: Georgia Historical Commission Arch-aeological Research Series Number 1.

Komar, D. A. & Buikstra, J. E. (2008). *Forensic Anthropology: Contemporary Theory and Practice*. Oxford: Oxford University Press.

Lanning, J. T. (1935). *The Spanish Missions of Georgia*. Chapel Hill: University of North Carolina Press.

Lewis, B. (1953). Comments on the Spanish Mission Site. *Southeastern Archaeological Conference Newsletter*, **3**, 32–3.

(1967). Fort King George. *Georgia Magazine*, October/November, 22–4.

(2002). *They Called Their Town Darien*. Privately published by the Lower Altamaha Historical Society.

López, A. (1931). *Relación Histórica de la Florida Escrita en el Siglo XVII*. Volume 1. Madrid.

Lorentz, K. O. (2008). From bodies to bones and back: theory and human bioarchaeol-ogy. In: Schutkowski, H. (ed.) *Between Biology and Culture*. Cambridge: Cam-bridge University Press, 273–303.

Magaña, R. (2011). Dead bodies. The deadly display of Mexican border politics. In: Masci-Alees, F. E. (ed.) *A Companion to the Anthropology of the Body and Embodiment*. Malden, MA: Blackwell Publishing, Ltd., 157–71.

Omaechevarría, I. (1955). Martires franciscanos de Georgia: informes y relaciones sobre su muerte. *Missionalia hispánica*, **XII**. Madrid: Instituto Santo Toribio de Mogrovejo, 12–35, 291–370.

Pou y Martí, J. M. (1927). Estado de la orden Franciscana y de sus misiones en América y extreme Oriente en el año de 1635 [Part 2]. *Archivo Ibero-Americano*, **28**, 43–92.

Rebay-Salisbury, K., Stig Sørensen, M. L. & Hughes, J. (2010). *Body Parts and Bodies Whole*. Oxford: Oxbow Books.

Saunders, R. (2009). Stability and ubiquity: Irene, Altamaha, and San Marcos pottery in time and space. In: Deagan, K. & Thomas, D. H. (eds.) *From Santa Elena to St. Augustine: Indigenous Ceramic Variability (A.D. 1400–1700): Proceedings of the Second Caldwell Conference. Anthropological Papers of the American Museum of Natural History Number 90*. New York: American Museum of Natural History, 83–111.

Scheper-Hughes, N. (2002). Commodity fetishism in organs trafficking. In: Scheper-Hughes, N. & Wacquant, L. (eds.) *Commodifying Bodies*. Los Angeles: Sage, 31–62.

Scheper-Hughes, N. & Lock, M. M. (1987). The mindful body: a prolegomenon to future work in medical anthropology. *Medical Anthropology Quarterly, New Series*, **1**, 6–41.

Shanks, C. & Tilley, M. (1982). Ideology, symbolic power, and ritual communication: a reinterpretation of neolithic mortuary practices. In: Hodder, I. (ed.) *Symbolic and Structural Archaeology*. Cambridge: Cambridge University Press, 129–54.

Sharp, L. (1995). Organ transplantation as a transformative experience: anthropological insights into the restructuring of the self. *Medical Anthropology Quarterly*, **9**, 357–89.

(2000). The commodification of the body and its parts. *Annual Review of Anthropology*, **29**, 287–328.

Shilling, C. (1993). *The Body and Social Theory*. London: Sage Publications.

Steinen, K. T. (1985). *Excavations at Fort King George 1984*. Manuscript on file, Fort King George Museum.

Stojanowski, C. M. & Duncan, W. N. (2008). *Anthropological Contributions to the Cause of the Georgia Martyrs*. Occasional Papers of the Georgia Southern Museum, number 3. Georgia Southern Museum.

(2009). Historiography and forensic analysis of the Fort King George "skull": craniometric assessment using the specific population approach. *American Journal of Physical Anthropology*, **140**, 275–89.

(2010). Heredity and cranial morphology: a forensic case study from Spanish colonial Georgia. In: Bonogofsky, M. (ed.) *The Bioarchaeology of the Human Head: Decapitation, Deformation, and Decoration*. Gainesville: University Press of Florida, 179–201.

Strathern, M. (1988). *The Gender of the Gift: Problems with Women and Problems with Society in Melanesia*. Berkeley: University of California Press.

Tarlow, S. (2008). The extraordinary history of Oliver Cromwell's head. In: Borić, D. & Robb, J. (eds.) *Past Bodies: Body-Centered Research in Archaeology*. Oxford: Oxbow books, 69–78.

Taussig, M. (1999). *Defacement: Public Secrecy and the Labor of the Negative*. Stanford: Stanford University Press.

Thomas, D. H. (1993). *Historic Indian Period Archaeology of the Georgia Coastal Zone*. Athens, GA: University of Georgia Laboratory of Archaeology Series Report No 13.

Torquemada, J. (1944). *Los Veinte y un Libros Rituales y Monarquia Indiana. Tomo III*. Facsimilar reprint edition, Salvador Chavez Hayhoe.

Ubelaker, D. H. (1996). The remains of Dr. Carl Austin Weiss: anthropological analysis. *Journal of Forensic Sciences*, **41**, 60–79.

Watkins, C. M. (1970). *Artifacts from the Sites of Three Nineteenth Century Houses and Ditches at Darien Bluff, Georgia*. Athens, GA: University of Georgia Laboratory of Archaeology Series Report No. 9.

Watkins, J. (2004). Becoming American or becoming Indian? NAGPRA, Kennewick and cultural affiliation. *Journal of Social Archaeology*, **4**, 60–80.

Worth, J. E. (1995). *The Struggle for the Georgia Coast: An Eighteenth-Century Spanish Retrospective on Guale and Mocama*. New York: American Museum of Natural History, Anthropological Papers, Number 75.

  (2004a). *Evidence for the Locations of Guale Missions in 1597 (with Notes on Possible Locations for Physical Remains of the Martyrs)*. Report submitted to Father Conrad Harkins, Vice Postulator for the Cause of the Georgia Martyrs. Manuscript in possession of the authors.

  (2004b). *Guale. Handbook of North American Indians. Volume. 14, Southeast*. Washington, D.C.: Smithsonian Institution Press, 238–44.

Wyse, A. (1982). The martyrs of Georgia: Fr. Pedro De Corpa, O.F.M. and his companions. In: Tylenda, J. N. (ed.) *Portraits in American Sanctity*. Chicago: Franciscan Herald Press, 76–88.

  (1985). The five Franciscan martyrs of Georgia. *Provincial Annals*, **34**, 30–7.

Sonora, Mexico. With an estimated population of 30 000, the Yaquis were the largest indigenous group in northwest Mexico at the time (Hu-DeHart 1974). Areas of Yaqui settlement were generally rich farmland in the otherwise arid region.

The first major violent conflict between the Yaqui and the Spanish occurred when the forces of Diego de Guzmán dispersed some Yaqui settlements on the Yaqui River soon after the Spanish arrived in the region in 1533. The Yaquis "resisted armed intrusion in their territory from the first" (Spicer 1962: 46), but for the most part tolerated the presence of the Jesuit missionaries, many of whom consciously refrained from bearing arms.

In spite of the continuous expansion of Spanish outposts in the region through the remainder of the sixteenth century, the Yaqui managed to remain independent. By the early 1600s some 20 000 Indigenous peoples in north-western Mexico were under Spanish control, with the exception of the Yaqui, the Mayo, and a few smaller Indigenous populations (Spicer 1962). During the first two centuries of Spanish conquest, the Mayo retained their autonomy through friendly relations with the Spanish while the Yaqui, often supported and protected by the Jesuits, consistently rebelled against efforts to bring them under Spanish control (Hu-DeHart 1974).

By 1623 nearly all Yaquis had been baptized by the Jesuits, who also established eight missions along the Yaqui River (Spicer 1980). As 80+ scattered small communities were consolidated into these eight mission communities, the "Yaquis' incipient consciousness of being a nation" was heightened (Hu-DeHart 1984: 4). The Jesuit missionaries actually reshaped Yaqui military, political, and cultural practices in a manner that intensified the Yaquis' autonomous identity and offered a degree of protection from Spanish control (Hu-DeHart 1984; Spicer 1980). The Jesuits taught the Yaquis to become surplus producers yet encouraged them to retain their egalitarian social organization and communal control of their land. As a result, the Yaqui developed a flexible, resilient culture that was still centered on control of their homeland.

11.2.2   Yaqui revolt and cultural revision

By 1740 relations between the Mayo and the Spanish had broken down, and the Yaqui and the Mayo joined together to rebel against Spanish oppression. While the Spanish were ultimately victorious, the conflict drove all missionaries in the region out; fatalities numbered over 1000 for the Spanish and over 5000 for the indigenous allies (Spicer 1962). The Jesuits eventually returned and resumed their work in the region (Spicer 1962). The Jesuits encouraged the Yaqui to produce surpluses on their farmlands as a means of economic protection but, when the Jesuits were permanently expelled in 1767, the Yaqui no longer saw a need to maintain this practice. By this point they were able to participate as wage laborers in mines opened in the region, which offered greater economic benefits (Hu-DeHart 1984). For a period the Yaqui were able to utilize the autonomy that the Jesuits encouraged, supplemented economically by their surpluses or work as wage laborers, to resist Spanish domination and retain control of their homeland. They maintained this separation during the War for Independence, during which the Yaqui and Mayo were essentially passive observers and refrained from taking sides (Spicer 1962).

11.2.3   Formation of haciendas and oppression of the Yaqui

After Mexico gained independence, the Yaqui, along with all other indigenous groups, were made citizens of the new nation and were therefore required to pay taxes to and live under the authority of the Mexican government. The Yaqui resisted these requirements and in 1825 Mexican troops were sent to Sonora to collect taxes, protect non-Yaqui settlers, and force the Yaqui to submit to the control of the Mexican government. This marked the beginning of an extended period of oppression by the Mexican government and continued resistance by the Yaqui, who organized revolts in 1825, 1827, 1857–62, and 1899. Each of the Yaqui rebellions in the nineteenth century was met with efforts by the Mexican government to maintain "peace by force" (Spicer 1962: 66), including several massacres of Yaquis and the persecution and occasional execution of Yaqui leaders. The Yaqui continuously responded by reorganizing their leadership and intensifying their resistance efforts, including continued collaboration with the Mayo. A new state constitution was enacted in Sonora in 1873, which decreed that Yaquis and Mayos be denied citizenship if they "maintain the anomalous organization that they have in their towns and rancherías, but allowing the enjoyment [of those rights] to individuals of the same tribes who reside in the organized pueblos of the state" (quoted in Spicer 1962: 67).

Political changes imposed by the Mexican government were compounded by economic changes fueled by an influx of foreign capital. President Porfirio Díaz prioritized national economic development during his rule (1876–1911, a period in Mexican history known as the *Porfiriato*). Díaz, with the cooperation of Luis Torres, the governor of Sonora, established a development program in Sonora that called for "colonization and fruitful exploitation of the rich river lands of the Yaqui and Mayo" (Hu-DeHart 1984: 99).

In particular, the construction of the Sonoran Railroad intensified the oppression of the Yaqui. The Yaqui revolts and general hostility towards the

Mexican government, as covered by the US press, were identified as a hazard to development projects and travel in Sonora. The Yaqui were thus seen as a problem that needed to be controlled, which "justified a violent institutional response" (Guidotti-Hernández 2011: 181). Torres saw a double benefit in colonization efforts – once Yaqui were removed from their land they could provide the necessary labor for the railroad and other capital projects and could be paid less than other Mexican workers given their increasingly limited options for economic sustainability (Hu-DeHart 1984).

It is estimated that by 1890 "less than one-quarter of the entire Yaqui population still lived in their home communities," with many Yaqui left "marginalized and landless" (Erickson 2008: 42). This landless existence resulted in food shortages (Forbes 1957), and several waves of communicable diseases such as yellow fever added further biological stress. In response to food shortages and continued hostility from Mexican troops, some Yaqui began to migrate across the US border to Arizona in 1882 (Spicer 1967). For several decades at the end of the nineteenth century, individual Yaquis were generally either rebels or exploited laborers.

Postcolonial struggles in Sonora mirrored postcolonial political and economic changes around Mexico. These changes were aimed at accelerating assimilation of autonomous groups under the Mexican government. Communal land holdings were dissolved and debt peonage laws were strengthened, both of which facilitated the expansion of haciendas (Meyers *et al.* 2008). Haciendas were predominantly owned by European-descended individuals or families, who employed or enslaved indigenous peoples to produce surpluses for export (Meyers and Carlson 2002; Meyers *et al.* 2008). Haciendas were most common in the Yucatán and primarily employed/enslaved Mayans. However, the Yaqui, along with other indigenous people, were subject to the same treatment in Sonora or sent from Sonora to haciendas in the Yucatán or elsewhere.

By 1902 all Yaquis were required to carry passports as identification; any individual caught without a passport was either subject to arrest and deportation to haciendas in the Yucatán, executed immediately, or sent to labor camps or haciendas in Sonora. More than 2000 adults were deported under these policies; children of those who were deported were sent to live as servants with local families or left to die (Hu-DeHart 1974). Historian Evelyn Hu-DeHart (1974: 83) observes: "One tragic consequence of these procedures was the splitting up of the families, all the more devastating in a society in which the family had been such a strong cultural institution."

Specific practices at the haciendas in Sonora and the Yucatán further amplified the atmosphere of fear and intimidation. A Yaqui man describes in his memoirs the weekly scene at the haciendas: "Out in the middle of the cuartel, Yaqui men were sorted into three lines. Men in one line were to be killed; men in the second line were to be deported; men in the third line were released to work another week" (Moisés *et al.* 1971: 25). The forced labor, deportations, and splitting up of families characteristic of this time resulted in several rescue-style raids on haciendas in Sonora by Yaqui warriors. On May 31, 1902, the *New York Times* (1902c) ran the following story:

> YAQUI INDIANS ON WARPATH
> Kill the Governor of a Ranch and Make Several Raids
>
> TUCSON, Arizona, May 30.-The Yaqui Indians are again on the warpath. On Tuesday a band of Yaquis visited La Carmen, a hacienda near Hermosillo, and killed the governor of the ranch and a servant, besides carrying off the provisions and taking away the best stock on the place. Another band visited the ranch of Don Juan Maytorena, near Guaymas, and raided it. The occupants escaped when they saw the Indians approaching. Several other haciendas were visited and robbed. The situation is serious.

11.2.4 1902 Massacre

Our bioarchaeological research focuses on the skeletal remains of 12 Yaqui individuals involved in one of these rescue-style raids (the *New York Times* story quoted above does not appear to be connected to this rescue raid but does give a sense of the tone utilized in media coverage of Yaqui activities). This rescue raid was followed by a violent encounter between the Yaqui and the Mexican army. Hrdlička (1904: 65–6) provides a brief but detailed account of the events:

> In June, 1902, a force of 200 to 300 free and armed Yaquis descended one evening on four haciendas near Hermosillo and, without doing any damage, took away, partly by force, over 600 Yaqui there employed. The whole party proceeded in the direction of Ures, with the intention of reaching the safe upper Yaqui country. A little southwest of Ures the party had a skirmish with soldiers, whom they defeated. Shortly afterward the Yaquis reached the isolated, rough, but not very high mountain called Sierra de Mazatán, nearly south of Ures. Here they waited for the soldiers. The armed party separated from the rest and took up a strong position on a rugged ridge facing westward. The men, women, and children from the haciendas, with a guard of about a score of armed men, made camp on sloping ground, thickly overgrown with visaches, etc., separated from the ridge by a rough though not very deep barranca. It was in this camp that some of the men commenced to make bows and arrows, rude spears consisting of pointed sticks, and clubs. On the night of June 15th [Note: the correct date is June 8th] a force of about 900 Mexican soldiers, under General Luis Torres, instead of attacking the armed Yaquis from the

front, as the latter expected, rounded the mountain and in the morning surprised the camp of Indians from the haciendas. At the first volley the entire party, except those who were wounded or killed on the spot, ran down the mountain, most of the women and the armed guard directing their flight through the barranca. The soldiers following killed many here and took the rest prisoner. In one part of the gulch resistance was offered by the armed guard. The main armed body of the Yaquis was too far away to actively participate, and when the panic began, that part, with some of the men from the haciendas, escaped over the mountain.

General Luis Torres's official account of this encounter records the Yaqui fatalities: 78 men, 26 women, and 20 children. He records 234 Yaqui taken as prisoners – but does not include in that number male children under the age of 10 – and one injury and no fatalities among the Mexican troops (Troncoso 1977).

11.2.5   Hrdlička in Mexico

The US papers of the time began reporting on the Yaqui fighting around Sierra de Mazatán on June 5, 1902. The *New York Times* (1902b) ran a story entitled "Yaqui Indian Uprising," which mentions the Yaqui fighting in the Mazatán Mountains specifically. The article also states that it was estimated that there were 1000 well-armed Yaqui assembled in the foothills and that the Mexican soldiers were outnumbered and short of both arms and ammunition. On June 8, the same day as the massacre at Sierra de Mazatán, the *New York Times* (1902a) ran another article entitled "No War with Yaqui Indians," in which General Torres denounced the reports of war between the Yaqui and the Mexican troops in Sonora. Torres insisted that the only war that existed was in the mind of the correspondents along the border and that all that was going on was minor skirmishes. As stated above, both President Diáz and General Torres had a vested interest in maintaining regional stability (or at least the image of stability) to keep the influx of foreign capital flowing into Sonora.

All of this might have remained simply a footnote in history had it not been for the actions of Aleš Hrdlička. Hrdlička, an American physical anthropologist, was traveling in Mexico at the time, conducting research for the American Museum of Natural History (AMNH) under the auspices of the Hyde expedition. Three weeks after the Sierra de Mazatán event, Hrdlička, escorted by rurales, traveled to the site and found the bodies of the Yaqui lying where they had fallen. In one area the bodies of 12 women and a little girl were heaped together; he also found two areas in which rows of men had been executed and a cradle-board with the body of a dead infant still secured to it. Hrdlička (1904: 66) stated: "My object in visiting the place was to obtain skeletal material, in which I was successful; but most of the skulls, whether from a peculiar effect of the Mauser cartridges or from the closeness of the range, were so shattered as to be of no use." He collected skeletal remains from 12 individuals, packed them in a zinc-lined box filled with sawdust and shipped them to AMNH (Hrdlička n.d.: 452). He also collected weapons, articles of clothing and jewelry, and the cradle-board (Hrdlička 1904).

On his way to Sierra de Mazatán, Hrdlička passed the body of a Yaqui man, who had been executed the day before, hanging from a tree. He photographed the man from three different angles, taking the time to pose the body (he removes the man's hat for one photograph and then places it back on the man's head in another photograph). Days later he collected the man's cranium after the man's body had been cut down and partially burned.

In 1904 Hrdlička reported on his trip to Sonora in the *American Anthropologist* article "Notes on the Indians of Sonora, Mexico." He referenced his trip to Sierra de Mazatán and the battle that had taken place prior to his arrival (quoted earlier in this chapter). He showcased the artifacts collected and made reference to the 12 skulls in a table highlighting cranial measurements designed to identify "tribal differences in the various body dimensions"; he argued that "when these [differences] can be eliminated or explained, there is good prospect of reducing all the numerous ethnic divisions" of Sonora (Hrdlička 1904: 86).

11.3   Research methods and findings

As stated in the Introduction to this volume, one way to gain a deeper understanding of the motivations and consequences of violence for different categories of participants (e.g. victims, aggressors, captives, warriors) is to examine the different roles that individual agents and groups play and how they interact in a specific location. In our research, we found it critical to analyze our data in context with additional lines of evidence to understand how to categorize the participation of various groups and individuals in the June 8, 1902, event at Sierra de Mazatán. However, we were also mindful of the need to explore bioarchaeological evidence of antemortem stress and trauma to counter the tendency to categorize the entire life history of these individuals based on their roles (e.g. victim, perpetrator) during the June 8, 1902 event. Keeping in mind Klaus's (2012: 37) warning to avoid categorizing victims of structural violence as "passive," we utilized multiple lines of evidence, relying heavily on bioarchaeological data and the historical context outlined earlier in this chapter, to understand the lives of these 13 individuals, not just the circumstances surrounding their deaths.

The violence experienced by the Yaqui was an attempt to reconfigure their social environment. This type of structural violence[1] must never be viewed as a transitory punctuated event that leaves only a memory with no lasting effects. This sort of violence becomes a determining factor that shapes future realities for both individuals and cultures through the imposition of social, political, and economic structures imposed by the dominant (in this case, colonial) powers. Thus we must examine the cultural realities of the Yaqui during this period by their daily practice and not as some static historical event.

Our bioarchaeological analysis focused on cranial remains from 12 individuals and postcranial remains from one individual collected in Sonora by Hrdlička (Table 11.1). The remains (as well as the other material Hrdlička collected) were curated at AMNH from 1902 until their repatriation in 2009.

Individual #99–3972 is the executed man; #99–3982 is a set of postcranial remains from Sierra de Mazatán; the remainder are cranial remains from Sierra de Mazatán. Eleven of the twelve crania include at least a partial mandible. (AMNH located a twelfth mandible after these skeletal remains had been repatriated; as of the time of preparation of this chapter the authors have not had a chance to examine this mandible.) The set of postcranial remains includes all long bones from the right side, the left scapula and clavicle, a cervical vertebra, the fifth lumbar vertebra, the sacrum, and a partial hand and foot. Other than noting that many of the skulls were "so shattered as to be of no use" Hrdlička (1904: 66) did not record how he selected which bones to send to AMNH. However, in the case of the postcranial remains, the inclusion of all the limbs from the right side of the body suggests use as comparative specimens.

Sex was estimated using standard variation in features of the cranium and sacrum (Buikstra and Ubelaker 1994); all 13 individuals were identified as male. Age at death could be estimated for two individuals: #99–3979 was estimated to be less than 17 years based on the fact that the third molars had not yet erupted (Ubelaker 1999) and the spheno-occipital synchondrosis was unfused (Scheuer and Black 2000); #99–3982 was estimated to be 30–39 years based on features of the auricular surface and pubic symphysis (Ubelaker 1999). The remainder of the cranial remains lacked intact cranial sutures due to damage from trauma or missing skeletal elements which, combined with the lack of postcranial remains, left no diagnostic features from which to estimate age. Therefore age for the remaining 10 individuals could only be roughly categorized based on degree of dental wear (e.g. younger adult, older adult).

---

[1] Here we are constructing the idea of structural violence around Bourgois' (2003) idea of "social suffering," Farmer's (2004 and 2006 *et al.*) concept of "structural violence," and Scheper-Hughes's (1992) ideas of "everyday violence."

Table 11.1. *Trauma and pathology analysis of cranial remains from 12 individuals and postcranial remains from one individual collected at Sierra de Mazatán by Hrdlička in 1902.*

Accession number	Trauma	Pathologies
99–3972	Charred cranium	Healed porotic hyperostosis
99–3973	Projectile trauma R parietal boss	Healed porotic hyperostosis
99–3974	Projectile trauma L mastoid; blunt force trauma L side of occipital	Healing cribra orbitalia; 18 LEH on 11 teeth
99–3975	Healed broken nose; healed fracture on frontal	Healed porotic hyperostosis
99–3976	Healed broken nose	Possible periostitis on mandible; two LEH on two teeth
99–3977	Possible healed depression fracture on sagittal suture	Possible healed porotic hyperostosis; nine LEH on five teeth
99–3978	Multiple sites of sharp force trauma/ cut marks	One LEH on one tooth
99–3979	Blunt force trauma R side of occipital and R temporal	Healing porotic hyperostosis; three LEH on three teeth
99–3980	Blunt force trauma on occipital	Healed porotic hyperostosis; three LEH on three teeth
99–3981	No trauma exhibited	No pathologies exhibited
99–3982	No trauma exhibited	Lipping on fifth lumbar vertebrae and body of sacrum
99–3983	No trauma exhibited	Healing porotic hyperostosis and cribra orbitalia; two LEH on one tooth
99–3984	Multiple cut marks	Healed porotic hyperostosis; 12 LEH on eight teeth

LEH, Linear enamel hypoplasia.

All skeletal remains were examined for evidence of pathologies and ante-mortem and perimortem trauma. Again, the small number of skeletal elements present limited the data that could be collected. Our data do allow us to explore individual-level evidence of stress and trauma, and, indeed, every one of the 13 individuals displays evidence of biological stress and/or trauma. Of the individuals represented by a cranium, two-thirds (8 of 12) exhibited at least one linear enamel hypoplasia (LEH) and two-thirds (8 of 12) exhibited healed or healing porotic hyperostosis or cribra orbitalia; 42% (5 of 12) exhibited both. Our ability to contextualize these indicators of stress (Goodman and Rose 1991; Walker *et al.* 2009) is limited, but historical accounts indicate that oppression of the Yaqui continuously intensified after the 1825 Yaqui revolt, the time period that would have encompassed the lifetimes of these 13 individuals. Forbes (1957) estimates that over 75% of the Yaqui population of Sonora was landless by 1890 and those not settled on Yaqui homeland experienced food shortages. In addition, the pattern of LEH distribution suggests multiple stressful episodes within an individual's lifetime: four individuals display more than one LEH on the same tooth. Evidence of antemortem trauma includes two individuals with healed broken noses; one of these individuals also exhibits a healed cranial fracture. The postcranial remains exhibit lipping on L5 and the base of the sacrum.

These data provide individual-level glimpses of stress, yet limitations of the skeletal sample (e.g. small size, limited range of skeletal elements present, exclusively male) restrict our ability to identify population-level patterns regarding trauma and health. In addition, there are no skeletal datasets available with which to make specific comparisons about the biological health of the Yaqui pre- and post-contact or during different periods after the time of European contact. Interpretation of these data is further complicated by the fact that porotic hyperostosis and enamel hypoplasias are prevalent in other populations from the broader geographic region dating from both pre- and post-contact periods (see, for example, Martin *et al.* 1985; Palkovich 1987; Stodder 1994; Stodder *et al.* 2002) and reflect a variety of etiologies. Thus biological markers of stress as evident on the skeletal remains that we examined are not on their own sufficient evidence to theorize structural and direct violence as experienced by the Yaqui. In summary, our biological data allow us to suggest that the individuals we observed were subject to stressful episodes, while our historical research suggests that much of this stress experienced by the Yaqui was related to cultural marginalization. The complexities of the biological and historical data underscore the value of considering these forms of evidence holistically.

11.3.1 *Bioarchaeological understandings of the 1902 massacre*

In our analysis of perimortem trauma related to the 1902 encounter, we excluded data from #99–3972, as this individual was the executed man and was thus not involved in the event. Of the remaining 12 individuals, five exhibit clear evidence of perimortem trauma. Two individuals exhibit projectile trauma consistent with a gunshot wound. One individual (#99–3973) was likely shot while kneeling or lying on the ground, based on the location and angle of the entrance wound. The bullet entered the right side of the skull and exited the left side just behind the ear (Figure 11.2). The extensive trauma produced around the entrance wound is consistent with a high-velocity contact wound to the head. In the second individual (#99–3974), the bullet entered the left side of the skull just behind the ear and exited near the right

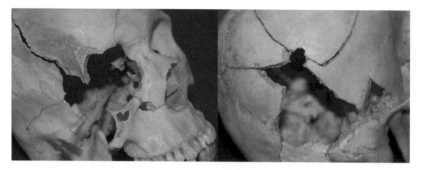

Figure 11.2. Exit wound for 99–3974 (left); entrance wound of 99–3973 (right).

eye (Figure 11.2). The entrance wound is consistent with a high-velocity round entering the skull with minimal deformation because of rapid penetration and absorption of the kinetic energy by the primary fracture or entrance wound.

Two individuals exhibit evidence of blunt force trauma. One individual (99–3980) exhibits two fractures: one on the occipital near lambda and one radiating fracture extending up and around the right parietal nearly to the coronal suture. The shape and dimensions of the fracture (Figure 11.3) are consistent with the butt of a Mauser rifle (as measured by the authors from an example in the National Firearms Collection at the Smithsonian Museum of American History), which was standard issue for the Mexican army at this time. Individual 99–3979 exhibits evidence of blunt force trauma on the right occipital and temporal. This individual also exhibits at least three radiating fractures and additional fractures on the opposite side of the cranium. The severity of the fractures on both of these skulls suggests the assailant was striking the victim with a heavy weapon propelled with great force.

Three individuals exhibit evidence of sharp force trauma with a total of 23 cut marks identified. For each incidence of sharp force trauma we recorded the location, position, length, width, depth, shape, and direction. After data were collected, a vinyl polysiloxane impression was made of the cut marks. Positive casts were then produced, creating an exact replica of the cut marks. These in turn were thin-sectioned and examined microscopically. Microscopic analysis allowed us to identify the geometry of the cut marks as well as to verify the maximum depth and width. These measurements allowed the determination of the amount of soft tissue present on the remains during the time of processing.

Of the three individuals displaying sharp force trauma we identified one incident of perimortem sharp force trauma likely related to the massacre event. In this individual the cut marks are clustered around the right side of the cranium near the external auditory meatus. Two of these cut marks were

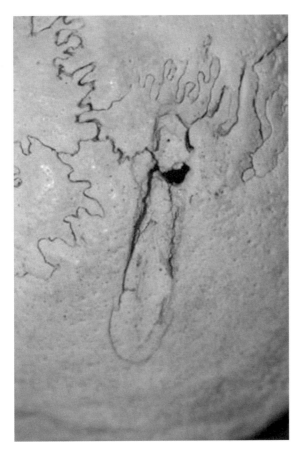

Figure 11.3. Blunt force trauma on individual 99–3980.

produced by a slicing motion; the cut mark pattern and location suggest that the ear was cut off around the time of death. The two other individuals exhibit cut marks that appear to be associated with Hrdlička's actions when collecting the skeletal remains. One individual exhibits a chop mark located on the left lateral aspect of the posterior portion of the ascending ramus. This was likely produced as Hrdlička was removing the cranium from the body. Additional cut marks on these two individuals appear to be related to Hrdlička's efforts to deflesh his specimens after his return to AMNH.

These skeletal data were analyzed in context with four additional lines of evidence to categorize the participation of various groups and individuals in the June 8, 1902, event at Sierra de Mazatán. These were: (1) material culture collected from Sierra de Mazatán by Hrdlička; (2) historical documents;

(3) Hrdlička's journal and photographs; and (4) existing literature on the Yaqui of Sonora. These multiple lines of evidence suggest that this encounter between Mexican troops and the Yaqui should be classified as a massacre rather than a battle. The Yaqui were overpowered by the Mexican army and had significantly fewer and less sophisticated weapons than the soldiers. Approximately 900 Mexican troops attacked a group of Yaqui that likely included a greater number of people, but it is important to remember that the number of Yaqui included men, women, children, and elderly individuals. Recall also that at the time of the encounter the Yaqui were split into two groups – the group that eventually faced the Mexican army included only 20 armed men.

Perhaps more significant than the number of individuals involved is the weaponry each side had at its disposal. Historical accounts, including Hrdlička's journal and his 1904 article, indicate that only the 20 Yaqui guards were armed with guns and ammunition. The rest were armed with bows and arrows, spears, and a macana (a type of knob-headed club) collected by Hrdlička.

Hrdlička's written accounts and photographs detail the aftermath of an extremely violent event – he labels one photograph of victims as the "Slaughter Den." However, without the context of unequal resources – both people-power and weapons – these sources of evidence could be viewed as the remnants of a hard-fought battle resulting in casualties for both sides. As stated earlier, there were no fatalities reported among the Mexican troops, yet the army reported 124 Yaqui fatalities. In addition, it is interesting to note that Hrdlička describes the massacre in no uncertain terms in his journal: "It was a massacre here and more than one of the rocks was still bespattered with dried blood or brains of the victims. But the most pathetic sight was th[e] heap of bodies of killed women among the rocks to one side of the gulch." (n.d.: 451). Yet in his 1904 publication for *American Anthropologist* Hrdlička does not use the term massacre and in fact refers to the site at Sierra de Mazatán as a battlefield. Our historical research suggests that the Yaqui were outnumbered by an army with vastly superior firepower, thus the level of trauma evident in Hrdlička's records, the material culture, and the skeletal remains become further evidence for a massacre of the Yaqui by the Mexican army rather than a battle fought with relatively equal resources on both sides.

11.4   Repatriation

After completing our analysis of the human remains we brought this information to the attention of Robert Valencia (Vice Chairman of the Yaqui tribe), and he in turn brought it to the Pascua Yaqui tribal council. This started the repatriation process. Complex negotiations were required to establish how various Yaqui tribal groups in the USA and Mexico would be involved before a formal request was made to AMNH for repatriation of the Yaqui skeletal remains and objects of material culture. AMNH agreed that they would return the human remains and material culture to the Yaqui if the National Institute of Anthropology and History (INAH) in Mexico would permit it.

After several long negotiations with the regional INAH office in Sonora and the national office in Mexico City it was decided that AMNH would turn the material over to INAH and they would then return the material to the Yaqui. It was also decided that this transfer of power would take place during a formal signing ceremony in New York at AMNH during the fall of 2009. After the ceremony the Yaqui delegation brought the Yaqui remains back to their homeland. The delegation was met by ceremonial dancers and the Yoeme American legion post color guard who then processed with the remains to the church so the community could pay homage to their relatives. Vice Chairman Valencia observed that even though we (the bioarchaeologists) could not provide specific identifications for any of these individuals, the community felt that they deserved the full honors generally reserved for elders in high standing (Figure 11.4).

The repatriation of the *guerreros* ("warriors") Yaqui had tremendous impact beyond the descendant community via coverage and discussion in countless

Figure 11.4. On November 16, 2009, the remains of the Yaqui were baptized and ceremonially interred in Viacam, Mexico.

blogs, websites, and news articles. This is because the cooperation and speed of this international repatriation was unprecedented. However, it was not precedent-setting. It is important to remember that one of the principal reasons this repatriation was allowed to go forward is that the collection was not considered archaeological material by AMNH or INAH but rather it was seen as a historic massacre site and thus a human rights issue. Thus AMNH did not give material collected in Mexico to a culturally affiliated US federally recognized tribe as part of the Native American Graves Protection and Repatriation Act (NAGPRA), and INAH did not return archaeological material to a Mexican tribe.

For the Yaqui people this repatriation had a profound impact on the community and reopened old wounds and traumatic memories. The social reality of the Yaqui people was affected by the lives, deaths, and prolonged burial and grieving process for *los guerreros*. Their repatriation and their stories stirred memories of violence that had a profound impact on generations of people who had not directly experienced the violence but whose mothers, fathers, and grandparents had.

11.5   Body as heritage

> We often ask ourselves what would have happened if our ancestors had not fought to conserve our territory for the generations of today? A great uncertainty comes over us, and we deeply value the bravery of our ancestors who gave their lives to inherit a wide area of land that, to us, clearly denotes the "Yaqui territory". These stories are the ones that sustain us on a daily basis. All Yaquis, from a very tender age, listen to tales that speak not only of the struggle and resistance of our distant ancestors but also of our living old folk. (Molina 2000: 99)

This quote demonstrates the tremendous value that the Yaqui place on knowing and understanding their heritage. Heritage values and activities make the past a dynamic part of the present and future. In the case of the Yaqui skeletal remains, the bioarchaeological analysis provided a framework under which the bodies of the dead become a site of heritage. Human remains are themselves "objects" of material culture, as they can bear artifacts of cultural, political, social, and historical experiences (Douglas 1966; Foucault 1973; Pérez 2012; Scheper-Hughes and Lock 1987; Sofaer 2006; Verdery 1999). This includes tangible proof of violent pasts that can attest to various forms of suffering (Moore 2009; Moshenska 2009) and serve as a form of "truth-telling" when violent pasts are ignored or denied (Williams 2007).

During ceremonies and activities associated with the repatriation of the Yaqui remains, one of the authors of this chapter (VRP) was asked, along with a colleague, Dr. J. Andrew Darling, to give a series of presentations to the tribe. We were given the great honor of sharing the story of *los guerreros* with

Figure 11.5. As part of ceremonies and activities associated with the repatriation Ventura Pérez was asked to show the children the skeletal remains and explain the evidence of violence so that the children could understand the sacrifice of the earlier generation.

the children of the Rio Yaqui at the pueblo of Vicam, including showing them how we (bioarchaeologists) learn about their ancestors by studying the skeletal remains (Figure 11.5).

Meanings and knowledge associated with the bodies of the dead are recognized and shared to convey particular messages – in the case of the Yaqui, the body becomes a vehicle for telling the story of past violence because the body itself reflects evidence of that violence. Because "the skeleton represents human life at its most universal, stripped of the apparent differences that can divide the living" (Alberti *et al.* 2009: 135) there is perhaps no more powerful political statement than to use the bodies of victims of violence as a means for others to reflect on the meanings and impacts of violence.

11.6   Conclusion

Considering political, social, and economic factors has allowed us to expand our bioarchaeological analysis of the skeletal remains of 13 Yaqui individuals from Sonora, Mexico. Based on various lines of evidence we concluded that evidence of biological stress and trauma in these individuals demonstrates the persistent and pervasive nature of structural and direct violence experienced by the Yaqui in the nineteenth and early twentieth centuries. In addition, while we are mindful of the need to refrain from characterizing these individuals' lives based on the circumstances of their deaths, we concluded that the 12 individuals collected from Sierra de Mazatán in 1902 were victims of a violent massacre perpetrated by Mexican troops.

Oppression and persecution of the Yaqui continued through the Mexican revolution and beyond. The last armed conflict between Yaquis in the USA and US troops occurred in 1918; in 1927 the Yaquis of Sonora engaged in their last major battle with Mexican troops and lost. While Yaqui tribes on both sides of the border have been granted recognition by their respective governments, the Yaquis characterize their history as a "long history of struggle" (Molina 2000: 98). Our bioarchaeological analysis and the 2009 repatriation activities brought this heritage of Yaqui resistance and resilience to younger generations, making the past a dynamic part of the present.

Acknowledgments

We thank Dr. Debra Martin and Cheryl Anderson for inviting us to participate in the special poster session at the 81st Annual Meeting of the American Association of Physical Anthropologists and contribute to this volume. We are grateful to the leadership of the Pascua Yaqui and traditional Yaqui in Mexico, particularly Vice Chairman Robert Valencia, for their guidance and collaboration on this project and allowing us to use photographs of the skeletal remains and reburial of their ancestors. This research benefited significantly from the efforts of our colleague Dr. J. Andrew Darling. We would also like to thank Dr. Randall McGuire and María Elisa Villalpando Canchola. Finally, we are grateful for the helpful comments offered by one anonymous reviewer. Any errors or omissions remain our responsibility.

References

Agarwal, S. C. & Glencross, B. A. (2011). Building a social bioarchaeology. In: Agarwal, S. C. & Glencross, B. A. (eds.) *Social Bioarchaeology*. Malden: Wiley-Blackwell, 1–11.

Alberti, S. J. M. M., Bienkowski, P. & Chapman, M. J. (2009). Should we display the dead? *Museum and Society*, **7**, 133–49.

Bourgois, P. (2003). Crack and the political economy of social suffering. *Addiction Research and Theory*, **11**, 31–7.

Buikstra, J. E. & Ubelaker, D. H. (eds.) (1994). *Standards for Data Collection from Human Skeletal Remains. Proceedings of a Seminar at the Field Museum of Natural History*. Fayetteville: Arkansas Archaeological Survey, Research Series, No. 44.

Douglas, M. (1966). *Purity and Danger: An Analysis of the Concepts of Pollution and Taboo*. London: Routledge and Keegan Paul.

Erickson, K. C. (2008). *Yaqui Homeland and Homeplace: The Everyday Production of Ethnic Identity*. Tucson: University of Arizona Press.

Farmer, P. (2004). An anthropology of structural violence. *Current Anthropology*, **45**, 305–25.

Farmer, P., Nizeye, B., Stulac, S. & Ksehavjee, S. (2006). Structural violence and clinical medicine. *PLoS Medicine*, **3**, 1686–91.

Forbes, J. D. (1957). Historical survey of the Indians of Sonora, 1821–1910. *Ethnohistory*, **4**, 335–68.

Foucault, M. (1973). *The Birth of the Clinic: An Archaeology of Medical Perception*. New York: Pantheon Books.

Goodman, A. H. & Leatherman, T. L. (eds.) (1998). *Building a New Biocultural Synthesis: Political-Economic Perspectives on Human Biology*. Ann Arbor: University of Michigan Press.

Goodman, A. H. & Rose, J. C. (1991). Dental enamel hypoplasias as indicators of nutritional status. In: Kelley, M. A. & Larsen, C. S. (eds.) *Advances in Dental Anthropology*. New York: Wiley-Liss, 279–93.

Guidotti-Hernández, N. M. (2011). *Unspeakable Violence: Remapping U.S. and Mexican National Imaginaries*. Durham: Duke University Press.

Hrdlička, A. (1904). Notes on the Indians of Sonora, Mexico. *American Anthropologist*, **6**, 51–89.

(n.d.). *Personal Journal*. Unpublished.

Hu-DeHart, E. (1974). Development and rural rebellion: pacification of the Yaquis in the late Porfiriato. *The Hispanic American Historical Review*, **54**, 72–93.

(1984). *Yaqui Resistance and Survival: The Struggle for Land and Autonomy 1821–1910*. Madison: University of Wisconsin Press.

Klaus, H. D. (2012). The bioarchaeology of structural violence: a theoretical model and a case study. In: Martin, D. L., Harrod, R. P. & Pérez, V. R. (eds.) *The Bioarchaeology of Violence*. Gainesville: University of Florida Press, 29–62.

Larsen, C. S. (1999). *Bioarchaeology: Interpreting Behavior from the Human Skeleton*. Cambridge: Cambridge University Press.

Martin, D. L. & Frayer, D. W. (eds.) (1997). *Troubled Times: Violence and Warfare in the Past*. Amsterdam: Gordon and Breach.

Martin, D. L., Goodman, A. H. & Armelagos, G. J. (1985). Skeletal pathologies as indicators of quality and quantity of diet. In: Gilbert, R. I. & Mielke, J. H. (eds.) *The Analysis of Prehistoric Diets*. Orlando: Academic Press, 227–79.

Martin, D. L., Harrod, R. P. & Pérez, V. R. (eds.) (2012a). *The Bioarchaeology of Violence*. Gainesville: University Press of Florida.

Martin, D. L., Harrod, R. P. & Pérez, V. R. (2012b). Introduction: bioarchaeology and the study of violence. In: Martin, D. L., Harrod, R. P. & Pérez, V. R. (eds.) *The Bioarchaeology of Violence*. Gainesville: University of Florida Press, 1–10.

Meyers, A. D. & Carlson, D. L. (2002). Peonage, power relations, and the built environment at Hacienda Tabi, Yucatán, Mexico. *International Journal of Historical Archaeology*, **6**, 225–52.

Meyers, A. D., Harvey, A. S. & Levithol, S. A. (2008). Houselot refuse disposal and geochemistry at a late 19th century hacienda village in Yucatán, Mexico. *Journal of Field Archaeology*, **33**, 371–88.

Moisés, R., Kelley, J. H. & Holden, W. C. (1971). *A Yaqui Life: The Personal Chronicle of a Yaqui Indian*. Lincoln: University of Nebraska Press.

Molina, H. (2000). Historic autonomies: Yaqui autonomy. In: Mayor, A. B. C. Y. (ed.) *Indigenous Autonomy in Mexico*. Copenhagen: International Work Group for Indigenous Affairs, 98–116.

Moore, L. M. (2009). (Re)Covering the past, remembering trauma: the politics of commemoration at sites of atrocity. *Journal of Public and International Affairs*, **20**, 47–64.

Moshenska, G. (2009). Resonant materiality and violent remembering: archaeology, memory and bombing. *International Journal of Heritage Studies*, **15**, 44–56.

New York Times. (1902a). No War with Yaqui Indians, June 8.

    (1902b). Yaqui Indian Uprising, June 5.

    (1902c). Yaqui Indians on the Warpath, May 31.

Palkovich, A. M. (1987). Endemic disease patterns in paleopathology: porotic hyperostosis. *American Journal of Physical Anthropology*, **74**, 527–37.

Pérez, V. R. (2012). The politicization of the dead: violence as performance, politics as usual. In: Martin, D. L., Harrod, R. P. & Pérez, V. R. (eds.) *The Bioarchaeology of Violence*. Gainesville: University of Florida Press, 13–28.

Sandoval, E. Q. (2009). Yaqui history. Available: www.pascuayaqui-nsn.gov. [Accessed November 10, 2012.]

Scheper-Hughes, N. (1992). *Death without Weeping: The Violence of Everday Life in Brazil*. Berkeley: University of California Press.

Scheper-Hughes, N. & Lock, M. M. (1987). The mindful body: a prolegomenon to future work in medical anthropology. *Medical Anthropology Quarterly, New Series*, **1**, 6–41.

Scheuer, L. & Black, S. M. (2000). *Developmental Juvenile Osteology*. San Diego: Elsevier Academic Press.

Sofaer, J. R. (2006). *The Body as Material Culture: A Theoretical Osteoarchaeology*. Cambridge: Cambridge University Press.

Spicer, E. H. (1962). *Cycles of Conquest: The Impact of Spain, Mexico, and the United States on the Indians of the Southwest, 1533–1960*. Tucson: University of Arizona Press.

    (1967). *Pasqua: A Yaqui Village in Arizona*. Tucson: University of Arizona Press.

    (1980). *The Yaquis: A Cultural History*. Tucson: University of Arizona Press.

Steckel, R. H. & Rose, J. C. (eds.) (2002). *The Backbone of History: Health and Nutrition in the Western Hemisphere*. Cambridge: Cambridge University Press.

Stodder, A. L. W. (1994). Bioarchaeological investigations of protohistoric Pueblo health and demography. In: Larsen, C. S. & Milner, G. R. (eds.) *In the Wake of Contact: Biological Responses to Conquest*. New York: Wiley-Liss, 97–107.

Stodder, A. L. W., Martin, D. L., Goodman, A. H. & Reff, D. T. (2002). Cultural longevity in the face of biological stress: the Anasazi of the American Southwest. In: Steckel, R. H. & Rose, J. C. (eds.) *The Backbone of History: Health and Nutrition in the Western Hemisphere.* Cambridge: Cambridge University Press, 481–505.

Troncoso, F. D. (1977). *Las Guerros Con Las Tribus Yaqui Y Mayo, Tomo Ii.* Mexico: Instituto Nacional Indigenista.

Tung, T. A. (2012). Violence against women: differential treatment of local and foreign females in the heartland of the Wari Empire, Peru. In: Martin, D. L., Harrod, R. P. & Pérez, V. R. (eds.) *The Bioarchaeology of Violence.* Gainesville: University of Florida Press, 180–98.

Ubelaker, D. H. (1999). *Human Skeletal Remains: Excavation, Analysis, Interpretation,* 3rd edn. New Brunswick, Aldine Transaction.

Verdery, K. (1999). *The Political Lives of Dead Bodies: Reburial and Postsocialist Change.* New York: Columbia University Press.

Walker, P. L., Bathurst, R. R., Richman, R., Gjerdrum, T. & Andrushko, V. A. (2009). The causes of porotic hyperostosis and cribra orbitalia: a reappraisal of the iron-deficiency-anemia hypothesis. *American Journal of Physical Anthropology,* **139**, 109–25.

Williams, P. (2007). *Memorial Museums: The Global Rush to Commemorate Atrocities.* Oxford: Berg.

12 Interpreting skeletal trauma and violence at Grasshopper Pueblo (AD 1275–1400)

KATHRYN M. BAUSTIAN

12.1 Introduction: bioarchaeology and violence

Within archaeological contexts, evidence of warfare and interpersonal violence is most frequently observed in weaponry, defensive site layout and architecture, and catastrophic site abandonment and/or destruction (Kuckelman *et al.* 2002; LeBlanc 1999; LeBlanc and Rice 2001; Tuggle and Reid 2001). Bioarchaeological evidence of violence is most easily observed in perimortem lethal trauma to the skeleton (i.e. projectiles embedded in bone, scalping, etc.) and mortuary treatments that suggest social differentiation of subjugated members of a community. Analysis of human skeletal remains can contribute additional information for reconstructions of human response to environmental change, population aggregation, and changing social relationships. Increases in violence in the American Southwest during the late prehistoric period have been attributed to degrading environments and greater competition over scarce resources, particularly food (LeBlanc 1999; 2006; LeBlanc and Register 2003).

This chapter examines the impact of rapid cultural change at the prehistoric settlement of Grasshopper Pueblo in the American Southwest. This community provides an excellent opportunity to interpret the role and meaning of violence because of the culmination of multiethnic encounters, environmental marginality, agricultural intensification, and climatic stress due to droughts during its occupation that could have led to conflict and warfare. Violence at Grasshopper has previously been downplayed or dismissed as researchers carried out analyses that considered only single or a few factors as evidence (Allen *et al.* 1985; Birkby 1982; Reid and Whittlesey 1999; Tuggle and Reid

Bioarchaeological and Forensic Perspectives on Violence: How Violent Death is Interpreted from Skeletal Remains, ed. D. L. Martin and C. P. Anderson. Published by Cambridge University Press. © Cambridge University Press 2014.

2001; Whittlesey 1978). Collective consideration of factors is necessary in violence studies, and the addition of bioarchaeological data can greatly enhance interpretation and reconstructions of the past. The ability to bring together a great deal of archaeological contextual information and biological data from human skeletal remains at Grasshopper Pueblo provides an opportunity to better understand the role of violence in this community.

Using bioarchaeological data, including osteological indicators of trauma and stress, this systematic analysis explores the use of lethal and non-lethal violence within the multiethnic population at the pueblo. It uses a biocultural model to integrate osteological data with cultural and environmental variables to increase understanding of the community. Analysis of the human remains from Grasshopper Pueblo has been undertaken by many previous researchers. Aspects of child health (Berry 1985; Hinkes 1983; Schultz *et al.* 2007), adult diet (Ezzo 1994), and musculoskeletal indicators (Perry 2004) have shown the population to be under stress during occupation of the community. Isotope data and biodistance data (Birkby 1982; McClelland 2003) have been useful to demonstrate migration in the region and to distinguish local from non-local individuals. The results of this analysis are complementary to these prior investigations of Grasshopper Pueblo and build on the interpretation of the social dynamics of the community in particular and the greater region as well.

12.2   Background

This case study examines evidence for shifts in social structure among mountain Mogollon Pueblo populations during the fourteenth century AD. The specific region of study is the Grasshopper Plateau, located in the mountains of east-central Arizona. Populations occupying this region engaged in a hunting and gathering subsistence early in their chronology and shifted toward a reliance on agriculture later on. The mountainous landscape has been described as poorly suited for intense agriculture (Reid and Whittlesey 1999), therefore adaptation was likely a key factor for successful life in the region. Unsuccessful adaptation to such a lifestyle may have ultimately led to depopulation of the area by AD 1400, however.

The Grasshopper community experienced major growth during the late thirteenth and early fourteenth centuries AD. Three major room blocks (1, 2, and 3) and several smaller room blocks were constructed and expanded as migration in the region led to aggregation of a large population (Figure 12.1). Movement of both Ancestral Puebloan and Mogollon populations during this time resulted in several multiethnic communities, Grasshopper Pueblo being the largest (Riggs 2001). Archaeological excavation of a large portion of the

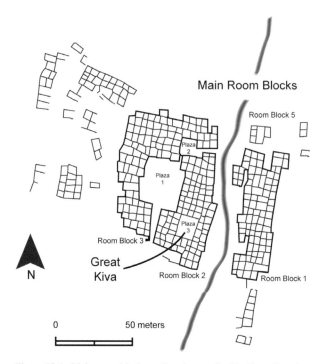

Figure 12.1. Main room blocks at Grasshopper Pueblo (from Baustian *et al.* 2012).

community revealed materials (e.g. ceramics) and architectural features (e.g. wall openings) of both Mogollon and Ancestral Puebloan culture groups. Room Block 2 was home to local and nearby regional people while more migrants from the Mogollon Rim, Chevelon Valley, and more distant Grasshopper regions mostly occupied Room Blocks 1 and 3 (Ezzo and Price 2002).

Although Grasshopper Pueblo experienced a large influx of outsiders, the community appears to have remained relatively egalitarian (Reid 1989; Whittlesey and Reid 2001). Mortuary patterns do not suggest strict social hierarchies with subordinate subgroups in the population (Whittlesey 1978). Whittlesey (1978) found mortuary patterns to be mostly homogenous among Grasshopper burials. Studies (Clark 1967; Griffin 1969; Whittlesey 1978) have debated the presence of higher status groups; however, only a few burials (such as Burial 140) with numerous grave goods indicate differential social status in the community. Alternatively, inference of social ranking through number of grave items may be inaccurate as Whittlesey's ethnographic review of Puebloan mortuary rites suggested that items in a burial can be more reflective of those performing the mortuary rites than the individual buried. Based upon grave location, those buried in the Great Kiva may have been members of a distinct group, possibly characterized by ceremonial or social importance (Whittlesey 1978). Isotope data from Ezzo (1991; 1992; Ezzo and Price 2002) demonstrate that both local and non-local people were buried in the Great Kiva. Considering information from both Ezzo and Whittlesey, those in the Great Kiva may have been members of the same kin group and that afforded them a particular social significance in the community (Whittlesey 1978). This would have been especially important if non-local females were marrying local males through intermarriage practices (Ezzo and Price 2002; Whittlesey 2002).

Other forms of data have not yet indicated hierarchical subgroups (based on social ranking, ethnic group, or other criteria) at Grasshopper Pueblo. Only Ezzo's (1991; 1993) data indicate that differential access to foods occurred between early period males and females at Grasshopper Pueblo. This finding does not prove higher status among males, however, and both sexes had similar diets later on in the occupation.

The data from this analysis present another measure of social interaction and organization of the population at Grasshopper Pueblo. By examining evidence of trauma and health and comparing results with archaeological contextual data and other biological indicators, this analysis further explores the presence of separate groups in the community. An understanding of the social dynamics of Grasshopper Pueblo will allow better interpretation of patterns of violence.

12.3   Analysis

The skeletal assemblage from Grasshopper Pueblo was analyzed at the Arizona State Museum in Tucson, Arizona. Of the 674 burials in the assemblage, individuals of approximately 15 years and older were analyzed. Poor preservation and extensive fragmentation prevented inclusion of some individuals and ultimately a sample of 187 adult skeletons was included in the analysis. Individuals in the sample had been excavated from numerous areas of the settlement, including room blocks, plazas, extramural areas, and the Great Kiva. These individuals represent both early and late period Grasshopper burials.

A biological profile was established for each individual using standard osteological techniques outlined by Buikstra and Ubelaker (1994). Pathological processes such as infectious disease and evidence of physical stress were documented, and additional analyses were completed to document traumatic injuries of the cranium and postcranial skeleton. Both lethal (unhealed) and non-lethal (healed) injuries can offer information about interpersonal conflict and the use of violence among past populations (Brink *et al.* 1998; Scott and Buckley 2010; Walker 1989, 1997, 2001). For communities such as that at Grasshopper Pueblo, documenting patterns of injuries has the potential to trace behavioral patterns of individuals as well as groups (e.g. different sexes or subgroups) and the community as a whole. Non-lethal trauma, in particular, is especially informative for assessing the scale and duration of violence within a time period and/or region.

Non-lethal cranial trauma was categorized as facial fractures (e.g. nasal, zygomatic, mandibular) or cranial depression fractures (CDFs). CDFs occur in fairly predictable ways when a blunt object strikes the cranial vault. When the injury does not kill the victim, the bone slowly heals and the CDF remains as a permanent marker of the injury (Merbs 1989; Walker 1989). All CDFs were assessed for size and severity as well as location and state of healing. Injuries were measured with digital calipers for length, width, and depth. Healing was scored on an ordinal scale of 0 to 4 to indicate no healing up to completely healed. The larger and deeper the injury, the more likely it was to be qualified as severe. Severe CDFs were quantified by depths greater than 0.7 mm and having a total area of 150.0 mm^2 or greater (although most had areas much larger). Lastly, the location of each injury was noted with respect to the bone(s) affected and the specific area of trauma.

Postcranial fractures were categorized using standards described by Lovell (1997; 2008) and Galloway (1999). Of most interest was the location and state of healing of each injury. Documentation of trauma to the postcranial skeleton was important for interpretation of behavior of the individual, particularly if the cranium also had non-lethal trauma – research has shown that these injuries can have neurological effects that predispose the individual to recurring injury which may not be violent in nature (Blackmer and Marshall 1999; Caufeild *et al.* 2004; Hedges *et al.* 1995). Lastly, if any information regarding the sequence of injuries could be obtained, it was noted.

Finally, select musculoskeletal stress markers (MSMs) were assessed for level of development so that evidence of activity patterns might be inferred for the individuals at Grasshopper Pueblo. MSMs were analyzed through a ranked scoring of development (Mariotti *et al.* 2007) and identification of presence or absence of specific changes in bone morphology (Capasso *et al.* 1999). Development of MSMs on the major long bones of the arms and legs (e.g. pectoralis major, deltoideus, brachioradialis, gluteus maximus, iliopsoas) was documented to tease out patterns in activities varying by sex and social status.

12.4   Results

Results of the analysis of the Grasshopper Pueblo sample have previously been reported by Baustian and colleagues (2012), but are summarized here again.

Table 12.1. *Distribution of CDFs by sex and age groups.*

Sex	Young adult	Middle adult	Old adult	Adult	Total
Male	40% (8/20)	30% (12/40)	31% (5/16)	50% (1/2)	33% (26/78)
Female	41% (17/41)	17% (6/36)	33% (7/21)	80% (4/5)	33% (34/103)
Indeterminate sex	67% (2/3)	0% (0/1)	50% (1/2)	0% (0/0)	50% (3/6)
Total	42% (27/64)	23% (18/77)	33% (13/39)	71% (5/7)	34% (63/187)

The relationship of CDFs and distribution among subgroups of the population is of most importance for interpreting behaviors and relationships. The occurrence of CDFs for both sexes and all age groups is presented in Table 12.1.

The distribution of CDFs among the sample of 187 individuals was fairly equal for both sexes. Approximately one-third (34%; $n = 63$) of crania exhibited at least one CDF. This included 34 females (33% of 103 females), 26 males (33% of 78 males), and three individuals of unknown sex (50% of six individuals). No statistical difference was found for presence of CDFs among either sex (Fisher's exact two-tailed test; $P = 0.8739$). For the 63 individuals exhibiting CDFs, 38% ($n = 24$) had multiple injuries while the rest had only one. Both males and females had similar occurrences of single or multiple cranial injuries. The majority of CDFs were not severe; only five CDFs were larger in size and deep enough to be qualified as severe.

Analysis of cranial trauma by age at death showed that young adults (15–34 years of age) frequently incurred injuries (42%; $n = 27/64$). Those who died as middle (35–49 years of age) and old (over 50 years of age) adults also had CDFs but at lower frequencies (23% and 33%, respectively). It cannot be determined when in the lives of these older age groups each CDF occurred as almost all were completely healed. Only one old male and four young females had cranial injuries that could be categorized as perimortem, or occurring around the time of death. It is possible that these five CDFs contributed to the deaths of the individuals.

All but three individuals in the dataset could be linked with Ezzo's (1991) isotope data for temporal occupation (Early or Late), and 53 individuals could be linked to isotope data for geographic origin (Table 12.2). Once again, there was approximately equal distribution of individuals with CDFs from the Early period (33%; $n = 43/130$) and from the Late period (36%; $n = 19/53$). For the 53 individuals in the sample that were determined to be local ($n = 21$) and non-local ($n = 32$), rates of CDF trauma were somewhat different between groups. Although the sex ratio was approximately equal for both groups, 48% ($n = 10/21$) of individuals with local geographic origin had CDFs, while 28% ($n = 9/32$) of non-locals had CDFs. These results do not suggest that non-locals were targeted for violent attack.

Table 12.2. *Grasshopper Pueblo burial dataset.*

Burial number	Sex	Age: lower estimate	Age: upper estimate	Age category	CDFs present	Origin	Burial location	Occupation period	Average depth of CDFs
1	Probable female	20	29	Young adult	0	N/A	Extramural?	Early	N/A
2	Male	15	24	Young adult	1	N/A	Extramural	Early	1.20 mm
3	Female	30	35	Young adult	2	N/A	Extramural	Early	1.39 mm
5	Female	25	29	Young adult	0	N/A	Extramural	Early	N/A
6	Female	40	49	Middle adult	3	N/A	Extramural	Late	0.54 mm
7	Male	60	100	Old adult	0	N/A	Extramural	Early	N/A
8	Female	30	34	Middle adult	3	N/A	Extramural	Early	0.46 mm
10	Male	25	35	Young adult	0	N/A	Extramural	Early	N/A
14	Female	Indeterminate	Indeterminate	Young adult	1	N/A	Extramural	Early	0.78 mm
15	Female	30	35	Middle adult	0	N/A	Extramural	Early	N/A
17	Female	18	25	Young adult	1	N/A	Extramural	Early	0.70 mm
20	Female	45	49	Middle adult	0	N/A	Room Block 1	Early	N/A
26	Probable male	44	50	Middle adult	0	N/A	Extramural	Late	N/A
30	Female	28	39	Middle adult	1	N/A	Room Block 1	Early	0.80 mm
35	Probable female	50	59	Old adult	2	N/A	Extramural	Early	0.83 mm
36	Male	Indeterminate	Indeterminate	Adult	2	N/A	Extramural	Early	N/A
38	Female	25	30	Young adult	1	N/A	Extramural	Early	0.57 mm
39	Probable male	50	100	Old adult	4	N/A	Extramural	Early	0.72 mm
40	Probable male	45	49	Middle adult	0	N/A	Extramural	Early	N/A
41	Female	25	29	Young adult	0	N/A	Extramural	Early	N/A
42	Probable male	25	34	Young adult	0	N/A	Extramural	Early	N/A
43	Probable female	30	34	Middle adult	1	N/A	Extramural	Late	0.39 mm
51A	Probable female	Indeterminate	Indeterminate	Adult	2	N/A	Room Block 2	Early	0.62 mm
52	Female	40	50	Middle adult	0	N/A	Room Block 2	Early	N/A
56	Female	18	22	Young adult	0	Local	Room Block 2	Early	N/A
57	Female	30	39	Middle adult	0	Non-local	Room Block 1	Early	N/A

	Sex			Age			Provenience		
62	Male	40	49	Middle adult	0	N/A	Room Block 1	Late	N/A
63	Female	25	29	Young adult	0	N/A	Room Block 2	Early	N/A
64	Female	35	39	Middle adult	0	N/A	Extramural	Late	N/A
65	Probable male	Indeterminate	Indeterminate	Adult	0	N/A	Room Block 1	Early	0.54 mm
68	Female	Indeterminate	Indeterminate	Adult	2	Local	Great Kiva	Early	N/A
76	Male	50	100	Old adult	1	N/A	Great Kiva	Early	1.04 mm
80	Female	25	29	Young adult	0	N/A	Plaza 1	Late	N/A
81	Female	18	21	Young adult	0	N/A	Extramural	Early	N/A
82	Male	20	25	Young adult	0	N/A	Extramural	Early	N/A
83	Indeterminate	20	25	Young adult	0	N/A	Extramural	Early	N/A
84	Female	25	30	Young adult	0	N/A	Extramural	Early	N/A
88	Female	20	25	Young adult	0	N/A	Extramural	Early	N/A
89	Probable male	50	60	Old adult	0	N/A	Extramural	Late	N/A
91	Probable female	40	50	Middle adult	0	N/A	Extramural	Late	N/A
93A	Indeterminate	44	50	Middle adult	0	N/A	Extramural	Late	N/A
112	Female	35	45	Middle adult	3	Non-local	Great Kiva	Early	0.58 mm
115	Female	20	25	Young adult	1	Non-local	Room Block 2	Early	2.06 mm
116	Male	45	55	Middle adult	0	N/A	Room Block 2	Early	N/A
129	Male	22	28	Young adult	0	Local	Great Kiva	Early	N/A
133	Indeterminate	30	35	Young adult	1	N/A	Room Block 2	Early	0.79 mm
140	Male	40	45	Middle adult	0	N/A	Great Kiva	Early	N/A
141	Male	20	24	Young adult	1	N/A	Room Block 2	Early	0.78 mm
142	Probable female	30	34	Young adult	1	Local	Great Kiva	Early	0.53 mm
143	Female	18	21	Young adult	1	Local	Great Kiva	Early	3.38 mm
144	Probable female	40	55	Middle adult	0	N/A	Great Kiva	Early	N/A
150	Female	25	30	Young adult	0	Local	Room Block 2	Early	N/A
152	Female	15	18	Young adult	1	Local	Great Kiva	Early	0.78 mm
158	Male	25	30	Young adult	0	Non-local	Room Block 2	Early	N/A
163	Probable male	45	55	Middle adult	0	N/A	Great Kiva	Early	N/A
164	Female	16	20	Young adult	0	Non-local	Great Kiva	Early	N/A
166	Male	35	39	Middle adult	0	N/A	Extramural	Early	N/A

Table 12.2. (*cont.*)

Burial number	Sex	Age: lower estimate	Age: upper estimate	Age category	CDFs present	Origin	Burial location	Occupation period	Average depth of CDFs
168	Male	45	49	Middle adult	0	N/A	Room Block 2	Early	N/A
171	Indeterminate	50	100	Old adult	0	N/A	Great Kiva	Early	N/A
174	Female	50	100	Old adult	0	N/A	Great Kiva	Early	N/A
175	Female	45	55	Middle adult	0	N/A	Great Kiva	Early	N/A
178	Female	23	30	Young adult	0	Non-local	Great Kiva	Early	N/A
184	Female	35	50	Middle adult	0	N/A	Great Kiva	Early	N/A
187	Female	40	50	Middle adult	0	Non-local	Great Kiva	Early	N/A
188	Female	22	30	Young adult	0	Local	Great Kiva	Early	N/A
190	Male	30	39	Middle adult	0	Local	Great Kiva	Early	N/A
194	Female	50	100	Old adult	0	N/A	Great Kiva	Early	N/A
195	Female	40	50	Middle adult	0	N/A	Great Kiva	Early	N/A
196	Male	35	40	Middle adult	1	N/A	Great Kiva	Early	0.32 mm
198	Female	40	50	Old adult	0	N/A	Great Kiva	Early	N/A
199	Male	23	30	Young adult	2	N/A	Extramural	Late	1.09 mm
200	Male	45	100	Old adult	0	N/A	Extramural	Late	N/A
201	Female	50	100	Old adult	0	N/A	Extramural	Late	N/A
203	Female	19	23	Young adult	0	N/A	Extramural	Late	N/A
206	Female	30	40	Middle adult	0	N/A	Extramural	Late	N/A
208	Male	35	45	Middle adult	0	Local	Room Block 2	Early	N/A
209	Male	40	50	Middle adult	0	N/A	Room Block 2	Early	N/A
210	Female	45	60	Old adult	0	N/A	Room Block 2	Early	N/A
211	Male	40	50	Middle adult	0	N/A	Room Block 2	Early	N/A
216	Female	45	55	Middle adult	0	N/A	Room Block 2	Early	N/A
217	Probable female	50	59	Old adult	0	N/A	Room Block 2	Early	N/A
222	Indeterminate	45	60	Old adult	1	N/A	Room Block 2	Early	2.11 mm
225A	Probable female	30	39	Middle adult	0	Non-local	Room Block 2	Early	N/A

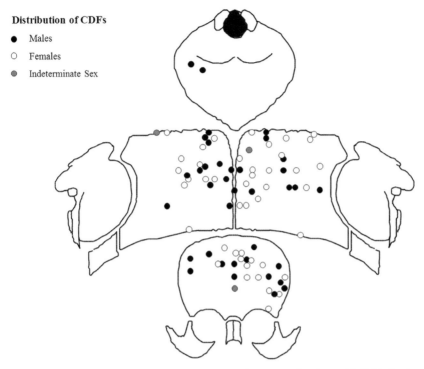

Distribution of CDFs

● Males
○ Females
◉ Indeterminate Sex

Figure 12.2. Distribution of CDFs on crania from males, females, and individuals of indeterminate sex (Baustian *et al.* 2012).

CDFs were not incurred in any particular patterns among the crania of either males or females. Most CDFs were located on the front and sides of the head, affecting the frontal and left and right parietal bones (see Figure 12.2 for a composite distribution of all CDFs). There was approximately the same number of injuries to each bone for males and females; however, the left parietal was an exception, with twice as many ($n = 16$) CDFs among women than among males ($n = 8$).

MSMs were assessed to determine patterns in physicality among the assemblage. No major patterns were observed and differences in development between the sexes and age groups were as expected (Milella *et al.* 2011); males exhibited slightly higher rugosity levels than females and older adults had slightly higher rugosity levels than younger adults. Comparing MSM development with presence or absence of CDFs, results did not indicate frequent co-occurrence. These data do not show any patterns among the Grasshopper Pueblo assemblage and the MSM data in particular, and are generally consistent with findings by Perry (2008).

Table 12.3. *Burials demonstrating scalping.*

Burial	Sex	Age	Number of CDFs	Time period	Origin	Comments
10	M	Young adult	0	Early	N/A	Grave goods present
38	F	Young adult	1	Early	N/A	Grave goods present
236	F	Young adult	3	Early	N/A	Possible antemortem scalping; 1 CDF is perimortem; grave goods present
543	M	Middle adult	0	Late	Local	
611	F	Young adult	0	N/A	N/A	14–18 years of age

Postcranial injuries were minimal among the Grasshopper Pueblo assemblage. Healed broken long bones of the arms and legs were observed among 7% of the sample, which included eight females and five males. The majority of the injuries were not severe but some healing occurred in all postcranial trauma. Violent injuries are not suspected for all but one individual (Burial 201, an older female), who had a healed parry fracture of the right forearm, which is sometimes associated with defensive maneuvers (Galloway 1999). Each of the postcranial injuries observed could have resulted from accidents. Only four individuals had both cranial and postcranial injuries. Research has shown that behavioral effects such as poor balance can result from non-lethal cranial trauma (Martin *et al.* 2008), which could potentially lead to subsequent accidental injuries of both the cranium and postcranial body.

Like postcranial trauma, sharp force trauma was not frequently observed. Three males and three females had sharp force trauma. For five of these individuals, this presented as scalping cut marks on the frontal, parietal, and temporal bones (the sixth individual with sharp force trauma had a possible chop mark on the occipital bone). Those potentially scalped were mostly young adults who lived in the community during the early period (Table 12.3). One young adult female (Burial 236) possibly survived scalping earlier in life. The co-occurrence of cranial trauma and scalping affected this same young female and another young adult female (see Table 12.3). The results of this analysis corroborate those of Allen and colleagues (1985), who also documented likely scalping. The significance of scalped individuals among the Grasshopper population will be explored further in the following section.

12.5   Discussion

The data presented are useful in consideration of theories regarding the role of violence at Grasshopper Pueblo. Trauma observed among the human skeletal remains indicates that many people (approximately one-third of the males and females) experienced direct interpersonal violence at some point in their lives. The following discussion addresses possible contexts in which cranial injuries occurred.

12.5.1   Warfare

Warfare in the Grasshopper Plateau region has not been identified as easily as that in other regions farther north (i.e. San Juan region) (LeBlanc 1999). During the Pueblo IV period, conflict increased throughout the northern Southwest as the environment deteriorated and tension rose among populations. Tuggle and Reid (2001) agree that this increasing conflict played a role in population migration and aggregation of pueblos on the Grasshopper Plateau. These authors describe the location of sites and architectural design as evidence of defensive intent. They do not, however, believe that internal violence and external aggression were present at Grasshopper Pueblo during its occupation or throughout abandonment of the community. Acts of large-scale warfare have not been identified at Grasshopper Pueblo (Reid and Whittlesey 1999; Tuggle and Reid 2001). The trauma data in this analysis include only a few occurrences of perimortem or lethal injuries (e.g. scalp marks, unhealed cranial fractures) commonly observed in warfare contexts.

12.5.2   Hostility between locals and non-locals

Using several isotope signatures among the human remains at Grasshopper Pueblo, Ezzo (1991; 1992; 1993) and Price (Ezzo and Price 2002) have demonstrated when individuals lived in the community and if they originated locally. Early period (AD 1275–1330) individuals ($n = 164$) outnumber late period (AD 1330–1400) individuals ($n = 67$) (Ezzo 1992). A subsample ($n = 53$) of burials from the assemblage resulted in 21 locals and 32 non-locals, of which most were from the early period (Ezzo 1992; Ezzo and Price 2002). Considering the distribution of CDFs among the whole sample and the subsample, there was again a similar frequency of affected individuals for both time periods and local/non-local status. There was also a similar distribution of CDFs among each sex. The results therefore suggest that violence between locals and non-locals was equally experienced.

Stone (2003) used multiple types of data to make similar conclusions that multiethnic groups at Grasshopper Pueblo coexisted well throughout their occupation without stark delineation of respective cultural practices. Evidence at Point of Pines suggests that aggregated ethnic groups did not always maintain peaceful relationships (Haury 1958; Reid 1989), but evidence at Grasshopper Pueblo indicates better interaction. Integration is indicated by several types of data but most relevant to this study is the biological evidence of local and non-local people living together in the same room blocks (Ezzo 1993; Ezzo and Price 2002; McClelland 2003). Both Ezzo and Price (2002) and McClelland (2003) documented burials of both groups in all areas of the community, although a concentration of locals was found in Room Block 2 and the Great Kiva. These findings suggest that non-locals were being integrated into the community and had similar experiences as those originating locally.

Cohesion of ethnic groups in the Grasshopper community appears likely; however, the high rates of trauma contradict this. Determining exactly how people became integrated into the community could be difficult and potentially impossible, but perhaps violence played a role. Violence related to integration practices could explain how all factions of the adult community demonstrate high rates of non-lethal trauma. Injuries might be incurred through ritual acts or other practices that aim to subdue an individual rather than kill him/her (Walker 1989). While analyzing Chumash skeletal remains from the Channel Island region of California, Walker (1989) proposed ritualized fighting to resolve disputes and maintain order among the population during times of limited resources. Data from that study showed high rates of non-lethal trauma to the cranium and low rates of postcranial injuries. This is consistent with the findings at Grasshopper, therefore injury through ritual activity should be considered.

12.5.3   *Raided captives and refugees of war*

The taking of captives, intentionally or as a corollary to warfare, is described throughout prehistory among pre-state societies (Cameron 2011; Keeley 1996). Although the high number of females and children among the Grasshopper burials is consistent with models of captives (Cameron 2011; Harrod and Martin in press; Martin and Cameron 2012), raided captives can likely be excluded as an explanation for this dataset. Several forms of data support this assessment. Most importantly, skeletal evidence of poor health can indicate the presence of captives in a population. Captives are often treated poorly by captors and exhibit higher rates of health problems and injuries (Harrod and Martin in press; Keeley 1996; Martin and Cameron 2012; Martin et al. 2008, 2010). The results of this study demonstrate similar rates of cranial and postcranial injuries, disease, and musculoskeletal development among all factions of the population. Co-occurrence of these maladies and skeletal features was not common either. This most likely suggests that captives were not present at Grasshopper, but other studies have documented similar patterns in which captives became fully integrated or adopted into the society of their captors (Wilkinson 1997). Even when physical abuse was part of that process, captives often were treated as all others in the community for many activities, including burial practices. At Grasshopper Pueblo, burial styles among individuals do not deviate from typical patterns (see also Allen *et al.* 1985). Collectively, this evidence does not indicate subgroups in the sample that might represent captives but it cannot exclude them either if they were assimilated into the larger community.

The differential sex and age representation among the burial population and other data have also suggested the possibility of warfare refugees at Grasshopper Pueblo (Lowell 2007). The presence of non-local women and children has been confirmed by isotope data by Ezzo (1991; 1993); however, he asserts that intermarriage with non-local women can explain many of the migrants present (Ezzo and Price 2002). This study demonstrates the presence of conflict in the region which can lend support to theories of war refugees at Grasshopper Pueblo. If, as Lowell (2007) suggests, males were engaged in warfare farther away from the community, the observed sex and age distribution in the sample may be a result. Ultimately, however, refugees of war cannot be excluded as members of the community and the data from this study cannot refute their presence because healed cranial injuries among non-locals could have occurred at any point during their lifetime.

12.5.4   Scalping as evidence of violence between groups

Evidence of scalping among the Grasshopper skeletal sample is potentially indicative of aggressive violence between groups in the region. As discussed by Allen and colleagues (1985), the presence of scalping victims suggests minimally that small-scale raiding took place in the nearby area. Conflict over limited resources could have taken the form of opportunistic raids in which members of the Grasshopper community became involved. It is possible that they were aggressors at some times and victims at others. Populations engaged in raiding, even at low levels, participate in a cycle of attacking as aggressors, retreating, and defending against raids by others (Maschner and Reedy-Maschner 1998). For those who were scalped at Grasshopper, burial patterns indicate that the individuals were community members and isotope data from Ezzo and Price (2002) demonstrate that at least one person was a local. These findings imply victimization by outsiders, but who these aggressors were is undetermined. It is unlikely that members of their own community were engaged in scalping of their own neighbors. Furthermore, four of the five scalped individuals lived at Grasshopper during the early period (AD 1275–1330). Human suffering (via worse dietary breadth, greater infectious disease, and poor sanitation) increased throughout the occupation of the community (Ezzo 1993), therefore the presence of scalping prior to serious problems indicates that violence was already a factor in daily life.

12.6   Conclusions

The rate of cranial injuries among the Grasshopper population is high, and this cannot be ignored. Compared to rates of non-lethal cranial trauma among other western North American populations, Grasshopper is the highest, at approximately 34%. A survey by Walker (1989) noted high rates of 18% for the northern Channel Islands and 30% for the Baja California region, but only 1–9% for all other western North American populations. It is surprising that the numerous analyses of Grasshopper human skeletal remains have not noted the extent of cranial trauma documented in this study (see also Baustian *et al.* 2012). Whittlesey (1978) noted a lack of violent deaths as indicated by skeletal markers such as scalping cut marks or unhealed fractures. One study of 163 crania (Birkby 1982) even went so far as to discuss the *lack* of violently induced trauma as evidence of peaceful and cooperative alliances between populations in the region during this time of environmental degradation. Even if warfare was not a frequent occurrence, data from this analysis indicate that violence was common in daily affairs.

Because all factions of adults in the community experienced cranial trauma equally, it is difficult to contextualize these results and form definitive explanations for the violence that is indicated. Ubiquitous interpersonal conflict likely explains much of the non-lethal trauma among the Grasshopper Pueblo population. Studies of health suggest worsening health throughout occupation of the region (Berry 1985; Hinkes 1983), and larger population size could have precipitated greater infectious disease, poor sanitation (Ezzo 1993), and increased competition for resources. These factors collectively indicate an environment of heightened stress that could have promoted opportunistic raiding.

The fact that little perimortem trauma was observed indicates that it either did not occur frequently or injuries were intended to subdue rather than kill an individual. It does not seem that lethal violence was prominent in this community; however, scalping data suggest otherwise. It is important to note that trauma to the body may only affect the skeleton up to 40% of the time, with the majority of injuries affecting soft tissue only; therefore skeletal analysis likely underestimates physical impairment in the past (Judd 2002; Walker 2001).

Fatalities, particularly those associated with violence, are thus underestimated by the bioarchaeological record and this may be the case at Grasshopper as well.

Interpreting the motivations and social context within which CDFs and scalping took place is very difficult, as revealed by this study. Contrary to the popular adage that the bones speak for themselves, in this case they do not. There are several alternative hypotheses which must be kept in the mix of potential explanatory models, including small-scale warfare and raiding, the possibility of internal interpersonal violence based on ethnicity, immigrant status, or kinship, as well as the possibility for class divisions that kept nonlethal violence at a fairly steady pace throughout the occupation.

Violence at some level is apparent at Grasshopper Pueblo. Even if underestimated because of lack of skeletal evidence, the population experienced conflict at high rates. The data in this analysis demonstrate that internal conflict was possible but certainly not the root of all traumatic injury. External conflict was most likely a factor in the lives of at least some in the community, particularly those who were scalped. This conclusion directly challenges previous notions of peace for this and other nearby communities. Determining who might have been the enemy is difficult given the level of cohesion and integration indicated by archaeological and biological data for this and other sites in the region. The Grasshopper Plateau and neighboring areas were very much in flux during the late prehistoric period and stress would have been ubiquitous for all communities. That high-level violence has *not* been well documented for this immediate region and time period is perhaps more surprising than the high rates observed by this and the previous study (Baustian *et al.* 2012). Future analysis of other skeletal assemblages from nearby sites will be necessary to reach a better understanding of the extent and role of violence for this region.

References

Allen, W., Merbs, C. F. & Birkby, W. H. (1985). Evidence for prehistoric scalping at Nuvakwewtaqa (Chavez Pass) and Grasshopper Ruin, Arizona. In: Merbs, C. F. & Miller, R. J. (eds.) *Health and Disease in the Prehistoric Southwest.* Tempe: Arizona State University, 23–42.

Baustian, K. M., Harrod, R. P., Osterholtz, A. J. & Martin, D. L. (2012). Battered and abused: analysis of trauma at Grasshopper Pueblo (AD 1275–1400). *International Journal of Paleopathology,* **2,** 102–11.

Berry, D. R. (1985). Dental pathology of Grasshopper Pueblo, Arizona. In: Merbs, C. F. & Miller, R. J. (eds.) *Health and Disease in the Prehistoric Southwest.* Tempe: Arizona State University, 253–74.

Birkby, W. H. (1982). Biosocial interpretations from cranial non-metric traits of Grasshopper Pueblo skeletal remains. In: Longacre, W. A., Holbrook, S. J. &

Graves, M. W. (eds.) *Multidisciplinary Research at Grasshopper Pueblo Arizona.* Tucson: Anthropological Papers of the University of Arizona, No. 40, University of Arizona Press, 36–41.

Blackmer, J. & Marshall, S. C. (1999). A comparison of traumatic brain injury in the Saskatchewan native North American and non-native North American populations. *Brain Injury*, **13**, 627–35.

Brink, O., Vesterby, A. & Jensen, J. (1998). Patterns of injuries due to interpersonal violence. *Injury: International Journal of the Care of the Injured*, **29**, 705–9.

Buikstra, J. E. & Ubelaker, D. H. (1994). *Standards for Data Collection from Human Skeletal Remains: Proceedings of a Seminar at the Field Museum of Natural History.* Fayetteville: Arkansas Archeological Survey.

Cameron, C. M. (2011). Captives and culture change: implications for archaeology. *Current Anthropology*, **52**, 169–209.

Capasso, L., Kennedy, K. A. R. & Wilczak, C. A. (1999). *Atlas of Occupational Markers on Human Remains.* Teramo: Edigrafital S.P.A.

Caufeild, J., Singhal, A., Moulton, R., Brenneman, F., Redelmeier, D. & Baker, A. J. (2004). Trauma recidivism in a large urban Canadian population. *The Journal of Trauma: Injury, Infection, and Critical Care*, **57**, 872–6.

Clark, G. A. (1967). A preliminary analysis of burial clusters at the Grasshopper Site, East-Central Arizona. University of Arizona: Unpublished MA thesis.

Ezzo, J. A. (1992). Dietary change and variability at Grasshopper Pueblo. *Journal of Anthropological Archaeology*, **11**, 219–89.

Ezzo, J. A., Jr. (1991). Dietary change at Grasshopper Pueblo, Arizona: the evidence from bone chemistry analysis. University of Wisconsin: Unpublished PhD dissertation.

   (1993). *Human Adaptation at Grasshopper Pueblo, Arizona: Social and Ecological Perspecives.* Ann Arbor: Archaeological Series, No. 4, International Monographs in Prehistory.

   (1994). Paleonutrition at Grasshopper Pueblo, Arizona. In: Sobolik, K. D. (ed.) *The Diet and Health of Prehistoric Americans.* Carbondale: Occasional Papers, No. 22, Center for Archaeological Investigations, Southern Illinois University, 265–79.

Ezzo, J. A., Jr. & Price, T. D. (2002). Migration, regional reorganization, and spatial group composition at Grasshopper Pueblo, Arizona. *Journal of Archaeological Science*, **29**, 499–520.

Galloway, A. (1999). *Broken Bones: Anthropological Analysis of Blunt Force Trauma.* Springfield: Charles C. Thomas.

Griffin, P. B. (1969). Late Mogollon readaptation in East-Central Arizona. University of Arizona: Unpublished PhD dissertation.

Harrod, R. P. & Martin, D. L. (in press). Bioarchaeological case studies of slavery, captivity, and other forms of exploitation. In: Marshall, L. W. (ed.) *The Archaeology of Slavery: A Comparative Approach to Captivity and Coercion.* Carbondale: Southern Illinois University Press.

Haury, E. W. (1958). Evidence at Point of Pines for a prehistoric migration from Northern Arizona. In: Thompson, R. H. (ed.) *Migrations in New World Culture History*. Tucson: University of Arizona Press, 1–8.

Hedges, B. E., Dimsdale, J. E., Hoyt, D. B., Berry, C. & Leitz, K. (1995). Characteristics of repeat trauma patients, San Diego County. *American Journal of Public Health*, **85**, 1008–10.

Hinkes, M. J. (1983). Skeletal evidence of Stress in subadults: trying to come of age at Grasshopper Pueblo. Tucson: University of Arizona: Unpublished PhD dissertation.

Judd, M. A. (2002). Ancient injury recidivism: an example from the Kerma Period of Ancient Nubia. *International Journal of Osteoarchaeology*, **12**, 89–106.

Keeley, L. H. (1996). *War before Civilization*. New York: Oxford University Press.

Kuckelman, K. A., Lightfoot, R. R. & Martin, D. L. (2002). The bioarchaeology and taphonomy of violence at Castle Rock and Sand Canyon Pueblos, Southwestern Colorado. *American Antiquity*, **67**, 486–513.

LeBlanc, S. A. (1999). *Prehistoric Warfare in the American Southwest*. Salt Lake City: The University of Utah Press.

(2006). Who made the Mimbres bowls? Implications of recognizing individual artists for craft specialization and social networks. In: Powell-Marti, V. S. & Gilman, P. A. (eds) *Mimbres Society*. Tucson: University of Arizona Press, 109–50.

LeBlanc, S. A. & Register, K. E. (2003). *Constant Battles: The Myth of the Peaceful, Noble Savage*. New York: St. Martin's Press.

LeBlanc, S. A. & Rice, G. E. (2001). Southwestern warfare: the value of case studies. In: Leblanc, S. A. & Rice, G. E. (eds.) *Deadly Landscapes: Case Studies in Prehistoric Southwestern Warfare*. Salt Lake City: University of Utah Press, 1–18.

Lovell, N. C. (1997). Trauma analysis in paleopathology. *Yearbook of Physical Anthropology*, **40**, 139–70.

(2008). Analysis and interpretation of skeletal trauma. In: Katzenberg, M. A. & Saunders, S. R. (eds.) *Biological Anthropology of the Human Skeleton*, 2nd edn. Hoboken: John Wiley & Sons, Inc., 341–86.

Lowell, J. C. (2007). Women and men in warfare and migration: implications of gender imbalance in the Grasshopper Region of Arizona. *American Antiquity*, **72**, 95–123.

Mariotti, V., Facchini, F. & Belcastro, M. G. (2007). The study of entheses: proposal of a standardised scoring method for twenty-three entheses of the postcranial skeleton. *Collegium Antropologicum*, **31**, 291–313.

Martin, D. L. & Cameron, C. M. (2012). Archaeological and bioarchaeological perspectives on captivity and slavery. *Anthropology News*, **53**, 4–5.

Martin, D. L., Akins, N. J., Crenshaw, B. J. & Stone, P. K. (2008). Inscribed on the body, written in the bones: the consequences of social violence at La Plata. In: Nichols, D. L. & Crown, P. L. (eds.) *Social Violence in the Prehispanic American Southwest*. Tucson: University of Arizona Press, 98–122.

Martin, D. L., Harrod, R. P. & Fields, M. (2010). Beaten down and worked to the bone: bioarchaeological investigations of women and violence in the Ancient Southwest. *Landscapes of Violence*, **1**, Article 3.

Maschner, H. D. & Reedy-Maschner, K. L. (1998). Raid, retreat, defend (repeat): the archaeology and ethnohistory of warfare on the North Pacific Rim. *Journal of Anthropological Archaeology*, **17**, 19–51.

McClelland, J. A. (2003). Refining the resolution of biological distance studies based on the analysis of dental morphology: detecting subpopulations at Grasshopper Pueblo. University of Arizona: Unpublished PhD dissertation.

Merbs, C. F. (1989). Trauma. In: Iscan, M. Y. & Kennedy, K. A. R. (eds.) *Reconstruction of Life from the Skeleton*. New York: Alan R. Liss, 161–99.

Milella, M., Mariotti, V. & Belcastro, M. (2011). *You Can't Tell a Book by Its Cover: The Effects of Age, Sex and Physical Activity on Theseal Changes in an Italian Contemporary Skeletal Collection*. 80th Annual Meeting of the American Association of Physical Anthropologists. Minneapolis, MN.

Perry, E. M. (2004). Bioarchaeology of labor and gender in the prehispanic American Southwest. University of Arizona: Unpublished PhD dissertation.

(2008). Gender, labor, and inequality at Grasshopper Pueblo. In: Stodder, A. L. W. (ed.) *Reanalysis and Reinterpretation in Southwestern Bioarchaeology*. Tempe: Arizona State University, Anthropological Research Papers, 151–66.

Reid, J. J. (1989). A Grasshopper perspective on the Mogollon of the Arizona Mountains. In: Cordell, L. S. & Gumerman, G. J. (eds.) *Dynamics of Southwest Prehistory*. Santa Fe: School of American Research, 65–97.

Reid, J. J. & Whittlesey, S. (1999). *Grasshopper Pueblo: A Story of Archaeology and Ancient Life*. Tucson: University of Arizona Press.

Riggs, C. R. (2001). *The Architecture of Grasshopper Pueblo: Dynamics of Form, Function, and Use of Space in a Prehistoric Community*. Salt Lake City: The University of Utah Press.

Schultz, M., Timme, U. & Schmidt-Schultz, T. H. (2007). Infancy and childhood in the pre-Columbian North American Southwest–first results of the palaeopathological investigation of the skeletons from the Grasshopper Pueblo, Arizona. *International Journal of Osteoarchaeology*, **17**, 369–79.

Scott, R. M. & Buckley, H. R. (2010). Biocultural interpretations of trauma in two prehistoric Pacific Island populations from Papua New Guinea and the Solomon Islands. *American Journal of Physical Anthropology*, **142**, 509–18.

Stone, T. (2003). Social identity and ethnic interaction in the Western Pueblos of the American Southwest. *Journal of Archaeological Method and Theory*, **10**, 31–67.

Tuggle, H. D. & Reid, J. J. (2001). Conflict and defense in the Grasshopper region of East-Central Arizona. In: Leblanc, S. A. & Rice, G. E. (eds.) *Deadly Landscapes: Case Studies in Prehistoric Southwestern Warfare*. Salt Lake City: University of Utah Press, 85–107.

Walker, P. L. (1989). Cranial injuries as evidence of violence in prehistoric Southern California. *American Journal of Physical Anthropology*, **80**, 313–23.

(1997). Wife beating, boxing, and broken noses: skeletal evidence for the cultural patterning of violence. In: Martin, D. L. & Frayer, D. W. (eds.) *Troubled Times: Violence and Warfare in the Past*. Amsterdam: Gordon and Breach, 145–80.

(2001). A bioarchaeological perspective on the history of violence. *Annual Review of Anthropology*, **30**, 573–96.

Whittlesey, S. M. (1978). Status and death at Grasshopper Pueblo: experiments toward an archaeological theory of correlates. University of Arizona: Unpublished PhD dissertation.

(2002). The cradle of death. In: Kamp, K. A. (ed.) *Children in the Prehistoric Puebloan Southwest*. Salt Lake City: The University of Utah Press, 152–68.

Whittlesey, S. M. & Reid, J. J. (2001). Mortuary ritual and organizational inferences at Grasshopper Pueblo, Arizona. In: Mitchell, D. R. & Brunson-Hadley, J. L. (eds.) *Ancient Burial Practices in the American Southwest: Archaeology, Physical Anthropology, and Native American Perspectives*. Albuquerque: University of New Mexico Press, 68–96.

Wilkinson, R. G. (1997). Violence against women: raiding and abduction in prehistoric Michigan. In: Martin, D. L. & Frayer, D. W. (eds.) *Troubled Times: Violence and Warfare in the Past*. Amsterdam: Gordon and Breach, 21–44.

13   The contribution of forensic anthropology to national identity in Chile: a case study from Patio 29

ELIZABETH M. DEVISSER,

KRISTA E. LATHAM, AND

MARISOL INTRIAGO LEIVA

13.1   Introduction

On September 11, 1973 the military coup overthrowing socialist president Salvador Allende transformed Chilean identity forever. Little did the Chilean people realize at that point in time how drastically their lives would change. Officially, the military claimed to be restoring peace and order to a chaotic nation after the disastrous consequences of Allende's government tore the country apart. However, the reality is that the military dictatorship suppressed the opposition by utilizing extreme extermination efforts such as detainment, torture, and murder. Pinochet showed so little regard for his victims that he ordered many of them thrown in clandestine graves, rivers, the sea, and cemeteries, to be effectively removed from the historical record and collective memory. One such site, Patio 29, stands as a symbol of the systematic extermination of Chilean citizens.

The bodies and memories of his victims remained silent during his 17-year tenure, engendering a sense of fear and mistrust in the government. Recent efforts altered the landscape, allowing the victims' voices to be heard, recognized, and acknowledged. One of the most important endeavors involved the formation of a special branch of the Department of Justice assigned to identify all missing persons from the Pinochet dictatorship. The efforts of a multi-disciplinary forensic team at the Servicio Medico Legal (SML) have helped rebuild the identity of a fractured nation by identifying a large number of the

Bioarchaeological and Forensic Perspectives on Violence: How Violent Death is Interpreted from Skeletal Remains, ed. D. L. Martin and C. P. Anderson. Published by Cambridge University Press.
© Cambridge University Press 2014.

victims and returning them to their families. The history of Patio 29 and the forensic team at the SML are inextricably linked.

Fundamental changes in national identity resulted as a direct outcome of the Patio 29 identification efforts. The SML underwent an extraordinary transformation in 2006, all because of the devastating consequences of misidentifications of Patio 29 victims. The SML emerged more informed and dedicated to employing comprehensive contemporary scientific protocols to human identification in Chile.

National identity requires membership in the collective memories of the nation. Fear and aggression break the bonds of national identity. Systematic extermination destroys it. The forensic team, including anthropologists at the SML provide a necessary function to restoring membership by giving a name to the victims.

13.2   On national identity

National identity is dynamic and cannot be defined by a clear set of definitive traits. Neither can it simply be substituted with personal identity. National identity is a symbolic construction beginning when the nation was first formed. Anderson (1991) describes national identity as an "imagined community" where a sense of fraternity is prompted by the collective memory of heroic deeds and landscapes, but also shared suffering and common memories of brutality and trauma. When a large body of the nation, the Chilean military, seeks out and demonizes a subset of citizens (supporters of Allende, communists, socialists) within the community, the sense of fraternity is negated. The "others," who were once members of the community, are vilified, disrespected, and ignored (Larraín 2006). The military regime eliminated the corporeal body from existence, effectively removing individuals and families from the collective memory of society. Overcoming the effects of a fractured national identity requires justice, reparation, and reconciliation by influential members of the community to strengthen the identity of the whole community (Barsalou 2005).

Every dimension of identity, from the individual to the global level, affects national identity. Self-identity is influenced by perceptions of the body and definitions of the self, such as familial relationships, socioeconomic class, religious beliefs, ethnic affiliations, and gender roles (Brison 2002; Larraín 2006). A person's physical body provides the vital ingredient of sentient self-actualization. Self-identity allows humans to define an "us" versus "them" mentality. Group identity requires membership within the group that carries with it an emotional attachment significant to one's self (Anderson 1991). Group identity thus can be construed as a core construct because it carries with it great significance to the individual (Bell 2003). Shared kinship, education, geographic location, and religions catalyze the formation of communities, allowing "them" to become "us." This sharing of common values and designing rituals constitutes a collective memory. Collective memory represents a powerful construct of national identity as historical circumstances can alter the substance of national identity. Shared ideas, values, and interpretations of traumatic events signify a shared history made resonant through symbols and rituals (Reimers 1999). When the "them" becomes "us" on a national level, it serves to unify humans as a nation. A nation (and by extension national identity) can then be defined as "a named human population sharing an historic territory, common myths and historical memories, a mass, public culture, a common economy and common legal rights and duties for all members" (Smith 1991).

Traumatic events such as genocide, ethnic cleaning, or mass extermination profoundly influence national identity. Trauma disrupts the status quo, generating feelings of fear, vulnerability, and resentment (Hutchison and Bleiker 2008). Trauma shatters the sense of belonging and fear undermines a community. When the body (or self) is threatened, naturally a person feels vulnerable. When the body of a group member is threatened in such a systematic way as mass extermination by a ruling government, not only is the personal identity of the individual negated, but the collective identity is threatened as well (Bell 2003). Obliterating the memory and bodies of the victims from the historical record was corrosive to the Chilean national identity (Larraín 2006). A traumatized society emerged, devastated by the blatant and systematic violations of human rights and the attempts to silence the collective memories of those who were eliminated (Mendeloff 2009).

In post-conflict Chile, the government applied transitional justice mechanisms such as truth commissions, institutional changes, and memorials to rebuild their society. Those who were persecuted cannot feel as though they are members of the community until justice has been done. Justice may take the form of reparations to the victims and their families, but also acknowledgment by those directly responsible for the atrocities (Black 2002; Mendeloff 2009). Recognition of injustice by the government reincorporates the victims' families, allowing them to once more re-enter the community and become part of the shared national collective memory (Barsalou 2005). Preservation of a national identity occurs by creating rituals (such as anniversaries, monuments, art, and ceremonies) meant to build a national memory. Chile is rife with symbols reflecting the shared memory of trauma caused by the Pinochet regime (Larraín 2006). As a result, President Allende is glorified in memory through art, his mausoleum in the General Cemetery, in books, and in conversation. The power of these rituals rests in their ability to elicit emotions, and their capacity to symbolize shared communal memories that can be relived, translated, and, often, contested.

An important contribution to the process of transitional justice regards identification of the victims of mass atrocities. Chile was already torn apart from years of repression and censorship, and the physical elimination of thousands of people rendered national identity damaged. However, identity is dynamic, and changes in the relationships between victims' families and the government have contributed to a restored unity in Chilean national identity. Forensic experts have restored a feeling of peace and justice to families by reinstating the identity of the disappeared back into the Chilean collective memory. The case study from Patio 29 later in this chapter exemplifies these complex relationships between families and forensic experts, and the evolution of a dynamic national identity.

13.3   Historical context

Unidad Popular (UP), Allende's coalition of leftist political parties, became highly distrusted during its short 3-year tenure as a direct consequence of poor economic strategies which alienated a broad base of the populace. The Allende government made impressive improvements in areas such as health and unemployment, but these were overshadowed by the outstanding disregard the government showed for the consequences of their policies as Allende strived to socialize Chile (Rector 2003).

The nationalization of major revenue-producing institutions, such as copper mining and agriculture, would provide Chile with much needed profits. Benefits included an increase in workers' wages, a growing economy, and a drop in unemployment, which were looked on favorably (Loveman 1986; Rector 2003). However, unintended consequences quickly hampered the path to Chilean socialism. For the middle class, nationalization increased jobs, which eased financial burdens. However, factions with diametrically opposed values developed within the middle class. For example, an important influencing factor for urban middle class citizens was rent control, whereas the rural middle class favored an agenda that increased property values. The UP immediately put rural real estate (farms) and industrial investments under governmental control, which frustrated the landowners. While worker benefits increased and provided support and reassurance to a large proportion of the Chilean population, the country's wealthiest landowners felt betrayed by the new agenda and began transferring funds out of Chile. Moving money overseas reduced the amount of taxes the government could impose on the landowners. To gain much needed revenue for his nationalization program, Allende sought funding from foreign countries, primarily the USA (Collier and Sater 2004; Loveman 1986; Rector 2003).

The UP mistakenly intensified the pace of socialism since public opinion looked upon the agenda favorably. However, accelerating its socialist agenda resulted in unexpected consequences that would prove fatal for many Chilean citizens. The UP increased agrarian reform, which disrupted agriculture. While the government was expropriating land, campesinos (farmers/peasants) began taking up arms and expropriating property for themselves without government oversight. While the campesinos stood with arms at the gates of elite homes, the Mapuche (the native community of Chile) took back lands taken from them earlier. Landowners armed themselves against the campesinos and the Mapuche, further escalating the conflict. Allende did not involve the government in these disputes. Alienating rural workers was anathema since they were the recipients of his socialist policies. Expropriations resulted in a supply decrease and black markets arose because of agricultural scarcity. Allende could never allay the fear that the scarcity would end. By 1972 Chile was an unstable country as struggles between the elite and the lower classes increased. Businesses were concerned over increased property seizures by the UP, and the middle and lower classes were afraid of the scarcity of agricultural supplies (Rector 2003).

Two monumental uprisings further decreased the faith in Allende's policies. The first national strike occurred in 1972. Businesses closed their doors due to the scarcity imposed by conflicts in the rural and industrial regions. Truckers went on strike first, followed by merchants and industrial workers, and, finally, professionals. Allende invited the military into his cabinet in an effort to end the strike and increase confidence in his government. Augusto Pinochet was appointed as Defense Minister in 1973. The next major strike occurred when miners wanted increased wages. The UP denied a wage increase and ultimately spent $80 000 000 (US) to end the strike 77 days later, but the damage to the Chilean economy was already done (Rector 2003).

Allende's policies destabilized the national economy. Gross domestic product decreased because of massive strikes and a scarcity of raw materials. Wages decreased after only 2 years while, conversely, prices and scarcity increased. The UP was so fractured ideologically that they could not agree on a common policy (Collier and Sater 2004; Rector 2003). By then the financial situation in Chile was already out of control. Believing that Allende and the UP could no longer effectively govern the nation, the military was urged by many political factions to overthrow the government.

13.4   Military coup and the Pinochet regime

On September 11, 1973 Chilean democracy was replaced by a fascist regime that used coercion, torture, and violence to assume control. A junta, with representatives from each branch of the military, served as the executive and legislative branches of the nation. Immediately following the coup, between 2000 and 10 000 civilian casualties resulted from junta violence (Kornbluh 2004), though they admitted to only 244 fatalities. The military junta detained over 13 000 people and specifically targeted individuals who were officials of the Allende government, politicians who did not support the coup, activists, union members, and factory employees (Loveman 1986; Wyndham and Read 2010). Over 1100 detention camps were constructed across the Chilean landscape. Prisoners were also housed at the National Stadium (Estadio Nacional) and Chile Stadium (Estadio Chile), where they were interrogated and tortured (Kornbluh 2004; Rector 2003; Zalaquett 1985). In many circumstances detention resulted in execution, with the bodies of the deceased dumped in the street, left in the Mapocho River, thrown into the ocean, or buried in secret in mass graves (Wyndham and Read 2010). Over 3215 (according to the Valech Report, 2011 version) people disappeared during the militarized government, most of them between 1973 and 1978 (Grandin 2005; Reconciliación and Berryman 1993). The Chilean secret police, the Directorate of National Intelligence (DINA) and later the National Center for Information (CNI), covered up the crimes, stating that the magnitude of human rights violations was a natural consequence of being at war. According to the "official" record, the military coup saved Chile from socialism and communism while bringing Chile back from the brink of chaos. Defeating Communism and the "Marxist cancer" that had invaded Chile became the regime's primary goal, and enemies of the state were effectively removed from existence (Loveman 1986; Spooner 2011).

Pinochet controlled the populace through mass media interventions, firmly establishing a fear campaign designed to eliminate any supporters of socialism. Censorship became the regime's tool to calm the public and keep their clandestine activities secret (Loveman 1986). Many prominent authors, writers, journalists, and musicians, most notably Victor Jara, were murdered. Anything that "endangered morality, public order, national security or the private life of citizenry" (Montaner 1988) was silenced. The military junta was successful in keeping this tight control over subversives and succeeded in silencing the voices of the opposition for 17 years.

The factual history of the atrocities caused by Pinochet's regime did not officially surface until after Pinochet relinquished power in 1989. When President Patricio Aylwin was inaugurated in 1990, he assumed power of a nation that had experienced tremendous changes and pressures over the past 17 years. The economy was growing, yet 40% of the population fell below the poverty line (Rector 2003). President Aylwin also had to confront the most difficult challenge created by Pinochet's regime – the fate of over 3000 Chileans was still unknown.

The 1990s marked Chile's transition back to a democracy, but numerous obstacles conspired against the new administrations and prevented them from reconciling the demands of the families with quick resolution. Either because of sly judgment, or perhaps anticipating future accountability, Pinochet decreed in 1978 that the state agents who committed crimes between September 11, 1973 and March 10, 1978 be given amnesty under the constitution (Brody 2008; Collier and Sater 2004; Kornbluh 2004; Rector 2003). The Supreme Court upheld the decree but declared that the government could investigate instances of human rights abuses. President Aylwin, with an emphasis on "truth and justice as far as possible," appointed an investigative congressional committee, the National Truth and Reconciliation Commission (NTRC), which had investigative power but lacked prosecutorial authority (Ensalaco 1994; Zalaquett 1993). Jose Zalaquett, a leader of the commission, notes that the commission "was the cornerstone of a transitional policy aimed at the moral (and political) reconstruction of our society after a period of tragic breakdown..." (Grandin 2005; Reconciliación and Berryman 1993).

According to Benedict Anderson (1991), modern-day truth commissions have been powerful instruments in the creation of nationalism. The NTRC, or "Rettig Commission," named for the head of the commission, Raul Rettig, obtained testimonies from thousands of detainees and family members of the disappeared. The report documented the violence executed by the military under the auspices of General Pinochet and the DINA/CNI that resulted in death. The NTRC was the first effort by a governmental agency in the post-dictatorship government to address and publicly acknowledge the atrocities of the Pinochet regime. The Rettig Report not only uncovered the nefarious deeds of the Pinochet regime, but also unearthed sites of numerous mass graves located throughout Chile (Zalaquett 1993).

13.5   Patio 29

Patio 29 stands as one of the most notorious and well-known large burial sites in Chile. The burial ground rests within the heart of Santiago in the country's largest cemetery, Cementerio General. The General Cemetery is not simply a graveyard, but a small city with tree-lined avenues and parks often named after famous Chilean leaders, thinkers, and artists. The cemetery is sectioned into patios, or courtyards. The more prosperous sections contain mausoleums, marble statues, and formal masonry. The humbler areas to the north are reserved for those of lower socioeconomic status (Wilde 2008). Nestled within this area is Patio 29 (Figure 13.1), a large overgrown field of simple tin crosses, all bearing the initials "N.N." for "No men Nescio" Latin 8 or "Name unknown."

Patio 29 was the largest collective effort by the Pinochet regime to hide their crimes. Directly following the coup, bodies began piling up in the city morgue

Figure 13.1. Patio 29 mass grave. Santiago, Chile.

as they were recovered from the middle of streets, alleyways, and even floating in the river. The bodies decomposed in the hallways of the morgue as the freezers began to fill. Urgency, combined with pressure from the administration, forced morgue employees to perform "economic autopsies" (Servicio Medico Legal 2010). Such autopsies were incomplete and many of the reports did not even contain identifying information for the decedent. Nonetheless, in most cases fingerprints were taken if the state of decomposition allowed and stored with the individual's file (Servicio Medico Legal 2010; Wyndham and Read 2010).

Disposal of these bodies was a primary concern. Orders came in to cremate the remains, but were quickly rescinded. The military regime ordered secret burials and a perfect site was Patio 29. Seclusion, adjacency to the morgue, and the availability of 320 open plots provided a hiding spot in plain sight. Regular coffins were in short supply, so morgue staff created makeshift coffins from whatever materials were available. Some of the makeshift coffins contained two or more individuals. When presented with this information, Pinochet remarked "Qué economía tan grande!" – 'Such amazing economy!' (Wyndham and Read 2010). Military personnel supervised the interments, which occurred over the course of several months. The military warned the workers against notifying anyone of Patio 29's new residents, but families of the victims received news of the graves in spite of the military threats. Rumors concerning Patio 29 spread through Santiago and the site increasingly became one of horror, but of hope as well (Wyndham and Read 2010). As long as the victims remained in the cemetery, there existed a chance that someday they might be identified and returned home.

The military was not yet through with Patio 29. The Vicariate of Solidarity, a human rights advocacy group in Chile, gathered detailed testimony about the Patio 29 burials and publicly presented their findings. Although the judge recused himself, stating that he was incompetent to carry on the case, he ordered the Patio 29 graves were not to be touched, moved, or exhumed further. However, the Cemetery began to remove the victims in order to reuse the graves, and this was conducted without alerting the victims' families (Kornbluh 2004; Wyndham and Read 2010). The illegal exhumations would have remained secret had it not been for an anonymous phone call to the Vicariate from a cemetery employee. The Vicariate was unable to prevent the exhumations, however, and the victims were either reinterred in another location or cremated, and their whereabouts are still unknown (Wyndham and Read 2010).

After the appointment of President Aylwin, the families of the "N.N." people in Patio 29 would finally have answers. In 1991 he appointed several forensic specialists to exhume and identify the remains. In an effort to appease the military and ensure success, the recovery of Patio 29 had to be a military-led process. Additionally, no military personnel were to be held accountable for the people identified in Patio 29, a necessary caveat if the scientists were to proceed without interruption or interference (Wyndham and Read 2010). Compromises of this sort suited both the military and the families. The military controlled the recovery efforts while seeming to mollify the families, and the families could find closure. Exhumation and identification of the remains was seen as a form of restitution and acknowledgment for the country (Servicio Medico Legal 2010; Wyndham and Read 2010). Patio 29 was not simply a resting place for the disappeared, but had become a symbol of remembrance.

The forensic identification of Patio 29 individuals took from 2 to 10 years. Medical doctors and forensic anthropologists at the SML performed morphological analyses to generate a biological profile consisting of sex, age, stature, ancestry, and any other special identifying characteristics, including dental and skeletal radiograph comparisons. Only 108 of the original 320 graves were located and only 126 people were recovered. Individuals exhumed from Patio 29 ranged in age from 14 to 60+, but the majority of them were between the ages of 20 and 30 years old. All individuals except four were male. Ninety-six of the decedents were returned to their families by 1998, but many could not be identified and were kept under the custody of the SML. New information surfaced in 2006 suggesting that 48 of the 96 individuals had been clearly misidentified (Servicio Medico Legal 2010; Wyndham and Read 2010). This crisis led to a complete restructuring of the human rights identification division of the SML and presented a dilemma for future identification efforts.

13.6   Servicio Medico Legal

The SML is a department of the Ministry of Justice and is responsible for conducting investigations into all forensic matters in the country. A specific branch of the SML, Unidad de Identificación y Museo, was instituted in 1994 to address the ubiquitous human rights issues rampant throughout the nation. This department was responsible for identifying the disappeared around the nation. The SML responds to the demands of families through an active and organized search for victims, along with laboratory analysis of remains. In 2006 the Identification branch was completely restructured as a result of the Patio 29 scandal. This branch was restructured once more in 2010. The SML had expanded their professional staff and were able to handle human rights and modern forensic cases (Servicio Medico Legal 2010).

Patio 29 played a pivotal role in re-establishing faith in government institutions. During the initial identification process in the 1990s, the families of the Patio 29 victims were brought in by the SML, and medical doctors and anthropologists explained in great detail the fate of their family member. Every aspect of the investigation was explained, down to the smallest detail: trajectory of the bullet(s), broken limbs, and evidence of torture. Truth and unbiased disclosure allowed families to include the deceased in family history while also fostering trust in the government (Avruch 2010; Barsalou 2005; Kriesberg 1993).

DNA profiling technologies were just emerging in the early 1990s, especially in Latin America. In 2001, a special section of the SML was dedicated to generating the mitochondrial DNA profiles of the victims. During this process the team found inconsistencies between several of the genetic profiles and the identified victims. In March of 2005, the courts ordered that all decedents of the Patio 29 graves be exhumed for genetic testing. Genetic tests revealed that at least 48 of the cases were misidentified and 37 were inconclusive (Servicio Medico Legal 2010). The impact of these results was staggering, not only for the families who had subsequently moved on in the grief process, but for the public and for the SML.

Trust had slowly begun eroding since the exhumations occurred and became a reality in 2006, when the misidentifications became public. The government suppressed two reports that revealed systematic incompetence within the SML. A report on the Patio 29 recoveries issued in 1994 urged the SML to change their processes of identification drastically, as they were found to be inadequate and out of date. An independent forensic agency released another report in 2002 stating that the credentials of the experts in charge of identification had not been assessed and urged that all recoveries and identification procedures be suspended. Families had to endure two separate disappearances and begin the grieving process again. Victims' families directly targeted the SML director and accused the government of gross indifference, calling for the director's resignation despite a public apology. The blame then fell to two officers not working at the SML at the time, but closely associated with identification efforts. The officers exonerated themselves, stating that they did what they could with the tools provided them. The inadvertent misidentifications were a direct result of the inadequate identification protocols and pressure from the government to identify the victims quickly and were believed to be accidental. Nonetheless, the damage was already done – public opinion deemed the SML negligent and indifferent.

Restructuring of the human rights division was the direct result of the misidentifications of the Patio 29 victims; it was deemed that insufficient scientific standards and insufficiently trained professional personnel contributed to the misidentifications of the victims (Servicio Medico Legal 2010; Wyndham and Read 2010). To address these issues, the SML commissioned international professionals to audit the processes of identification and provide guidelines for the recovery and analysis of human remains. The SML modernized their identification system by hiring professional forensic senior management and providing adequate training for all new staff. Additionally, the SML provided auditing and training protocols as a system of checks and balances and offered continuing education programs for their scientists with institutions in the USA and Europe. As of 2010, 30 individuals from Patio 29 have been identified by genetic analysis (Servicio Medico Legal 2010; Wyndham and Read 2010). The case study below is representative of the tremendous work of the restructured Identification division and of the methodical and meticulous forensic team most recently employed at the SML.

13.7   Case study

The forensic experts at the SML generate biological profiles for victims of human rights abuses all across the country. Using the previous autopsy, anthropology, and genetic profiles, the anthropologists attempt to reconstruct the history of unidentified remains. Patio 29 victims remain a priority owing to the high profile nature of the graves and continued support from the government. The case study presented here provides an interesting example of the initial Patio 29 identification issues. Further, this case demonstrates the complex relationship that the forensic experts, particularly the anthropologists, have with the victims' families and the effect of bringing the deceased back into the collective memory of the nation.

This individual was exhumed and identified by the SML staff in 1994 prior to genetic testing. The decedent was returned to his family and subsequently reburied. However, the parents did not truly believe this was their son and the mother routinely called professionals at the SML voicing her opinion. The individual was later returned to the SML when the court ordered genetic testing for all Patio 29 victims.

The new biological profile generated by the SML suggested the decedent was a young male between the ages of 16 and 24, stood about 168.0 cm (5.5 feet) tall and was in generally good dental health. This young man was originally interred in Patio 29 and buried in a makeshift coffin with another person in 1973. Evidence of at least two bullet wounds were found in his cranium and other gunshot trauma shattered his pelvis, left tibia, clavicle, humerus, scapula, and vertebral column, particularly in the midthoracic region (Figures 13.2 and 13.3).

The newly generated profile was compared to the biological profile constructed in the 1990s and several inconsistencies arose. First, prior age estimates differed by approximately half a decade. Additionally, comparisons to the original autopsy noted a healing fracture of the right clavicle, yet no trauma to the right clavicle was observed on this skeleton. Finally, the DNA did not match this individual to the family of the previously identified male. The anthropologists returned to their files for any leads on the identification of the skeletal remains and a match was discovered.

The newly identified decedent died several days after September 11, 1973. As a known follower of President Allende, the military targeted the decedent for execution. Found floating near the banks of the Mapocho River, gunshot wounds had riddled his body. The morgue documented his fingerprints and he was buried in Patio 29. He was identified and his records were on file at the SML for over 30 years. Nonetheless, his extermination and clandestine burial were obliterated from the collective memory and he was lost. After 37 years of remaining in the darkness, the decedent finally has his name and identity returned to his family.

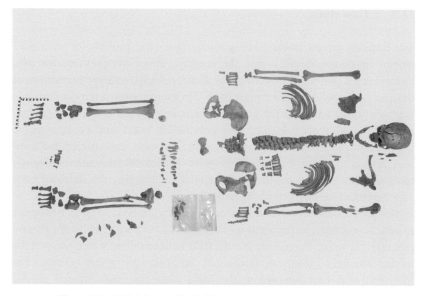

Figure 13.2. Full skeleton of Patio 29 victim.

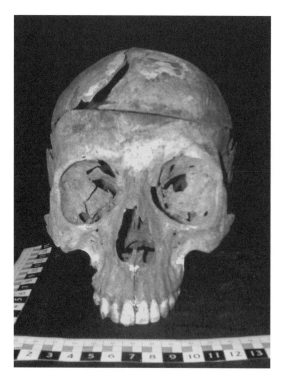

Figure 13.3. Cranium of Patio 29 victim.

The above case study was chosen to highlight in this chapter for several reasons. First, this case is representative of the enormous task facing the forensic anthropologists at the SML. Most individuals from Patio 29 have a common biological profile: they are males between the ages of 20 and 40 and have severe gunshot trauma. Additionally, when confronted with few identifying characteristics, the biological profile does not narrow the number of possible matches and the forensic anthropologists must utilize a suite of other documents fortunately retained by the previous SML staff. This case represents the horror that too many Chileans endured but also stands as a symbol of the reconciliation efforts of the Chilean government. Successful identification of each individual exterminated during the Pinochet era remains the ultimate goal of the anthropologists and staff at the SML. The forensic team return the lost identity of victims, give peace to the grieving families by aiding in repairing the old wounds of a fractured society, and act to restore faith in the government.

13.8   Changes in Chilean national identity

Chilean identity was drastically altered during the shift from a democratic society free from involuntary exclusion to one where systematic violations of human rights reigned. In the Pinochet regime, an entire faction of the population was eliminated. Fear, torture, aggression, and oppression resulted in a fractured nation. To heal this rift, families of the disappeared and those who experienced torture and abuse needed once again to feel acknowledged as full members of the community. Examples in transitional justice have demonstrated that concerted effort of public acknowledgment, reconciliation, and reparation must be given to the sufferers for the families to begin healing (Aukerman 2002; Barsalou 2005; Waldorf 2006).

Prior to the rise of the Pinochet dictatorship, Chileans had already experienced a fracture in national identity (Miller 2006). Forced expropriations and economic instability of the nation contributed to the growing fear of the nation. The UP's economic policies disenfranchised a large group of people, and any sense of shared fraternity was effectively weakened. Fear and aggression threatened the unity necessary to sustain a strong national identity. Forced expropriations, strikes, and armed warfare in the rural regions set Chileans against one another. When the government neglected to thwart such conflict, fear increased among the people (Larraín 2006; Rector 2003). Fear is a powerful motivator to action. Once fear takes hold, rational discourse is limited and hostilities are intensified (Hutchison and Bleiker 2008). The Allende opposition manipulated this fear, allowing the military to take hostile action.

The Allende administration made conserving a unified national identity difficult, but the Pinochet regime escalated and manipulated these tensions. People were excluded from the community; some people were exiled, others were denied their nationality yet were unable to leave the country. Exclusion from the community also extended to any individual who supported the UP but could not leave the country. These people were vilified, spied upon by family and neighbors, and even called enemies or "humanoids" (Wyndham and Read 2010). The military regime added a new element to their policy of brutal repression and exclusion. Victims suffered not only the loss of freedom and community, but the most tangible aspect of their identity. Victims were killed and the military sought to obliterate their very existence from the collective identity. These actions by the military and sanctioned by Pinochet traumatized a nation. The military regime severed any ties that bound these communities together through torture and extermination of the defeated "other."

Discourses regarding the period leading up to the coup are naturally varied because not all citizens experienced elimination and/or torture (Black 2002). Tremendous fear and rage was rampant throughout the country during Allende's presidency. Lands that had been in families for generations were expropriated, feeding a sense of injustice, fear, and impotence. On the other hand, Allende's policies had many supporters. This dichotomy is clearly demonstrated in an article published by *El Mercurio*, the nation's largest newspaper. Isabel Allende (Salvador Allende's daughter) remembers her father fondly, regarding him as a national hero whose sacrifice will never be forgotten. Countering this view, Alberto Wurmann remembers his father, who worked his entire life building his dream, only to have it cruelly expropriated (Larraín 2006; Wurmann 2003). If one accepts that material possessions can be a projection of the bodily self, and the body is a central construct of personal identity, then any threat to the property is a threat to personal identity. This breach of trust strikes at the core of human dignity and self-worth. If Wurmann's view can be understood and sympathized with, then it is not a far leap to understand, though not justify, the violent reaction to the UP policies.

Long-term violence enacts profound changes in the behavior of groups and individuals in the community. At the national level, evidence has shown that re-establishing the rule of law, viable political institutions, security, and access to information all play a role in restoring individuals' sense of control over their lives (August 1996; Avruch and Vejarano 2001; Mendeloff 2009). The necessity for truth about the fate of the victims cannot be understated. Identifying the disappeared makes it possible for the members of a community to begin to heal. Reclaiming the dead allows families to rejoin the community and take part in the narrative of the collective memory.

Pinochet's attempt to erase the collective memories about his atrocities did not succeed. While many people are still missing, there has been a concerted effort by the successive administrations to address and acknowledge the human rights violations. Although his hands were tied because of judiciary inaction and impunity, President Aylwin set up the NTRC, which informed the public about the truth of Pinochet's duplicity. In 2004 the Valech Report was issued, which registered over 35 000 cases of torture, and resulted in formal recognition by the Commander of the Army of its responsibility for these human rights violations (Comisión Nacional de Verdad y Reconciliación 2004).

A forensic anthropologist's job in Chile is not limited to human identification. Anthropologists at the SML work very closely with families, and the development of that relationship has a direct effect on public opinion concerning identification efforts and reconciliation. The circumstances surrounding the Patio 29 debacle demonstrate how tenuous the thread is that links forensic anthropologists to victims' trust in the government. Anthropologists and families share a collective memory that strengthens group identity and, by extension, national identity.

Fragile threads of trust eroded until the newly elected president, Michelle Bachelet, matched government actions to the rhetoric. Previous administrations failed to address the issue of Patio 29 effectively. Appointing a well-meaning but untrained forensic team and ignoring international recommendations set the agenda for a succession of failures in a high profile human rights situation. Restructuring the SML allowed the government to demonstrate its dedication to ensuring that victims and their families were recognized. The professionals at the SML act as liaisons between the government and the victims, and each human rights case offers an opportunity to heal the fractured community. If the body is a core component in self-identity, and self-identity is core to belonging in a community, then, if change occurs with the self, over time these changes can affect relationships within the community. Thus, if a family can find peace through identification of their missing relation, then their feelings toward the government, and, by extension, the nation, can change. The anthropologists at the SML work hard to mend this rift by re-initializing the core of human identity into the community.

The dynamic shift of national identity specifically with regard to human rights is realized in the cultural manifestations and shared symbols of the nation. Historic symbols of Chilean identity have lost their power, primarily because of their ubiquitous use by the Pinochet regime (Meade 2001). For example, the extensive presentation of the Chilean flag now invokes memories of repression and trauma in some Chileans. The same can be said for national icons, such as La Moneda, which retain the memory of tragedy even today. Not all symbols evoke negative feelings, however. The Chile Stadium (previously Estadio Chile) has been renamed Estadio Victor Jara in honor of the notable musician who died in that location. President Bachelet inaugurated a museum in Santiago in 2010 dedicated to commemorating victims of the human rights atrocities (The Museum of Memory and Human Rights). Further, President Bachelet proclaimed Patio 29 to be a historic national landmark.

Memorials are not simply about commemorating the dead, however. A recent shift in the utilization of human rights memorials gives insight into how Chile is changing. Villa Grimaldi is a former concentration camp used by DINA to torture and execute the opposition. In 1997 the camp was redesigned as a "park for peace" (Consejo de Monumentos Nacionales Ministerio de Educación Gobierno de Chile, n.d.; Hite and Collins 2009). An example of the shift in significance of Villa Grimaldi lies in the construction of a wooden water tower that was once used to house prisoners. The water tower was originally rebuilt to be viewed from all vantage points and serve as a constant reminder of the atrocities that occurred. Currently, however, the water tower is obscured from view by a large stage constructed for public events (Meade 2001). This historic landmark now serves a variety of purposes. Victims and families gather to remember, mourn, and heal, while others use the site to educate and even entertain as theater groups and musicians have begun performing there (Hite and Collins 2009). Chilean national identity is dynamic, an imagined community that responds to evolving relationships between the victims, families, and the rest of the nation. Since monuments and commemorations are symbolic representations and a public acknowledgment of identity, then the utility of the monument is also dynamic. This transformation is evidence that the national dialog of Chile is also changing.

Human rights issues were once a fringe movement in Chile. Recently, the dialog has shifted and human rights issues are now of primary concern to a large group of Chileans. Pinochet's arrest in the late 1990s electrified victims' rights advocates. Pioneered by the Rettig Report, numerous reports have surfaced detailing the atrocities of the Pinochet regime. The reports established the profundity of Pinochet's clandestine operations and allowed the Justice Department finally to take legal action. Pinochet was arrested in England and extradited to Chile to begin trial hearings, but he was deemed unfit and was never convicted. Armed forces personnel did not go unscathed, however. Members of the armed forces were directly held accountable in national tribunals and trials. The head of DINA, Manuel Contreras, is currently serving 25 life sentences totaling 289 years after he was convicted for his numerous human rights violations, specifically torture, rape, and murder, and his involvement in political assassinations in Chile and abroad. The government has consistently made frequent efforts since 2006 to make reparations to the victims' families and to put all effort into finding truth and obtaining justice.

but, nevertheless, the Empire's retraction is thought to have created a political vacuum which transformed local intergroup relationships; these relationships were antagonistic and consequently involved physical violence.

This study investigates how violence was experienced among newly formed social groups in the Andahuaylas region of south-central Peru following Wari imperial fragmentation. Human crania excavated from Middle Horizon and LIP mortuary contexts were systematically assessed. To discern how violence was experienced in Andahuaylas before and after the era of Wari fragmentation, crania from both eras were examined for evidence of head wounds, a reliable proxy for physical conflict. Trauma data were correlated with attributes including age, sex, and cranial modification, to determine how violence may have variably impacted different subpopulation groupings.

14.2   Historical context

14.2.1   The post-imperial Chanka of Andahuaylas, Peru

Following Wari fragmentation in the Andahuaylas region, a near-hinterland province located about a 2-day walk southeast from the old imperial capital, the Chanka society coalesced as a formidable and distinctive presence (Bauer *et al.* 2010) (Figure 14.1). Chanka social organization during the LIP was likely structured by the *ayllu*, a complex amalgam of nested and complementary ranked groups. Practically speaking, *ayllu* members collectively managed corporate landholdings, shared communal burial crypts, and claimed descent from a common mythohistoric ancestor (Isbell 1997). Bioaffinity data derived from analysis of cranial non-metric traits show that the Chanka are directly descended from earlier, Wari-era populations in Andahuaylas (Pink and Kurin 2011).

Archaeological data suggest that the Chanka experienced significant levels of violence. Hilltop settlements were built and occupied in Andahuaylas just after Wari fragmentation between AD 1000 and 1100 (Bauer *et al.* 2010: 80; Bauer and Kellett 2010; Kellett 2010). Settlements were isolated and lacked water sources; many consisted of defensive features such as walls, ditches, precipices on three sides, and lookouts. Caches of used, functional weaponry have been found at many Chanka sites (Gómez 2009).

Similarly, recent ethnohistoric research indicates fierce competition among different Chanka groups (Hyland and Amado Gonzalez 2010). For instance, several early colonial testimonies relate that Chanka leaders dispossessed rivals by "pulling crops from the root and slinging stones" (Hostnig *et al.* 2007 [1612]: 491). Although historic portrayals depict the Chanka as

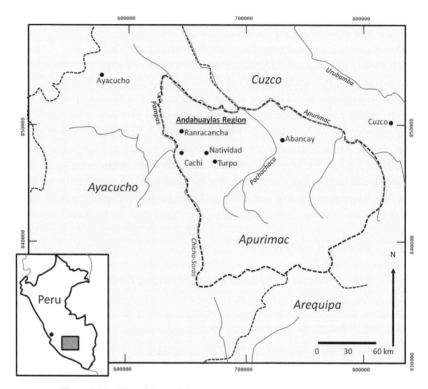

Figure 14.1. Map of the Andahuaylas region. Study sites include Ranracancha, Cachi, Natividad, and Turpo.

a capriciously bellicose society which emerged from the ashes of a crumbling archaic empire, the relationship between Chanka social groupings and violence remains poorly understood.

14.2.2   *The emergence of cranial modification in Andahuaylas: novel affiliations*

Among the many distinctive cultural attributes that structured Chanka society was the practice of cranial modification. Cranial modification, the intentional deformation of the infant skull using pads, bands, and boards (O'Brien and Stanley 2011), is perhaps the most salient corporeal indicator of social identity in the ancient Andes. Indeed, Spanish and Mestizo chroniclers, including Betanzos (2004 [1557]), Cieza de Leon (1984 [1553]), and Garcilaso de la Vega (1966 [1609–1613]), all related that cranial modification signaled some type of affiliation.

Today, many anthropologists interpret cranial modification not just as an artifact of normative child-rearing practices (see Shimada *et al.* 2004; Verano 1994) but as a marker of a social identity and group affiliation. In the Andes, studies have consistently demonstrated that cranial modification was often employed to demarcate different sectors of the population, including occupational groups (Lozada and Buikstra 2002), social or ethnic groups (Torres-Rouff 2002), moiety and residential descent groups (Hoshower *et al.* 1995), lineages (Blom 2005), and even elites (Dembo and Imbelloni 1938). Previous research in Andahuaylas has revealed several significant trends in cranial modification. For instance, cranial modification was practiced in Andahuaylas only after Wari's fragmentation. None of 36 individuals from the Middle Horizon evinces modified crania. However, during the early LIP, cranial modification rates increased significantly to 76% (208/273) (Fisher's exact; $P = 0.0001$; $n = 309$). Modification rates remained high throughout the LIP.

Discerning the meaning of cranial modification in Andahuaylas has been tricky. Modified head shapes are not significantly associated with sex, burial cave, historically documented *ayllu* or moiety, diet (revealed through carbon isotope analysis), residential origin (as determined through strontium isotope analysis), biological affinity (informed by cranial non-metric traits), or status (as indicated through grave goods) (Kurin 2012). Presently, the consensus among scholars in Andahuaylas is that cranial modification signals affiliation with a historically contingent social group. This social group may have been structured to some extent by lineage, kinship category (i.e. primogeniture), or an ethnic or "ethnic-like" identity.

Regardless of the type of social identity and affiliation demarcated through a modified head, the implementation of this boundary-marking practice (separating "us" and "them") is noteworthy (see Barth 1969). The sudden, novel use of cranial modification in post-imperial Andahuaylas appears to be part of a larger process of ethnogenesis during the nascent LIP. In this case, ethnogenesis refers to invented or reformulated traditions which come to prominence as social boundary markers, integrated with surviving or vestigial elements of past societies that become stitched together in such a way that the boundaries between groups are radically redefined compared to previous generations (see also Knudson and Stojanowski 2009).

Ethnogenesis is a common feature in eras emerging from dramatic societal restructuring. In highland Peru, tightly imbricated social, political, and economic relationships unraveled at the end of the Middle Horizon, and new social affiliations were necessarily forged. During the LIP, fraught with unforeseen challenges, solidarity groups would have to have been maintained, occasionally activated, and (re)created in each generation. Certain practices of affiliation may have been necessary so that in-group members could make legitimate claims to access natural resources and social networks. Modification may have been one strategy that facilitated this process. Yet, although cranial modification could have promoted solidarity among in-group members, it may have simultaneously provoked further balkanization with those outside the group (Torres-Rouff 2002). These antagonisms could have become violent (see Sen 2008; Taylor 2010). Thus, an important question remains: what were the consequences of ethnogenesis with respect to experiences of violence during the tumultuous LIP?

14.3   Materials and methods

To better understand how Andahuaylan lifeways were impacted by Wari fragmentation and the ensuing sociocultural and political machinations, human skeletal remains (minimum number of individuals [MNI] = 477) were systematically excavated from one late Middle Horizon tomb (*c.* AD 700–1000) and 14 early LIP burial caves in the region (*c.* AD 1000–1250) (Figure 14.2).

14.3.1   Site descriptions

Turpo (Middle Horizon)

Rescue excavations at Qatun Rumi (3206 meters above sea level [m.a.s.l.]) in Turpo District, Andahuaylas Province, focused on the recovery of human

Figure 14.2. Typical burial cave in Andahuaylas.

remains and artifacts from a stone-lined, circular, semi-subterranean tomb. In all, crania representing at least 36 individuals were recovered from the circular tomb, and 26 of them were at least 15 years old. Within the tomb, a bone bed of disarticulated human remains was deposited above a fully articulated middle adult male (35–50 years old). This "apical" male was buried face down in a tightly flexed position on a thin-beamed wooden pallet, likely fabricated for the occasion. A sample of wood from the burial pallet was radiocarbon dated to cal AD 880–990 (2σ), placing it squarely in the twilight of Wari's imperial existence during the later Middle Horizon.

The style of the tomb was similar to those uncovered elsewhere in both the Wari heartland and hinterland (Ochatoma Paravicino 2007; Tung 2007b: 251). Poorly preserved, culturally unaffiliated terraces are also located near the tomb, and a pre-Hispanic road runs next to the site. Several classes of artifacts recovered during excavation affirm that Wari's influence was pervasive in western Andahuaylas. High-quality Viñaque style ceramics (Menzel 1968: 143) were present, along with locally produced vessels with emulated Wari motifs. Excavations also uncovered high-status Wari goods, including a figurine pendant depicting an elite, collared individual wearing a four-cornered hat with crossed arms (Ochatoma Paravicino 2007: 203) and pupil-less eyes (Cook 1992). A fragment of a face-neck jar depicts Wari Agent 102 (Knobloch 2002), an individual who played an integral role in the proselytization and subjugation of distant regions during Epoch 1B/2 (*c.* AD 700). In the lab, the well-contextualized human remains from Turpo were assessed to provide insight on both mortuary practices and lifeways during the twilight of the Wari Empire.

Natividad (LIP Chanka)

The Natividad Museum collection consists of skeletal remains of 24 individuals, 19 of whom were over 15 years of age. Remains derive from a burial cave on the Qasiachi plateau in Turpo District (3405 m.a.s.l.). Reconnaissance survey work and loosely associated ceramics suggest the caves were used during the LIP. According to colonial documents, Turpo was governed by a powerful upper moiety Chanka lord named Guasco, whose family maintained leadership in the region for at least five centuries (Cieza de Leon 1996 [1553]; Hostnig *et al.* 2007 [1612]; Julien 2002 [1539]).

Cachi (LIP Chanka)

Located in San Antonio de Cachi District, Andahuaylas Province, the archaeological complex at Cachi was home to a historically documented upper moiety Chanka community. Radiocarbon dating and Wari-style pottery indicate that Cachi witnessed significant Wari investment in mining, agriculture, and pastoralism between cal AD 690–973 (2σ). During the eleventh century AD, burial caves in Cachi were cleaned out and refurbished. Subsequently caves were used for internment for about a century on average, between cal AD 1123 and 1290 (2σ). LIP mortuary assemblages included small personal items (e.g. spindle whorls and *tupu* mantle pins) marking gender-based (Silverblatt, 1987) or social collectives. Offerings of non-functional artifacts like paired miniature ceramics, curated carnivore skulls, and camelid *conopas* (talismans) were commonly encountered and likely formed part of a mortuary assemblage that signaled patrilineal affiliation (Arriaga 1968 [1621]: 29; Betanzos 2004 [1557]: 109). Finally, paired stone weapons like *liwis, aillos,* and *porras* were uncovered and are important indirect signatures of warfare and violence (Nielsen and Walker 2009).

At Cachi, skeletal remains were excavated from three sectors and, in total, 162 individuals over the age of 15 were assessed in the lab. The largest sector at Cachi, called Sonhuayo (3365 m.a.s.l.), is a 5-ha. fortified habitation located on a promontory that has commanding views of the surrounding region. The accessible south side of the site is protected by a wide ditch and a series of concentric walls. Several dozen agglutinated circular houses were arranged into haphazard patio groups and burial caves were carved out of the existing bedrock nearby. Three intact mortuary caves were excavated within this sector, and surface remains were collected from an additional six caves that were all badly looted, yielding 129 crania amenable to analysis. At the nearby Masumachay sector (3380 m.a.s.l.), burial caves were hewn from bedrock outcrops in the middle part of a butte-like hill that has poorly preserved terraces. Four crania from three caves were assessed from this sector. Finally, the Mina Cachihuancaray sector (3530 m.a.s.l.) is characterized by the Mina rock salt mine, where extraction by hand has continued unabated for some 10 centuries. A few meters downslope of this mine are burial caves. In all, 56 crania were recovered from two caves in this sector.

Ranracancha (LIP Chanka)

Finally, 42 crania were assessed from a looted burial cave at Ranracancha (3436 m.a.s.l.) (Chincheros Province) called Ayamachay. Thirty-seven individuals from this cave were at least 15 years old. Sixteenth-century documents relate that Ranracancha was populated by members of the Anccohuallyo *ayllu* (Bauer *et al.* 2010; Kellett 2010), a group that conformed to the lower moiety Chanka. Ceramic styles and radiocarbon dates indicate internment during the early LIP (AD 1160–1260). There are no visible signs of pre-Hispanic architecture near Ayamachay Cave, but there are extensive LIP terraces 3.0 km east.

14.3.2   Methods

Although excavations yielded cranial and postcranial remains, this article only presents data derived from analysis of human crania. This unit of analysis was selected because crania afford information on age, sex, and the absence or presence of cranial modification. Moreover, head trauma in particular is often attributed to violent physical confrontations rather than accidental injury (Tung 2007a, 2012; Walker 2001). Cranial MNIs were determined based on the number of diagnostic crania (at least 75% complete). Age-at-death estimations were made using standard methods (Buikstra and Ubelaker 1994). Cranial vault suture closure scores were summed to determine an S value correlated with mean ages, and maxillary dental wear scores were employed to determine broad age categories which could be compared to other south-central Peruvian populations (Tung 2012). For subadults, dental development and eruption were used to determine the age at death (Hillson 1996; Ubelaker 1989). Finally, sex estimation was based on dimorphic features on the cranium; crania were designated as male, female, probable male or female, or unknown (Buikstra and Ubelaker 1994: 21). Because sexually dimorphic features are not expressed in individuals until after puberty, juveniles under 15 years of age were designated as "unknown."

Anthropogenic features of the crania were also evaluated. Evidence for cranial modification was assessed anthroposcopically, and confirmed through the measurement of cranial arcs and chords (Kurin 2012; see Torres-Rouff 2002). Heads were classified as either modified or unmodified ("normal").

Bioarchaeologists have had much success in discerning the social contexts of violent interactions based on trauma frequency, location, and distribution (Frayer 1997; Martin and Frayer 1997; Tung 2012; Walker 1997). To ascertain how violence was experienced in Andahuaylas, crania were examined for evidence of head wounds. Despite remodeling, evidence of injury becomes sedimented in bone for several years, usually leaving residual defects that allow us to see the accumulated effects of violence over the life of an individual (Agarwal and Glencross 2011). Trauma data were collected on the location of affected areas on bone, including the side, region, and aspect. The number and types of fractures or defects were calculated from the inventory and distribution of wound impacts (Jurmain 1999; Lovell 1997), and concomitant abnormal bone changes were described. Trauma frequency sheds light on rates of violence within a population, while the location and distribution of wounds informs on the victim's position relevant to the direction of force (Galloway 1999) and may illuminate normative patterns of aggression that targeted specific regions of the head. For instance, multiple perimortem facial injuries on a single individual may be an example of excessive rage-filled "overkill" violence (Rautman and Fenton 2005), while lethal wounds directed to the base of the skull may signal execution blows (Ta'ala *et al.* 2006). Thus, used in conjunction with wound distribution and frequency, trauma lethality can signal whether the potential intent of an assailant during a violent confrontation was to injure or kill an opponent. Following standard practices, head wounds were classified as either antemortem, which bear evidence of bone remodeling (healing), or unhealed perimortem wounds, which occur at or around the time of death (Lovell 1997). The presence of both antemortem and perimortem wounds is an unambiguous sign of consecutive assault. Finally, because the experience of adults and subadults may deviate, infant/child (0–14 years) and late adolescent/adult (15–50+ years) trauma rates were calculated separately following Tung (2003; 2012).

14.4   Results: trauma and violence in Andahuaylas

14.4.1   *Trauma during imperial and post-imperial eras*

Remains at Turpo were radiocarbon dated to the late tenth century (AD 880–990). Of 26 late adolescent/adult diagnostic crania examined, only two (7.7%) have traumatic injuries (Table 14.1). All injuries were non-lethal, and showed signs of long-term healing. In sharp contrast, during the subsequent early LIP (AMS dated *c.* AD 1080–1290), trauma rates increase significantly: 53.7% (117/218) of late adolescent/adult crania have at least one wound (Fisher's exact; $P < 0.0001$; $n = 244$). Trauma also became significantly more lethal over time. While there are no late adolescent/adult individuals with perimortem fractures from the Middle Horizon population, the Chanka sites occupied during the twelfth and thirteenth centuries apparently experienced substantial lethal violence. Fifty of 218 (22.9%) late adolescents/adult Chanka crania have at least one perimortem wound; 39% (88/225) of all wounds observed occurred at or around the time of death (Fisher's exact; $P = 0.0034$).

14.4.2   *Sex and violence in Chanka communities*

Trauma patterns between Chanka males and females are similar across Andahuaylas (Figure 14.3). There are no sex-based differences in trauma

Table 14.1. *Trauma among late adolescent/adults in Andahuaylas.*

Site	Sex	Cranial MNI	Number w/ trauma	% w/ trauma	Total number of wounds	Average number of wounds	Antemortem: perimortem trauma	Total trauma rates
Turpo (Wari-affiliated)	Males	11	2	18.1	4	2.00	N/A	7.7% (2/26)
	Females	5	0	0	0	N/A	N/A	
	Unknown	10	0	0	0	N/A	N/A	
Ranracancha (Chanka)	Males	19	11	57.9	31	2.81	2.44:1	62.1% (23/37)
	Females	17	11	64.7	13	1.18	2.25:1	
	Unknown	1	1	100	2	2.00	n/a	
Natividad (Chanka)	Males	16	7	43.7	9	1.29	0.5:1	52.6% (10/19)
	Females	3	3	100	3	1.00	0.5:1	
Cachi (Chanka)	Males	63	36	57.1	64	1.78	2.05:1	51.8% (84/162)
	Females	72	45	62.5	92	2.04	1.34:1	
	Unknown	27	3	11.1	7	2.33	0.4:1	
Total		244	119	48.8	225			

Table 14.2. *Summary table of wound distribution on Andahuaylan males and females.*

	Left	Right	Anterior	Posterior	Superior	Inferior	Total
Middle Horizon							
Antemortem	0	0	3	1	0	0	4
Perimortem	0	0	0	0	0	0	0
Total wounded males	0	0	3	1	0	0	**4**
($n = 2$)							
Antemortem	0	0	0	0	0	0	0
Perimortem	0	0	0	0	0	0	0
Total wounded females	0	0	0	0	0	0	**0**
($n = 0$)							
Late Intermediate Period							
Antemortem	11	12	26	17	5	0	71
Perimortem	7	7	13	3	1	2	33
Total wounded males	18	19	39	20	6	2	**104**
($n = 54$)							
Antemortem	14	10	17	14	9	0	64
Perimortem	7	8	15	8	0	5	43
Total wounded females	21	18	32	22	9	5	**107**
($n = 56$)							

Table 14.3. *Wound tally and distribution on modified and unmodified individuals.*

	Left	Right	Anterior	Posterior	Superior	Inferior	Total
Antemortem (mod.)	24	18	40	26	14	0	122
Perimortem (mod.)	9	12	23	10	2	7	63
Total modified (n)	33	30	63	36	16	7	**185**
Modified (%)	(17.8%)	(16.2%)	(34.1%)	(19.5%)	(8.6%)	(3.8%)	
Antemortem (unmod.)	2	4	4	5	0	0	15
Perimortem (unmod.)	4	3	5	1	0	0	13
Total unmodified (n)	6	7	9	6	0	0	**28**
Unmodified (%)	(21.4%)	(25%)	(32.1%)	(21.4%)	(0%)	(0%)	

frequencies (males $= 52.9\%$, females $= 75.7\%$; Fisher's exact; $P = 0.2378$; $n = 190$), the ratio of lethal to sublethal wounds (Table 14.2; Fisher's exact; $P = 0.2512$; $n = 211$), or the average number of wounds (males $= 1.96$, females $= 1.40$; unpaired t test; $P = 0.9685$). Finally, male and female trauma distribution patterns were similar; sex is not correlated with trauma on a particular region of the head (Table 14.2).

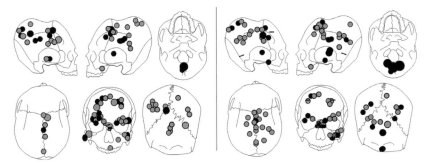

Figure 14.3. Trauma lethality and distribution between Chanka males (left) and females (right). Grey circles signal antemortem trauma; black circles indicate perimortem trauma.

Trauma frequencies, lethality, and wound distribution are not significantly different between Chanka males and females. These results suggest that both males and females were experiencing violence in similar social contexts, or that sex did not mediate the frequency, location, or lethality of attack. This pattern is distinct from traditional cases of Andean warfare, where males tend to display significantly more trauma than females (Tung 2007a; 2012). Instead, trauma data from Andahuaylas appear to be strongly associated with cranial modification.

14.4.3   Trauma among modified and unmodified adults

Thus far, trauma data from Andahuaylas have shown that Chanka individuals experienced significantly more violence then earlier Middle Horizon populations. Moreover, Chanka late adolescent/adult males and females experienced physical attacks that were congruent in their frequency, lethality, and location.

However, not all Chanka late adolescent/adults were targeted for attack. While some individuals were singled out for head trauma, others did not experience violence severe enough to break bone. In this case, the difference appears to have been primarily based on whether or not an individual had a modified head. Trauma rates among modified and unmodified Chanka are significantly different. Of 160 modified individuals, 97 (60.6%) had at least one traumatic wound, while only 16 of 50 (32%) unmodified crania had at least one instance of trauma (Fisher's exact; $P = 0.0006$; $n = 210$) (Figure 14.4).

14.4.4   Trauma among modified and unmodified juveniles

Head wound trends for late adolescents and adults in Andahuaylas also extend to subadults under 15 years of age. Juvenile trauma rates increased overall

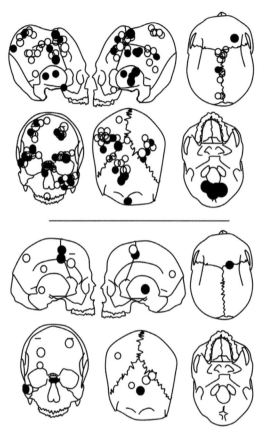

Figure 14.4. Trauma among Chanka individuals with modified crania (top) and unmodified crania (bottom). Clear circles signal antemortem trauma; black circles indicate perimortem trauma.

from 0% (0/10) during the Wari era to 14.3% (3/21) during the post-imperial period (Fisher's exact; $P = 0.5328$; $n = 31$). Relative to the preceding Wari era when no juveniles exhibited head trauma (Tung 2012), this is a striking change that further demonstrates that the Chanka lived during a violent and tumultuous time, both for adults as well as children. Intriguingly, in Andahuaylas, wounded children were only present at Chanka sites; juvenile crania ($n = 12$) from other contemporaneous (non-Chanka) cultural groups in the region do not display head wounds (Kurin 2012).

Similar to the older group, cranial modification appears to have structured experiences of violence among Chanka juveniles. All three wounded Chanka subadults also had cranial modification; wounds were all higher impact blunt force trauma with characteristic depression and radiating fractures. Linear fractures, which are usually caused by lower forces and stem from accidental injury (Lovell 1997), were not observed. The lone unmodified child cranium in the sample had no trauma. Because of the small sample size, trauma differences between modified and unmodified juveniles are not statistically significant (Fisher's exact; $P = 1.000$; $n = 21$). However, the trend suggests that traumatic injuries were not restricted to modified individuals within a specific age cateogry. Regardless of age, those who displayed cranial modification (a practice that must occur in infancy) were predisposed to a higher level of violence.

14.4.5 Distribution of trauma in modified and unmodified groups

The location of trauma can inform on the social context of the encounter and intent of the assailant (Ta'ala *et al.* 2006). This study compared the distribution of wounds between the modified and unmodified groups (Table 14.3). Significant differences are apparent: only individuals with cranial modification had wounds targeting the superior and inferior portions of the vault (Fisher's exact; $P = 0.0322$; $n = 213$).

Furthermore, only Chanka crania with modification demonstrated unsurvivable basal skull wounds, called ring fractures. With this type of wound, impact forces caused the basilar portion of the occipital to separate from the rest of the vault. Radiating fractures split dense features terminating at the foramen magnum, and posterior fracture margins on the occipital squama displayed internal beveling. With this type of wound, the brainstem is often lacerated, and death is almost always immediate (DiMaio and DiMaio 2001). Biomechanically, ring fractures can be caused by vertical loading and impact forces transmitted up through the cervical spine and occipital condyles, as experienced in high falls (Lovell 1997). However, ring fractures from falls are usually associated with cervical vertebrae compression fractures. In Andahuaylas, not a single cervical vertebra of more than 2224 observed had this type of fracture. Because there is no evidence that ring fractures are from falls, the likely etiology of these wounds in Andahuaylas is violent blunt force trauma. The location of the wound indicates that the victims likely had their heads bowed, exposing the base of the skull. Several strikes to the base of the skull of a kneeling, subdued individual by a standing assailant would lead to the ring fractures observed on Andahuaylan crania. A similar pattern of lethal injury, characterized as execution blows, was found on crania from post-imperial contexts at the former Wari capital city in Ayacucho (Tung 2008) and at the Khmer Rouge killing fields (Ta'ala *et al.* 2006).

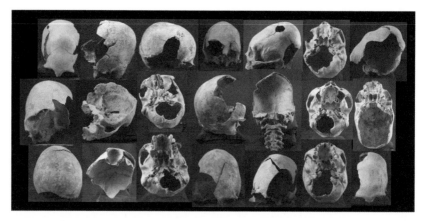

Figure 14.5. Excessive trauma and ring fractures on modified Chanka crania.

14.4.6   Head shape and excessive trauma

When Chanka individuals were targeted for violence, those with cranial modification tended to be the victims of consecutive violent encounters, unambigu-
ously evinced by the presence of both antemortem and perimortem trauma. Of
97 modified individuals with trauma, 16 (16.5%) have both antemortem and
perimortem wounds, while none of the unmodified individuals (0/16) were the
victims of repeated aggression. This difference is nearly significant (Fisher's
exact; $P = 0.0715$; $n = 113$). Given this trend, it appears that Chanka men and
women with cranial modification were victims of recidivism, while the group
with unmodified, "normal," head shapes evaded repeated attacks.

Finally, synchronic, excessive violence was also enacted within Chanka
communities. This type of violence may be identified by the presence of
multiple perimortem blunt force traumas that are redundant and physically
destructive (Figure 14.5). In post-imperial Andahuaylas, these repetitive, high
impact, overkill blows were mostly directed towards the face. Although crania
($n = 34$) from contemporaneous, non-Chanka sites in the region were also
examined to provide a comparison (Kurin 2012), excessive wounds were only
observed during the post-imperial era, exclusively in Chanka communities,
and only on modified crania.

14.5   Discussion: exploring motivations of violence in Andahuaylas

14.5.1   Interpreting trauma during the Wari era

Compared to other contemporaneous Andean hinterland communities (Tung
2012), cranial trauma among Wari-era populations in Andahuaylas was low

and non-lethal. This suggests that assailants may have intended to injure – but not kill – the victim during the assaults. Moreover, given that trauma only impacted males, what sort of violence might have been taking place?

Sublethal anterior cranial injuries in the Andes are often attributed to a form of ritualized conflict called *tinku* (Tung 2012: 139), or *takanakuy* in Andahuaylas. In cases of *takanakuy*, combatants from different *ayllus* meet at a central location to face off. During these yearly events, community tensions are released as fighters trade blows. Ethnographic observations of over three dozen *takanakuy* encounters in Andahuaylas revealed that jabs, crosses, and uppercuts were never used, while hooks and bolo punches were only thrown in a few bouts. In almost all cases, combatants lunged with wild, uncontrolled, roundhouse blows. This type of fighting significantly impacted the nasal bones, lateral eye orbits, zygomatics, greater wings of the sphenoid and temporal bones; medial areas around the frontal bosses and superior coronal suture tended to evade impact. Although hands were bandaged, combatants also tended to display broken metatarsals ("boxer's fractures") (see Lovell 1997). Assuming traditional fighting styles have remained relatively unchanged over several centuries, the lack of wounds to the sides of the face and broken hand bones at Turpo suggest *takanakuy* was not the cause of injuries.

Sublethal violence on males may be evidence of more acrimonious encounters. For instance, Tung's (2012: 125) research on trauma in the Wari southern hinterlands documented injuries on the frontal bones and facial area of males as well as concomitant parry fractures of the radius and ulna. These data were interpreted as evidence of face-to-face physical conflict and possibly raiding. Yet, in Wari-era Andahuaylas, the low trauma rate and the lack of clear evidence of parry fractures suggests that violence at Turpo did not take the form of malevolent attacks either. Because trauma data largely rule out other forms of violence, it appears that males at Turpo may have occasionally fallen victim to interpersonal conflict resolution with prescribed rules of engagement (Chagnon 1992), or perhaps some form of community sanctioned corporal punishment (Tung 2012: 144–5). Overall, there is no evidence at present to suggest that the later Wari era (Middle Horizon) in Andahuaylas was a time of endemic conflict.

14.5.2   Interpreting trauma among the Chanka

Trauma patterns at the three LIP Chanka sites are distinct. Ranracancha, Natividad, and Cachi were engaged in a context of violence distinct from earlier Wari-era populations. The striking similarity in trauma patterning between males and females, and between juveniles and late adolescents/adults, informs on the type of violence that the Chanka may have experienced.

Violence from raiding and traditional warfare tends to be associated with disparate trauma rates, distribution, and lethality between males and females, and old and young. This is not the case among the Chanka. Instead, violence seems to be structured by the performance of cranial modification. Given the significant disparities in trauma patterning between those with and without cranial modification, it appears that modifying the shape of one's head was a culturally meaningful practice, one that denoted a specific type of ethnic, social, or cultural identity. Conspicuously demarcated through head shape (among other archaeologically unidentifiable indicators), the identity embodied by those with modified crania apparently signaled their status as potential victims of violence to as-of-yet unknown assailants. This type of selective assault has few analogs in the prehistoric past. In contemporary societies, violence that targets particular social, cultural, or ethnic groupings has been characterized as intergroup violence, sectarian conflict, civil war, ethnocide, and genocide (see Bhavnani and Backer 2000; Gould 1999; Hinton 2002; Horowitz 1985; Potter and Chuipka 2010; United Nations General Assembly 1948). The evidence from ancient Andahuaylas strongly suggests that a similar iteration of selective violence was occurring during the tumultuous milieu that constituted the post-imperial Chanka era. There are several lines of data that support this interpretation.

High trauma rates among males, females, and juveniles with cranial modification

Foremost, late adolescents/adults with cranial modification have significantly more trauma than their unmodified counterparts. These results strongly suggest that, within post-imperial Chanka communities, victims of violence were primarily and disproportionately singled out for attack based on identification and recognition of head shape. In sharp contrast, unmodified individuals led less violent lives. The stark disparity in trauma rates between groups is a fundamental correlate of violence that singles out certain subpopulations within society.

Trauma enacted against children is another key indicator of intergroup violence. The frequency of childhood trauma among the prehistoric Chanka (14.3%) is high even among modern populations (c.f. United Nations 2009). Although abuse is a common etiology of trauma in children and may increase in times of stress (Korbin 2003), only children from Chanka communities with modified crania demonstrated head wounds. The disparate treatment of children is commonly seen in ethnographic examples of genocidal behavior (vs. traditional warfare), where children are actually targeted for killing. This seems to have been the case for Chanka juveniles with modified crania; they, like their adult counterparts, were singled out for violence.

Executions, recidivism, and excessive trauma among those with cranial modification

Unique locations or mechanisms of injury can become normative for groups of aggressors. For these reasons, violent acts can sometimes be attributed to a particular segment of society. For instance, in Peru during the 1980–2000 civil war, different causes of death could be associated with agents of the state (e.g. military, secret police), who tended to use small arms fire, compared to the Shining Path *Senderista* terrorists, who overwhelmingly employed blunt force trauma to subdue victims (Comisión de la Verdad y Reconciliación 2003). While the identity of aggressors in Andahuaylas remains unknown, the similarity in targets and methods across the region may point to a common enemy.

Beside informing on possible motivations for violence, wound patterning also indicates the victim's position at the moment of impact. In Andahuaylas, the presence of ring fractures on Chanka men, women, and juveniles with cranial modification indicates that those individuals were possibly incapacitated when they received deadly, close range, blunt force trauma. The victims were ultimately interred collectively in burial caves with uninjured and unmodified men, women, and children. The lack of any specialized mortuary treatment for individuals with excessive trauma points to violent behavior not commonly associated with ritual sacrifice in the Andes (see Benson and Cook 2001). Moreover, individuals with ring fractures were found at different Chanka sites; this evidence does not support a single mass killing or massacre scenario (Frayer 1997; Slaus *et al.* 2010; Tung 2008; Verano 1986; Willey and Emerson 1993). Rather, ring fractures arising from efficient, depersonalized executions of defenseless victims have been noted in cases of modern genocide (Ta'ala *et al.* 2006).

In addition to execution blows, other trauma patterns are consistent with selective intergroup violence. For instance, only individuals with cranial modification demonstrated both antemortem and perimortem wounds, unambiguous evidence of injury recidivism. Apparently, individuals with modified head shapes were more likely to become the victims of repeated aggression. Finally, the fact that excessive "overkill" violence was solely directed towards Chanka men, women, and children with cranial modification is especially significant. This type of trauma is deeply symbolic. Repeated blunt force injury is meant to increase the suffering of a victim (Kimmerle and Baraybar 2008), and the intentional fragmentation of the skull (but not the postcranial skeleton) suggests destruction and dehumanization, distinct from cases of dispatched witches (see Darling 1998). In post-imperial Chanka communities, the physical destruction of modified crania would have been a potent method of obliterating a victim's identity. This form of trauma has deep roots in the Peruvian highlands: witness testimony from Andahuaylas relates how *Senderistas* in the late 1980s would almost always smash the faces of victims with large rocks to symbolically destroy their identities, as well as inhibit the positive identification of victims (Theidon 2001). Centuries earlier, chronicler Juan de Betanzos (2004 [1557]: 244) reported that battle axes were used to "smash heads to pieces," as the final step in a longer process of genocidal torture. Osteological evidence from Andahuaylas appears to confirm at least part of the chronicler's account.

14.6   The social dimension of intergroup conflict in post-imperial Andahuaylas

Coalescing in the wake of Wari fragmentation, the Chanka appear to have employed cranial modification as a novel form of demarcating intergroup differences. This active process of ethnogenesis was not a matter of biology, but rather structured by historically and politically contingent and embedded conventions. These groups became socially relevant as distinctions were acknowledged – tacitly or implicitly – as people went about their day-to-day lives.

As a permanent process, cranial modification may have provided a solid basis for forming coalitions. This boundary-marking tradition persisted for hundreds of years despite the very real risk of violence associated with the affiliation signaled by an intentionally elongated head. Motivations for violence are still unclear, but selective, intergroup violence may have been a strategic mechanism used to gain access over resources, build allegiances with like-minded members, completely eliminate rivals, and legitimize dominant authority and beliefs (see Fearon and Laitin 1996) during a tumultuous era that witnessed the disintegration of Wari hegemony and infrastructure as well as the coalescence of novel, regional societies in the early LIP.

Human remains were used to evaluate this scenario. This study hypothesized that violence increased after Wari collapse, and cranial trauma data appear to support this hypothesis. Compared to the late Wari imperial era, trauma rates increased significantly during the post-imperial Chanka period. Violence also became significantly more lethal in the post-imperial era, as illustrated by a dramatic increase in perimortem trauma.

Within Chanka communities, wound frequency, lethality, and distribution are similar between males and females. This indicates that they experienced violence in similar encounters. Importantly, trauma rates and patterns diverged significantly between individuals with cranial modification and those with "normal-shaped" heads. Males, females, and juveniles with cranial modification had significantly (or nearly significantly) more trauma than their contemporaneous, unmodified neighbors. They were also more likely to be the victims of successive violent encounters. The fact that all members of this subpopulation group appear to have been equally impacted by attack is an indispensable correlate of genocidal behavior in modern societies.

The distribution of head wounds also points to violence that singled out a particular group within Chanka communities. Only modified individuals had trauma directed at the inferior portions of the vault. These deadly ring fractures on the skull base indicate that those individuals were likely incapacitated when they became the victims of close range, execution-style blunt force trauma. Moreover, repeated, high impact, lethal, overkill blows were used to physically and symbolically extirpate the identity of modified victims.

As victims of selective intergroup violence, Chanka men, women, and children with cranial modification endured fundamentally different social contexts of conflict than both their unmodified neighbors and their Wari-era ancestors. The skeletal data from Andahuaylas clearly indicate that local intergroup relationships were profoundly transformed in the decades following Wari imperial fragmentation. Notably, cranial modification emerged as a newly significant and highly conspicuous means of group differentiation. However, with this distinction came the systematic, targeted killing of those newly identifiable group members. In sum, skeletal data strongly support a scenario whereby group identities were reformulated and, correspondingly, violent physical interactions were restructured. Connections between cranial modification and cranial trauma point to the creation of new social boundaries as well as the intentional, physical destruction of the very individuals who employed those boundary-marking practices in this region of the Andes.

Acknowledgments

This research was supported by funding from a National Science Foundation DDIG, a Fulbright-Hays DDRA fellowship, and Vanderbilt University. The Peruvian Ministry of Culture and the Municipality of Andahuaylas provided research permits and lab space. Lic. Emmanuel Gómez helped lead excavations and direct the Proyecto Bioarqueologico Andahuaylas research team. Many thanks to Debra Martin and Cheryl Anderson for inviting me to participate in this volume and for offering suggestions that greatly improved the quality of the manuscript. All errors herein are my own.

References

Agarwal, S.C. & Glencross, B.A. (eds.) (2011). *Social Bioarchaeology*. Malden: Wiley-Blackwell.

Arkush, E.N. (2008). War, chronology, and causality in the Titicaca Basin. *Latin American Antiquity*, **19**, 339–73.

(2009). Warfare, space and identity in the South-Central Andes: constraints and choices. In: Nielsen, A. & Walker, W. (eds.) *Warfare in Cultural Context: Practice Agency, and the Archaeology of Conflict*. Tucson: University of Arizona Press, Amerind Foundation Advanced Seminar Series, 190–217.

Arkush, E. N. & Stanish, C. (2005). Interpreting conflict in the ancient Andes. *Current Anthropology*, **46**, 3–28.

Arkush, E. N. & Tung, T. A. (2013). Patterns of war in the Andes from the archaic to the late horizon: insights from settlement patterns and cranial trauma. *Journal of Archaeological Research*, DOI: 10.1007/s10814–013–9065–1.

Arriaga, P. J. (1968) [1621]. *The Extirpation of Idolatry in Peru*. Lexington: University of Kentucky Press.

Bamforth, D. B. (1994). Indigenous people, indigenous violence: precontact warfare on the North American great plains. *Man, New Series*, **29**, 95–115.

Barth, F. (1969). *Ethnic Groups and Boundaries: The Social Organization of Culture Difference*. New York: Waveland Press.

Bauer, B. S. & Kellett, L. C. (2010). Cultural transformations of the Chanka Homeland (Andahuaylas, Peru) during the late intermediate period (AD 1000–1400). *Latin American Antiquity*, **21**, 87–111.

Bauer, B. S., Kellett, L. C. & Silva, M. A. (2010). *The Chanka, Archaeological Research in Andahuaylas (Apurimac), Peru*. Los Angeles: Cotsen Institute of Archaeology, UCLA.

Benson, E. P. & Cook, A. G. (eds.) (2001). *Ritual Sacrifice in Ancient Peru*. Austin: University of Texas Press.

Bhavnani, R. & Backer, D. (2000). Localized ethnic conflict and genocide: accounting for differences in Rwanda and Burundi. *Journal of Conflict Resolution*, **44**, 283–306.

Blom, D. E. (2005). Embodying borders: human body modification and diversity in Tiwanaku society. *Journal of Anthropological Archaeology*, **24**, 1–24.

Brubaker, R. & Laitin, D. D. (1998). Ethnic and nationalist violence. *Annual Review of Sociology*, **24**, 423–52.

Buikstra, J. E. & Ubelaker, D. H. (eds.) (1994). *Standards for Data Collection from Human Skeletal Remains. Proceedings of a Seminar at the Field Museum of Natural History*. Fayetteville: Arkansas Archaeological Survey, Research Series, No. 44.

Cahill, D. (2010). Advanced Andeans and backward Europeans: structure and agency in the collapse of the Inca Empire. In: McAnany, P. A. & Yoffee, N. (eds.) *Questioning Collapse: Human Resilience, Ecological Vulnerability, and the Aftermath of Empire*. Cambridge: Cambridge University Press, 207–38.

Chagnon, N. (1992). *Yanomamo*. New York: Harcourt-Brace College Publishers.

Chase-Dunn, C. & Taylor, P. (1994). Hegemony and social change. *Mershon International Studies Review*, **38**, 361–6.

Cieza de Leon, P. (1984) [1553]. *La Crónica Del Peru: Primera Parte*. Lima: Fondo Editorial, Pontificia Universidad Catolica del Peru.

(1996) [1553]. *La Crónica Del Perú*. Madrid: Cornices de America.

Comisión de la Verdad y Reconciliación. (2003). *Informe Final* [Online]. Available: www.cverdad.org.pe. [Accessed September 28, 2013.]

Cook, A. G. (1992). The stone ancestors: idioms of imperial attire and rank among Huari figurines. *Latin American Antiquity*, **3**, 341–64.

Covey, R. A. (2008). Multiregional perspectives on the archaeology of the Andes during the late intermediate period (C. A.D. 1000–1400). *Journal of Archaeological Research*, **16**, 287–338.

Darling, A. J. (1998). Mass inhumation and the execution of witches in the American Southwest. *American Anthropologist, New Series*, **100**, 732–52.

De Betanzos, J. (2004) [1557]. *Suma y Narración de los Incas*. Lima: Polifemo.

Dembo, A. & Imbelloni, J. (1938). Deformaciones intencionales del cuerpo humano de carácter étnico. *Humanior. Buenos Aires, Sección A, Tomo*, **3**, 1–348.

DiMaio, D. & DiMaio, V. (2001). *Forensic Pathology*, 2nd edn. Boca Raton: CRC Press.

Fearon, J. D. & Laitin, D. D. (1996). Weak states, rough terrain, and large-scale ethnic violence since 1945. *Paper presented at the 1999 Annual Meeting of the American Political Science Association*.

(2003). Ethnicity, insurgency, and civil war. *American Political Science Review*, **97**, 75–90.

Frayer, D. W. (1997). Ofnet: evidence for a mesolithic massacre. In: Martin, D. L. & Frayer, D. W. (eds.) *Troubled Times: Violence and Warfare in the Past*. Amsterdam: Gordon and Breach, 181–216.

Galloway, A. (ed.) (1999). *Broken Bones: Anthropological Analysis of Blunt Force Trauma*. Springfield: Charles C. Thomas.

Garcilaso de la Vega, I. (1966) [1609–1613]. *Comentarios Reales: El Origen De Los Incas*. Madrid: Bruguera.

Gómez, D. E. (2009). Investigaciones en sitios de inhumación en Andahuaylas. Universidad Nacional San Cristóbal de Huamanga: Unpublished Lic. thesis.

Gould, R. (1999). Collective violence and group solidarity: evidence from a feuding society. *American Sociological Review*, **64**, 356–80.

Hillson, S. W. (1996). *Dental Anthropology*. Cambridge: Cambridge University Press.

Hinton, A. (ed.) (2002). *The Annihilation of Difference: The Anthropology of Genocide*. Berkeley: University of California Press.

Horowitz, D. L. (1985). *Ethnic Groups in Conflict*. Berkeley: University of California Press.

Hoshower, L. M., Buikstra, J. E., Goldstein, P. S. & Webster, A. D. (1995). Artificial cranial deformation at the Omo M10 site: a Tiwanaku complex from the Moquegua Valley, Peru. *Latin American Antiquity*, **6**, 145–64.

Hostnig, R., Palomino, P. D. & Decoster, J. J. (2007) [1612]. *Proceso De Composición Y Titulación De Tierras En Apurimac*. Cuzco: Instituto de Investigaciones Jurídicas y Asesoramiento.

Hyland, S. & Amado Gonzalez, D. (2010). Marriage and conflict among Chanka Kurakas, 1570–1775. *Paper presented at the 38th Annual Midwest Andean Conference on Andean and Amazonian Archaeology and Ethnohistory*. Indiana University–Purdue University Fort Wayne. February 21.

Isbell, W. H. (1997). *Mummies and Mortuary Monuments: A Postprocessual Prehistory of Central Andean Social Organization*. Austin: University of Texas Press.

Julien, C. (2002) [1539]. Diego Maldonado y los Chancas. *Revista Andina*, **34**, 183–97.

Jurmain, R. (1999). *Stories from the Skeleton: Behavioral Reconstruction in Osteoarchaeology*. Amsterdam: Gordon and Breach Publishers.

Kellett, L. C. (2010). Chanka settlement ecology: hilltop sites, land use and warfare in late prehispanic Andahuaylas, Peru. University of New Mexico: Unpublished PhD dissertation.

Kimmerle, E. H. & Baraybar, J. P. (eds.) (2008). *Skeletal Trauma: Identification of Injuries Resulting from Human Remains Abuse and Armed Conflict*. Boca Raton: CRC Press.

Knobloch, P. J. (2002). *Who Was Who in the Middle Horizon Andean Prehistory* [Online]. Available: www-rohan.sdsu.edu/~bharley/WWWHome.html. [Accessed September 10, 2012.]

Knudson, K. J. & Stojanowski, C. M. (eds.) (2009). *Bioarchaeology and Identity in the Americas*. Gainesville: University Press of Florida.

Korbin, J. (2003). Children, childhoods, and violence. *Annual Review of Anthropology*, **32**, 431–46.

Kurin, D. S. (2012). The bioarchaeology of collapse: ethnogenesis and ethnocide in Post-Imperial Andahuaylas, Peru (AD 900–1200). Vanderbilt University: Unpublished PhD dissertation.

LaLone, D. (2000). Rise, fall and semiperipheral development in the Andean world system. *Journal of World-Systems Research*, **1**, 67–98.

Lofaro, E. M., Kurin, D. S., Krigbaum, J. & Kamenov, G. (2011). Isotopic analysis of Chanka mobility in the central highlands of Peru (Ca. AD 1000–1450). University of Florida: Unpublished MA thesis.

Lovell, N. C. (1997). Trauma analysis in paleopathology. *Yearbook of Physical Anthropology*, **40**, 139–70.

Lozada, M. C. & Buikstra, J. E. (2002). *El Senorio Chiribaya En La Costa Sur Del Peru*. Lima: Instituto de Estudios Peranos.

Martin, D. L. & Frayer, D. W. (eds.) (1997). *Troubled Times: Violence and Warfare in the Past*. Amsterdam: Gordon and Breach.

Menzel, D. (1968). *La Cultura Huari*. Lima: Compañía de Seguros y Reaseguros Peruano-Suiza.

Nielsen, A. E. & Walker, W. H. (2009). *Warfare in Cultural Context: Practice, Agency, and the Archaeology of Violence*. Tucson: University of Arizona Press.

O'Brien, T. G. & Stanley, A. M. (2011). Boards and cords: discriminating types of artificial cranial deformation in prehispanic South Central Andean Populations. *International Journal of Osteoarchaeology*, **23**, 459–70.

Ochatoma Paravicino, J. A. (2007). *Alfareros Del Imperio Huari: Vida Cotidiana Y Areas De Actividad En Conchopata*. Ayacucho, Peru: Universidad Nacional de San Cristobal de Huamanga Facultad de Ciencias Sociales.

Pink, C. & Kurin, D. S. (2011). Beyond the grave: continuity among Chanka populations in Andahuaylas Province, Peru. *Paper presented at the 76th Annual Meeting of the Society for American Archaeology*. Sacramento, CA.

Potter, J. M. & Chuipka, J. P. (2010). Perimortem mutilation of human remains in an early village in the American Southwest: a case for ethnic violence. *Journal of Anthropological Archaeology*, **29**, 507–23.

Rautman, A. E. & Fenton, T. W. (2005). A case of historic cannibalism in the American West: implications for southwestern archaeology. *American Antiquity*, **70**, 321–41.

Rowe, J. H. (1945). Absolute chronology in the Andean area. *American Antiquity*, **10**, 265–84.

Sen, A. (2008). Violence in identity. In: Karawan, I. A., Mccormack, W. & Reynolds, S. E. (eds.) *Values and Violence*. New York: Springer Press, 3–14.

Shimada, I., Shinoda, K., Farnum, J., Corruccini, R. & Watanabe, H. (2004). An integrated analysis of pre-hispanic mortuary practices: a middle Sican case study. *Current Anthropology*, **3**, 369–402.

Silverblatt, I. (1987). *Moon, Sun, and Witches: Gender Ideologies and Class in Colonial Peru*. Princeton: Princeton University Press.

Slaus, M., Novak, M., Vyroubal, V. & Bedic, Z. (2010). The harsh life on the 15th century Croatia-Ottoman empire military border: analyzing and identifying the reasons for the massacre in Cepin. *American Journal of Physical Anthropology*, **141**, 358–72.

Ta'ala, S. C., Berg, G. E. & Haden, K. (2006). Blunt force cranial trauma in the Cambodian killing fields. *Journal of Forensic Sciences*, **51**, 996–1001.

Tainter, J. A. (1988). *The Collapse of Complex Societies*. Cambridge: Cambridge University Press.

Taylor, C. C. (2010). Rwandan genocide: toward an explanation in which history and culture matter. In: Mcanany, P. A. & Yoffee, N. (eds.) *Questioning Collapse: Human Resilience, Ecological Aftermath of Empire*. Cambridge: Cambridge University Press, 239–68.

Theidon, K. (2001). How we learned to kill our brother: memory, morality and reconciliation in Peru. In: Sanchez, G. & Lair, E. (eds.) *Bulletin De L'institut Français Des Études Andines, No. 3 (29)*. Bogota: Colombia, 539–54.

Torres-Rouff, C. (2002). Cranial vault modification and ethnicity in middle horizon San Pedro De Atacama, North Chile. *Current Anthropology*, **43**, 163–71.

Torres-Rouff, C. & Costa Junqueira, M. A. (2006). Interpersonal violence in prehistoric San Pedro De Atacama, Chile: behavioral implications of environmental stress. *American Journal of Physical Anthropology*, **130**, 60–70.

Tung, T. A. (2003). A bioarchaeological perspective on Wari imperialism in the Andes of Peru: a view from heartland and hinterland skeletal populations. University of North Carolina, Chapel Hill: Unpublished PhD dissertation.

(2007a). Trauma and violence in the Wari Empire of the Peruvian Andes: warfare, raids, and ritual fights. *American Journal of Physical Anthropology*, **133**, 941–56.

(2007b). The village of Beringa at the periphery of the Wari empire: a site overview and new radiocarbon dates. *Andean Past*, **8**, 253–86.

(2008). Violence after imperial collapse: a study of cranial trauma among late intermediate period burials from the former Huari Capital, Ayacucho, Peru. *Ñawpa Pacha*, **29**, 101–18.

(2012). *Violence, Ritual, and the Wari Empire: A Social Bioarchaeology of Imperialism in the Ancient Andes*. Gainesville: University Press of Florida.

Ubelaker, D. H. (1989). *Human Skeletal Remains: Excavation, Analysis, Interpretation*. Washington: Taraxacum Press.

United Nations (2009). *Progress for Children: A Report Card on Child Protection*. New York: United Nations Publications.

United Nations General Assembly (1948). Convention on the Prevention and Punishment of the Crime of Genocide. Adopted December 9.

Verano, J. W. (1986). A mass burial of mutilated individuals at Pacatnamu. In: Donnan, C. B. & Cock, G. A. (eds.) *The Pacatnamu Papers, Volume 1*. Los Angeles: Museum of Cultural History, University of California, 117–38.

(1994). Características físicas y biología osteológica de Los Moche. In: Uceda, S. & Mujica, E. (eds.) *Propuestas Y Perspectivas*, Vol. 79. Lima: Travaux de l'Institut Frances d'Etudes Andines, 307–26.

Walker, P. L. (1997). Wife beating, boxing, and broken noses: skeletal evidence for the cultural patterning of violence. In: Martin, D. L. & Frayer, D. W. (eds.) *Troubled Times: Violence and Warfare in the Past*. Amsterdam: Gordon and Breach, 145–80.

(2001). A bioarchaeological perspective on the history of violence. *Annual Review of Anthropology*, **30**, 573–96.

Willey, P. & Emerson, T. E. (1993). The osteology and archaeology of the Crow Creek massacre. *Plains Anthropologist*, **38**, 227–69.

Williams, R. P. (2002). Rethinking disaster-induced collapse in the demise of the Andean Highland states: Wari and Tiwanaku. *World Archaeology*, **33**, 361–74.

Yoffee, N. (2005). *Myths of the Archaic State: Evolution of the Earliest Cities, States and Civilizations*. Cambridge: Cambridge University Press.

15 Allies today, enemies tomorrow. A comparative analysis of perimortem injuries along the biomechanical continuum

MELISSA SCOTT MURPHY, BRIAN SPATOLA, AND RICK WEATHERMON

15.1 Introduction

The historical record often guides the understanding of the violence perpetrated by the Spanish during the conquest of the Inca Empire; however, a critical close reading of the record combined with nuanced skeletal analysis is required to evaluate the victims of violence properly and to understand the social contexts of those violent encounters. For example, evidence of injuries from European weapons, such as firearms or steel-edged weapons (blunt and sharp), indicates that the victims were injured after the arrival of the Spanish; however, the perpetrators could have been Spaniards, indigenous Andean allies of the Spanish armed with European weapons, or even allies recruited from different parts of the Americas. Furthermore, the effects of sixteenth-century European weapons on human skeletal remains are little known, so the interpretation of the correspondence between the weapon and the injury is particularly challenging. In this chapter, we examine characteristics of perimortem skeletal injuries, weapon class, and mechanism of injury from historical and forensic case studies to aid in interpretation of the high frequencies of perimortem traumatic injuries (25.0%) among 120 individuals, and injuries consistent with European weapons from a sample of indigenous human skeletal remains from Puruchuco-Huaquerones (PH), Peru (Murphy *et al.* 2010). Our analysis attempts: (1) to interpret trauma characteristics based on their association with the types of weapons available before and after the arrival of the Spanish; and (2) to illuminate the context of the violence of the Spanish Conquest.

Bioarchaeological and Forensic Perspectives on Violence: How Violent Death is Interpreted from Skeletal Remains, ed. D. L. Martin and C. P. Anderson. Published by Cambridge University Press. © Cambridge University Press 2014.

15.2   Bioarchaeological trauma analysis

In this study documented historic and modern injuries are compared with historic and prehistoric unknown injuries of similar character from cemeteries at the archaeological site of PH, Peru (AD 1470–1540). The purpose of this exercise is to explore the interface between contextual and forensic anthropological approaches to interpretation of wounds from unidentified weapons. The effects of sixteenth-century European weapons on human skeletal remains are not as widely documented as those of their modern counterparts and the evidence should be approached with due caution. We examine characteristics of perimortem skull injuries, documentation of Spanish and Inca weapons, and forensic case studies to assist with interpretation of perimortem traumatic cranial injuries from PH, Peru.

15.3   Perpetrators or victims? Violence and Spanish Conquest

Warfare, raiding, and battles have been reported from pre-Hispanic contexts in the Central Andes (Andrushko 2007; Andrushko and Torres 2011; Torres-Rouff and Costa Junqueira 2006; Tung 2007; Verano 2001). Typical pre-Hispanic Andean weapons included maces, slings with sling stones, large wooden axe-like implements, bolas, tumi knives, and large wooden spears (macana) (D'Altroy 2002; Del Busto Duthurburu 1978; Himmerich and Valencia 1998; Rowe 1957). The Inca attached edges or points made of animal bone, copper, silver, or bronze to their weapons (D'Altroy 2002; Hemming 1970; Himmerich and Valencia 1998; Pizarro 1978; Rowe 1946; Salas 1950). As armor, the Incas donned lightweight cotton or textile padding.

During the conquest and invasion of the Inca Empire, the Spanish armed themselves with steel-edged swords, pikes, pole arms (such as a halberd), war hammers, crossbows, longbows, metal clubs and maces, and some firearms (arquebus, pistol, falconet) (Guilmartin 1991; Hemming 1970; Salas 1950). When musket balls were in short supply, the Spanish loaded their firearms and small cannons with rocks and metal objects (Guilmartin 1991; Salas 1950). The Spanish also discharged "branched balls" or wire balls, which were two hemispheres of lead joined together with a wire (Salas 1950: 211–12). Indigenous allies, including the Lima chiefdom from the central coast of Peru, as well as from other regions, supported the Spanish in their quest to subdue the Inca (Rostworowski 1977; 2002: 238; Spalding 1999).

In our efforts to understand the perpetrators and victims of violence in the samples from PH and to illuminate the context of violence of the Spanish Conquest, we used historic cases, forensic studies, and the biomechanical principles that apply to bone under physical stress to aid in the interpretation of trauma. Based on ethnohistoric accounts of the Spanish Conquest of the Inca Empire (D'Altroy 2002; Del Busto Duthurburu 1966, 1978; Rostworowski 2002; Spalding 1999), indigenous Andean peoples were both perpetrators and victims of violence. Other bioarchaeological studies have reported heightened levels of violence associated with the Spanish Conquest, between the Spanish and indigenous peoples and heightened internecine violence between indigenous peoples (Hutchinson 2009; Larsen *et al.* 1996; Stodder and Martin 1992). Therefore, we expected that the indigenous community at PH also experienced heightened levels of violence associated with the Spanish Conquest and warfare. Previous analysis of the perimortem injuries on individuals from PH has shown that the injuries are consistent with trauma sustained by a variety of indigenous and European weapons (Murphy *et al.* 2010). We expect that injuries or combinations of injuries with conflicting characteristics will pose significant challenges to interpretation.

15.4   Samples: archaeological, historic, and modern cases

The archaeological zone of PH is located on the Central Coast of Peru approximately 12 km southeast of the center of Lima in the middle of the Rímac valley. The archaeological zone contains several cemeteries, two of which, Huaquerones and 57AS03, are contemporaneous and located less than 1 mile from one another. Over 1200 burials have been recovered from the cemeteries. The presence of Inca-style ceramic vessels, a small number of Early Colonial ceramic vessels, as well as Inca stylistic patterns and details on textile bags, date the majority of the burials to the arrival of the Inca in the Rímac valley shortly after the arrival of the Europeans, or approximately AD 1470–1540 (Cock 2006; Cock and Goycochea 2004: 185). Previous publications have reported that the nature and frequency of perimortem injuries is different at the two cemeteries of Huaquerones and 57AS03 (13% vs. 25%, respectively), with multiple perimortem injuries observed on many individuals at 57AS03, including children (Gaither and Murphy 2012; Murphy *et al.* 2010). The higher frequency of injuries at 57AS03 may have resulted from violence associated with the Spanish Conquest, and several individuals possess injuries that may have been caused by sixteenth-century European weapons (Murphy *et al.* 2010).

For this study, a total of 53 (of which 31 are shown in Table 15.1) adult individuals (≥15 years of age) previously identified as displaying perimortem injuries to the cranium were compared to documented specimens from various collections (Table 15.1) (Murphy *et al.* 2010: 640).

Table 15.1. *Individuals with perimortem injuries to the cranium (Huaquerones and 57AS03) (Modified from Murphy* et al. *2010: 640).*

Burial number	Age	Sex	Burial type	Description of perimortem trauma
HP01–11	35–49	M	Late Horizon	Majority of cranium
HP01–32	20–34	M	Late Horizon	Right frontal
HP01–33	15–20	M	Late Horizon	Majority of left side of cranium, right mandible
HP01–76	15–20	F	Late Horizon	Left side and midline of cranium (parietal, occipital)
HP01–84	35–49	M	Late Horizon	Majority of cranium
HP01–86	20–34	M	Late Horizon	Occipital
HP01–107	35–49	M	Late Horizon	Right parietal, right temporal
HP01–123	20–34	M	Late Horizon	Mandible
HP02–170	20–34	M	Late Horizon	Majority of cranium
HP02–174	20–34	M	Late Horizon	Majority of right side of cranium
HP02–187	20–34	F	Indeterminate	Majority of cranium
HP02–193	16–18	I	Late Horizon	Left parietal
HP02–199	16–18	F	Late Horizon	Mostly to left side of cranium, some damage on right side
57AS03E048	15–20	F	Atypical	Left parietal
57AS03E073	20–34	M	Atypical	Extensive damage to left side of cranium, occipital
57AS03E107	20–34	F	Late Horizon	Multiple injuries to cranium (frontal, mandible)
57AS03119A	35–49	F	Atypical	Injuries to right frontal, zygomatic, sphenoid, and maxilla
57AS03E121	20–34	M	Atypical	Extensive damage to entire cranium
57AS03E123	20–34	M	Atypical	Possible projectile entrance and exit wounds; related damage to cranium
57AS03E145	15–20	F	Atypical	Occipital, right parietal
57AS03E160	20–34	M	Atypical	Craniofacial region
57AS03E175	35–49	M	Atypical	Maxillae and mandible
57AS03E176	50+	F	Atypical	Extensive damage to cranium
57AS03E218	20–34	M	Atypical	Occipital
57AS03E231	15–20	F	Atypical	Ovoid defect to left frontal; extensive damage to entire cranium
57AS03E248	15–20	M	Atypical	Quadrangular defects to left, posterior of cranium
57AS03E366	35–49	F	Atypical	Left temporal, parietal
57AS03E368	35–49	M	Atypical	Mandible, atlas
57AS03E449	35–49	M	Atypical	Frontal, left maxilla
57AS03E459	20–34	M	Atypical	Occipital
57AS03E479	15–20	I	Atypical	Extensive damage to entire cranium

I, Indeterminate.

Reference specimens from the National Museum of Health and Medicine (NMHM) consist of documented historic and modern examples of cranial trauma. The NMHM curates skeletal remains with a range of traumatic injuries that include a large collection of nineteenth- and twentieth-century gunshot, sharp force, and blunt force injuries from military and civilian contexts. Modern examples are drawn from the Milton Helpern Collection from the early to mid-twentieth-century cases of the New York City Medical Examiner curated at the museum. In addition to NMHM cases, this study is augmented by a reference specimen from a forensic case of a crossbow injury investigated by law enforcement from southeastern Wyoming, the county coroner, and forensic scientists from the University of Wyoming.

Documented specimens were selected to demonstrate the range of characteristics that may be seen in bone trauma through historic time from various types of objects and surfaces. The appearance of different episodes of trauma inflicted using similar weapons varies with regard to unknown factors such as striking angle and velocity. Reference specimens of documented injuries are bona fide exemplars of the typological features of trauma. They are not diagnostic tools for matching to unknown injuries; rather they display similarities and differences in characteristics that may assist in highlighting salient features for comparison with the injuries from PH.

Selected historic and modern forensic examples from civilian and military sources provide references for a broad range of wound characteristics. References are presented for comparison and contrast with the injuries seen from the cemeteries at Huaquerones and 57AS03. The reference specimens represent the evidence of injuries spanning prehistoric and historic contexts. They include injuries from early firearms, as well as metal and stone implements. Two instances of suicidal injury to the cranium are also included, each from different contexts, including a broad depressed fracture from a fatal leap from a building and another from a localized injury caused by being struck by a moving subway train.

Early firearm injuries show characteristics of trauma from the American Civil War (1861–5) and the Mexican–American War (1846–8). Both of these wars utilized firearms that delivered large-caliber, unjacketed projectiles using a black powder charge at velocities that were considerably lower than those of which modern rifles are capable (LaGarde 1916; Ragsdale 1984; see Table 15.2). Conical-shaped projectiles were introduced just prior to the Civil War while only round ball ammunition was used during the Mexican–American War. The velocity of projectiles from firearms used during the Spanish Conquest would not have been significantly larger than some mid-nineteenth-century firearms. The rifling of barrels and technological improvements of conical bullets slightly increased velocity and improved accuracy.

Table 15.2. *Velocity and foot-pounds of various weapons and implements discussed in text.*

Projectile/firearm	Velocity (meters per second)	Velocity (feet per second)	Foot-pounds (at impact)
	Thrown projectiles		
Sling stones (2314.9–12346 grains[1])	29.9–40.2[2]	98–132	49.4–477.6
Baseball (2284 grains)	40.2	132 (90 mph)	88.4
sixteenth-century crossbow bolt (1095.7 grains[3])	36.6–54.9	120–180	35.0–78.8
	Antique firearms		
.58 caliber arquebus match-lock (smoothbore, 280 grain ball[4])	198.1–259.7[5]	650–850	262.7–449.2
.75 caliber flintlock (smoothbore, 545 grain ball[5])	173.4–306.6	569–1006	391.8–1224.6
.58 caliber rifle minie ball (510 grain bullet[5])	283.5–369.1	930–1211	979.3–1660.6
	Modern firearms		
.22 caliber – 5.56 mm long rifle (40 grain bullet[6])	304.8	1000	88.8
Colt 1911.45 caliber ACP (200 grain bullet[6])	283.5	930	384.1
.44 Smith & Wesson magnum (240 grain bullet[6])	475.5	1560	1296.8
M16 – 5.56 mm NATO (70 grain bullet[6])	960.1	3150	1542.1

Weights and/or velocities adapted from: [1] Mullins 2012; [2] Richardson 1998; [3] Watson 2009; [4] Alderney Maritime Trust 2012; [5] Fadala 2005; [6] Barnes 1989.
Note: 437.5 grains = 1 ounce.

Stones, hammers, and sling ammunition are technologically similar to traditional stone and Bronze Age pre-Hispanic weapons and produce blunt force injuries. Spanish swords, halberds, and pikes would have been capable of introducing sharp force injuries with cut edges, penetrating injuries, and combinations of blunt injuries from sharp instruments and possibly patterned injuries consistent with weapon size and shape.

Extrinsic factors such as mass, velocity, and energy-absorbing potential of objects involved in an injury can vary significantly, affecting the extent and magnitude of wound expression; however, the patterning of injuries and degree of localization are assumed to be consistent with overall size, shape, and design characteristics of a range of weapon types and to be in accordance with biomechanical principles.

15.5   Trauma classification

Forensic anthropologists use a classification system of traumatic bone injury originally conceived by forensic pathologists that has proven to be accurate in categorizing the mechanism of skeletal injuries in the majority of cases. The categories are blunt force trauma (BFT), sharp force trauma (SFT), and gunshot (projectile) wounds (GSWs) (DiMaio and DiMaio 2001; Galloway 1999; Gonzales *et al.* 1954; Spitz 1993; Symes *et al.* 2012). Injuries can be further subclassified as either penetrating (impaling) or non-penetrating (Shkrum and Ramsay 2007). The classification system has been recognized as being overly weapon-centric in light of the biomechanical continuum of force, surface area, and acceleration that contributes to wound production (Kroman 2007). It has also been pointed out that, without an estimate of the type of weapon involved, trauma analysis in forensic cases would not be very useful in a medicolegal context (Berryman *et al.* 2013). Likewise, the need to classify trauma in archaeological research is unavoidable; however, interpretation should follow the same best practice standards as forensic trauma analysis. The tendency in archaeological and historical trauma analysis is to support findings with written and archaeological references to specific weapons used during the period under examination. In any instance where interpretation is questionable, a detailed description of the wound and context of discovery is acceptable.

BFT is the classification for injuries involving low-velocity mechanical forces from broad and blunt surfaces. They are slow-loading injuries that typically exhibit a ductile response in bone prior to fracturing, creating the irreversible deformation of bone material (plastic deformation). Blunt force fractures can be classified as either linear or depressed (Itabashi *et al.* 2007). Linear fractures can be single or multiple radiating or stellate patterned injuries where point of impact is often clearly indicated, particularly if there was only a single impact (Gurdjian and Webster 1958). Depressed fractures are those where bone is forced below its original anatomical location. Many different fracture characteristics can be present within a single injury. Patterns of injury are also influenced by surface area of the object, with broad impacts more likely to cause linear and comminuted fractures and narrow impacts often resulting in depressed and potentially penetrating fractures (Galloway 1999). Overall, blunt injuries are less likely to result in penetrating injuries than injury caused by stabbing or gunshot (Gonzales *et al.* 1954). Wounding by a blunt instrument tears, shears, and crushes tissue (Spitz 1993).

SFT to bone is characterized by narrow or broad defects with at least one incised or straight-line cut edge produced by narrowly focused, slow-loading compressive forces from a tool or instrument with a beveled edge (Symes *et al.* 2012). Examples of actions related to SFT involve stabbing, cutting, sawing, or hacking of tissue (Spitz 1993; Symes *et al.* 2012). SFT often has characteristics of blunt force injuries, such as radiating fractures and plastic deformation, and can be described as BFT with a sharp implement (Symes *et al.* 2012). Sharp force may or may not result in a penetrating injury. Hacking and deep penetrating injuries with sharpened blades, such as slashes, usually have one polished side (Humphrey and Hutchinson 2001; Hutchinson 1996; Milner *et al.* 2000: 358; Williamson *et al.* 2003) that is diagnostic of sharp force injury.

GSWs are typically high-velocity penetrating or perforating wounds caused by projectiles accelerated by a charge of gunpowder. Kinetic energy transferred to bone through GSWs results in the "brittle" fracture response of rapidly loaded bone, with little to no deformation during fracturing. Characteristics of GSWs are affected by the design of the weapon, projectile, and the density of affected body tissues (Hollerman *et al.* 1990). Entrance wounds are typically round to oval punched-out defects with sharp uncrushed edges externally with internal beveling (DiMaio 1985). Bone beveling is recognized as a circumscribed radius of exposed diploe at the gunshot injury site on the side opposite the direction of force. These features are reversed for exit wounds. External beveling of entrances may be found in tangential bullet strikes, resulting in "keyhole" defects. In rare instances entrance wounds can display external beveling that resembles an exit wound (Coe 1982; Peterson 1991). GSWs may also be classified as penetrating (entrance only) or perforating (entrance and exit). In historic contexts and instances of diminished velocity of projectiles, GSWs can be indistinguishable from blunt force injuries (LaGarde 1916; Otis 1870). Standard radiography can be used to locate evidence of metal fragments in such cases.

Underlying the defined categories is the fact that wound production in reality occurs on a continuum. Wounding potential of a given object is commensurate with the amount of kinetic energy conveyed to the body and is further influenced by the physical and dynamic characteristics (i.e. velocity, surface area, and acceleration/deceleration rates) of both the tissues and impacting object (Kroman 2007; Moritz 1954). A critical factor in analyzing bone trauma is recognizing the gross characteristics of slow vs. rapid loading of bone, which demonstrates the rate at which the kinetic energy associated with impact was resisted by anatomical structures (Symes *et al.* 2012). In most documented wounds to bone, plastic deformation indicates slow-load blunt force injuries. Round-shaped beveled edge holes with little to no plastic deformation indicate GSWs. However, not all injuries are amenable to interpretations that seek to identify weapon type. For example, decelerated or slow-moving projectiles can produce blunt injuries (LaGarde 1916; Otis 1870), and narrowly focused (i.e. small surface area) penetrating blunt injuries (Perdekamp *et al.* 2010) with sheared entrance margins can resemble GSWs. Such injuries are technically blunt (low-velocity) but conceptually somewhere between traditional classifications of a blunt wound vs. a GSW. Situations such as these demonstrate how implement characteristics can produce injuries that do not conform with standard classifications based on weapon type.

A projectile with reduced or lost velocity, such as one from a historic weapon or one that passes through an intermediary target, conveys lower kinetic energy and therefore elicits less resistance from tissues, prolonging deceleration time and decreasing the loading rate of impact when compared with textbook GSWs. Such a situation may produce an injury indistinguishable from a blunt force injury. Likewise, some smaller accelerated blunt objects traveling at lower than gunshot velocities (for example, captive bolt guns used to stun livestock) may produce internal beveling (Perdekamp *et al.* 2010). Knowledge of special circumstances such as these demonstrates the need for caution in the interpretation of skeletal injuries, particularly when dealing with uncertain armament technologies.

15.6   Wound descriptions and comparisons

The characteristics of injuries from PH were analyzed and wounds were classified using standard anthropological methods (Murphy *et al.* 2010). The majority of perimortem injuries to the cranium were consistent with the comminuted and circular depressed blunt force injuries previously reported from the region (Andrushko and Torres 2011; Torres-Rouff and Costa Junqueira 2006; Tung 2007, 2012). Notable exceptions, however, were found in individuals from the site of 57AS03. Several of these individuals demonstrated injuries that were more consistent with localized penetrating injuries from projectiles and blunt-edged weapons rather than the broad surface area impacts reported from perimortem injuries from previous investigations of traumatic injuries in the pre-Hispanic Andes (Andrushko 2007; Andrushko and Torres 2011; Torres-Rouff and Costa Junqueira 2006; Tung 2007, 2012).

Many individuals from the archaeological sample display depressed fractures of the neurocranium coupled with extensive fracturing of the upper face and mandible, often also displaying cranial base fractures. Multiple blunt force injuries were observed in both cemeteries (Figure 15.1). The majority of these blunt force injuries display fracture margins typical of non-penetrating wounds, with some noteworthy exceptions. Individuals with penetrating

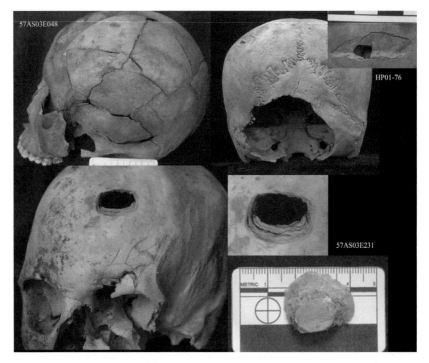

Figure 15.1. Top panel: examples of typical blunt force injuries from Puruchuco-Huaquerones (57AS03E048, HP01–76). Skull with multiple perimortem injuries on the left parietal eminence with others on the occipital region and cranial base. Inset: close-up of oval-shaped depressed fracture with a punched-in central hole with depressed margins on parietal. Bottom panel: 57AS03E231. Ovoid defect of left frontal with endocranial and ectocranial views of bone plug.

injuries were only found in 57AS03. Four individuals from this cemetery show injuries that are penetrating (E123, E231, and E248) or have rectilinear margins (E248 and E107) or both (E248) (Figures15.1–3).

57AS03E231 (female, 15–20 years) had an ovoid defect on the left frontal (23.0 × 10.8 mm) (Figure 15.1). The anterior rim of the defect consisted of roughly parallel terrace or stair-step fractures. The plug from this injury was recovered from the anterior edge of the defect, hinging inside the cranium at the time of its discovery. The defect exhibited internal beveling and the endocranial surface of the plug was larger than the ectocranial surface (i.e. funnel-shaped). No tension fractures were on the endocranial surface of the plug (Murphy *et al.* 2010). The cranium had additional blunt force perimortem injuries to the left frontal, left maxilla (tripod fracture), and the left parasymphyseal region of the mandible and there was also a small, depressed ovoid

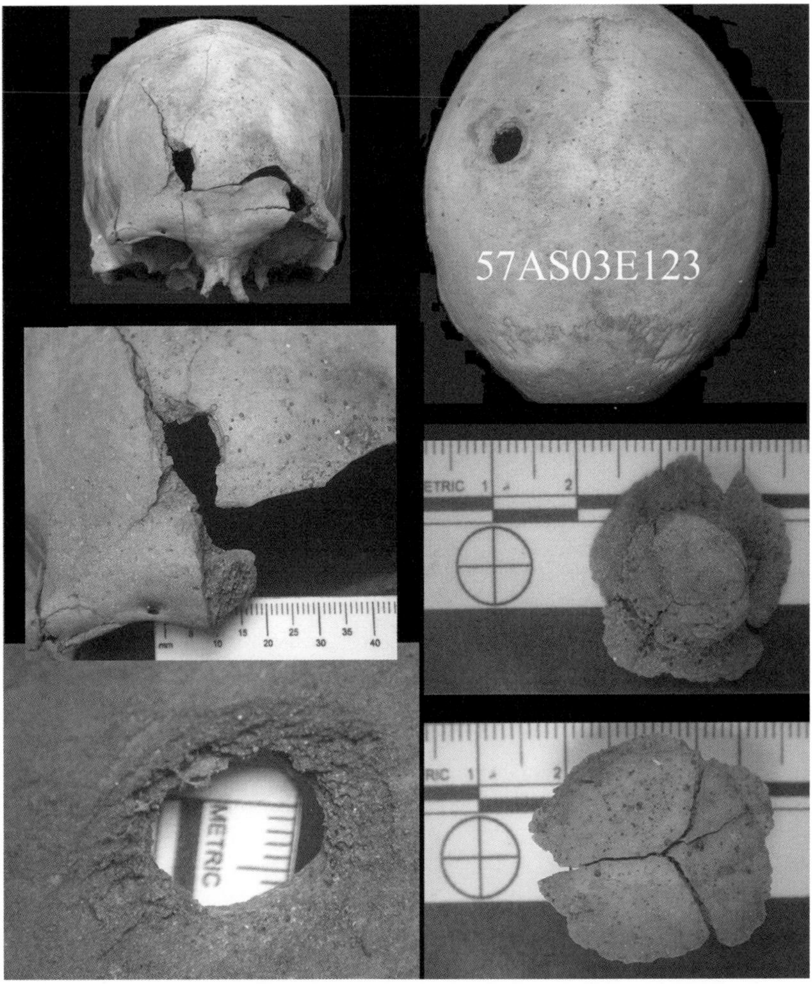

Figure 15.2. 57AS03E123. Clockwise from top right. Top right: superior view with ovoid defect consistent with a perimortem penetrating injury. Right middle: compressed ectocranial surface of the plug. Right bottom: endocranial surface of the plug. Left lower: endocranial view. Left middle: close-up of defect on frontal. Top left: defect with delamination, depressed edge, and radiating fractures on frontal.

defect on the occipital. Standard radiography did not detect any metal residues on the cranium.

57AS03E123 (male, 20–34 years) had a circular injury on the left parietal (15.5 × 17.1 mm) (Figure 15.2). The exterior margins of approximately half of the defect's circumference display parallel curvilinear "terraced" or

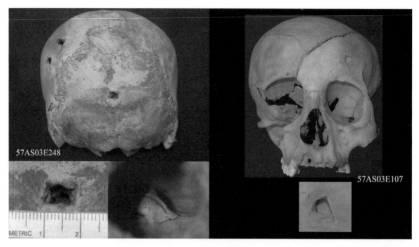

Figure 15.3. Top left: 57AS03E248. Quadrangular defects to the left parietal and occipital. Bottom left: close-up of quadrangular defect on occipital. Bottom right: interior of the quadrangular defect on the occipital viewed from the foramen magnum. Right: 57AS03E107. Anterior view of triangular defect to left frontal and extensive perimortem trauma to the right zygoma, the parietal and temporal bones, the occipital, and the mandible.

stair-step depressed fractures. The interior of the injury displayed internal beveling of the inner table of the endocranium and a plug of bone was recovered among the facial bone fragments with intact endocranial and ectocranial surfaces. The ectocranial surface of this plug of bone is slightly compressed, but no impact points are discernible. The endocranial surface of the plug has four tension fractures in a stellate pattern, radiating from the center and towards the edges of the plug. Standard radiography did not detect any metal residues on the cranium. 57AS03E123 also has a smaller (~5.0 mm) fracture on the right frontal with a single depressed edge and adjacent delamination of the outer table. Several fractures surround this defect. Multiple blunt injuries of the adjacent upper face preclude accurate assessment of the association of fractures and the depressed fracture. The hole superficially resembles an exit wound (Murphy *et al.* 2010), but as it possesses a depressed edge it could also be consistent with a blunt force depressed fracture (Saukko and Knight 2004). The adjacent injuries to the face may account for the presence of delamination of the outer table (Berryman and Symes 1998). Other fractures include separate blunt force injuries to the left and right zygomaticofrontal regions and right parasymphyseal region of the mandible and alveolar bone with crowns from anterior teeth sheared from their roots.

57AS03E248 (male, 18–20 years) displayed three rectangular-shaped defects to the left parietal and occipital representing penetrating injuries (Figure 15.3). The size and shape of all three defects were mutually consistent and averaged approximately 8.0 × 5.25 mm. The angles of the margins of the inferiormost parietal defect are approximately 90°, giving the appearance of a nearly perfect rectangle. A small hinging fracture of the outer table of the cranium was found on the superior edge of one of the defects on the left parietal. Plastic deformation at the cruciform eminence of the occipital was observed on the interior of the defect, indicating that the weapon did not completely penetrate the inner table.

The cranium of 57AS03E107 (female, 20–34 years) has multiple blunt force injuries, primarily to the left side, causing radiating fractures on the frontal, parietals, occipital, mandible, and temporal bones. A depressed fracture of particular interest is found on the left frontal bone just above the zygomatic process (Figure 15.3). In the deepest portion of the injury the margin displays two linear crushed margins at an approximately 90° angle. This punched-in defect is triangular-shaped and measures 15.0 × 14.0 × 11.0 mm, with a maximum depression depth of 3.0 mm.

To begin the comparison of the samples from PH with documented samples from historic and modern cases, we examined the cranium AFIP 1000776, which shows a penetrating GSW of the left parietal from the American Civil War entering around the approximate parietal eminence with an incomplete exit in the right parietal above the temporal squama (Figure 15.4, left top and bottom). The bullet traveled from the posterior to anterior and from left to right. The skull shows a large ovoid entrance wound with a single radiating fracture extending first to the frontal bone and then across the frontal in the region of the frontal eminences, terminating on the right parietal just above the temporal squama where it meets with the fractures of the incomplete "exit" wound in the form of a blunt force injury on the opposite side (Figure 15.4, left bottom). The initial fracture preceded the exit fractures and one of the fragments of bone was secured with metal wire by museum staff.

Similarly, specimen AFIP 1002808, from the Mexican–American War, shows a perforating GSW to the cranium (Figure 15.4, top right). This injury is typical of mid-nineteenth-century rifles, showing extensive fracturing from larger-caliber, unjacketed round ball lead projectiles. The slightly oblate entrance on the right temporal varies between 19.0 and 22.0 mm in diameter with several radiating fractures. The exit wound (not pictured) in the left occipital is irregular, externally beveled, and measures 25.0 × 20.0 mm.

Cranium AFIP 1001829, from nineteenth-century Patagonia, sustained an injury from a metal bola tied to a length of cord that was hurled. The skull has a

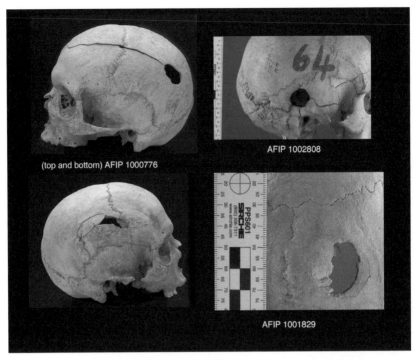

Figure 15.4. Left top and bottom: AFIP 1000776. Cranium from the Civil War with a penetrating gunshot injury to the left parietal and an incomplete exit wound of the right parietal. Top right: AFIP 1002808. Cranium with gunshot injury from the Mexican-American War. Bottom right: AFIP 1001829. Cranium, bola injury (metal ball), nineteenth-century Patagonia.

roughly circular 30.0 × 38.0 mm depressed fracture near the anterior superior angle of the right parietal. There are multiple concentric depressed fractures within the main fracture. A jagged fracture bisects the injury to the right, of which less than half of the injured bone is missing (Figure 15.4, bottom right). Although fragments of bone are missing, this does not appear to be a penetrating injury.

A skullcap from a modern forensic case (1990.0003.1688) shows a non-penetrating blunt force injury from the head of a ball peen hammer (rounded hemispherical head). There is a depressed oval-shaped injury 10.0 mm above the right parietal eminence measuring 30.0 × 25.0 mm, with a central area of crushed and depressed bone consisting of comminuted bone within a concentric fracture (Figure 15.5, top).

The skull section specimen PS 10074 has an injury from a rock thrown to the head (Figure 15.5, bottom). The specimen shows a circular depressed

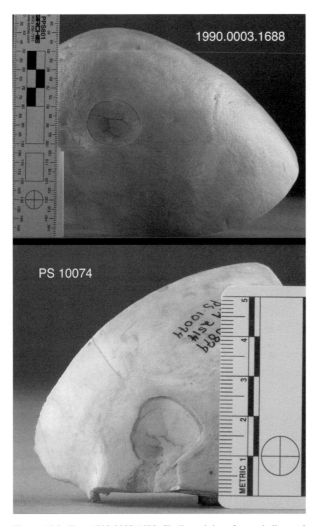

Figure 15.5. Top: 1990.0003.1688. Skullcap, injury from a ball peen hammer, twentieth century. Bottom: PS 10074. Frontal bone struck by a thrown stone.

fracture of the frontal bone with comminuted bone, a crushed edge, and fractures radiating to the face. The injury measures 20.0 × 20.0 mm. The delaminated portion appears to be an artifact of the sawing of bone to remove the specimen.

Specimen 1990.0003.1819 is a parietal bone of an adult male struck by a subway train. The injury is a 27.0 × 22.0 mm circular defect with an angular 12.5-mm crushed edge with stair-step parallel fractures. The injury produced

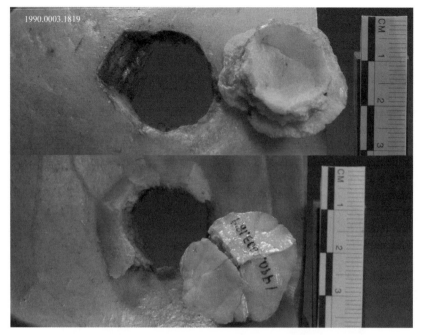

Figure 15.6. 1990.0003.1819. Cranium. Blunt force injury and bone plug from train.

a bone plug with both tables intact and having buckled internal margins corresponding to the crushed external portion (Figure 15.6).

Specimen AFIP 1002456 (saber injury, nineteenth century, Chile) has multiple sharp injuries with associated blunt force characteristics concentrated in the left parietal area. Four separate blows can be seen in the photo with three parallel cuts spaced roughly 45.0 mm apart with an inferior cut across the left lambdoid suture (Figure 15.7). Each blow shows a clear polished appearance of the edges of cut bone on one side, with chipped and fractured bone on the opposite side. Areas with multiple blows have large blunt force fractures, which removed large fragments of bone that were not recovered.

Specimen PS 5721 (suicide, jumped from window, 1870, Washington, D.C.) is a cranium with extensive museum wiring of fractured bone and a hinged left half skullcap for viewing the endocranium. On the right side of the skull is a 9.0 × 10.0 cm depressed fracture comprised in large part by a stellate fracture circumscribed by a concentric fracture. An additional adjacent 2.5-cm area of depressed bone is seen on the frontal bone just lateral to the frontal eminence. A fracture of the right zygomatic process and LeFort III fractures to the upper face are seen. Inferior to the stellate fracture is an

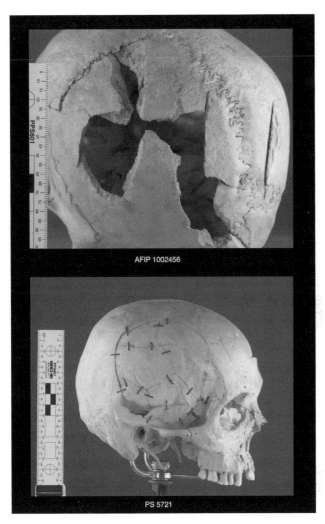

Figure 15.7. Top: AFIP 1002456. Saber injury, nineteenth century, Chile. Bottom: PS 5721. Adult male cranium, blunt force injury, suicide. Jumped from window, 1870, Washington, D.C.

area of comminuted temporal and sphenoid bone with a radiating fracture to the right middle fossa (Figure 15.7).

During forensic examination of a skeletonized fragmentary cranium from southeastern Wyoming in 2002, anthropologists from the University of Wyoming identified multiple blunt force injuries caused by at least two different weapons (modern crossbow injury, southeastern Wyoming)

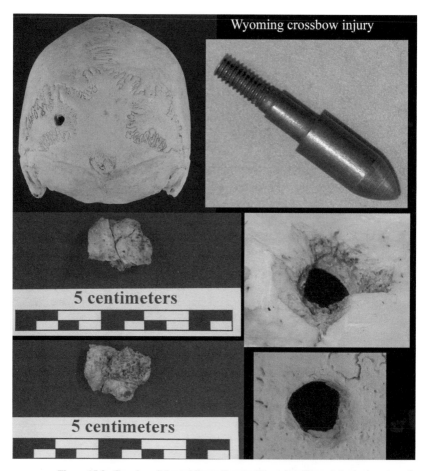

Figure 15.8. Crossbow injury, Albany County, Wyoming. Upper left: the location of
the entrance defect. Upper right: crossbow dart tip. Bottom right: endocranial view of
entrance defect and ectocranial view of entrance defect. Bottom left: endocranial and
ectocranial views of the bone plug.

(Figure 15.8). Subsequent criminal proceedings documented the two implements used in the attack.

The majority of the blunt force injuries were radiating fractures and impact
flutes originating in and near the superior eye orbits. According to statements
by the perpetrator, these injuries were caused by repeated blows from a metal
pipe directed into the face (Furgeson *et al.* 2009; Gill and Weathermon 2003;
Snyder 2008). An additional injury, a circular defect with a corresponding
bone plug, was noted on the left side of the occipital (Figure 15.8). This injury
was caused by a lightweight crossbow bolt released at a range of 3–4 m.

The crossbow used was a small pistol-type (Furgeson 2008; Furgeson *et al.* 2009), which can produce velocities up to 50 m/s (Tremayne 2009: 28). Photographs of bolts at the crime scene indicate that the puncture was caused by an aluminum arrow shaft 33.0 cm with a solid metal ogive-tipped target point (Figure 15.8) (Furgeson 2008). Dart mass has been estimated at between 17.8 and 21.1 g (274.7–325.6 grains), given the above. Maximum diameter of the metal point is approximately 8.9 mm; the hollow shaft of the bolt is about 0.15 mm less. The ectocranial puncture has a maximum diameter of about 5.9 mm. Grellner and colleagues (2004) report that crossbow bolts at relatively high velocities can completely transect human crania. In this case, the taper of the projectile point and the external wound diameter indicate a penetration of <6.0 mm into the bone, or about two-thirds the length of the ogive portion of the tip. Deformed inward, the plug shows a crushed external surface with compression of the diploe. The endocranial surface of the plug, measuring approximately 1.5 cm in maximum dimension, exhibits radiating fractures with wedge-shaped splinters of bone.

Using the information above, estimates of the bolt's kinetic energy indicate that a very low yield impact caused the trauma. The ballistic formula, kinetic energy $= \frac{1}{2} \times$ mass $\times$ velocity^2, is used to calculate the work (kinetic energy in foot-pounds) of an object traveling at X velocity with Y mass (see Carlucci 2008). At 50 m (164 feet) per second and with a mass of 325.6 grains, the bolt exerted a maximum of 19.45 foot-pounds at impact. At lower velocity and lower mass, the kinetic energy is significantly less (see Table 15.2 for comparative velocities and foot-pounds at impact). Note that diameters of the .22 caliber and 5.56 NATO bullets are slightly smaller than the defect caused by the ogive dart tip. The relatively low velocity and energy impact of the bolt resulted in the formation of the bone plug. With the higher velocities and energies of these bullets, the bone plug would probably have been shattered into multiple and smaller fragments on impact.

15.7   Discussion: comparing injuries of known cause to the unknown injuries

Positive identification of weapons used in skeletal trauma cases may aid in the interpretation of unknown bone injuries. However, identification of specific implements is often not possible when blunt force trauma to the cranium is evident in archaeological and forensic cases (Symes *et al.* 2012: 353). The majority of wounds from the archaeological sample are consistent with extensive multiple blunt force injuries to the face and head. Three broad types of injuries can be seen in the archaeological samples from PH. The first type comprises two subtypes and consists of the multiple broad and localized blunt force injuries typical of the pre-conquest Peru (see E048 and HP01–76 in Figure 15.1). Second are the penetrating circular and ovoid penetrating injuries with terraced margins from 57AS03 (E231 [Figure 15.1] and E123 [Figure 15.2]). Third are penetrating localized injuries with rectilinear margins (E248, E107 [Figure 15.3]).

Broad depressed fractures in the typical Peruvian samples were similar in character to those from a documented impact with a broad surface (PS 5721) with displayed characteristics of stellate and concentric fractures typical of blunt force injury. Localized shallow depressed fractures such as those seen in HP01–76 are similar to lower-velocity blunt objects with localized application of force such as seen in reference samples for stone, metal bola, and ball peen hammer, though each injury is expectedly influenced by differences in size and shape of implement. Such comparisons are hardly unexpected and unremarkable. However, the next two classes of specimens from four individuals in 57AS03 arguably possess injuries with unexpected penetrating and/or rectilinear pattern characteristics that imply a different armament type from those seen previously in other pre-Hispanic contexts.

Two specimens show round to oval penetrating depressed fractures with internal beveling and terraced fracture margins (E123 and E231). The injuries of the two examples of nineteenth-century GSWs do not have terraced fracture margins and demonstrate radiating fractures. However, blunt force injuries from firearms can and do occur under some circumstances (LaGarde 1916; Otis 1870; Spatola in press). These injuries are consistent with the example from that caused by the subway train (1990.0003.1819) to include plug formation without spalling, internal beveling, and marginal terracing. As a result, we conclude that, although there is no conclusive evidence of a gunshot injury (based on our comparative historic cases), a reduced-velocity gunshot injury cannot be ruled out for the injury seen on E123, owing to its rounded shape consistent with round ball ammunition. To a lesser degree, E123 also shares characteristics of a slow-loading injury when compared with the crossbow injury (Figure 15.8), such as evidence of crushed margin and internal beveling and a partial plug formation. Taken as a whole, these specimens demonstrate that similar injuries can be produced from vastly different contexts, but where the localization and magnitude of biomechanical forces are similar.

E248 and E107 show injuries with rectilinear patterns not documented previously in pre-Hispanic contexts from the Central Andes. Penetrating injuries from this context are rare. We believe the injuries on E248 in particular are inconsistent with pre-Hispanic weapons as they are uniformly rectangular on all sides and consistent across three separate impacts. Two of the three impacts on E248 are penetrating injuries, while the third is incompletely penetrating; however, we did not classify the injuries as arising from sharp force as the rectilinear sides are not incised or polished. They are more accurately described as BFT with an angular edged implement. Future experimental investigations may illuminate why these injuries are distinct from the majority of pre-Hispanic injuries from the Central Andes.

Using historic documented cases, we set out to demonstrate the broad range of injuries that can be caused by slow-loading lower-velocity implements and how the biomechanical continuum should be taken into account when examining injuries from unknown weapons, particularly from armaments without exemplars. We do not advocate using documented cases to determine perimortem traumatic injuries in bioarchaeological cases; however, appropriate comparisons may provide more insights than those interpretations based solely on textbook weapon-centered classifications.

Forensic analysis in the medicolegal context requires scientific and legally defensible interpretations whereas archaeological investigations do not. To avoid over-reaching interpretations we advise bioarchaeologists that, if the injury demonstrates confounding characteristics (i.e. terraced or depressed fractures in a suspected GSW), it might be best to follow forensic best practices (SWGANTH 2011) and describe the injuries and defects in question and provide these descriptions along with photos and accompanied by a discussion of the various potential interpretations. This is particularly prudent if the variation of injuries from a particular source is unknown or little studied, such as in the case of sixteenth-century weapons or the discharge of rocks or "branched balls" from sixteenth-century firearms. More replication studies are needed to illuminate the variation of wounds caused by prehistoric and early weapons. The atypical injuries from the archaeological samples in our study indicate to us that a different milieu of armaments may have been present when these individuals were killed. Exactly what these weapons were and who wielded them is difficult to determine.

When the editors of the volume organized the symposium at the 2012 American Association of Physical Anthropologists (AAPA), they tasked the participants with contextualizing "the skeletal data within the larger social, political, economic, and historical context, specifically by examining the roles of individual agents and groups and how they interact in a specific geopolitical or geographical area" (Anderson and Martin 2012). As the authors point out, by its very nature, bioarchaeological investigations of human skeletal remains with traumatic injuries emphasize the victims of violence, with scant attention to the initiators, perpetrators, or aggressors. Also potentially absent from these investigations is the acknowledgment of the fluidity and instability of individuals and groups in these roles of aggressor or victim and, therefore, the often unconscious assumption of a dichotomy (i.e. one is either an aggressor or a victim), rather than the inherent ambiguity and chaos attached to certain contexts of violence, such as, as in this case, the European colonialism of indigenous populations in the Americas. Along these lines, ethnohistoric and historical sources indicate that not all native Andeans fought against the Spanish during the Spanish Conquest of the Inca Empire, and that some groups, including the local lord (curaca) of the chiefdom of Lima on the central coast of Peru (Rostworowski 2002: 238), backed and supported Pizarro and the Spanish (Rostworowski 2002; Spalding 1999). Therefore, discerning the victims from aggressors and the exact roles of native Andeans in violence after the Spanish Conquest and invasion is an extremely daunting task. Individuals and communities may have shifted their positions vis-á-vis the Spanish and those that were formerly allies may have become enemies (or vice versa).

In the archaeological sample from 57AS03, there is an extraordinary degree of multiple, lethal perimortem injuries (Murphy *et al.* 2010), which are particularly excessive and could be attributed to the brutality of the Spanish as described by historical accounts. However, brutality, violence, sacrifice, and corpse mutilation are not unknown from the Central Andes, so the Spaniards were not the only perpetrators of violence and it could be that native Andeans caused these injuries (e.g. Andrushko *et al.* 2011; Blom 2005; Klaus *et al.* 2010; Toyne 2009, 2011; Tung 2008; Tung and Knudson 2010; Verano 1986, 2001, 2007, 2008). The frequency of individuals from 57AS03 affected by perimortem injuries is relatively high; men, women, and children possessed these injuries and many individuals possessed multiple injuries. The frequency and pattern of perimortem injuries coupled with their atypical mortuary treatment distinguishes them from the other contexts of violence reported from the pre-Hispanic Andes.

Unfortunately, the archaeological context and historical contexts cannot definitively clarify the aggressors and their relationship to the victims. Although the archaeological context of the burials is well understood, it is a cemetery and not a battlefield or a battlefield cemetery, and the early accounts of Spanish Conquest and invasion are extremely sparse and limited. These victims may have been participants in the attack on the Spanish during the siege of Lima, which was the second of two sieges that the Inca leader Manco Inca organized and led against the Spaniards. The first uprising began in Cusco and, based on its success, Manco Inca ordered one of his generals to surround and attack the new Spanish capital at Lima (Del Busto Duthurburu 1978; Vega 1980). The Spanish routed the Inca forces and the survivors fled back to the highlands (Del Busto Duthurburu 1978; Vega 1980). If these individuals were participants, then they were interred alongside other native Andeans from the central coast. The Spanish and their allies may have subjected these victims to retributive violence after the siege or they could have been involved in internecine violence (native vs. native violence) in the aftermath of the Spanish Conquest, a phenomenon that has also been described in post-conquest contexts from North America (Stodder and Martin 1992).

From the bioarchaeological and forensic perspectives taken here, pinpointing the perpetrators is an extremely daunting task. With the archaeological sample described, while we may be able to isolate an implement that may have caused an atypical injury, we cannot identify the exact perpetrators of this violence: the high frequency of blunt force injuries in the archaeological sample is consistent with the use of blunt force implements. These injuries could, however, have been caused by European maces or clubs wielded by the Spanish or their native allies or the injuries could have been caused by indigenous maces or clubs. It is widely known that the Spanish were allied with native warriors who were armed with traditional weapons (Cieza de León 1998; Del Busto Duthurburu 1966; Hemming 1970; Lockhart 1972; Restall 2004). The injuries to E107, E248, and E123 could have been caused by Spanish or by native Andeans armed with European weapons, but we cannot ascertain whether they were allies or enemies of the Spanish.

Disclaimer

The opinions and assertions contained herein are those of the authors and do not necessarily represent the views of the National Museum of Health and Medicine or the Department of Defense (DoD), any of the military services or other DoD components or any other government agencies, and do not constitute an endorsement by the DoD of any of the opinions expressed, or any information, products, or services contained therein.

Acknowledgments

Funding for this research (MSM) was provided by Bryn Mawr College, the University of Wyoming, the National Science Foundation (grant #0618192), and The Wenner-Gren Foundation for Anthropological Research (grant #6791). We thank the anonymous reviewers for their constructive comments. We are especially grateful to our editors, Debra Martin and Cheryl Anderson, who graciously invited us to participate in the AAPA symposium and to contribute to this volume. We thank them for their patience with our editorial process. MSM would like to thank the curators and staff at the National Museum of Health and Medicine for their assistance during her visit. Thanks to Matthew Breitbart and Merissa Olmer for photography of the NMHM specimens.

References

Alderney Maritime Trust. (2012). *An Elizabethan Shipwreck Off the Island of Alderney* [Online]. Available: http://www.alderneywreck.com. [Accessed November 22, 2012.]

Anderson, C. P. & Martin, D. L. (2012). Bioarchaeology and forensic case studies of sectarian violence, revolts, and small-scale warfare: reconstructing and explaining complex human behavior. *American Journal of Physical Anthropology*, **S54**, 361 (Abstract).

Andrushko, V. (2007). The bioarchaeology of Inca imperialism in the heartland: An analysis of prehistoric burials from the Cuzco region of Peru. University of California Santa Barbara: Unpublished PhD dissertation.

Andrushko, V. & Torres, V. (2011). Skeletal evidence for Inca warfare from the Cuzco region of Peru. *American Journal of Physical Anthropology*, **146**, 361–72.

Andrushko, V., Buzon, M., Gibaja, A., McEwan, G., Simonetti, A. & Creaser, R. (2011). Investigating a child sacrifice event from the Inca heartland. *Journal of Archaeological Science*, **38**, 323–33.

Barnes, F. C. (1989). *Cartridges of the World*. Northfield, IL: DBI Books, Inc.

Berryman, H. E. & Symes, S. A. (1998). Recognizing gunshot and blunt cranial trauma through fracture interpretation. In: Reichs, K. J. (ed.) *Forensic Osteology: Advances in the Identification of Human Remains*, 2nd edn. Springfield: Charles C. Thomas, 333–52.

Berryman, H. E., Shirley, N. R. & Lanfear, A. K. (2013). Low velocity trauma. In: Tersigni-Tarrant, M. T. A. & Shirley, N. R. (eds.) *Forensic Anthropology: An Introduction*. Boca Raton: CRC Press, 271–90.

Blom, D. E. (2005). Embodying borders: human body modification and diversity in Tiwanaku Society. *Journal of Anthropological Archaeology*, **24**, 1–24.

Carlucci, D. E. (2008). *Ballistics: Theory and Design of Guns and Ammunition*. Boca Raton: CRC Press/Taylor & Francis Group.

Cieza de León, P. (1998). *The Discovery and Conquest of Peru*. Chapel Hill: Duke University.

Cock, G. A. (2006). *Proyecto De Recuperación De Contextos Funerarios En El Cementerio 57as03 – Zona Arqueológica Puruchuco-Huaquerones*. Lima: Instituto Nacional de Cultura.

Cock, G. A. & Goycochea, C. E. (2004). Puruchuco y el cementerio Inca de la quebrada de huaquerones. In: Villacorta Ostolaza, L. F., Vetter Parodi, L. & Ausejo Castillo, C. (eds.) *Puruchuco Y La Sociedad De Lima: Un Homenaje a Arturo Jiménez Borja*. Lima: Concytec, 179–97.

Coe, J. I. (1982). External beveling of handgun wounds. *American Journal of Forensic Medicine and Pathology*, **3**, 215–19.

D'Altroy, T. (2002). *The Incas*. Malden: Blackwell.

Del Busto Duthurburu, J. A. (1966). *Francisco Pizarro. El Marques Gobernador*. Madrid: Ediciones RIALP, S.A.

(1978). *Peru Incaico*. Lima: Libreria Studium.

DiMaio, D. & DiMaio, V. (2001). *Forensic Pathology*, 2nd edn. Boca Raton: CRC Press.

DiMaio, V. J. M. (1985). *Gunshot Wounds: Practical Aspects of Firearms, Ballistics and Forensic Techniques*. New York: Elsevier.

Fadala, S. (2005). *Black Powder Handbook & Loading Manual*, 2nd edn. Middletown: Lyman Books.

Furgeson, T. A. (2008). Identification of multiple cranial traumas in a recently closed homicide investigation. *Paper presented at the Mountain, Desert & Coastal Physical Anthropologists Annual Meeting, Echo Bay Resort, Nevada*.

Furgeson, T. A., Gill, G. W. & Weathermon, R. L. (2009). Identification of multiple cranial traumas in a recently closed homicide investigation. *Paper presented at American Academy of Forensic Sciences Annual Scientific Meeting, Denver, CO*.

Gaither, C. & Murphy, M. S. (2012). Consequences of conquest? Subadult trauma at Puruchuco-Huaquerones, Peru. *Journal of Archaeological Science*, **39**, 467–78.

Galloway, A. (ed.) (1999). *Broken Bones: Anthropological Analysis of Blunt Force Trauma*. Springfield: Charles C. Thomas.

Gill, G. W. & Weathermon, R. L. (2003). *Forensic Case Reports on File, Anthropology Department – Human Remains Repository*. Laramie: University of Wyoming.

Gonzales, T. A., Vance, M., Helpern, M. & Umberger, C. J. (1954). *Legal Medicine: Pathology and Toxicology*, 2nd edn. New York: Appleton, Century-Crofts, Inc.

Grellner, W., Buhmann, D., Giese, A., Gehrke, G., Koops, E. & Püschel, K. (2004). Fatal and non-fatal injuries caused by crossbows. *Forensic Science International*, **142**, 17–23.

Guilmartin, J. F. (1991). The cutting edge: an analysis of the Spanish invasion and overthrow of the Inca Empire, 1532–1539. In: Andrien, K. & Adorno, R. (eds.) *Transatlantic Encounters: Europeans and Andeans in the Sixteenth Century*. Berkeley: University of California, 40–69.

Gurdjian, E. S. & Webster, J. E. (1958). *Head Injuries: Mechanisms, Diagnosis and Management*. Boston: Little Brown and Co.

Hemming, J. (1970). *The Conquest of the Incas*. London: Macmillan.

Himmerich, Y. & Valencia, R. (1998). The 1536 siege of Cuzco: an analysis of Inca and Spanish warfare. *Colonial Latin American Historical Review*, **7**, 387–418.

Hollerman, J. J., Fackler, M., Coldwell, D. M. & Ben-Menachem, Y. (1990). Gunshot wounds: 1. Bullets, ballistics, and mechanisms of injury. *American Journal of Roentgenology*, **155**, 685–90.

Humphrey, J. H. & Hutchinson, D. L. (2001). Macroscopic characteristics of hacking trauma. *Journal of Forensic Sciences*, **46**, 228–33.

Hutchinson, D. L. (1996). Brief encounters: Tatham Mound and the evidence for Spanish and Native American confrontation. *International Journal of Osteoarchaeology*, **6**, 51–65.

  (2009). *Tatham Mound and the Bioarchaeology of European Contact: Depopulation in Central Gulf Coast Florida*. Gainesville: University of Florida.

Itabashi, H., Andrews, J. M., Tomiyasu, U., Erlich, S. S. & Sathyavagiswaran, L. (2007). *Forensic Neuropathology*. New York: Elsevier, Academic Press.

Klaus, H. D., Centurión, J. & Curo, M. (2010). Bioarchaeology of human sacrifice: an integrated study of health, identity, and ritual violence at Cerro Cerrillos, Peru. *Antiquity*, **84**, 1102–22.

Kroman, A. (2007). Fracture biomechanics of the human skeleton. University of Tennessee: Unpublished PhD dissertation.

LaGarde, L. A. (1916). *Gunshot Injuries: How They Are Inflicted; Their Complications and Treatment*, 2nd edn. New York: William Wood and Co.

Larsen, C. S., Huynh, H. P. & McEwan, B. G. (1996). Death by gunshot: biocultural implications of trauma at Mission San Luis. *International Journal of Osteoarchaeology*, **6**, 42–50.

Lockhart, J. (1972). *The Men of Cajamarca*. Austin: University of Texas.

Milner, G. R., Larsen, C. S., Hutchinson, D. L., Williamson, M. A. & Humpf, D. A. (2000). Conquistadors, excavators or rodents: what damaged the King Site skeletons? *American Antiquity*, **65**, 355–63.

Moritz, A. R. (1954). *The Pathology of Trauma*. Philadelphia: Lea and Febiger.

Mullins, P. (2012). Fortaleza de Quirihuac: a Chimú Fortress in the Middle Moche Valley. University of North Carolina at Chapel Hill: Unpublished Honors Thesis.

Murphy, M. S., Gaither, C., Goycochea, E., Verano, J. W. & Cock, G. (2010). Violence and weapon-related trauma at Puruchuco-Huaquerones, Peru. *American Journal of Physical Anthropology*, **142**, 636–49.

Otis, G. A. (1870). *The Medical and Surgical History of the War of the Rebellion (1861–65). Part 1. Vol. II. Surgical History*. Washington, D.C.: Government Printing Office.

Perdekamp, M. G., Kneubuehl, B. P., Ishikawa, T., Najdem, H., Kromeier, J., Pollak, S., & Thierauf, A. (2010). Secondary fractures in head wounds inflicted by captive bolt guns: autopsy findings and experimental simulation. *International Journal of Legal Medicine*, **124**, 605–12.

Peterson, B. L. (1991). External beveling of gunshot entrance wounds. *Journal of Forensic Sciences*, **36**, 1592–5.

Pizarro, P. (1978). *Relacion Del Descubrimiento Y Conquista Del Peru*. Lima: Pontificia del Catolica del Peru.

Ragsdale, B. D. (1984). Gunshot wounds: a historical perspective. *Military Medicine*, **149**, 301–15.

Restall, M. (2004). *Seven Myths of the Spanish Conquest*. NewYork: Oxford University Press.

Richardson, T. (1998). The ballistics of the sling. *Royal Armouries Yearbook*, **3**, 44–9.

Rostworowski, M. (1977). *Etnia Y Sociedad. Costa Peruana Prehispánica*. Lima: Instituto de Estudios Peruanos.

(2002). *Pachacamac. Obras Completas Ii*. Lima: Instituto de Estudios Peruanos.

Rowe, J. H. (1946). Inca culture at the time of the Spanish conquest. In: Steward, J. (ed.) *Handbook of South American Indians*. Washington, D.C.: Smithsonian Institution, Bureau of American Ethnology, 183–330.

(1957). The Incas under Spanish colonial institutions. *Hispanic American Historical Review*, **37**, 155–99.

Salas, A. M. (1950). *Las Armas De La Conquista*. Buenos Aires: Emecé Editores.

Saukko, P. J. & Knight, B. (2004). *Knight's Forensic Pathology*, 3rd edn. Boca Raton: CRC Press.

Shkrum, M. & Ramsay, D. (2007). *Forensic Pathology of Trauma*. New York: Humana Press.

Snyder, C. (2008). Man pleads guilty to '98 murder. *Wyoming Tribune-Eagle*, January 9, 2008.

Spalding, K. (1999). The crises and transformations of invaded societies: Andean Area (1500–1580). In: Salomon, F. & Schawrtz, S. B. (eds.) *The Cambridge History of the Native Peoples of the Americas*. Cambridge: Cambridge University, 904–72.

Spatola, B. S. (in press). Atypical gunshot and blunt force injuries: wounds along the biomechanical continuum. In: Passalacqua, N. V. & Rainwater, C. W. (eds.) *Skeletal Trauma Analysis: Case Studies in Context*. Hoboken, NJ: Wiley-Blackwell.

Spitz, W. (1993). *Spitz and Fisher's Medicolegal Investigation of Death: Guidelines for the Application of Pathology to Crime Investigation*, 3rd edn. Springfield: Charles C. Thomas.

Stodder, A. L. W. & Martin, D. L. (1992). Native health and disease in the American southwest before and after Spanish contact. In: Verano, J. W. & Ubelaker, D. H. (eds.) *Disease and Demography in the Americas*. Washington, D.C.: Smithsonian Institution Press, 55–73.

SWGANTH. (2011). *Trauma Analysis* [Online]. Available: http://swganth.startlogic. com/Trauma%20Rev0.pdf. [Accessed September 28, 2013.]

Symes, S. A., L'abbé, E., Chapman, E., Wolff, I. & Dirkmaat, D. (2012). Interpreting traumatic injury to bone in medicolegal investigations. In: Dirkmaat, D. (ed.) *A Companion to Forensic Anthropology*. Malden: Blackwell Publishing, 340–89.

Torres-Rouff, C. & Costa Junqueira, M. A. (2006). Interpersonal violence in prehistoric San Pedro de Atacama, Chile: behavioral implications of environmental stress. *American Journal of Physical Anthropology*, **130**, 60–70.

Toyne, J. M. (2009). Offering their hearts and their heads: a bioarchaeological analysis of ancient human sacrifice on the northern coast of Peru. Tulane University: Unpublished PhD dissertation.

(2011). Cut mark analysis and activity signature interpretations of pre-hispanic ritual violence in northern Peru. *Latin American Antiquity*, **22**, 505–23.

Tremayne, V. (2009). Pistol crossbow injuries. *Emergency Nurse*, **17**, 28–30.

Tung, T. A. (2007). Trauma and violence in the Wari Empire of the Peruvian Andes: warfare, raids, and ritual fights. *American Journal of Physical Anthropology*, **133**, 941–56.

(2008). Dismembering bodies for display: a bioarchaeological study of trophy heads from the Wari site of Conchopata, Peru. *American Journal of Physical Anthropology*, **136**, 294–308.

(2012). *Violence, Ritual, and the Wari Empire: A Social Bioarchaeology of Imperialism in the Ancient Andes*. Gainesville: University Press of Florida.

Tung, T. A. & Knudson, K. J. (2010). Childhood lost: abductions, sacrifice, and trophy heads of children in the Wari Empire of the ancient Andes. *Latin American Antiquity*, **21**, 44–66.

Vega, J. J. (1980). *Incas Contra Españoles*. Lima: Pacific Press.

Verano, J. W. (1986). A mass burial of mutilated individuals at Pacatnamu. In: Donnan, C. B. & Cock, G. A. (eds.) *The Pacatnamu Papers, Volume 1*. Los Angeles: Museum of Cultural History, University of California, 117–38.

(2001). War and death in the Moche World: osteological evidence and visual discourse. In: Pillsbury J. (ed.) *Moche Art and Archaeology in Ancient Peru*. New Haven: Yale University, 111–26.

(2007). Conflict and conquest in pre-hispanic Andean South America. In: Chacon, R. J. & Mendoza, R. G. (eds.) *Latin American Indigenous Warfare and Ritual Violence*. Tucson: University of Arizona, 105–15.

(2008). Communality and diversity in Moche human sacrifice. In: Bourget, S. & Jones, K. L. (eds.) *The Art and Archaeology of the Moche: An Ancient Andean Society of the Peruvian North Coast*. Austin: University of Texas Press, 195–213.

Watson, D. R. (2009). *Iolo's First Book of Crossbows*, 2nd edn. Austin: Gwasg Caeseg Wen Press.

Williamson, M. A., Johnson, C. A., Symes, S. A. & Schultz, J. J. (2003). Interpersonal violence between 18th century native Americans and Europeans in Ohio. *American Journal of Physical Anthropology*, **122**, 113–22.

16 Interpreting gunshot trauma as context clue: a case study from historic North Las Vegas, Nevada

JOHN J. CRANDALL, RYAN P. HARROD,
CHERYL P. ANDERSON, AND KATHRYN
M. BAUSTIAN

16.1 Introduction

Traumatic injuries found on human skeletal remains, whether recently deceased or from long ago, are a direct source of evidence for anthropologists to generate information concerning the nature of violent human interactions among victims, witnesses, and aggressors. An anthropological approach to understanding instances of violence is important because it can help to advance theories which explain the causes and common consequences of warfare and violence among humans, as the bones offer data to validate or nullify hypotheses about violent human behavior in the past (Walker 2001). However, anthropology is not always simply a theoretical endeavor as the work done by forensic anthropologists has practical applications and directly impacts the living. Anthropological methods can also be used to identify traumatic injuries to assist in reconstructing the circumstances around an individual's death. In cases where whole communities are suspected to have been violently murdered, trauma data generated by forensic anthropologists can be invaluable in advancing human rights action on behalf of victimized communities (Komar and Buikstra 2008).

The intent of this chapter is to show how both of these goals can be addressed when analyzing populations with skeletal trauma. The case study used to accomplish this involves burials that represent a historic ranching family living in the "Wild West" at the turn of the twentieth century. The individuals were two brothers who were excavated from a small historic cemetery in North Las Vegas in southern Nevada. The burials were disinterred

Bioarchaeological and Forensic Perspectives on Violence: How Violent Death is Interpreted from Skeletal Remains, ed. D. L. Martin and C. P. Anderson. Published by Cambridge University Press.
© Cambridge University Press 2014.

because of discontinued use of the Kiel Ranch where the cemetery was located, as well as the economic and demographic growth of the Las Vegas metropolitan area in the 1970s (Escobar 2005).

The Kiel Ranch burials offer an interesting case study because they represent one of the earliest pioneer settlements in southern Nevada. Additionally, two of the burials were victims of lethal trauma involving two distinct firearms. Skeletal injuries resulting from firearms or high-velocity projectile weapons such as handguns, shotguns, and rifles are commonly seen by forensic anthropologists working in a legal context as well as bioarchaeologists working in historical contexts. In both circumstances, trauma data related to gunshot wounds (GSWs) obtained from careful examination of human skeletal remains can generate information regarding the details surrounding an individual's death as well as the setting in which they lived when carefully contextualized against other data. When judiciously used, trauma data can be integrated into anthropological hypotheses testing the role of violence among a past group. For forensic experts, such information may help narrow down the identity of unidentified injured remains or assist investigators in deciding the cause and manner of death. For bioarchaeologists, this same dataset can carefully be integrated into larger biohistorical analyses seeking to investigate the political function of violence among past communities.

The focus of this chapter is the analysis of the ways that trauma related to GSWs can be integrated into anthropological research. This could help interpretations that at least partially identify the witnesses, victims, and perpetrators of past violence. Using models and frameworks that integrate osteological, archival, and archaeological data will greatly benefit the ability to interpret how violence functions. This contextual information is key to understanding the nature of past violence (Martin *et al.* 2012). This investigation of lethal trauma associated with the Kiel Ranch brothers provides a unique opportunity to demonstrate how trauma is key to a better understanding of the context regarding the death of early frontier men in the growing cities of the American West.

16.2   The context of the Kiel Ranch: violent frontiers in the historic American West

In 1879, one of southern Nevada's earliest frontiersmen, Octavius Decatur Gass, made two decisions that changed southern Nevada and set the stage for the formation of Las Vegas' growth (Moehring and Green 2005). Pressured by his unhappy family, the former Ohioan invited Conrad Kiel, his wife, and children to move to southern Nevada and take over an experimental Paiute farm near the Old Mormon fort that had been established in the 1850s. The second decision Gass made in an attempt to please his family, who missed the amenities of Ohio life, was a grave financial mistake. Gass, the owner of nearly 1000 acres of land (in what was at the time Arizona territory), had come into debt. Between the taxes he owed the fledgling state of Nevada, the pressure of nearby Army soldiers bartering for his produce, and lawsuits concerning land south of Los Angeles, Gass mortgaged his property to manage his debt. Turning to businessman Archibald Stewart in Pioche, a mining town north of Las Vegas, Gass mortgaged his ranch for 5000 dollars in gold. Within 3 years, Gass defaulted on the mortgage and the ranch became Stewart's property (Moehring and Green 2005).

With both the Stewart and Kiel families now owning separate ranches in Las Vegas, the small market of soldiers, settling pioneer families, and travelers making their way to the Pacific coast began to compete. Strife between the ranch families was exacerbated by two conflicts that erupted in 1884. First, Kiel aggravated relationships with the Stewarts by accusing Archibald of swindling his friend Gass out of land. Second, a Kiel family ranch hand by the name of Schuyler Henry inflamed the conflict by allegedly spreading gossip about Mrs. Stewart, his former employer. On June 13, 1884, Archibald returned home and rode out with his gun to confront his former employee about the gossip that he had heard. He never returned. Helen Stewart, a debutante who played a key role in later developing Las Vegas, received a note from Conrad Kiel that afternoon that her husband was dead. Burying him on a hill in a coffin fashioned from two doors of their ranch house, Helen Stewart forever blamed the Kiels for her husband's death, noting that she believed her neighbors and the gunslingers they associated with had ambushed Archibald (Townley 1973).

Some say that Archibald's death was what motivated additional violence that erupted on the Kiel Ranch in 1899 (Martin 1988). That year, Conrad Kiel's nephews and heirs to his property, Edwin and William Kiel, assumed management of the ranch. Edwin had just moved west and together the brothers joined the list of neighbors with whom Helen refused to speak. One morning in October 1900, Helen's new suitor Frank Roger Stewart and his son William went to the Kiel Ranch. Supposedly visiting to report the arrival of wagon wheels in town, they found the two brothers' bodies near the adobe house that still stands in North Las Vegas today. A coroner rapidly determined that the brothers had engaged in a murder–suicide and the bodies were promptly buried. Edwin, accused of killing his brother William with a shotgun and ending his own life with a handgun, was buried facing east so that he would not face Christ on judgment day (Brooks and Brooks 1984).

Archibald Stewart, William Kiel, and Edwin Kiel's deaths are not the only violent incidents that occurred around the Kiel Ranch, though they seem to be the best remembered. Carrie Marie Townley, in writing the biography of Helen Stewart, documented the everyday violence that appears to have been common in frontier life (Townley 1973: 230–1). She writes:

> ...If Parish enjoyed the reputation of a gunslinger, the reputation of the Kiel Ranch was not much better. It was not uncommon for a rough crowd to congregate there. On December 1, 1894, a man named Gibbons was maimed when the side of his face was shot off during a quarrel over a card game by two men with a price on their heads, Gay and Butcher. Henry Hudson Lee, long time resident of Lincoln County and one-time county recorder, remembered that Jack Longstreet, another gunslinger residing in Lincoln County was known to hang out frequently at the Kiels. According to Lee, the Kiel Family did not enjoy a good reputation; people did not speak well of them.

This account of "rough crowds" congregating around the ranch seems accurate given the way in which tension erupted in fatal shootouts such as the ones in which both Stewart and Kiel blood was spilled between 1894 and 1900. One can only wonder how commonly such violence may also have affected the Paiute and other Native American laborers working in and around these North Las Vegas ranches (see Blackhawk 2006).

16.2.1   The fate of the Kiel family

William and Edwin's deaths signaled the formal close of the Kiel tenure in Las Vegas. Conrad's wife passed away in 1899 and this left no one invested in the farm, general store, and small estate, consisting of about 250 acres of land, one horse, and cattle left behind by the brothers (Townley 1974: 11). The remaining Kiel heirs sold the ranch to the Utah, Nevada, and California Railroad Company in 1901. The ranch passed through many hands, ending with the City of North Las Vegas. In 1975, the City of North Las Vegas contacted anthropologists at the University of Nevada, Las Vegas, to remove a small cemetery on the land associated with the historical Kiel Ranch. The city had acquired the property in preparation for a 1976 Bicentennial project in which the city would transform the Kiel Ranch into a historic site that would honor the history of American expansion, patriotism, and the formation of the state of Nevada. However, the violent deaths of two long-forgotten brothers would rewrite this history. The bodies of William and Edwin revealed the violence that occurred in the 1890s on the ranch. These skeletonized bodies were not found until 1976 when they were excavated (ranch history up until 1980s provided in Martin 1988).

16.2.2   The Brooks' analysis of the burials

With consent of the relatives at the time of exhumation, the remains recovered from Kiel Ranch were analyzed and described by Sheilagh and Richard Brooks, anthropologists at the University of Nevada, Las Vegas (for a full description of this analysis see Brooks and Brooks 1984).

Using a backhoe, five burials were excavated from the small plot. With student volunteers, all four adult burials and one infant burial were carefully excavated, photographed, inventoried, and analyzed. Using historic dental records, former coroner's reports, archival research, and forensic osteological techniques, each burial was positively identified as a member of the Kiel family. Brooks and Brooks (1984) noted that two of the four adult burials (identified as Edward and William Kiel using dental records and historical context) exhibited evidence of gunshot-related trauma to the crania. One of these two individuals also exhibited a possible injury to the bones of the left forearm. This injury is not identified as being associated with the gunshot trauma.

In their analysis, the Brooks suggest that the brothers did not die of a murder–suicide but more likely were victims of a double homicide. Their discussion of cause of death, however, was based only on the osteological information and did not consider weapons found with the burials, broader context of the crime scene as documented in a 1900 coroner's report, or broader comparative data regarding GSWs throughout the historic West. Additionally, given that the analysis was conducted a number of decades ago, much of the information about GSWs has changed as forensic anthropologists have continued to refine the techniques of identifying and interpreting trauma related to projectiles fired from firearms.

16.2.3   A reanalysis of the Kiel brothers

After government funded excavation in 1976 and reanalysis by the Brooks, the bones of William and Edwin Kiel remained curated at the University of Nevada, Las Vegas, and were all but lost in the archives for over three decades. However, in light of new techniques in osteological analysis and forensic science related to GSWs, as well as a greater emphasis on context and integration of multiple lines of evidence in bioarchaeology (Martin *et al.* 2012), a partially blind reanalysis was conducted. The analysis is considered partially blind because the investigators analyzed the adult remains without matching them up to the previous information provided by the Brooks. The goal of the reanalysis was to generate additional information regarding the lives and deaths of the individuals interred at the ranch and to see if contextualization of gunshot-related trauma into broader bioarchaeological and historical literature could further shed light on why these individuals died violently.

16.3   Methods

The reanalysis of the human remains from Kiel Ranch was performed using osteological techniques widely applied in both bioarchaeological and forensic contexts. Biological profiles, including estimation of age at death and sex, were established macroscopically using the pubic symphysis, cranial suture closure, and visual assessment of skeletal morphology in conjunction with sex estimation metric analyses (Brooks and Suchey 1990; Buikstra and Mielke 1985; Buikstra and Ubelaker 1994; Lovejoy *et al.* 1985; Meindl and Lovejoy 1985; Phenice 1969). Living stature was estimated through the use of the FORDISC 3.0 computer software (Ousley and Jantz 2005). All of the individuals from this site were examined for signs of bony pathology and antemortem and perimortem trauma, and, when present, this was recorded. Trauma was identified as perimortem or antemortem based on fracture morphology and whether or not signs of healing were observed (Galloway 1999; Lovell 2008). Pathological conditions were identified by unusual bone formation or destruction as well as abnormal bone shape, size, or density (Ortner 2003). Detailed descriptions of any pathological bone were recorded during the analysis. The information was then compared to paleopathological reference texts (Aufderheide and Rodríguez-Martin 2003; Ortner 2003).

The interpretation of gunshot injuries in bioarchaeology is largely manifested in the literature as case studies. These case studies have greatly advanced careful analysis and remain useful given the paucity of large historical skeletal assemblages rich in contextual information. It is key, however, that scholars begin to present data objectively so that comparative analyses, such as the one presented by Crist (2006), can be advanced and used to test theories regarding the function and consequences of violence in an anthropological context. Discussion of fracture pattern analysis in an osteological context is presented in Berryman and Symes (1998). Novak and Kopp (2003) present an excellent population-level analysis of GSW trauma in a fragmentary, commingled skeletal assemblage derived from the Mountain Meadows massacre. Their research and the subsequent biohistory of the massacre, which situated trauma data in the context of American history and culture (Novak 2008), provide an excellent model for future bioarchaeological research.

16.3.1 Interpreting gunshot wounds in the skeletal record

Traditionally, skeletal trauma resulting from projectiles has been seen as a unique category of traumatic injury separate from sharp force or blunt force injuries. Recently, however, experimental research, as well as reflection on increasing forensic anthropology casework, has emphasized that trauma caused by GSWs is simply a specialized form of blunt force injury and should be interpreted in a similar manner (Kroman and Symes 2012). This approach, informed by injury biomechanics, skeletal biology, and field research, is a holistic approach to trauma analysis that may advance the accurate collection of skeletal trauma data in both bioarchaeological and forensic contexts.

The reason that GSWs are always considered different from other forms of blunt force trauma is because of the way the bone reacts to the impact. An extensive review of bone structure and biomechanics can be found in Currey (2002), but what is of importance is to understand that, because of its structure, bone can only react in a limited number of ways. Bone is defined as a hard tissue, but, in reality, it is rich in collagen and other organics that make it quite elastic or flexible while an organism is alive. Additionally, bones within the body and between different organisms have notable variability in structural density, integrity, and composition. The result is that bone is often quite dynamic, making differential diagnosis of changes to its structure challenging. With most instances of blunt force trauma, forensics experts can only approximate the force involved because the low velocity of the impact allows the bone time to absorb some of the force, causing deformation prior to fracture, which can be difficult to reconstruct. However, with GSWs, the velocity of the impact is much greater and the bone does not have time to deform (Passalacqua and Fenton 2012: 400–1). The result is that the reconstruction of the skull is generally easier than in cases where blunt force injuries have caused great plastic deformation of the remains (Berryman and Symes 1998). Thus, because of the great force used to launch projectiles and the way that such concentrated force impacts skeletal tissue, it is possible to differentiate high-velocity projectile (i.e. gunshot) wounds from trauma caused by some other mechanism.

Just as when reporting pathological lesions in human remains, trauma analysis is best begun with a thorough description that avoids determining whether a wound resulted from a rifle or handgun, for example, and simply describes injuries in such a way that future scholars and other forensic experts can adequately evaluate the interpretations made from such data. It is important to document the size, shape, location, and placement of all injuries and related fractures. It is most common to begin the identification of skeletal trauma by examining the present remains for taphonomic changes. Key to the interpretation of skeletal injuries is determining whether an injury is truly antemortem or perimortem in nature and, more importantly, whether an injury is caused by a human agent rather than being the result of an animal or some other non-human force. These topics have been addressed elsewhere (Lovell 1997, 2008; Ortner 2008; Sauer 1998; Spencer 2012). The most obvious sign of gunshot-related trauma is the presence of an entrance and exit wound. These wounds are generally circular with fractures relative to the surface of bone first struck by the projectile and beveling on the opposite surface. These injuries, because great force strikes the bone rapidly in a smaller area of application, are different in morphology from other blunt force injuries (Berryman and Haun 1996).

Because of the variable preservation of human remains, particularly in prehistory, it is important not to look solely for evidence of entrance or exit wounds when collecting trauma data in any skeletal assemblage. Entry wounds are generally more variable in their morphology than exit wounds (Kimmerle and Baraybar 2008: Table 7.2). Examination of beveling, the sequence of fracturing, and comparison of wounds can help to identify which are entrance wounds and which are the result of a projectile exiting the body.

A secondary characteristic associated with GSWs is fractures with smooth edges that radiate out from such wounds at very high velocities. In fact, the fractures spread at such a rapid rate that they often reach the other side of the bone before the bullet, resulting in a hidden or missing exit wound (Smith *et al.* 1987). Thus, the possibility that bullets could ricochet, exit without injuring bone, or become lodged in the body and then move should the individual have momentarily survived the trauma was considered.

16.3.2 *Recording and quantifying gunshot wounds*

For the Kiel brothers the following data were collected from the available bones: anatomical location of the wound, number of wounds, wound size, wound morphology, and direction of wounds. This information allows an estimation of range of fire, caliber, and projectile type to be made (Komar and Buikstra 2008: 176).

Once all data were collected, the kinds of projectile, the nature of each wound, and the relative range and force of the injury were carefully estimated. First, entry and exit wounds should be differentiated based on the nature of the defects observed. To determine the anatomical location and number of wounds, the bones were rearticulated, even if only temporarily, to enable the reconstruction of the fracture pattern and identify missing bone. While reconstructed, the remains were photographed and drawn to provide others with data from which they can consider the interpretations presented in this chapter. Collectively these data allowed for the reconstruction of the wound track or the

Table 16.1. *Biological profile of the Kiel brothers.*

Biological profile			
Known age at death		Osteological estimation of age	
William Kiel	Edwin Kiel	KHUR 4	KHUR 3
53 years old	51 years old	50–60 years old	45–55 years old

Known age at death information from Brooks and Brooks (1984).

path the projectiles took through the body, the direction in which the projectile was fired, as well as the anatomical position the individual was in when shot.

The path taken by a projectile, as well as the order of injuries (in cases of multiple injury), was estimated by reconstructing the radiating direction of fractures, the nature of the beveling around the edges of the wound, and the orientation of exit and entry wounds to the anatomical position of the body in different postures.

Finally, to analyze the injuries associated with the projectiles fired from the shotgun, special consideration was needed because of the nature of the projectiles, as these consist of small pellets in a casing that are designed to spread out when shot. Given that they fire differently than the projectiles fired from a handgun or rifle, the effect is that subsequent injuries are more or less severe depending on the extent of the spread (Nag and Sinha 1992). Using these criteria and ethnohistoric information about the type of ammunition and firearms available during a particular period of time, it was possible to narrow down the possible kinds of projectiles and weapons that might have been involved in the shooting of the Kiel brothers.

16.4   Results

The results of the skeletal analysis demonstrated that the burials designated KHUR 3 and KHUR 4 in the University of Nevada, Las Vegas, osteological collection are consistent with both the findings for the known age at death records for the two Kiel brothers, Edwin and William, as well as the 1976 analysis performed by Brooks and Brooks (1984). In terms of the biological profile, both individuals are middle-aged adult males of European ancestry. Furthermore, the burial designated as KHUR 3 is slightly younger than the burial designated as KHUR 4, which is consistent with the fact that William Kiel was slightly older than his brother Edwin Kiel (see Table 16.1).

The patterning of trauma found on both burials is consistent with the injuries noted on the bodies in the coroner's report in 1900 as well as the trauma recorded

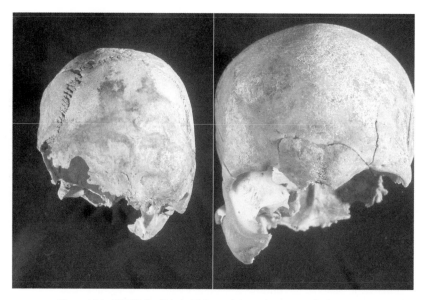

Figure 16.1. KHUR 3 – Edwin Kiel: cranial gunshot trauma. Left: entrance wound located on the inferior occipital. Right: extensive facial fracturing where bullet exited.

by Brooks and Brooks (1984). KHUR 3/Edwin Kiel has a perimortem GSW on the skull. The entrance wound for this gunshot is located on the inferior occipital. The distance from major bony landmarks was measured with a tape measure and this defect was found to be 94.0 mm inferior and to the left of lambda and 43.0 mm inferior and to the left of the inion. The exit wound from the gunshot is located in the face, with much of the face broken away during the bullet exit. This defect is shown in Figure 16.1. KHUR 4/William Kiel also has evidence of perimortem gunshot trauma. The cranium is extensively fractured and has pitting on the endocranial surface, which is shown in Figure 16.2.

16.5   Discussion

The two KHUR burials at the University of Nevada, Las Vegas, are the long-forgotten bodies of William and Edwin Kiel, who died at their ranch in Nevada at the turn of the twentieth century. The importance of this analysis is that it supports the previous analysis and interpretation of the death of these two brothers provided by Brooks and Brooks (1984). Additionally, this analysis identified a previously undocumented traumatic injury that may suggest a different reconstruction of the events that occurred on the day that Edwin and William Kiel were killed.

 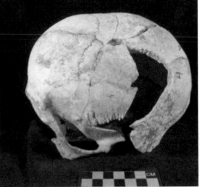

Figure 16.2. KHUR 4 – William Kiel: cranial gunshot trauma. Left: shotgun trauma evidenced by a fractured skull with pits on the endocranial surface. Right: two shotgun entrance wounds.

Looking first at Edwin Kiel, the size of the entrance wound in addition to the extensive fracturing (see Figure 16.1) suggests that the GSW was the result of either a large-caliber bullet or a high-velocity bullet (i.e. a rifle). The importance of wound size is that it has been known to be useful for identifying what type of weapon may have been used to cause a given wound (Ross 1996). While size alone cannot differentiate the caliber of the bullet or identify a specific gun (because of significant overlap in the size of injuries resulting from bullets of differing calibers [Berryman et al. 1995]), it can provide a general idea of whether or not it was a smaller or larger caliber bullet. For example, it is possible to differentiate between a .44-caliber and a .22-caliber bullet.

Analysis of radiating fracture lines is useful because the extent of fracturing can help to determine the type of firearm that was used. Clinical literature demonstrates that the patterning of fractures is variable, and is based on the biomechanics of the tissue where it impacts, the velocity at which it was fired, and the composition and mass of the bullet (Courtney and Courtney 2012; Hofbauer et al. 2010; Nunamaker and Berg 1985; Smith et al. 1987). A second benefit of analyzing the extent of fracturing is that it can help determine the general range or distance at which the gun was fired. Range can also be determined by the presence of soot, abrasion rings, and other unique kinds of wound morphology assist in interpreting whether an injury occurred at close contact, intermediate, or distant range. The problem with this burial is that the lack of soft tissue made it very difficult to identify if a gun was used at close or long range. One possible solution is to look for soot staining and periosteal lifting on the bone. Unfortunately, preservation is an issue as both natural and laboratory taphonomy have made it difficult to determine if soot staining is present. Therefore, simply considering the size of the entrance wound and the extent of fracturing, it is likely that either a high-velocity rifle or large-caliber handgun was used to murder Edwin Kiel.

The results of the analysis of the cranial wounds on William Kiel were consistent with those reported by Brooks and Brooks (1984), which suggests two shotgun blasts to the head. The first shotgun wound likely entered through the face and the second shot entered on the right side of the skull (Brooks and Brooks 1984). The cranium was destroyed by two shotgun blasts, which caused the dimples found on the endocranial surface of the skull (see Figure 16.2). The depressions left by the shot on the inside of the skull cannot be used to determine the distance at which William was shot. Given that spread is a product of both the weight of the pellets and the distance at which they are fired (Kimmerle and Baraybar 2008), it is likely, given the depth of these depressions, that he was shot at close range. However, care must be taken to ensure that the impact of the "billiard ball" effect does not disrupt accurate interpretation of the distance at which the gun was fired. In skeletonized remains, it is difficult to know if soft tissue inhibited the initial pellets that entered the body and therefore enabled later pellets to strike these farther throughout bony tissues. One more indication that William was shot at close range is the fact that the left radius and ulna were fractured by one of the shots. This is interpreted here to indicate that William Kiel attempted to block one of the shots with his forearm. However, new findings not reported during the analysis by Brooks and Brooks (1984) indicate that he was likely shot at some distance before being shot at close range. This analysis revealed that there was lead shotgun pellet lodged in the spinous process of the sixth thoracic vertebra (see Figure 16.3). Given the location of the shot at a spot in the body that would not occur from a shot to the head, this pellet either represents a third GSW or is the result of ricochet. The latter is less likely given the depth to which the pellet is embedded in the vertebra.

Based on the morphology and location of the trauma on these two individuals, possible scenarios were considered to explain the events that occurred on the Kiel Ranch. The results of this study confirm the interpretation made by Brooks and Brooks (1984): these two individuals represent victims of a double homicide instead of a murder–suicide. While it is difficult to reconstruct the exact sequence of events, it is suggested here that some sort of ambush or shootout may have occurred. It seems likely that at least two perpetrators were involved as two types of weapons were used. Also, it would have been difficult for one perpetrator to ambush both brothers, who were also possibly armed, successfully using two different weapons. If the shotgun pellet in the spine of William Kiel is the result of a long-distance shot and not ricochet, then it is

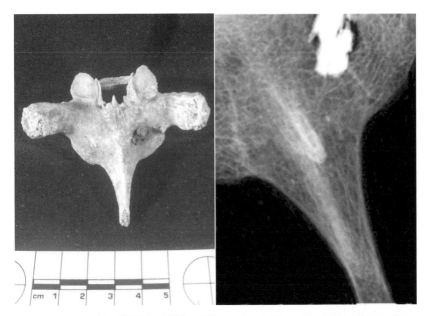

Figure 16.3. KHUR 3 – William Kiel: gunshot trauma on the vertebra. Left: lead shot embedded in the sixth thoracic vertebra. Right: X-ray of the vertebra and lead shot.

possible that he was attacked first from a distance, injured, and then approached by the perpetrator who shot him at close range. Again, it is unlikely that the bullet ricocheted as it entered the back of the body and was clearly lodged in the lamina of the vertebra, showing no sign of having entered via the neural canal or through the vertebral body. No other injuries to the thoracic region of the body suggest shotgun injuries from the sides or front of the body. Edwin Kiel, perhaps after hearing the sound of gunshots on his ranch, appears to have been ambushed at close range and shot in the back of the head by the second perpetrator. This just represents one of the many possible scenarios that could explain the trauma, however, and no definite conclusions can be made.

Interpreting traumatic injuries in the historic skeletal record is difficult. Skeletal data, paired with historical information and contextual clues derived from the 1900 crime scene investigation, permit us to posit that the Kiel brothers were the victims of a double homicide involving at least two perpetrators. The pattern of skeletal injuries identified in this study suggests a conflict that began at distance, with the perpetrators closing in on the brothers. Wounds to William's arm and the presence of jammed weaponry at the crime scene suggest that the brothers attempted to defend themselves. These findings allow us to suggest that perhaps the brothers were the victims of an ambush. We are not likely ever to know the true identity of the perpetrators; however, the tension between the Kiel and Stewart families certainly provides support for possible revenge by the Stewarts. Alternatively, the high prevalence of violence on the frontier and reported "gunslinger" activity around the Kiel Ranch may simply have put the brothers at increased risk of violent death for a series of other reasons that frontiersmen faced (see Courtwright 1998; White 1981).

Determining whether a violent event could have been foreseen by the victims is difficult in both archaeological and forensic contexts. For bioarchaeologists, such information could help to understand the nature of violence as it might be linked to political struggles. Yet, no method has to our knowledge been proposed by which to determine whether projectile trauma came as a surprise or was part of a planned "shootout." Bioarchaeological comparison to a growing body of literature documenting historical gunshot injuries should be useful in assisting in such interpretation.

16.5.1 Comparative analysis

A systematic, comparative analysis of historical gunshot injuries has not yet been attempted for the American West. Crist (2006), however, has compiled a list of 36 case studies of historic gunshot victims in a discussion of the modern gun culture debate. Expanding on his analysis, we documented the location of entry and exit wounds in each individual profiled by Crist (2006: Table 1). Using contextual information present in some cases, we could identify whether victims chose to engage in armed conflict (i.e. were part of a formal army or sought out a gunfight) or whether individuals were the victims of an ambush. In sum, the 36 individuals who were the victims of gunshots in the historic USA present 43 separate injuries as the result of gunshots. Of these, only two groups of individuals ($n = 10$; 27.7% of the victims profiled in Crist [2006]) are noted to present both contextual and bony evidence of having suffered injuries that have been interpreted as "point-blank execution" (Novak 2008: 161): Edwin and William Kiel and the eight individuals noted by Crist to have been killed as part of the 1857 Mountain Meadows massacre. Comparison to the victims of the Mountain Meadows massacre supports our interpretation that the Kiel brothers were ambushed, and provides a framework for formulating the osteological criteria of ambush.

In September 1857, some 120 men, women, and children migrating towards California were murdered in the Southern Utah Valley of Mountain Meadows. In 1999, the fragmentary remains of a mass grave comprised of many of these victims were reanalyzed by Shannon Novak and colleagues and have since been the subject of a number of bioarchaeological publications (e.g. Novak 2008; Novak and Kopp 2003). Projectile trauma, analyzed in Novak and Kopp (2003), provides useful comparison for interpreting the context of the Kiel brothers' deaths for a number of reasons. First, the Mountain Meadows massacre seems quite politically motivated (see Novak 2008; Novak and Rodseth 2006 for discussion), with the likely perpetrators defending what they saw as their sovereignty and livelihood through the event. If the Kiels were the victims of a revenge killing that stems from the strains of similar political or economic competition (see Moehring and Green 2005 on political competition in early southern Nevada), we might expect similar injury patterns. Second, the Mountain Meadows massacre yielded survivors whose recollections inform the interpretation of the violent events that occurred. Finally, the analyses conducted were thorough, and much information regarding the injuries of each victim is available for comparison.

The Mountain Meadows assemblage included some 1400 fragments of cranial bone. Of these, 25% exhibited radiating fractures, indicating perimortem trauma caused by blunt or projectile injuries. Gunshot entrance and exit wounds were also the most common lesions observed in the cranial remains. Of the five injuries for which locations of entrance and trajectory could be reconstructed, four consisted of injuries entering the back of the skull and exiting through the face (Novak and Kopp 2003: Figure 7). These injuries appear similar to those suffered by Edwin Kiel.

In interpreting the violent events at Mountain Meadows, Novak (2008: 161) notes that "the pattern of trauma is consistent with point-blank, execution-style shooting as opposed to a long-distance killing under battlefield conditions." Unlike injuries sustained in warfare, the wounds seen in Mountain Meadows largely occur at close range, are execution-style in many cases, and are not irregular or the result of long-distance shots. When considered alongside the blunt force trauma found at the massacre site, it is also clear that the assailants rapidly closed in on their victims and used rifle butts or other objects to bludgeon victims. The individuals appear to have been shot in the front of their bodies first at a distance and then, later, the victims were killed at close range.

This pattern of wounds (starting at a distance and ending in execution style) is seen at Kiel Ranch as well. William Kiel exhibits injuries to the back and arm that suggest some distance between his assailant(s?) and himself at the start of the fire fight. Yet, the final traumatic event that likely ended his life was a point-blank style injury from a shotgun to the side of his face. Edwin also exhibits a point-blank execution style shot to the back of the head that is similar to those documented by Novak and Kopp (2003).

This comparison, taken in the context of broader patterns of gunshot injury seen in the historic USA (Crist 2006), suggests that the Kiel brothers were ambushed and supports the interpretation of violent events that we posit above. Further, this comparative analysis suggests that ambush, or surprise attacks such as massacres, might yield an osteological signature. First, in both cases, initial injuries are sustained at a distance. These represent assailants rapidly closing in on unsuspecting victims. These injuries can be sustained across the body and from various angles such that many varieties of entrance wound morphology might be documented. As the victims are cornered, injuries change patterning. First, victims may attempt to defend themselves, using objects, nearby architecture, or their body positioning to shield against further injury. This is seen in the injuries to the arm sustained by William Kiel. Second, injuries become less random in how they are distributed across the body. Assailants attempt to kill their victims quickly so they can escape the scene of the crime in many cases. Injuries, in both the Mountain Meadows and Kiel Ranch chases, thus become focused on the head as rapid execution is the goal after the victims have been cornered or otherwise debilitated. Finally, point-blank execution seems to close out these ambush events. Unlike massacres, where political destruction of an "other" is the goal, in these contexts, perpetrators may seek to avoid signaling their identity in the crime and flee the scene without greatly mutilating the bodies, and may even attempt to make it difficult to interpret who caused the conflict by altering the crime scene.

16.6   Conclusion

Data obtained from GSWs can be judiciously used to contextualize human skeletal remains and aid both forensic anthropologists and bioarchaeologists in reconstructing violence in the past on many scales. As seen in the case of both the Kiel Ranch deaths as well as the Mountain Meadows massacre, trauma can be used to assist in reconstructing violence experienced first at the level of the individual. Here, skeletal trauma data are used to infer cause of death or generate data that other forensic experts may use to formally determine cause of death. At the level of the violent event, skeletal data assist in identifying the perpetrators, witnesses, and victims involved. The specific morphology of gunshot injuries can be used to reconstruct positioning of these actors. When partnered with contextual information, these kinds of reconstructions help formulate scenarios that other data can be used to test, thus allowing for the violent event to be reconstructed. Finally, and more broadly, skeletal trauma data can be used comparatively to begin to model the osteological signatures of various forms of violent conflict. In comparing Mountain Meadows and Kiel Ranch, we have suggested some preliminary osteological signatures of ambush that can be tested against additional forensic and historic cases and refined for use. Such kinds of models, generated from bioarchaeological and contextualized forensic data, are useful to bioarchaeology and forensic scholars attempting to establish the context of violence (for example, in human rights cases), where it is essential that ambush or massacre can be reliably identified. These kinds of models are also useful as they enable patterns of violence, such as ambushes, to be explored in a cultural context. Such investigations help link patterns of violence with social behavior and help us to understand how various types of violence, used by social groups to resolve power struggles on the frontier, manifest skeletally.

Acknowledgments

Funding to present preliminary versions of this work was provided by the Graduate and Professional Student Association of the University of Nevada, Las Vegas. We would also like to acknowledge the assistance of Dr. William Bauer and Dr. Debra Martin and attendees of the 2012 Mountain, Desert, and Coastal Forensic Anthropologists meeting for helpful comments and guidance in completing this project. Finally, we wish to acknowledge the late Drs. Sheilagh and Richard Brooks, whose notes, work, guidance, and insights led us to this project.

References

Aufderheide, A. C. & Rodríguez-Martin, C. (2003). *The Cambridge Encyclopedia of Human Paleopathology*, Reprint edition. Cambridge: Cambridge University Press.

Berryman, H. E. & Haun, S. J. (1996). Applying forensic techniques to interpret cranial fracture patterns in an archaeological specimen. *International Journal of Osteoarchaeology*, **6**, 2–9.

Berryman, H. E. & Symes, S. A. (1998). Recognizing gunshot and blunt cranial trauma through fracture interpretation. In: Reichs, K. J. (ed.) *Forensic Osteology: Advances in the Identification of Human Remains*, 2nd edn. Springfield: Charles C. Thomas, 333–52.

Berryman, H. E., Smith, O. C. & Symes, S. A. (1995). Diameter of cranial gunshot wounds as a function of bullet caliber. *Journal of Forensic Sciences*, **40**, 751–4.

Blackhawk, N. (2006). *Violence over the Land: Indians and Empires in the Early American West*. Cambridge: Harvard University Press.

Brooks, S. & Suchey, J. (1990). Skeletal age determination based on the os pubis: a comparison of the Acsadi-Nemskeri and Suchey-Brooks methods. *Human Evolution*, **5**, 227–38.

Brooks, S. T. & Brooks, R. H. (1984). Problems of burial exhumation, historical and forensic aspects. In: Brathbun, T. A. & Buikstra, J. E. (eds.) *Human Identification: Case Studies in Forensic Anthropology*. Springfield: Charles C. Thomas, 64–86.

Buikstra, J. E. & Mielke, J. H. (1985). Demography, diet, and health. In: Gilbert, R. I. & Mielke, J. H. (eds.) *The Analysis of Prehistoric Diets*. Orlando: Academic Press, 359–422.

Buikstra, J. E. & Ubelaker, D. H. (eds.) (1994). *Standards for Data Collection from Human Skeletal Remains*. Fayetteville: Arkansas Archeological Survey, Research Series, No. 44. A copy of Standards is required to fill out these forms accurately. It may be obtained from the Arkansas Archeological Survey, 2475 N. Hatch Ave., Fayetteville, AR 72704, http://www.uark.edu/campus-resources/archinfo/.

Courtney, A. & Courtney, M. (2012). *Physical Mechanisms of Soft Tissue Injury from Penetrating Ballistic Impact*. Colorado Springs: Air Force Academy, Report No. A408075. Published by Storming Media.

Courtwright, D. T. (1998). *Violent Land: Single Men and Social Disorder from the Frontier to the Inner City*. Cambridge: Harvard University Press.

Crist, T. A. (2006). The good, the bad, and the ugly: bioarchaeology and the modern gun culture debate. *Historical Archaeology*, **40**, 109–30.

Currey, J. D. (2002). *Bones: Structure and Mechanics*. Princeton: Princeton University Press.

Escobar, C. (2005). *The Status of Kiel Ranch: The City of North Las Vegas has Killed but Not yet Buried the Oldest Historic Site in the State*. Las Vegas: PACC, October 2005, Preservation Association of Clark County.

Galloway, A. (1999). The biomechanics of fracture production. In: Galloway, A. (ed.) *Broken Bones: Anthropological Analysis of Blunt Force Trauma*. Springfield: Charles C. Thomas, 35–62.

Hofbauer, M., Kdolsky, R., Figl, M., Grünauer, J., Aldrian, S., Ostermann, R. C. & Vècsei, V. (2010). Predictive factors influencing the outcome after gunshot injuries to the head – a retrospective cohort study. *Journal of Trauma*, **69**, 770–5.

Kimmerle, E. H. & Barrabar, J. P. (eds.) (2008). *Skeletal Trauma: Identification of Injuries Resulting from Human Remains Abuse and Armed Conflict*. Boca Raton: CRC Press.

Komar, D. A. & Buikstra, J. E. (2008). *Forensic Anthropology: Contemporary Theory and Practice*. Oxford: Oxford University Press.

Kroman, A. M. & Symes, S. A. (2012). Investigation of skeletal trauma. In: Digangi, E. A. & Moore, M. K. (eds.) *Research Methods in Human Skeletal Biology*. Oxford: Academic Press, 219–40.

Lovejoy, C. O., Meindl, R. S., Pryzbeck, T. R. & Mensforth, R. P. (1985). Chronological metamorphosis of the auricular surface of the ilium: a new method for the determination of adult skeletal age at death. *American Journal of Physical Anthropology*, **68**, 15–28.

Lovell, N. C. (1997). Trauma analysis in paleopathology. *Yearbook of Physical Anthropology*, **40**, 139–70.

(2008). Analysis and interpretation of skeletal trauma. In: Katzenberg, M. A. & Saunders, S. R. (eds.) *Biological Anthropology of the Human Skeleton*, 2nd edn. Hoboken: John Wiley & Sons, Inc., 341–86.

Martin, D. L., Harrod, R. P. & Pérez, V. R. (2012). Introduction: bioarchaeology and the study of violence. In: Martin, D. L., Harrod, R. P. & Pérez, V. R. (eds.) *The Bioarchaeology of Violence*. Gainesville: University of Florida Press, 1–10.

Martin, P. T. (1988). *Historic American Buildings Survey: Kiel Ranch, North Las Vegas, Nevada, HABS No. NV-19*. San Francisco: National Park Service, Western Region.

Meindl, R. S. & Lovejoy, C. O. (1985). Ectocranial suture closure: a revised method for the determination of skeletal age at death based on the lateral-anterior sutures. *American Journal of Physical Anthropology*, **68**, 57–66.

Moehring, E. P. & Green, M. S. (2005). *Las Vegas: A Centennial History*. Reno: University of Nevada Press.

Nag, N. K. & Sinha, P. (1992). A note on assessability of firing distance from gunshot residues. *Forensic Science International*, **56**, 1–17.

Novak, S. A. (2008). *House of Mourning: A Biocultural History of the Mountain Meadows Massacre*. Salt Lake City: The University of Utah Press.

Novak, S. A. & Kopp, D. (2003). To feed a tree in Zion: osteological analysis of the 185 Mountain Meadows Massacre. *Historical Archaeology*, **37**, 85–108.

Novak, S. A. & Rodseth, A. (2006). Remembering Mountain Meadows: collective violence and the manipulation of social boundaries. *Journal of Anthropological Research*, **62**, 1–25.

Nunamaker, D. M. & Berg, P. (1985). Open fractures and gunshot injuries. In: Newton, C. D. & Nunamaker, D. M. (eds.) *Textbook of Small Animal Orthopaedics*. Philadelphia: JB Lippincott, 481–97.

Ortner, D. J. (2003). *Identification of Pathological Conditions in Human Skeletal Remains*. London: Academic Press.

(2008). Differential diagnosis of skeletal injuries. In: Kimmerle, E. H. & Baraybar, J. P. (eds.) *Skeletal Trauma: Identification of Injuries Resulting from Human Remains Abuse and Armed Conflict*. Boca Raton: CRC Press, 21–93.

Ousley, S. D. & Jantz, R. L. (2005). *Fordisc 3.0: Personal Computer Forensic Discriminant Functions*. Knoxville: University of Tennessee.

Passalacqua, N. V. & Fenton, T. W. (2012). Developments in skeletal trauma: blunt-force trauma. In: Dirkmaat, D. C. (ed.) *A Companion to Forensic Anthropology*. Chichester: John Wiley & Sons, Ltd, 400–12.

Phenice, T. W. (1969). A newly developed visual method of sexing the os pubis. *American Journal of Physical Anthropology*, **30**, 297–301.

Ross, A. H. (1996). Caliber estimation from cranial entrance defect measurements. *Forensic Science International*, **41**, 629–33.

Sauer, N. J. (1998). The timing of injuries and manner of death: distinguishing among antemortem, perimortem, and postmortem trauma. In: Reichs, K. J. (ed.) *Forensic Osteology: Advances in the Identification of Human Remains*, 2nd edn. Springfield: Charles C. Thomas, 321–32.

Smith, O.C., Berryman, H.E. & Lahren, C.H. (1987). Cranial fracture patterns and estimate of direction from low velocity gunshot wounds. *Journal of Forensic Sciences*, **32**, 1416–21.

Spencer, S.D. (2012). Detecting violence in the archaeological record: clarifying the timing of trauma and manner of death in cases of cranial blunt force trauma among pre-Columbian Amerindians of West-Central Illinois. *International Journal of Paleopathology*, **2**, 112–22.

Townley, C.M. (1973). Helen J. Stewart: first lady of Las Vegas, Part I. *Nevada Historical Society Quarterly*, **16**, 214–44.

(1974). Helen J. Stewart: first lady of Las Vegas, Part II. *Nevada Historical Society Quarterly*, **17**, 2–32.

Walker, P.L. (2001). A bioarchaeological perspective on the history of violence. *Annual Review of Anthropology*, **30**, 573–96.

White, R. (1981). Outlaw gangs of the Middle Border: American social bandits. *The Western Historical Quarterly*, **12**, 387–408.

Part V

Concluding thoughts

17   *Living on the sidelines of death: anthropologists and violence*

A L I S O N G A L L O W A Y

17.1   Introduction

One of the most frequent questions I am asked at public presentations on forensic anthropology is how do I feel about death, having worked in this field for three decades. I respond by agreeing that exposure to death, dead bodies, and the consequences of violence has greatly changed the way in which I look at death. I value how precious life is and how quickly it can be snatched from us. I also know how desperately people cling to life as we see the evidence of people fighting to live and undergoing torture prior to their death.

When I was given the opportunity to provide a contribution for this volume, I sorted through the usual formats such as a case report or results of a research project. However, as I began writing, the current topic quickly spilled onto the page. I would attribute that to a number of factors: my own age and considerations of retirement; seeing my students embark on their own careers in forensic anthropology and bioarchaeology; and the loss of colleagues, family members, and friends. However, the most powerful factor is the sight of the many victims whose bodies we have examined and the opportunity we have to experience, in our minds, their last moments on earth.

The bioarchaeologist and forensic anthropologist experience death across a wide range of formats. For those of us working on contemporary material, we often participate in recovery efforts after mass disasters. During these times, we may see the bodies or body parts within the context of the death. This series of images is overlain by the sense of shock and dismay felt more broadly by the community/nation suffering the loss. It is accompanied by the strain of long hours and loss of our own support environment.

Bioarchaeological and Forensic Perspectives on Violence: How Violent Death is Interpreted from Skeletal Remains, ed. D. L. Martin and C. P. Anderson. Published by Cambridge University Press. © Cambridge University Press 2014.

For osteologists who specialize in examination of violence, we also spend long hours in the laboratory examining individual skeletons, identifying individual instances of damage to the bones, determining the means by which that damage occurred and when it occurred in relation to the individual's demise, and finally determining the sequence of events, if possible, from the remains and our knowledge of anatomy and human movement. The victims have come to us from situations in which the cause and manner of death may be unclear – suicide, homicide, accidental, or natural causes. The body is removed from the context but this act also exposes the vulnerability of the person. The cleaned bones are laid out on our table to be scrutinized, photographed, and documented. Stripped of context, all attention is focused on the evidence of violence.

In this chapter, I want to examine several aspects of how our examination of death also points inward. How does this change our own attitudes to death and dying? I will briefly discuss five specific aspects: (1) the isolation of our professional lives; (2) the lasting memories that this work produces; (3) the use of humor, specifically gallows or dark humor; (4) how the remains reveal information about the killer and how that knowledge is incorporated into our understanding of human nature; and (5) the potential for post-traumatic stress disorder (PTSD).

17.2   A professional life in isolation

Anthropologists who deal with death and violence often do so on an erratic schedule. Forensic anthropologists get cases intermittently – often going long periods without any work and then having multiple cases arriving within a week. Thrown into this mix are the fortunately less frequent events of mass disasters/multiple fatality incidents. These large-scale events may require many hours of work, often on 10–12-hour shifts, for weeks at a time, with the rest of one's life set to the side. Bioarchaeologists are more able to schedule the field season but not when and how bodies will be recovered. Often remains are uncovered at the close of a season, making recovery difficult and with little time to mentally process the more obvious evidence of violence. Only when remains are transported back to the laboratory do we have a chance to examine cases more closely. This uneven exposure, the need often to work at a quick pace, and the length of time that we will spend with the dead are part of the career choice we have made – but one that comes with other considerations.

One of the difficulties of working with forensic cases, in particular, is the inability to discuss these cases with the people who are the normal outlets one has for tension. While people may find working on forensic cases an intriguing topic of conversation, there is less willingness to hear the details – the maggots, the smell, the decomposed organs within the body cavity. Chills run up the spine when we say that we "cook the body," but visualizing a pot in which nail-polished hands bob up and down is a bit more than people want to know.

Family members often tire of hearing about cases in all the, often gory, detail. The choice of subject matter for work was ours, and not necessarily that of our families. This reticence to speak openly to family members about cases increases when there are younger children present. I stopped bringing my young daughter to the laboratory when she began asking if the stab wounds in the spine of a victim had hurt him. She did not return to the lab for many years after that, although she is now rather matter-of-fact about dead bodies.

The other factor that limits what we, as forensic anthropologists, can say to others is the problem of dealing with forensic evidence. Active cases require careful regulation of the release of information. Press coverage of cases will publicize certain details but often many intimate details are not included and may not be known beyond a small circle of investigators until the case goes to trial. Many cases never go to trial so this information remains concealed. While the wartime saying of "loose lips sink ships" now better applies to cyberspace, inappropriate talk can sink a legal case.

We are known to our colleagues, often in anthropology departments, for being a bit different. My colleagues in campus administration will acknowledge that something is odd about my response to bodies. I have been known to sit up sharply when a "burn pit" is mentioned in a campus planning activity – only to slump when it was evident that I could not use it for experimentation on thermal damage to remains. I also have a large number of non-human skeletal elements and El Dia de los Muertos artifacts in my office. It has become standard practice to give me skeleton cards, calendars, trinkets – anything as long as it has bones. Even my family has succumbed to the tradition and stopped trying to convert my décor to more acceptable designs of flowers or geometric patterns.

However, to revel too much in the dead is not appropriate and shows an indifference of the respect due to all individuals, living or dead. Our livelihood does, in part, depend on the deaths of others. So, we must temper our almost gleeful anticipation of a "good case" with the knowledge that, for a case to come our way, someone died.

So, how do we cope? We find ways to breach the boundaries of the isolation by reaching out to colleagues beyond our immediate circle. Some are fortunate to work in coroners' or medical examiners' units with colleagues who share the same experiences. However, many of us work in academia. These conversations are often not ones to share with our departmental colleagues. Our students share a part of this life, but until they have come to understand the world in which they are immersing themselves, we often do not confide fully in them. Revealing excessive vulnerability can also be problematic for a mentor to a mentee. Many of us hold things inside until we have the chance to share with like-minded colleagues.

The public often see professional conferences as a place where the latest information, processes, and practices are exchanged. Equally important for those of us who work with the dead is the opportunity to talk with others whose experience is comparable. Much of the time is spent "out-grossing" each other – an important release valve for the types of things we experience. I often spend some of the time with the entomologists since one of my areas of research has been decomposition. While we happily discuss the various attributes and accomplishments of maggots and other larvae, the neighboring tables begin to empty.

17.3   Lasting memories

Ask any forensic anthropologist or bioarchaeologist who deals with violence if they have any lasting memories of their victims and almost all will say yes. Many of these come from instances of mass disaster. It may be the image of the large "head-sized" impact marks on the underside of the folding trays after an airplane crash – especially when you have to fly the same type of plane on the same route; it may be seeing children getting on a plane, having just worked on a crash. In my case it was realizing that I was lifting a dead infant recovered from a plane crash just as I had lifted my own daughter – lifting the legs slightly and sliding my arm under the body to steady the head. In this case, there was no head.

Many of us also have specific cases that haunt us. Often it is where the complex pattern of defects seen on the bones can be matched to a story – either from an informant or the defendant. In one such case, we were able to identify blunt force blows to the head, multiple stab wounds in the lower back and ribcage, and linear cuts on the cervical vertebrae. As we found out after completing our analysis, the informant told of the victim being hit over the head, bound, and tortured before having his throat slit.

Then there are the bodies that are not even ours to examine. Since we often work in morgues, other remains pass before us. With each comes a story of how and where they died, with whom they were at the time. Many coroner cases are accidental deaths, often from drug or alcohol abuse, or suicides. I turned around from a skeletonized case once to see the body of a young man, with carefully sculpted and purple-dyed hair. He had been looking forward to a weekend of partying just hours before the heroin overdose claimed his life. I remember the hair.

Bioarchaeologists who work with victims of violence also capture images. The flesh may be long gone but the ages, the poses, the cut marks or blows are clearly visible. In these settings the reasoning behind why the people were killed and why they were placed as they were in death cannot be fully known. The investigator is left trying to reconstruct the unfathomable.

17.4   Seeing the funny side of death

Gary Larson has a lot of admirers among anthropologists – especially those who work with human bodies. It was a sad day when he retired in 1995. Fortunately his cartoons live on. I use them often in teaching, strongly favoring those that poke fun at death, decay, and scavenging. There are times when I relate particularly with his depiction of the child who brought in the head in a pickle jar for classroom "show and tell."

Humor is often used to break stressful situations but there are many unspoken rules about the use of such jokes. In general, joking about specific victims or attributing the cause of their death to their behavior or lifestyle is less acceptable than jokes that target death itself or the current circumstances, such as being in a roomful of decomposing bodies.

Gallows humor treats serious, even deadly, subjects as topics for satirical or light conversation (Watson 2011). Watson points out that gallows humor among physicians is often misunderstood as callousness and unprofessional behavior. Instead, she insists that we must recognize the humanity of those facing the stressful situation. About gallows humor among physicians, she states: "Moments when health care providers suddenly see the enormous gulf they're straddling between medical and lay culture are one source of gallows humor. Being off-balance can make us laugh, and sometimes laughing is what keeps us from falling over."

In a similar vein, Kuhlman (1988) describes humor used in a maximum security criminal mental health facility. The situations in which such humor surfaces share common features of unremitting or inescapable stressors and a sense of "existential incongruity." As anthropologists working on the dead, we cannot escape the task at hand without jeopardizing our careers and reputations. It has to be faced but we end up doing often socially unacceptable things (defleshing, dismemberment) to the dead while investigating what unspeakable things were done to get them that way in the first place.

The right to participate in gallows humor also marks the acceptance into a professional community. Students who overly joke about the bodies are eyed with suspicion, and senior practitioners either address the behavior or may decline to continue the association. It is often the mentor's role to initiate and set the level of humor for the students.

17.5   People less than human

For killers to be able to kill, they see their victims as less than human. Levin and Fox (2007) suggest that many sadistic killers do not fit the well-publicized stereotype of having an extreme personality disorder. Instead they argue that the killer is able to overcome his/her very normal forces of conscience by compartmentalizing his/her activities and by dehumanizing the victim.

For the anthropologist dealing with the remains of the victim, we witness the results of the dehumanization while simultaneously needing to dehumanize the victim so that we can conduct our studies. In order to perform our work, we must continue the desecration of the remains to reveal the information they contain. We strip the bones of their flesh, examine each bone microscopically, photograph it from every angle, and intrude into all the private areas of the remains. We, too, compartmentalize these activities away from the rest of our lives, and we must enter our scientific mode to remove the full humanity from the deceased individual.

In modern society, the murder of certain categories of people is considered more reprehensible. These include those individuals who are unable to provide even some level of defense – children, the severely handicapped, the elderly. Yet these are often the victims of violent crime, of mass disasters, and of genocide. In the bioarchaeology context, the discovery of the bodies of children as victims of either massacre or sacrifice is noted throughout the world. Again, as the osteologists, we can adopt the approach that these are scientific data as we complete the examinations and analyze the data. However, always lurking behind the screen we have mentally established is the understanding that other humans deliberately murdered people who we would now consider as innocent and harmless.

17.6   Post-traumatic stress

While post-traumatic stress may occur, most forensic anthropologists do not claim to suffer the classic symptoms, or, if they do, they do not find them as distressing. What we see are changes that are more subtle yet equally powerful.

These changes usually do not reach the level where symptoms become debilitating but they can interact with other aspects of our lives.

PTSD is an anxiety disorder commonly associated with those who have experienced life-threatening events, such as military combat or physical or sexual assaults. However, it can also be experienced by those who encounter death on a repeated basis, such as coroners, death investigators, and forensic experts. While the etiology is unknown, it is believed that the extreme exposure changes the biochemistry by which the person deals with emotions in the future. Changes in the transmission of neurotransmitters possibly underlie the symptoms.

Symptoms fall roughly into three categories. The first is the "reliving" of the event. Sufferers report flashbacks or dreams in which the events are repeated. Many of us in the field also experience dreams that have images most would find unpleasant. Decomposing bodies, skeletons, and evidence of terror may litter the dreams but not cause particular distress. However, there are times when circumstances do bring to mind the power of what we have witnessed. If I were to dream of a rotting corpse, I do not become distressed; however, if I dreamt of being murdered, or, worse, doing the murder, it is time to re-evaluate the situation.

The second major group of symptoms involves avoidance. This cluster includes an overall numbing of emotions and a retraction from circumstances that would trigger images. Many symptoms in this group are similar to those of depression. Finally, there is a cluster of symptoms around arousal in which those who suffer from PTSD have difficulty concentrating and are easily startled, constantly alert, irritable, and have difficulty sleeping.

Considerable work has been done on first responders, which may include anthropologists, especially in multifatality incidents. Brondolo and colleagues (2007) worked with the body handlers from the 9/11 incidents and noted that many were overwhelmed not only by the volume of remains but by the duration of the investigation that dragged on for over 4 years. In the immediate aftermath of the World Trade Center disaster, there was an airline crash with 275 victims, which overlapped with the other analyses. People whose professional work usually kept them separated from the survivors were thrust into roles of collecting antemortem data from families. Despite these circumstances, Brondolo notes that other studies show that the rates of PTSD are relatively low amongst World Trade Center workers. The incidence of acute stress disorder among those responding to air crashes may be as high as 25% (Fullerton *et al.* 2004), while officers involved with the World Trade Center showed rates of PTSD or partial PTSD up to 15% (Marmar *et al.* 2006).

Much of the psychological damage to workers on mass disasters can be avoided by preparation (Brondolo *et al.* 2007). While the events are unpredictable, training and practice sessions make the response more predictable. Mechanisms to provide information on progress and supporting performance are also beneficial. While mental health professionals would appreciate greater involvement in the support of body handlers, there is reluctance to seek these services. Much of this may lie in the perception of the isolated professional life (see above).

Less information is available about the effects on those who repeatedly see the results of violence over a long period of time, such as medical examiners, death investigators, autopsy technicians, and anthropologists. Probably the best to date is a study of volunteer workers in Israel who recover bodies and body parts after explosions, often perpetrated by suicide bombers (Solomon *et al.* 2007). Surprisingly, these individuals showed lower rates of PTSD than the general population. Furthermore, those individuals who employed a "repressive coping strategy," as defined by Weinberger *et al.* (1979), were better protected than others. Such body handlers report lower anxiety although they often exhibit higher levels of physiological anxiety (heart rate and blood pressure), a response pattern more fully explored by Mendolia *et al.* (1996) and Sparks *et al.* (1999). In other words, their anxieties are repressed. Solomon and associates (2007) noted that these individuals also reported a lower sense of danger in their work, although their sense of safety was no better than the other, non-repressive, individuals.

Self-selection may play a role in the relatively low incidence of mental health issues. As a professor, I have many students who express the intense desire to become forensic anthropologists – until their first experience with a decomposing body. Because the anxiety must be "put aside" when working on remains, those who choose to make it a career may be biased towards those whose coping strategies are, in general, better matched. As one matures in the field, the feeling of competence makes situations more controllable even though every case presents new circumstances.

There comes a time, however, when one gets tired of seeing dead bodies. It is not the dead themselves that cause the problem, it is the implication of what humans can do to each other. For each homicide we see as a corpse, there was someone or a group of people who were capable of putting aside their shared humanity to kill. It is not the death we seek to avoid seeing but the killing. I have known people in the field who have gotten so weary of death that they have given up the sport of hunting, which they previously enjoyed. I am addicted to a good murder mystery, whether in text or film, but routinely skip over any reference to the actual act of killing. My ability to repress only works so far and I make conscious choices to avoid situations that threaten to overwhelm my abilities to accommodate.

17.7   Conclusions

People ask me what it takes to be a good forensic anthropologist and I usually respond that it requires a weak nose and a strong stomach. In a sense, these are helpful traits but they also symbolize the broader qualities that it takes to work in this field. We have the responsibility to bear the burden of these deaths while also trying to protect ourselves so that the scent of death does not overwhelm us. We must remove ourselves emotionally from the immediate scene. I refer to this as going into "science mode" in which the analysis of the body takes priority over comprehending how the person died. The reality of the violence, however, does catch up to us. The sense of loss for a life cut short, the knowledge of the terror they experienced knowing that they would soon die, and the privilege of telling the story the victims can no longer speak require the anthropologist to be able and willing to bear the burden that comes with this knowledge.

What keeps those of us in the field is our sense of discovery, resolution, and contribution. When we examine a body, we are party to information about how that person spent their last moments. We become the mouthpiece through which that story can be told long after the decedent passed away. The ability to balance the emotion of knowing this very private information with the scientific investigation is key for a successful and lengthy career in the field.

A good colleague, a fellow forensic anthropologist, died recently. He left his body to the University of Tennessee decay facility and the skeletal remains, once cleaned, to the Smithsonian Institution. While we study death frequently, we know we will, at some time in the future, also be the remains subject to someone else's handling.

References

Brondolo, E., Wellington, R., Brady, N., Libby, D. & Brondolo, T. J. (2007). Mechanism and strategies for preventing post-traumatic stress disorder in forensic workers responding to mass fatality incidents. *Journal of Forensic and Legal Medicine*, **15**, 78–88.

Fullerton, C. S., Ursano, R. J. & Wang, L. (2004). Acute stress disorder, posttraumatic stress disorder, and depression in disaster or rescue workers. *American Journal of Psychiatry*, **161**, 1370–6.

Kuhlman, T. L. (1988). Gallows humor for a scaffold setting: managing aggressive patients on a maximum-security forensic uni. *Hospital and Community Psychiatry*, **39**, 1085–90.

Levin, J. & Fox, J. A. (2007). Normalcy in behavioral characteristics of the sadistic serial killer. In: Kocsis, R. N. (ed.) *Serial Murder and the Psychology of Violent Crimes*. Totowa: Humana Press Inc., 3–14.

Marmar, C. R., Metzler, T., Chemtob, C., Delucchi, K., Liberman, A., Fagan, J. *et al.* (2006) *Impact of the World Trade Center Attacks on the New York City Police Department: A Prospective Study. New York Academy of Sciences Conference Psychobiology of Post-Traumatic Stress Disorder: A Decade of Progress.* New York, NY: New York Academy of Sciences.

Mendolia, M., Moore, J. & Tesser, A. (1996). Dispositional and situational determinants of repression. *Journal of Personality and Social Psychology*, **70**, 856–67.

Solomon, Z., Berger, R. & Ginzburg, K. (2007). Resilience of Israeli body handlers: implications of repressive coping style. *Traumatology*, **13**, 64–74.

Sparks, G. G., Pellechia, M. & Irvine, C. (1999). The repressive coping style and fright reactions to mass media. *Communication Research*, **26**, 176–92.

Watson, K. (2011). "Gallows Humor in Medicine." *Hastings Center Report*, **41**, 37–45.

Weinberger, D. A., Schwartz, G. E. & Davidson, R. J. (1979). Low-anxious, high-anxious and repressive coping styles: psychometric patterns and behavioral and physiological responses to stress. *Journal of Abnormal Psychology*, **88**, 369–80.

Index

Page numbers in bold indicate – figures/tables